Holocaust Literature

*A Sarnat Library Book

HOLOCAUST
LITERATURE

[A HISTORY AND GUIDE]

DAVID G. ROSKIES AND
NAOMI DIAMANT

BRANDEIS UNIVERSITY PRESS

WALTHAM, MASSACHUSETTS

BRANDEIS UNIVERSITY PRESS
An imprint of University Press of New England
www.upne.com
© 2012 David G. Roskies
All rights reserved
Manufactured in the United States of America
Designed by Eric M. Brooks
Typeset in Dante and Aquarius by Passumpsic Publishing

University Press of New England is a member of the
Green Press Initiative. The paper used in this book meets
their minimum requirement for recycled paper.

The publication of this book was generously supported by the
Lucius N. Littauer Foundation.

For permission to reproduce any of the material in this book,
contact Permissions, University Press of New England, One Court
Street, Suite 250, Lebanon NH 03766; or visit www.upne.com

Library of Congress Cataloging-in-Publication Data
Roskies, David G., 1948–
Holocaust literature: a history and guide / David G. Roskies
and Naomi Diamant.
    p. cm. — (The Tauber Institute series for the study of
European Jewry)
ISBN 978-1-61168-357-8 (cloth: alk. paper) —
ISBN 978-1-61168-358-5 (pbk.: alk. paper) —
ISBN 978-1-61168-359-2
1. Holocaust, Jewish (1939–1945), in literature — History and criticism.
2. Holocaust, Jewish (1939–1945) — Influence. 3. Holocaust survivors
— Biography — History and criticism. I. Diamant, Naomi. II. Title.
PN56.H55R67   2012+
809'.93358405318 — dc23   2012021083

5 4 3 2 1

Can the dead mourn the dead?

ZALMEN GRADOWSKI

"The Czech Transport: A Chronicle of
the Auschwitz Sonderkommando"

Survivors: your legacy of gladness should be tentative,
Some of us still flicker in the straits of death.
Don't forget to keep our dying in your breath.
Don't forget, your martyrdom now will be to live.

ABRAHAM SUTZKEVER

"Epitaphs," translated by
C. K. Williams

On ne part pas de zéro.

MICHEL BORWICZ

Ecrits des condamnés à mort sous
l'occupation nazie, 1939–1945

Contents

Color plates appear after page 148.
A complete curriculum guide is available online
at www.brandeis.edu/tauber/roskies.html.

Illustrations

Preface

IN 1963, THE MONTREAL BRANCH OF THE JEWISH LABOR Bund marked the twentieth anniversary of the Warsaw ghetto uprising. Old-line Socialists, they commemorated the uprising by gathering on April 19, which fell on a Friday that year. No synagogue would host a secular event on the Sabbath, so they met in a school auditorium; the local Bundists had always gone their own way, since the time when they were the largest Jewish political party in Poland. I was fifteen years old, old enough to attend without my parents. My best friend Khaskl, who considered himself a Bundist and went to a Bundist summer camp in New York State, had brought me along.

There was no cantor to chant prayers in Hebrew, no prayers to a God that no one believed in anyway, and no concessions made to the Anglophones. Yiddish was the language spoken because the story happened to people who spoke Yiddish: the grandparents, parents, cousins, uncles, aunts, brothers, sisters, and comrades of the people sitting in the auditorium. That evening I heard about the heroic exploits of other ghetto fighters: not Mordecai Anielewicz but Abrasha Blum; not Mordecai Tenenbaum but Michal Klepfisz; of those who survived, not Antek Zuckerman and Zivia Lubetkin but Marek Edelman and Vladke Meed. Apparently, the Zionist and Bundist underground had been divided along party lines and joined forces only in the eleventh hour. This was a very different picture of the Warsaw ghetto uprising from the one I had learned at school, and I was now old enough to hear it, at a gathering that ended with the singing of two Yiddish hymns—the "Partisans' Hymn," which I already knew and the Bundist hymn, which I didn't.

But nothing prepared me for the centerpiece of the evening: a dramatic reading of an epic poem by someone named Simkhe Bunem Shayevitsh, a martyred poet from the Łódź ghetto. Abba Igelfeld, Khaskl's uncle, read from a large printed folio. Abba had been a semiprofessional actor in his youth, and he had real stage presence. *"Un atsind, Blimele, kind-leb,"* he began in a sepulchral tone—"And now Blimele, my child, / Restrain your childish joy . . . ," as if a father were interrupting an intimate conversation with his daughter to get her ready "for the unknown road," because just now, in the dead of winter, they've been ordered to leave their home, and besides packing what few belongings father, mother, and daughter can carry, they must also say goodbye to the thin wooden walls of their unheated ghetto room, to the table, the wardrobe, the conjugal bed, and above all the books, and there is just enough time to give Blimele instruction about those of her forebears who made similar journeys into the unknown, like Abraham of old, or like the poet Leivick who was exiled to Siberia, and Shayevitsh's poem, I noticed, rhymed the way that Yiddish folk songs rhymed, and there wasn't one word or reference that eluded me, so simply was the poem written, for even if I'd never heard of Tuwim or Yesenin, mentioned among the books that were being left behind, I could guess from the context that they were famous writers in some other language, and while Blimele was never taught the Torah directly, as a girl who grew up in a traditional home, I was old enough to know how Abraham leading Isaac to Mount Moriah and the prophet Jeremiah accompanying his people into exile were the biblical back story to the deportation of the Jews from the ghetto, and after Abba had been reading for a good fifteen minutes he raised his voice when the father said, *"Nor lomir nisht veynen, lomir nisht / yomern un lehakhis ale sonim— / shmeykhlen, nor shmeykhlen, az vundern / zoln zey zikh vos yidn konen"*—But now's not the time to weep, / Not the time to lament, but to spite all our foes / It's time to break into a smile, yes a smile / To astonish them at what the Jews can do," and in the poet's voice and through Abba's ventriloquism I recognized the call of Jewish defiance, the studied response of a stiff-necked, persecuted people.

From Abba's choice of poem and the stunned silence that followed his reading, I experienced before fully understanding it how public memory and mourning were bringing a new kind of liturgy into being. Such rites of commemoration had begun before I was born, and the works written during wartime were becoming a closed literary canon, like Scripture itself. Shayevitsh's poem was read aloud in solemn assembly as a sacred text, not only because he called it by the biblical name *"Lekh-lekho,"* God's command to Abraham to "go forth" from his native land; and not only because the poet turned the covenantal narrative on its head, rereading the beginning as the end, the patriarch's journey to the Promised Land as the ghetto father accompanying his wife and daughter on the road to perdition; but also because such texts were written specifically for us, the survivors. What gave this writing its feeling of authenticity was the voice of the dead writing for the living. When I was really old enough, I made it my business to learn about the group of Yiddish writers in the Łódź ghetto; to learn why writers and artists were a protected class in all the major ghettos, insofar as it was possible to protect any Jew inside the Jewish zone from disease, starvation, deportation, and violent death. Abba, I was later to discover, had found Shayevitsh's poem reprinted in a literary journal published in Toronto called *Tint un feder* which—like other Yiddish newspapers and journals—became a purveyor of Holocaust memory. Those who participated in this postwar ritual called *geto-akademye*, or ghetto commemoration, were scattered all over the world, from Buenos Aires to the Bronx, from

Paris to Tel Aviv, from Melbourne to Mexico City and Montreal. For them, it was a given that the unit of memory, the part that stood for the whole, was the lost city of Jews, the martyred community, the murdered party faithful, and equally a given that the way to keep their memory alive was to regroup, retell their story, read poetry written during or close to the catastrophe itself, and sing a few appropriate songs. The way to incubate memory and mourning was in the language(s) of the martyrs and fighters, and the literary forms that best lent themselves to public performance were epic and lyric poetry.

It was possible, of course, to commemorate the dead on other dates and in other ways. That Sunday night, my parents took me to the Public Tribute in Honor of the Jewish Martyrs, which was held at the Spanish and Portuguese Synagogue. Sunday night was the eve of Yom Hashoah, the twenty-seventh of Nissan, the date chosen in 1951 by the government of Israel to mark Holocaust and Ghetto Uprising Remembrance Day. The largest ghetto uprising, in Warsaw, had begun on the first day of Passover in the Hebrew month of Nissan, and the twenty-seventh would always fall twelve days after the observance of Passover and one week before Yom Hazikaron, Israeli Remembrance Day (Ofer 2000). By the mid-1960s, the twenty-seventh of Nissan had been adopted for community-wide observance in much of the Jewish world. Only two groups dissented: the Orthodox, who observed the tenth of Tevet, a traditional day of fasting, to memorialize the victims of the Holocaust whose date of death was unknown, and the Bundists, who stubbornly convened on April 19, even when this coincided with Passover. Meanwhile the *landslayt*, or compatriots, met on the anniversary of the liquidation of their respective ghettos: August for Białystok and Łódź, September for Vilna, and so on. The former inmates of Bergen-Belsen (both the concentration and displaced persons camp) gathered on the anniversary of its liberation.

The Spanish and Portuguese Synagogue was packed. The Canadian Jewish Congress had spared no expense, having brought in not one but two big-name speakers from New York: the celebrated Yiddish poet Jacob Glatstein and the popular Anglo-Jewish journalist Samuel Margoshes. Glatstein did not read from his own poetry on the theme of the great catastrophe. Presumably he wasn't being paid to do so. Each speaker spoke at length. Six fidgety schoolchildren each lit a memorial candle, one for each of the six million victims. Then we all stood up and bowed our heads as the cantor of the synagogue sang an operatic memorial prayer. Many of the men covered their heads. No work of Holocaust literature was read aloud, and nothing memorable was spoken. It felt like every other synagogue service I attended with my parents.

It was also possible not to remember the Holocaust at all. In 1965 I went off to college, the only Canadian and the only Yiddish speaker in the freshman class at Brandeis University. At the end of the fall semester I approached the

Jewish chaplain, a recent graduate of a Reform rabbinical seminary, to ask about his plans for Yom Hashoah and whether I could be of any help. "What's Yom Hashoah?" he replied.

Leaving home, I had moved from intense to attenuated group memory; from group memory divided along regional, ethnic, religious, and ideological lines to a zero-sum memory pool. I had moved from public remembering to public forgetting. At one end of the spectrum a culture of mourning was being incubated, with a separate calendar of memorial dates, a growing body of commemorative texts, a repertoire of songs, and competing historical narratives. At the other end, an invitation was extended to join the majority culture, where the slate of public memory was wiped clean every four years, on Election Day; where terrible wars were fought only abroad, and "we" were always on the winning side. From age fifteen to seventeen, in short, I had personally relived the jagged history of Holocaust literature.

DAVID G. ROSKIES

WHAT IS HOLOCAUST LITERATURE?

WHAT IS HOLOCAUST LITERATURE? WHERE DOES IT BELONG, and how is it changing? Is it to be read as a genre of literature about death, war, atrocity, or trauma? Does this vast outpouring of writing invite comparisons with responses to other Jewish catastrophes or with other forms of Jewish resistance? Is it sui generis, to be measured against itself alone and demanding a unique interpretive lens? How may its verbal art be related to the other arts—plastic, graphic, photographic, cinematic, pornographic, acoustic? And finally, why should readers care about this catastrophe when there are already so many others to compete for their attention? Why read literature when the facts can be gleaned from other sources? Why read at all when one can see the movie or watch the video testimony?

Who speaks for the Holocaust? For some, Holocaust literature is everything written, and especially sung, in Yiddish—the *loshn-hakdoyshim*, or language of the martyrs—by those who perished. For others, it is the distinct voice of the survivors, who speak in a language authentic to the Holocaust—Borowski speaking Polish, Celan speaking German, Delbo speaking French, Levi speaking Italian, Lustig speaking Czech—or those who speak a language that bears witness to the Holocaust—Appelfeld speaking Hebrew, Wiesel speaking English.

How shall they speak? We need this literature to be monumental, commensurate with its subject matter. "For I intend to write a great, immortal epic," Tadeusz Borowski resolved at the end of his first collection of concentration camp stories, "worthy of this unchanging, difficult world chiseled out of stone" (Borowski 1976, 180). "He told me his story," Primo Levi recalled, "and today I have forgotten it, but it was certainly a sorrowful, cruel and moving story; because so are all our stories, all different and all full of a tragic, disturbing necessity. We tell them to each other in the evening, and they take place in Norway, Italy, Algeria, the Ukraine and are simple and incomprehensible like the stories in the Bible. But are they not themselves stories of a new Bible?" (1985, 65–66). We, their readers, moreover, expect Borowski's great, immortal epic and Levi's stories of a new Bible to emerge, as they did, from the epicenter of evil, the locus of the crime—Auschwitz. Yet from the very beginning and increasingly in our own day, we are drawn to alternative landscapes—Anne Frank's Secret Annex, Momik's cellar in Jerusalem, the Spiegelman home in Rego Park, New York—that decenter the horror and play with our desire to domesticate it. There was a time when the heroes of the Holocaust were the fighters and resisters, each remembered by name and political affiliation. Today they are more likely to be Everysurvivor, whose very survival is heroism enough.

Enough questions for now. It is time to propose a working definition at once formal and flexible, true to the past and attentive to the present. And here it is, with its component parts discussed below: "Holocaust literature comprises all forms of writing, both documentary and discursive, and in any language, that have shaped the public memory of the Holocaust and been shaped by it."

All forms of writing, both documentary and discursive. Genre is the DNA of literature, so to view Holocaust writing through the lens of genre is anything but a dry, academic exercise. Diaries are universally acknowledged to be the core of wartime writing. By reading them in chronological order, we discover a specific type of diary that came into being when the confinement and enslavement of the Jews gave way to their mass extermination. It happened in year 4 of the war. By examining the corpus of wartime writing produced outside the war zone, we discover how literature was used to mobilize the public and then provided the same public with the means for mourning. Inside the war zone we discover reportage, second only to the diary in importance. By noting the recurrence of the coming-of-age story, the bildungsroman, in postwar writing, we recognize (and celebrate) the first such Holocaust story written in the collective voice. By starting from the beginning, we uncover the missing thread of fantasy and allegory. Certain genres rise to prominence, while others are consigned to oblivion. Then the chain may be broken beyond repair.

In any language. The multilingual scope of Holocaust writing makes maximal demands of its readers, none of whom could possibly read the entire corpus in the original. Works originally written in twelve languages are surveyed in this book. Each language is the bearer of religious symbolism, cultural memory and prejudice, national victory and defeat. Language is a mixture of high and low, declarative and cryptic, argot and dialect, doublespeak and "Jewspeak" (see below).

That have shaped the public memory of the Holocaust. Holocaust literature was born and bred in the habitat of public memory. Yet this did not come about all or everywhere at once. (My view of the Holocaust growing up in Yiddish-speaking Montreal was very different from the public perception of it among my cohort on American college campuses, just then engaged in a bitter protest against the war in Vietnam.) The growing public awareness of the Holocaust happened at the intersection of the private and public spheres: real and proxy witnesses began to write and publish, discovering new means of artistic expression and commemoration, but the public sphere was itself divided between Left and Right, East and West. When compiling the evidence of how *The World Reacts to the Holocaust* (Wyman 1996), the historian David Wyman proceeded country by country, and so do we.

Holocaust literature, as we shall see, unfolds both backward and forward: backward, as previously unknown works are published, annotated, translated, catalogued, and promptly forgotten; and forward, as new works of ever greater subtlety or simplicity come into being. How Holocaust literature came to be given that name is a large part of our story.

And been shaped by it. Holocaust memory unfolded in fits and starts because much of its narrative violated the horizon of expectations of a specific public. Instances of scandalous memory are a way of measuring these gaps, as when an uncensored piece of the Holocaust invaded the protected space of a readership that had made its peace with the past too eagerly and too soon. Fierce controversies over a Holocaust novel, a play, even a poem, moreover, tend to happen in nations that look to literature for self-definition: Russia, Poland, France, Italy, Mandatory Palestine (later the State of Israel), and Yiddishland (that is, the places where Yiddish is spoken). In these polities, the public looks to high culture and literary expression to bridge gaps between the generations. In Anglo-Saxon countries with a stronger and more unifying political culture, writers, poets, and playwrights are far less likely to shake things up or bring them back together. Either way, the course of Holocaust memory never did run smooth.

How This Book Is Different

Until now, Holocaust literature has been defined as belonging to a separate universe beyond normal beginning and end, and therefore demanding a unique interpretive lens. For some, this lens is transcendent, as everything—the *genizah* of fragments rescued from the ruins, the six million Jewish victims, the survivors, and their rescuers—has been rendered sacred. For others, the absolute extremity of the Holocaust has rendered obsolete, if not obscene, all accepted norms of beauty, human agency, and moral accountability.

This history and guide rejects all such essentialist claims. The push and pull between the sacred and profane, martyrdom and resistance, public memory and the unassimilable facts is the very story that cries out to be told. This being said, we limit our choice to works of secular literature. Be there no mistake about it: Chaim Grade, Jacob Glatstein, Uri Zvi Greenberg, Yitzhak Katzenelson, Zvi Kolitz, and Simkhe Bunem Shayevitsh are secular writers, however much they employ "God talk." The return to covenantal language is just that—a late return, a studied response, a chapter in literary history, of a piece with something that we shall call "Jewspeak," the invention of a superidiomatic Jewish voice in an otherwise silent universe. Jewish theological responses to the Holocaust—both during and after it—have their own genealogy, chronology, and audience, demanding a separate curriculum (Katz 2007). Where anthologizers have mixed literary and theological responses (Eliav 1965; A. Friedlander 1968; Roskies 1989), their agenda was explicitly restorative. The attempt to yoke the Good Book to the book is nothing less than utopian—itself a religiously inspired response to the Holocaust.

Cutting to the quick, cultural and literary critics in the West were driven by "a need to locate the epicenter of the earthquake." They went in anxious search of "a geographical, verbal or symbolic locus of the crime" (Ezrahi 2003, 319–20). Thus it was that Auschwitz was placed at the heart of the epistemological darkness, serving as the axis of a new world order, a pan-European dystopia, and the birthplace of a new language—what Borowski called "crematorium Esperanto" (1976, 35). For Western intellectuals, Auschwitz became the *telos*, the sum and substance of the Holocaust, the ultimate and exclusive reference point. Once Auschwitz was adopted as a master metaphor, the Jews—crammed into cattle cars at one end of the journey and dragged from the gas chambers as a mass of blue bodies at the other—ceased to be bearers of a distinct cultural identity. They became the Unknown Victims of the Second World War. With the myriad points on the map of the Holocaust reduced to one; with all personal effects plundered or destroyed on arrival at Auschwitz; and with all the inmates—men and women, Gypsies and Jews, the Kapos and *Muselmänner*—dressed in identical striped uniforms, there emerged a master narrative of absolute extremity and anonymity.

The named survivors of the camps were the ones who spoke for the nameless victims, and in the late 1970s, they in turn began to merge into a single composite identity. By that point, there were a sufficient number of survivors' testimonies published, translated, and catalogued to invite a collective biographer to step forward. Based on English translations of eyewitness accounts from the Nazi and Soviet concentration camps, Terrence Des Pres drew a group portrait of *The Survivor* (1976), whose emaciated, brutalized body could withstand the "excremental assault," survive nightmare and waking, survive "radical nakedness" (Des Pres 1976, chaps. 3, 7) through a kind of biological imperative. Countering this Darwinian scheme was Lawrence Langer, whose aesthetics of atrocity centered on the "choiceless choice," the denial of all human initiative or volition in Auschwitz (1982, 46; see also 67–129). Either way, on arrival the inmate was severed from spouse and children and then stripped of clothes, personal belongings, and name, so that reading the testimony of the camp survivors, the cultural critic came away with a new set of universal principles that transcended or subverted the existing moral, religious, and rational order. The "postmodern" world began in Auschwitz.

Just as we propose to study Holocaust literature as literature, to follow its meandering course of development wherever it may lead, so we abandon the search for an epicenter of evil. Rather than look to literature to create an "enduring, compelling narrative of mythical dimensions" that can answer all our needs (S. Friedlander 1992, 346), we shall introduce a new term of art, the "Jew-Zone," at the beginning of the next chapter. In this way we hope to redraw the boundaries of Holocaust literature in both time and space.

Then there is the matter of memory itself. "Memory" has become the new catchword of Holocaust studies, understood to be a species of trauma, and memoir has become the favored genre of Holocaust writing (see N. Levi and Rothberg 2003b, parts V and X). Before abdicating the field to psychoanalytic theory, we should like to take a long, hard look at the ongoing memory work of real and proxy witnesses who have tried since the very beginning to find the part that stands for the whole. The art of fearful metonymy and analogy—especially in its earliest iterations, before the full scale of the catastrophe was known—is another key to our story. We shall read Holocaust literature in the light of Jewish responses to catastrophe in ancient, medieval, and modern times (Ezrahi 1980, 96–148; Mintz 1984; Roskies 1984). That earlier research will inform our discussion of the art of countercommentary—the subtle, ironic, subversive, despairing, and defiant ways in which Scripture was used and abused during wartime, whether by chroniclers and poets in search of analogies to the unprecedented terror, by Soviet Jewish writers trying to suture their wounds, or by survivors and witnesses as different as Anthony Hecht, Primo Levi, Dan Pagis, and Y. D. Sheinson, who wished to translate the spatial into the temporal, and death into life. Shayevitsh's *Lekh-lekho* has already introduced us to the personal dynamic of Scriptural countermemory.

Finally, we come to the question of the timeline. "There is now broad consensus amongst scholars," we read in a definitive anthology of theoretical readings on the Holocaust, "that public awareness of the Holocaust was low in the first decade and a half after the end of World War II, an interval that many think of as a kind of 'latency period' but which might also be thought of in terms of what Marxist cultural theory describes as the inevitable 'cultural lag' between the emergence of the new and the development of a vocabulary—be it conceptual or artistic—to describe it" (N. Levi and Rothberg 2003a, 6). The new story line reconstructs what was actually written, conceptualized, and artistically developed in the order in which this vast and variegated literature came into being, in lands and languages both large and small. The new periodization of Holocaust literature, the backbone of our book, challenges the broad scholarly consensus on every score. By the time we reach the trial of Adolf Eichmann in 1961, the supposed point of origin of public consciousness of the Holocaust in the Western world, our story is half over.

To tell one story well requires that one not try to tell every story. In *The Black Seasons* (2005), Michał Głowiński traced his recuperation from wartime trauma and postwar fixation with the annihilation of the Jews to his reading of a Polish encyclopedia. There was still an orderly, alphabetical world out there that could be described in meticulous, boring detail. S. Lillian Kremer's two-volume *Holocaust Literature: An Encyclopedia of Writers and their Work* (2003) was supposed to be that kind of disinterested summation. Instead, the selection of authors and the allocation of space to each were based on celebrity, current fashion, and political correctness. There was a four-page entry for "Carl Friedman," the pseudonym of a Jewish author who never existed, and no entry for Davidson Draenger, Gebirtig, Glik, Gradowski, Gutfreund, Isacovici, Keilson, Kolitz, Kruk, Malaparte, Opoczynski, Orlev, Perle, Rochman, Rosenfeld, Zable, and Zelkowicz, to mention but a few letters in the alphabet. To set the record on a different course, this book starts from the beginning, giving artistic primacy and moral priority to what came first.

The encyclopedic approach to the Holocaust is based on the belief that more is better. As in certain of the Psalms or the Book of Lamentations, there is a deep belief that once one has covered all the letters of the alphabet, one has said it all. But no one reads a literature in alphabetical order. The uninitiated reader needs an annotated guide, and the guide needs a guiding hand—in our case, two. Adhering to the same chronology as the historical overview, we present a suggested reading list in our Guide to the First Hundred Books on an even playing field, with equal time given to all. Each book is there for a reason: it stands alone, surprising or dismaying us, as the case may be, and complicating the very notion of narrative history. Most writers, moreover, appear only once, requiring us to make a judgment call and select a writer's best or most representative work.

The story could have been told biographically, one writer at a time. It would have been easier for us to distinguish between those prose writers and poets who made the Holocaust their primary path—like Appelfeld, Auerbach, Borowski, Fink, Grynberg, Ka-Tzetnik, Kertész, Levi, Lustig, Rochman, Rosenfarb, Rudnicki, Semprún, Spiegel, and Wiesel—and those who, in Langer's phrase (1995), "admitted" the Holocaust into their literary and moral imagination, like Amichai, Bellow, Glatstein, Grade, Greenberg, Kiš, Orlev, Ozick, Pagis, Singer, Strigler, Sutzkever, Tournier, and many other writers on our list. Ruth Wisse (2003, 1234) has tackled the problem of biography by drawing a more useful distinction between those who became writers by virtue of their wartime experience and those whose approach to art, reality, and history determined their response to Hitler. There is a strong cultural bias nowadays to favor writers in the first category, since they alone are presumed to map the rupture in human values after Auschwitz. In contrast, in this book writers are prized for their ability to create their own space and establish their own precedent, regardless of where they belong on the Holocaust map or even if they do not belong there at all. Alone among the poets, prose writers, and purveyors of Holocaust memory, Abraham Sutzkever accompanies our story from start to finish.

Encyclopedia entries, despite the animus that provoked this project to begin with, have proved very useful when it came to fleshing out the relationships among writers. The fact that Edgar Hilsenrath met Yakov Lind while waiting in a long line of unemployed workers hoping for a day job in construction in Netanya, Israel (Klingenstein 2004), speaks volumes about the marginalization of German-language writers after the Holocaust, the politics of displacement, the formation of a new cohort, and the evolution of a new anti-aesthetic. Hilsenrath and Lind belong together, even though they subsequently moved far apart. Large as the cast of characters is, however, it is far from being exhaustive. The fact that some appear and reappear while others do not appear at all is both by design and by default. A good storyteller tries to keep the reader guessing.

Every writer "creates" his own precursors, Jorge Luis Borges famously said in his essay on Franz Kafka. "A great work modifies our conception of the past, as it will modify the future" (Borges 1951). Art Spiegelman ranks as such a creative force. The revelatory power of *Maus: A Survivor's Tale* (1986) made it imperative that some genealogy be found in the annals of graphic fiction. Even if they did not serve him as models, Kantor's 1945 *The Book of Alfred Kantor* (1971), Y. D. Sheinson's 1946 *Passover Service* (reprinted in *A Survivor's Haggadah*, 2000), and Hana Volavková's anthology of children's drawings and poems from Terezín (1959) suggest a creative trajectory that at the very least underscores how each artistic medium determines the message.

Some works, however, have neither precursor nor sequel. Such a singular masterpiece is Wojdowski's 1971 *Bread for the Departed* (1997) and Głowiński's *The Black Seasons* (2005). They suggest that Poland might be a breeding ground for a highly individualized approach to the Holocaust and provoke one to ask why this might be so.

Besides the artificial cutoff at the first 100 titles—why not some more iconic number, like 150, the number of chapters in the Book of Psalms?—another constraint we faced was linguistic. To make this a usable guide for readers of English, the selection was limited to books available (somewhere, somehow, and with one exception) in English translation. The books are presented in order of creation and completion. The chronology of creation is very different from the chronology of reception, however. Wartime writings from inside the war zone had long to wait before they were discovered, deciphered, and delivered. That is one story. The time lag between publication in the original language and translation into English is another. Those who wish to follow them both are advised to look carefully at all the dates.

The Four Phases of Holocaust Memory

It did not take a generation for a literary response to the Holocaust to be born. But it took at least two generations for its history to acquire a shape. Literary history is the sum of many stories, and it has taken this long for the stories within the story to be told—by no means all, by no means well, and, until now, never from start to finish.

This is the first attempt at a periodization of Holocaust literature worldwide. Chapters 2 through 6 constitute a preliminary map of where this literature comes from, how it has changed, and where it stands now. Beginning at the beginning, this part of the book reveals the cumulative though erratic process of mobilizing and consolidating the public memory of the Holocaust through literary means. This happened in four distinct phases: wartime writing (1938–45), communal memory (1945–60), provisional memory (1960–85), and authorized memory (1985–present). The new road map challenges the accepted story line, introduces a whole new cast of characters, and throws open dozens of new and heretofore unexplored directions. It is a story, moreover, without an ending.

WARTIME WRITING

A new literature of destruction emerged, both inside the war zone and without. The Holocaust became its own archetype—called *khurbn* in Yiddish and *shoah* in Hebrew—by the time of the Liberation.

COMMUNAL MEMORY

The first decade and a half after the end of the Second World War does indeed define a distinct phase in the history of Holocaust literature, second in importance only to the first. With astonishing speed, documentary and literary production resumed in the free memory zones carved out of Germany by the US and British armies and in parts of Poland. This new literature was born with full knowledge of Auschwitz, Treblinka, Majdanek, and Ponar. When the survivors, veterans, and former POWs trickled back, a small but significant window opened onto what was then called the last catastrophe—on both sides of the Iron Curtain, in Jewish Palestine, and in North America. In Yiddishland, the window that opened in 1945 was never shut.

"Communal" is an apt name for this second phase because the scandals that played out in the public sphere were very much directed inward, at other members of the same community. Following the momentous meeting in 1952 of Israeli Prime Minister David Ben-Gurion and German Chancellor Konrad Adenauer, a new scandalous term tore the Jewish community apart: *shilumim*, or reparations. Announcement of the plan for reparations was met with riots and mass rallies in Israel and spilled over to the Jewish street around the globe. In the Yiddish-language encyclopedia dealing with Jewish money, *shilumim-gelt* was defined as "the money that the Germans, may their name be blotted out, pay in recompense for the Nazi Holocaust and theft in the years 1938–1945 and their crime of Cain against the Jewish people" (Rivkin 1959, *s.v. shilumim-gelt*). To stand up and be counted among the naysayers, certain public figures refused inclusion in the *Biographical Dictionary of Modern Yiddish Literature*, one of many Yiddish cultural projects underwritten by the Conference on Jewish Material Claims against Germany. Among the most prominent were Isaac Bashevis Singer and Aaron Zeitlin. Yiddish—the language of the meek, the passive, and the pious—became in the wake of the Holocaust the repository of uncensored, unyielding, politically incorrect Jewish rage. The real conundrum, therefore, is to explain how and why the first two phases of Holocaust memory were so quickly forgotten and were replaced by the great scandal of all times: the presumed silence of those who could and should have responded to the Holocaust but failed to do so. The ultimate accusation levied against past generations is that the wartime and communal phases of Holocaust memory didn't exist at all.

Holocaust literature began to be called that during the communal phase.

The term was born in postwar Poland at a time of terrible stocktaking. Among the returning refugees and exiles, demobilized soldiers, former prisoners and partisans, and those who had somehow managed to survive in hiding was the poet and resistance fighter Michał Borwicz. Borwicz was the first anthologizer of Holocaust poetry (1947) and the first to map out the treacherous terrain of Jews in hiding (1954–55). He earned a doctorate at the Sorbonne in 1954 based on his study of wartime writing in occupied Europe (1973). Among those who remained in Poland after the Kielce pogrom of 1946 and the Communist seizure of power in 1948 was Ber Mark. Mark was responsible for publishing and promoting major works from the Warsaw ghetto and Auschwitz, but in doing so he had to negotiate the ups and downs of late Stalinism.

"Communal" also denotes a postwar landscape fiercely divided between East and West, Left and Right. Whoever tried to stake out a space for themselves on the memory map for the future was forced to take sides. The main purveyors of Holocaust memory in the immediate postwar period, as we shall see, were publishers and intellectuals on the Left, then at the height of its moral suasion both in Europe and abroad. All across Europe, in fact, from France and the Netherlands to the Communist-bloc countries, nations were "caught awkwardly between past and future," and the trauma of national identity was being forged through ignoring and forgetting (Gordon 1999, 51). The same, in large measure, was true in the nascent State of Israel. Holocaust memory had to negotiate between these narrow straits. The "communal" space was small, claustrophobic, and often inhospitable.

PROVISIONAL MEMORY

The next two phases were defined, not merely punctuated, by Holocaust-specific scandals. The third phase began with the Eichmann trial, which aroused fierce international debate before, during, and after it took place. Hannah Arendt's *Eichmann in Jerusalem* (1963) raised the stakes on Jewish self-blame by defining collaboration down. In the same year, a previously unknown playwright named Rolf Hochhuth shook the entire Catholic world, from Basle to Brooklyn, with *The Deputy* (1964). Daring to place the extermination of European Jewry center stage, Hochhuth proceeded to draw everyone into the limelight: Eichmann and Josef Mengele; the giants of German industry; staff sergeants and mere secretaries; abbots, cardinals, and Pope Pius XII. Appended to the published version of the play was a fifty-page historical exposition. *The Deputy* was banned and picketed, and performances of it were routinely interrupted (Whitfield 2010).

Provisional memory coincided with the 1960s, and Hochhuth's was very much the protest of the young, as was Jean-François Steiner's 1966 documentary novel, translated as *Treblinka: The Revolt of an Extermination Camp* (1967).

JEAN-FRANÇOIS STEINER

TREBLINKA

la révolte d'un camp d'extermination

Préface de
SIMONE
DE BEAUVOIR

FAYARD

FIGURE 1

Jean-François Steiner.
*Treblinka: la révolte d'un
camp d'extermination.*
Paris: Fayard, 1966.

Challenging the master narrative of the Resistance, with its scheme of one universalist model fits all, Steiner insisted on the particular fate—and heroism—of the Jews. Arrogating to himself true knowledge of what happened in Treblinka, he displaced the primary witnesses, those who had survived the camp or had first testified about the crimes perpetrated there, with his own agenda, angst, and addressee. The witnesses too rose up in protest. All of his informants demanded that their names be suppressed from all future editions of the book. Rachel Auerbach, who had given unstintingly of her time and expertise, launched a ferocious one-woman campaign aimed specifically at the American edition (Moyn 2005, 122–40). On the advice of his lawyers, Steiner added this disingenuous note to subsequent editions: "The events described in this book are so extraordinary in their nature that the author has chosen to change the names of the survivors in order to protect the privacy of these heroes and martyrs" (quoted in ibid., 132). But that was only to make his elders happy. "I do not regret anything," he boasted in the heat of the controversy, "because I am right," and he was right, he insisted, "because I am twenty-eight years old" (quoted in ibid., 93).

The 1970s and early 1980s were likewise a period of advocacy. The critics and cultural historians who appeared on the scene—Des Pres, Langer, Ezrahi, Rosenfeld, Young, and the first author of this book—each staked out and fiercely defended a separate turf. Each tried to create a different base line, be it the choiceless choice, the experience of displacement, or the death and rehabilitation of the idea of the human. It seemed as if the only way to convince the reader that the Holocaust mattered was by making some exclusive claim for its moral, existential, and otherwise subversive meaning.

As distinct from the communal phase, which was inward-looking and internecine, the provisional phase was marked by the first aggressive, albeit scattershot, attempts to reach beyond the borders of country, language, religion, political affiliation, and genealogy. As the survivor witnesses made the transition from refugee to landed immigrant, they became "writers in search of language" (Wisse 2000, 204), counting among their cohort the likes of Appelfeld, Kosinski, Rawicz and Wiesel. The children of Holocaust survivors made a tentative appearance on the scene.

AUTHORIZED MEMORY

Ushering in the fourth and last phase of public memory was a different kind of scandal. The Bitburg affair, as we shall see, marked the precise moment when the Holocaust entered the realm of "authorized memory"; it was unacceptable, even for a president of the United States, to equate fallen soldiers with the victims of Nazi genocide, let alone Germans and Jews. The Second World War and the Holocaust were coterminous but not morally equivalent.

Leading the charge was Elie Wiesel—who, like other members of his cohort, had by this time become a naturalized US citizen, his language loyalty now firmly established. Authorized, or sanctioned, to speak in the name of the Holocaust, survivors carried that name with pride; but it came at a price, for they were now subject to scrutiny. In 1987, both Jerzy Kosinski's life story and authorship were called into question, which sent him into psychological free fall. Equally precipitous was the fall from grace of Binjamin Wilkomirski's *Fragments* (1995). When it was revealed that both the author and his horrific tale had been invented out of whole cloth, the publisher and the critics were left with egg on their face, and the book was promptly taken out of circulation. When a work or author considered mainstream or cutting edge in Holocaust memory was revealed to be fabricated, it was as if a sacred trust had been broken. "Authorized memory" captures that sense of sacred trust.

Authorization finally came even to that part of the world where the memory of the Holocaust had been driven underground. Just when we might expect Holocaust memory to be moving inexorably from East to West, rendering Eastern Europe invisible and irrelevant once the memory found a permanent home in the United States, the world changed. With the collapse of what President Ronald Reagan called the evil empire, Czechoslovakia, Hungary, East Germany, Poland, Lithuania, Romania, and Russia became places where the past had to be reckoned with and could no longer be falsified and manipulated. The Soviet archives were opened. Ukraine and Belorussia became subject to scrutiny. Amid the upheaval, a new loanword, *Kho-lo-kost*, entered public and political discourse. The ever more global reach of Holocaust memory did not erase the distinctions between nations, religions, and ethnicities. Rather, it gave Holocaust literature a new lease on land, a renewed sense of being rooted in a specific territory.

After a long dry spell, seminal works of Holocaust writing in Polish, French, Italian, German, Dutch, Hungarian, and Serbo-Croatian began to appear in fluent English translations, many of them with critical introductions. The synergy between Holocaust literature and film became especially strong. The second generation claimed the mantle of moral authority from their survivor parents, spawning a whole new area of study. Gender as a category for analysis of the Holocaust became more accepted. Suddenly there was talk about the Americanization of the Holocaust, which also meant that the United States, for all its global power, was competing in an open market.

No sooner did the Iron Curtain fall, however, than it was replaced by a new and fearsome division. Cutting through the phase of Holocaust memory in which we live today is the geopolitical and religious divide between the Middle East and the West. In much of the Islamic world, the Jew has once again been classified as an infidel. Absent a threshold of shame, genocide too is a live option. In the world of radical Islam, Holocaust denial has become an article of faith, and everything in this book, from the epigraphs to the index, is anathema.

Classified Writing

Those who speak of a cultural or time lag between the emergence of the new and the development of a vocabulary to describe it are not completely misguided. In this case, they are pointing to the moment when the Holocaust was given that name, and when communal memory provisionally became the province of the whole world. Could anyone have known that the United States—so far removed from the landscapes and languages of the war, the fierce debates, and bloody divisions—would become the central repository and classifier of Holocaust writing? So great, in fact, was the volume of books and brochures deposited in the US Library of Congress that by 1968 librarians had to make a new entry in its subject catalog. A new rubric was needed to rationalize and organize the publications that were streaming in.

On September 25, 1968, the library's Humanities Section made the following new entry: "Holocaust, Jewish (1939–1945)." Three years later, to facilitate geographic subdivision, the heading was slightly revised. However, so many questions arose regarding both the specific time span of the Holocaust and the use of the qualifier "Jewish" that in October 1995, the library's Cataloguing Policy and Support Office conducted a survey on subject headings and classification numbers relating to the Holocaust. Among the respondents to the survey was the recently established US Holocaust Memorial Museum, which convened a miniconference to deliberate on the eight choices allowable under Library of Congress cataloguing guidelines. These were:

1. Holocaust, Jewish (1939–45)
2. Holocaust, 1939–45
3. Holocaust, 1933–45
4. Holocaust
5. Holocaust (Nazi genocide)
6. Jewish Holocaust, 1939–45
7. Jewish Holocaust, 1933–45
8. Jewish Holocaust

The first question debated was the accuracy and even necessity of the dates. Although historians have argued that the Holocaust began with the Nazi seizure of power on January 30, 1933, when Adolf Hitler was sworn in as chancellor of the German Republic, some respondents to the survey challenged headings 3 and 7 because the events of the period 1933–39 were antecedents of the Holocaust, not part of the Holocaust itself. Appending any dates, one respondent objected, implied that there could be other "Jewish holocausts." Did not the very qualifier "Jewish" obviate the need for a chronology? No, it did not, others argued, for insofar as "Holocaust, Jewish" was an "event" heading and a subset of the broader term "World War," it required that dates be provided; it followed, therefore, that the corresponding dates of the Second World War were the most logical choice (Bell 1996).

The second point of contention was the use of a qualifier. There was general consensus among the respondents that to define the Holocaust as "Nazi genocide" (heading 5) was both confusing and offensive, for it could be read as suggesting that Nazis, not Jews, were the victims. There were compelling arguments, however, in favor of retaining the qualifier "Jewish." It was likely that, in the future, "holocaust," whether capitalized or not, would be applied more broadly to describe atrocities against other ethnic groups. "Jewish" clearly identified the heading for the general public. In the final analysis, the seven alternative headings were rejected and the original subject heading,

"Holocaust, Jewish (1939–1945)," was upheld as being at once the most inclusive, because universally recognized, and the most exclusive.

The inverted structure had the added advantage of retaining "Holocaust" as the key term. Just as the volume of published works on the Holocaust had grown exponentially in the twenty-seven years since the subject heading was first adopted, so too had the number of works of Holocaust denial. Asked whether the current heading, "Holocaust, Jewish (1939–1945)—Errors, inventions, etc.," ought to be retained, the respondents were unanimous in selecting a new analytic breakdown with the following three headings:

— Literature: Holocaust denial literature, D804.35
— Phenomenon: Holocaust denial, D804.355
— Criticism of the literature: Holocaust denial literature—History and criticism, D804.355

Was Holocaust writing to be found only under the letter *D*, which in the Library of Congress classification covers the broad rubric of history? Certainly it was the place to begin. Those who went in search of antecedents in centuries past could start with DS102 ("1. Jews—Persecution—History; 2. Jewish Literature; 3. Holocaust, Jewish"). Alternatively, those who wished to consult the documentary sources at the bedrock of Holocaust memory might begin with DS135, which contained, for instance, rescued diaries and the oversized *yizkor* (memorial) books about the destruction of individual communities. The fastest-growing branch of Holocaust writing, personal narratives of Holocaust survivors and the growing body of literary analysis of them, were assembled in D804.3, while D810 was reserved for books with a focus on survival in the concentration camps. The event and its antecedents; history and memory; the individual and the collective; testimony and critical theory—all were contained within a single, capacious rubric. Yet the search for Holocaust literature led in many other directions as well.

Adhering to long-established practice, imaginative works pertaining to the Holocaust were assigned a completely different classification: "Holocaust Literature," PN56H.55, is housed alongside PN56.D4 ("Death and Literature") and PN.W3 ("War and Literature"). This by no means exhausted the relevant categories, for "Human Liberty in Extremis" was catalogued under HM271; "Passive Resistance" could be found under HM278; and "Art of the Holocaust" was classified in various places under the letter *N*. Overtly theological responses to the Holocaust were catalogued in BM645.H6, among the classics of rabbinic literature. Children's literature, a reader's first exposure to the meaning of history, was catalogued in D804.34 for nonfiction or in PZ for fiction.

Despite the best efforts of the Library of Congress to classify, segregate, and rationalize major works of Holocaust literature, like major works in any discipline, they defy easy categorization, either as literature or as history. This is because, from its very inception, Holocaust literature defied genre boundaries and crossed disciplines.

By housing "Holocaust Literature" alongside "Death and Literature" and not too far from "War and Literature," the Library of Congress has created a level playing field where one is encouraged to follow a comparative, cross-cultural, and transhistorical path. Shelved so close by, just a few decimals away, the literature and scholarship of the First World War, for example, has much to teach us about the literature of the Holocaust. It can teach us about the autonomy of great art, the evolution of generational consciousness, habits of reading, history as refracted through a cultural lens, and the difference a decade can make. It can teach us about the changing status of the eyewitness, the survivor, and the ex-soldier turned poet, playwright, or novelist. It can teach us how public memory pushes hard on private memory. It can teach us how a cataclysm of universal proportions, an unremitting disaster, can shape what it means to live in the modern world. This comparative work cries out to be undertaken.

How to Read Holocaust Literature

Most of this book's readers, like its authors, were born into a world in which the Holocaust had already happened and there existed a body of writing on the subject, if not a separate category in the Library of Congress cataloguing system. Most readers will probably remember their first exposure to this awesome subject, as young readers, perhaps, or as high-school students. For some, it will have been part of a compulsory curriculum, mediated by a certified teacher teaching in a prescribed manner. For others, learning about the Holocaust will have been like discovering some dirty secret about the depths of human depravity, a species of pornography. Still others might have come across the word in some contemporary setting, where it punctuated a rally against nuclear proliferation, described an atrocity perpetrated elsewhere in the world, or was otherwise marshaled as an inappropriate comparison to some current injustice. The Holocaust is so embedded in our psyche that it is hard to imagine living in the world as we know it without the counterknowledge of the ghettos, the killing fields, the trains, the gas chambers, the mounds of human hair. Some readers will have gone on pilgrimage to the death camps and will be left forever wondering how that reality and their own can possibly coexist.

For young readers, the Holocaust comes in small doses, sometimes cloaked in fantasy. It's mostly a story of personal loss and dislocation. Diaries and last letters are the preferred reading among adolescents because these are familiar, domesticated forms, which literally bring the wartime experience "home." This was true for the world at large, whose first exposure to the subject of the Holocaust was Anne Frank's 1947 *Het achterhuis* (The secret annex), better known as *The Diary of a Young Girl* (1952). To this day, many young girls identify with Anne and thrill at Peter's first kiss. Why, then, did the young lovers grow apart?

The Diary of a Young Girl is also the ideal point of entry to a curriculum on how to read Holocaust literature. To read ethically is to read in time. Our insistence on chronology rests on an ethic of unfolding, recovering, provoking, and revoking. Reading in time reveals the receding of narrative into past experience and history, the vertigo of the past recuperated or reinforced by language even as we continue to read fresh, as if from that time and place, and into this time and place.

How did Anne Frank become Everychild—and Everywoman? The canonical status she was accorded certainly had to do with the fact she was a nice, middle-class, Western European girl. Her closest confidante, the addressee of her diary, was "Kitty," a nonjudgmental, nonresponsive, and non-Jewish listener— a silent gentile to the Mistress Chatterbox Jewess. Kitty was an amalgam of her favorite heroine from an adolescent adventure story and the Dutch Christian classmates whom she had just begun to befriend before being forced to enroll in the Jewish Lyceum. Already a refugee from Germany and writing in a new language, Anne was the vulnerable heroine in a story of her own fashioning, her daily life rendered with its essential details and dramas. She conjured her fears away into the alluring Secret Annex. She described her three birthdays, her young womanhood unfolding as she recorded her thoughts, inspired by her reading, about the differences between women and men: "It's easy for men to talk—they don't and never will have to bear the woes that women do!" (Frank 1995, 320). This kind of reading and line of questioning have been made possible by the publication in 1995 of the so-called "definitive edition" of the work, by the rise of feminism and gender theory, and by the evolution of Holocaust memory itself.

In the United States, the nation's revered First Lady, Eleanor Roosevelt, wrote a brief introduction to the 1952 edition, which has been republished many times since. Like François Mauriac's introduction to Elie Wiesel's *Night* (1960), the First Lady's introduction to *The Diary of a Young Girl* is the authorizing voice that proclaims: This work has universal significance! Roosevelt, it should be recalled, was instrumental in creating the human rights declaration of the United Nations. Her introduction advanced the communal agenda of Holocaust memory in the immediate postwar period, which was the consistent and self-conscious campaign to downplay the Jewishness of Anne Frank, led, as we now know, by her father (Rosenfeld 2005). What happened in America was happening throughout Europe and, for different reasons, throughout the Communist bloc countries as well. To understand Anne Frank's reclamation as a symbol of ethnic pride and much more, we turn to her most critical reader, Philip Roth.

There is much controversy about the place of the Holocaust in American life. The historian Peter Novick (1999) attributes changes in the public memory of the Holocaust to the influence of Zionist leaders in particular and of the Jewish, pro-Israel establishment in general. Until recently, few have challenged the consensus view that awareness of the Holocaust began only in the wake of the Eichmann trial. An early dissenter was Roth, in the persona of Nathan Zuckerman. In *The Ghost Writer* (1979), Roth turns the clock back to the 1955 stage play of *The Diary of Anne Frank* and describes "the weeping and inconsolable audience" at the famous Cort Theater production of the play in New York City. Already then, according to Roth, the memory of the Holocaust had become sacralized, and attending the Broadway production had been turned into a communal rite of purgation. "If you have not yet seen the Broadway production of *The Diary of Anne Frank,*" Judge Leopold Wapter sternly counsels the rebellious Zuckerman, "I strongly advise that you do so" (Roth 1979, 102). At the same time as Roth satirizes the older generation for its soppy sentimentalism and naïve literalism, he uses Nathan's love affair with the reincarnated Anne Frank to expose another facet of her postwar image. The Anne of stage and screen is the eroticized female victim. Who wouldn't want to marry her if, in the same conjugal act, he could prove his loyalty to the tribe? Either as sacred icon or sex symbol, Anne Frank has become thoroughly domesticated.

With uncanny prescience, Roth's fantasy revealed a truth about the "real" Anne Frank that did not come to light until the publication of the definitive edition of her diary. Here the author was revealed to be an aspiring writer who, as early as September 21, 1942, began adding comments to her earlier diary entries, in advance of a thoroughgoing (unfinished) attempt to prepare the manuscript for postwar publication, not to mention the action-adventure story called "The Secret Annex" that she was planning to write. Conscious of her new role, she began signing her entries with her full name, "Anne Mary Frank," finally settling on "Anne M. Frank" as her official signature.

In the last acts of her many lives, Anne Frank appears in two mutually exclusive guises. One is Judith Goldstein's presentation of her as utterly exceptional, with her fate and that of her family differing radically from that of Dutch Jewry as a whole (Goldstein 2003). The other is the interpretation of Nelson Mandela, who read the *Diary* while in prison and saw Frank's "militant activism" as a model for the ongoing struggle for human rights (Mandela

2009). Not only are there many lives from which the reader is now invited to choose, there are also many points indicated by the compass of Holocaust memory where the reader may choose to tarry.

How to read Holocaust literature? In all languages. From the beginning: before time, in time, and against time.

WARTIME WRITING IN THE FREE ZONE 1938-45

The Two Zones of Wartime Writing

The classifiers at the Library of Congress dignified the Holocaust with a consistent name, identified its specific victims, defined its rough temporal boundaries, and parsed it into broad humanistic categories. But without a spatial grid it is impossible to retell its story from beginning to end, as tell it we must if we are ever to understand the unfolding of the Holocaust in public memory. "Holocaust, Jewish (1939–1945)" is an accurate rubric of the event as it was perceived long after the fact and from not quite halfway around the globe. It describes the event in reel time—that is, the place it came to occupy in popular culture, fitting nicely into the genre of the war movie. But the real-time narrative requires grounding in space, and that space requires a new name, one that will convey its ultimate purpose but that is so vulgar it may test the limits of free speech. The story of the Holocaust story begins at its point of entry: the Jew-Zone.

Hitler redrew the map of the world. His campaign for Lebensraum—ample "living space" for Aryan Germans—was contingent on making Europe *Judenrein*, free of Jews, so that by 1942 his solution to the Jewish problem extended its reach as far as Tunis. Hitler waged his relentless war against the Jews on a savagely leveled playing field in which the Jewish enemy was dispossessed, then segregated, and finally annihilated. The work of destruction proceeded at the intersection of time and ever-contracting space.

The chronology of Hitler's defeat on the military front was the opposite of his victory on the Jewish front. The battle of Stalingrad in the dead of winter 1943 marked the beginning of Hitler's end. But by then, the war against Europe's Jews was entering its final stage. By March 1943 all four gas chambers and crematoria in Auschwitz-Birkenau were running at full capacity. The April uprising in the Warsaw ghetto held the killers at bay for only a few weeks, just long enough to make the illustrated report that ss Police General Jürgen Stroop submitted in triplicate to Himmler that much more colorful. (In Gothic script, the title page read: *"Es gibt keinen judischen Wohnbezirt in Warschau mehr"*—"The Jewish Quarter of Warsaw is no more.") Hungarian Jewry, the last major holdout, did not know that a young Adolf Eichmann was waiting for them in the wings. Time for the Jews had simply run out.

Classifying the Holocaust as an "event" and making its time span the same as the Second World War was perhaps a necessary shortcut for the Library of Congress, but it does nothing to define the Holocaust's spatial boundaries. "Jewish," as the library's classifiers well knew, is not a geographical marker. Geography was destiny, and to render that objective and subjective reality, one needs a simple, brutal demarcation of space. What is needed is a new term of art, something so in-your-face and unsettling that it cannot be spoken of in polite company. What is needed is to restore the division of the globe in the years 1939–45 into two zones: a Free Zone and a Jew-Zone. Without such a Holocaust-specific map, it is impossible to imagine what it was like to live in that real time and space.

Which zone every Jewish man, woman, or child was in during the Second World War was literally a matter of life and death.

Just as it mattered for those Jews in uniform whether they were landing with American troops in Sicily, Casablanca, or Midway or fighting house-to-house with the Red Army in Stalingrad or in a tank in the Kursk Salient, so it mattered for Jewish noncombatants if they were interned in Westerbork, Drancy, or the Pawiak Prison.

It mattered if they were doing forced labor in Płaszów, Villa Emma, or Algiers.

It mattered if they were hiding on the Aryan side of Warsaw, in a village outside of Kovno, or in an annex in Amsterdam.

If they lived in the Polish city of Przemysl, it mattered on what side of the River San they lived. The Germans controlled one side, the Soviets the other.

It mattered whether their transport was heading for Sobibor, Dachau, or Auschwitz.

It mattered if their children were hidden in a monastery in the south of France or were living with them in the ghetto. It mattered if the children were evacuated to Fergana, Stalinobad, or Kuibyshev.

It mattered whether their children were studying in the north of England, in a camp in Teheran, or in a classroom in the Bronx.

It mattered if they were with German-speaking refugees on Riverside Drive, Washington Heights, or Beverly Hills.

It mattered whether they attended a rally in Red Square, Dizengoff Square, or Madison Square Garden.

Inside the Jew-Zone, the management of space was different from anywhere else. Concentrated Jew-zones called ghettos were established in over a thousand locales, putatively to protect the Aryan population from being polluted by the Jews. To make the work of segregating the Jews more efficient, the Germans imported them from exotic places, Jews who spoke foreign tongues. Jews who had been practicing Christians for two generations (sometimes more) were also included, as dictated by the Nuremberg Laws (Michman 2011).

The management of time was also different inside the Jew-Zone from anywhere else. The historian Michael Marrus, who cast his net across the European expanse of the Jew-Zone and went back in time to the mid-1930s, has made this amply clear. To begin with, in Germany, there was endurance time and emigration time. Wartime had its curfews and endless waits for bread and in offices of internal security; in hiding there was fugitive time; in ghettos there was the Judenrat's strategy of buying time, which ultimately did nor forestall deportation time; there was, for some, resistance time; and in the death camps, there was starvation time and, for most, killing time—the end of time (Marrus 2001).

The Jew-Zone is a geography beyond geography, the historical equivalent of Middle Earth. Just as fantasy literature pushes the human imagination beyond the boundaries of observable reality, so the wartime landscape requires a new topography. By this we mean not only the concentration camps, death camps, and killing fields whose very names fill one with horror—Auschwitz, Belsen, Babi Yar—but also the Alef-Beth of the annihilation (Blumental 1981):

Alef: arm band, Aryan papers, Aryan side
Beth: Bunker, Bath (euphemism for the gas chambers)
Gimmel: Ghetto, Gibraltar (the passageway between Żelazna and
    Chlodno streets in the Warsaw ghetto that connected its northern and
    southern parts), Generalgouvernement

To live inside the Jew-Zone was to lie. Censorship and encryption were the counterfeit currency of the realm.

"When I am not allowed to write anymore," Etty Hillesum instructed her friend Christine van Nooten in Amsterdam from the Westerbork transit camp on July 1, 1943,

> I'll still be able to send a postcard following the arrival of a parcel, with the words "Parcel received"—nothing else. So if a meaningless card like that comes, you'll know why. And something else: we are permitted to send telegrams to the Jewish Council to ask for things we need—also without further comment.
>
> But we are forbidden to be specific; we can only put something like "food" in the telegram. So let's agree from now on, for example: book = butter, writing = jam, ink = rye bread, shoelaces = fruit." (Hillesum 1986, 72)

Hillesum was forced to improvise. Native to her Yiddish-speaking coreligionists in the East, however, was an art of cryptic communication that had been perfected over generations. Every speaker of Yiddish knew that of the three components of the language—the Germanic, Slavic, and Hebraic—the last was the most "coded," because it was utterly foreign to one's non-Jewish neighbors. Both Emanuel Ringelblum in the Warsaw ghetto and Oskar Rosenfeld in Łódź-Litzmannstadt, for example, adopted the same code word, *Ashkenazim*, to signify the German rulers, which even added a touch of humor. In peace time, "Ashkenazim" denoted not the enemy but Jews who followed the Franco-German liturgy. "Naïve as he was," says the editor of the English edition of Herman Kruk's *Diary of the Vilna Ghetto*, "Kruk used various devices of conspiracy that anybody who reads Yiddish could easily decipher, . . . names are often given in reverse: Rebayrsh for Schreiber, Shtivelepets for Tsepelevitsh, and so on" (Harshav 2002, l). Little boys who studied in the traditional *heder*, the editor might have noted, routinely learned the Hebrew alphabet backward and forward. Rosenfeld—who wrote in German, the language of the enemy—had to be more careful than Kruk and Ringelblum, and sometimes he resorted to more elaborate word substitutions: "August 18. Ghetto again in a state of agitation because of events outside. *Milchome* in critical stage—the same time rumors: Horowitz-Hanoar to be brought from over there to us, pogrom, but ghetto administrator (Ashkenes) prevents it" (O. Rosenfeld 2002, 116). [My translation: "The war is in a critical stage. There are rumors that Hitler Youth were to be brought in from Germany to run wild inside the ghetto, but ghetto director Hans Biebow prevented this from happening."] This low cryptic style, with its comic dissonance between what is being encoded and how it is encoded, is another authenticating sign of Jewish discourse *in extremis* (Roskies 1984, 164–76).

Both collectives and individuals were forced to keep a double set of records. The Łódź ghetto is the best-known example. In addition to the meticulous communal record, the celebrated Polish-German *Chronicle of the Łódź Ghetto* (Dobroszycki 1984), which was surprisingly candid about everything except the German and Jewish overlords, we also have the hidden transcripts of two professional journalists: Oskar Rosenfeld, writing in German, and Josef Zelkowicz, writing in Yiddish. Rosenfeld's and Zelkowicz's private notebooks and journalistic sketches, which each man planned to publish after the war, are unfinished masterpieces of a new literature in the making.

To survive on the Aryan side required falsifying your record. Lying was a way of life for those who had secured Aryan papers. In the ghettos and camps, where physical contact with one's fellow inmates was unavoidable, the vast majority of Jews lived together and died together. Those few in number who went into hiding suffered the opposite fate, living a lonely existence of daily improvisation as they tried to pass by expunging their past and assuming false identities. In the ghettos and camps, "people were always surrounded by fellow-victims, with only the presence of the hangmen to break the monotony. Here—the opposite: surrounded and in constant contact with people from different spheres, of diverse intellectual, moral, and ideological levels" (Borwicz 1954–55, 1:13). Blending into one's surroundings involved mastering a foreign culture, different mannerisms, speech habits, body language, and dress. Since Jewish life was outlawed, to survive meant to live on the run, with even the smallest mistake spelling one's doom. Jewish women, trying to pass as Aryans, started bleaching their hair blond. No sooner did the Germans and their Polish stool pigeons get wise to this disguise than blondes became easy targets, and even natural blondes began dyeing their hair black (ibid., 1:93). Having "a good appearance" meant looking like a goy. A "bad appearance" was anything—anything at all—that gave you away as a Jew. "And what if you suddenly run in to somebody you know?" shouts a character in a novel who is trying to justify her survival. "All he has to do is call you by name. Just say one word, or show it on his face. Do you know how much courage it took to live on Aryan papers?" (Grynberg 2001, 84).

In this upside-down world, the most vulnerable part of the population— the children—became the most resilient, because they alone could slip under and over the ghetto walls and across forbidden borders, they could more easily adapt to living hand-to-mouth, and they suffered fewer moral qualms (Borwicz 1954–55, 1:70–91). "Playing an 'Aryan,'" Henryk Grynberg recalled, "meant fear and performance, like [being] on stage, constantly, each day and night," and if you were lucky enough to survive, "you'd never want to be a Jew again" (Grynberg 2004, 5).

There is no Library of Congress category for "Holocaust Literature: identity denial literature," but there ought to be. It would begin with *Justyna's Narrative* (Davidson Draenger 1996), about the heroic effort of young fighters to engage the enemy outside the ghetto walls, then proceed to the stories and novels of Louis Begley, Ida Fink, Michał Głowiński, Henryk Grynberg, Jerzy Kosinski, Arnošt Lustig, Uri Orlev, Adolf Rudnicki, and Jiří Weil, all of whom depict the machinations that ordinary men, women, and children used to survive by lying. It would catalog everything from the hallucinatory prose of Piotr Rawicz to the *Comedy in a Minor Key* by Hans Keilson; from *The Beautiful Mrs. Seidenman* (Szczypiorski 1989), who eluded her Polish stalker and a German interrogator by passing as the widow of a Polish army officer, to David Fremde joining a band of child smugglers in *Bread for the Departed* (Wojdowski 1997). There could be a cross-reference: see also *Wartime Lies*.

The Jew-Zone had no epicenter, no geographical, verbal, or symbolic locus of the crime. Each point on the Holocaust compass was an entire world. Surviving one was no guarantee to surviving another. It is through literature that we can learn the language, subjective reality, moral contingency, and symbolic significance of each one.

The Screamers: The Literature of Mobilization

Holocaust literature, it is universally believed, began with a conspiracy of silence. No one knew. No one cared. And no words could express what was happening. Yet the public record, now coming back to light, reveals a different point of origin. Throughout the Free Zone—in the United States, Britain, the Soviet Union, and Mandatory Palestine—the outlines of a new narrative concerning the annihilation of the Jews began to appear as the war was unfolding, a narrative that was the work of professional writers and public intellectuals, men and women who straddled the Old and New Worlds. Combining old and new forms of literary self-expression, their response ranged from protest to elegy, sometimes in the same person. At this early stage, the major obstacle was not the representation of events that had never been described before, of which there was as yet no firsthand knowledge. The problem was how to combat the apathy and matter-of-factness of one's fellow countrymen and women. Breaking through to public consciousness required that one find the appropriate means of expression and performance. The protest pageant, a new form of mass entertainment, was adapted for wartime use; a British novelist included the first description of mobile killing vans even as he railed against a disbelieving world; a famous Yiddish actor-director and a Yiddish poet were chosen to serve as Soviet ambassadors to the West; and Soviet Jewish soldiers become the first to report on the sites of slaughter in poetry and prose. Volumes in a paperback series dedicated to the war and the Jewish catastrophe began to appear in Mandatory Palestine, and the last letters to friends or relatives living in freedom that were published gave Hebrew readers a sense of the unfolding tragedy in real time. Literary production, in short, became a second line of defense; amid the screaming headlines, the still, small voice of the poet found ways to make itself heard.

Briefly (because there is so much material to cover), we shall survey the varied responses to the Holocaust in the countries adjacent to the Jew-Zone as a single, transnational literature. This follows the approach taken by the historian Yosef Gorny, who reads the response of the Jewish press in Palestine, Britain, the United States and the Soviet Union as one conversation in multiple voices, stretching across the globe (Gorny 2012). Despite fierce ideological differences between one newspaper and another, and very different political realities on the ground in the Free Zone, Gorny finds that the Jewish press outside the Jew-Zone entered an uncertain "in-between" phase of collective awareness, vacillating between concern and dread about the fate of European Jewry. By November 1942, however, the same press entered a second phase, a "time of horror," when rage was tempered by a sense of utter helplessness (ibid., 18). Going country by country and language by language, Gorny arrives at a composite and layered narrative of collective awareness of the Holocaust in the most public of media. Most of the writers we are about to discuss wrote for the press, and their other works were read by some of the same readers. Literature, from the start, was mobilized to help shape public awareness of the Holocaust even as it was shaped by it.

One of the first books of poetry written in direct response to the destruction of European Jewry was published in New York by the poet, novelist, journalist, and literary critic Jacob Glatstein, and its genesis was a protest poem that took the Yiddish world by storm when first published in April 1938 (Norich 2007, 42–73). "Good Night, World," the poet shouted angrily, as he demonstratively slammed shut the gate and went back, of his own accord, to the ghetto, there to don the yellow Jewish star with pride:

Prussian pig and hate-filled Pole,
Jew-killers, land of guzzle and gorge.
Flabby democracies, with your cold
sympathy compresses.
Good night, electro-impudent world. (Glatstein 1987a)

What could have happened in April 1938 to prompt such a dramatic about-face, such an aggressive stance toward the "Jesusmarxists," those apostate Jews who had misled the world? *Kristallnacht*, the night of broken glass, was still seven months away. No ghetto walls were to be built for another two years. Not since Hayyim Nahman Bialik in the wake of the Kishinev pogrom of

April 1903 had a Jewish poet provoked so much controversy, breast beating, and sheer awe by leading the charge against false hopes and false promises (Wisse 1996). In Bialik's "In the City of Slaughter" (1989), the prophet is ordered to stifle his rage, abandon the habitation of Jews, and make his way to the desert. "Within me weeps the joy of coming home," says the speaker at the end of Glatstein's poem (1987a). Better a diminished, darkened Jewish world than none at all.

This mock-prophetic poem, with the poet as his own Moses, was actually a long time in coming. In 1934, after a twenty-year absence, Glatstein returned to Poland to see his mother before she died, and that trip changed everything: he shifted suddenly from poetry to prose; he saw fascism face to face; and he bore witness to the imminent destruction of Polish Jewry, one way or another (Glatstein 2010). What, then, did it mean for this archetypally modernist poet to call for a voluntary return to the ghetto? It meant that the more he immersed himself in the cultural specificity of Yiddish, the more he discovered the wellsprings of his own creativity. The freer and more culturally autonomous he then became, the more he could stand proud, without fear or pretense, against the enemy within and without (Wisse 1996).

Called *Gedenklider*—meaning memorial poems or poems of remembrance—these poems (Glatstein 1943) attempted to anchor the shock of Jewish history within the personal experience of the poet, a poet who until then had snubbed his nose at overtly Jewish themes and had perfected the urbane sensibility and modernist style to go with it. In contrast, the *Gedenklider* were written in the weighty, witty, super-idiomatic style of a "national" poet. They were Exhibit A of what will be known throughout this book as "Jewspeak." The volume opened, in biblical cadence, with a section called "An Almond Staff Blossoms in the Desert," while the second part was devoted to the current crisis, some of the poems carrying specific dates: "Wagons" (June 1938), "On the Butcher Block" (June 1939), and "Lublin, 1941." The latter range in tone from ferocious to elegiac, from a Jew who awaits execution "On the Butcher Block" and faces down his accusers to a ghetto mother rocking her child to sleep in the absence of its father (Glatstein 1993). Now immersed in the not-so-ineffable self, the poet internalized the fate of the many: "I am I," he proclaims, "thousands of slaughtered I's" (Glatstein 1987c). "Such a wealth of gravestones," he is forced to admit, "I have never seen them before. / Day and night I shall mourn the names. // I have never been here before" (ibid.).

The first people who got the message out to the West were those who, like Glatstein and Arthur Koestler, consistently lived in two worlds. A Hungarian-born journalist in the German language, a war correspondent, a former Communist and a prisoner several times over, Koestler found final refuge in England. In January 1944 the *New York Times Magazine* ran a provocative article by him in which he laid bare the recurrent nightmare of the refugee survivor, who knew that his cries for help would remain unheeded (Koestler 1945). Koestler blamed his fellow countrymen for their "matter-of-fact unimaginativeness," which had become an almost racial characteristic. But in truth, he believed that there existed among all peoples a psychological split between "knowing" and "believing" that no amount of rhetoric, exhortation, or persistence could ever reconcile. The root cause of disbelief was the chronic inability of humans to bridge the "tragic plane" of history and the "trivial plane" of everyday life, and this Koestler knew both from his reading of the past and by dint of bitter personal experience. The biblical prophets Amos, Hosea, and Jeremiah had been no more heeded in their day than the "screamers" in his. "We, the screamers," he reported to his readers in the United States, "have been at it now for about ten years."

> At present we have the mania of trying to tell you about the killing—by hot steam, mass-electrocution, and live burial—of the total Jewish population of Europe. So far three million have died. It is the greatest mass killing in recorded history; and it goes on daily, hourly, as regularly as the ticking of your watch. I have photographs before me on the desk while I am writing this, and that accounts for my emotion and bitterness. (Ibid., 88–89)

Vowing to continue his efforts, Koestler was intent on finding a psychological explanation for his failure to bridge the gap between horrified public responses to the accidental loss of fifty lives and the planned murder of millions. It wasn't that people didn't know what was going on. Rather, such things were simply unimaginable.

Koestler had made the incommunicability of the horror a central theme of *Arrival and Departure*, originally published in 1943—his second work written in English (Koestler 1969). The work is flawed as a novel, but it contains a brilliantly imagined episode. Buried in the psyche of its semi-autobiographical hero, so deeply that only a psychoanalyst can pry it loose, is Peter's eyewitnessing of how a "Mixed Transport" of human cargo was divided up and dispensed with according to its usefulness to the Germans. Immediately consigned to the useless category were the last five carriages, containing old and sickly Jews—who, in defiance of all logic but with a premonition of what was to come, began singing at the top of their lungs a Yiddish question-and-answer song about the feast that awaited them in messianic times. Soon, Peter and the other useful prisoners watched from inside the train as the choir was herded into vans, where they were gassed to death (ibid., 78–87). The singing, then, was a communal speech act turned by the abandoned Jews into a spontaneous act of mass martyrdom. Until such time as an earlier text is found, this 1943 work marks the formal beginning of Holocaust fiction as we know it.

In the United States, other recent or almost-recent arrivals organized political action groups, exploiting the mass media and appealing to a different constituency to do battle against apathy, business as usual, and disbelief. The Committee for a Jewish Army of Stateless and Palestinian Jews changed its name as it changed its mission. Beginning in July 1943 it was known as the Emergency Committee to Save the Jews of Europe (Baumel 2005, 96, 113–14). Friends and enemies alike knew them as the Bergson Boys, six young members of the revisionist-Zionist military movement in Palestine whose mission it was to wake up the somnolent Jews of America. The most provocative American personality whom Peter Bergson succeeded in co-opting for the cause was Ben Hecht, a Hollywood scriptwriter, Broadway playwright, and man about town. After months of backroom politics aimed at blocking its publication, Hecht's global indictment finally appeared as a display ad in the *New York Times* on September 14, 1943. Billed as a "Ballad of the Doomed Jews of Europe" and written in doggerel, the last stanza read: "Oh world be patient / it will take / some time before the murder crews / Are done. By Christmas you can make / Your Peace on Earth / without the Jews" (quoted in Lukert 2002, 102–3). The American Jewish leadership was outraged.

Protest and elegy were the two poles of the early public response to the murder of European Jewry. In default of actual materials from the Jew-Zone, the vicarious witnesses appealed to their audience using any means at their disposal. Protest was the main engine of response because it answered to a three-pronged strategy, new in the annals of modern Jewry: to make the Jews front-page news, rescue the surviving remnant, and avenge the slaughter. Thus, among their growing arsenal of genres, the ad hoc advocacy groups (never large enough to constitute a movement) used petitions, paid ads, days of mourning, mass rallies, and a new form invented by the entertainment industry: the protest pageant (Whitfield 1996). The most famous and elaborate of these was Ben Hecht's "We Will Never Die: A Memorial Dedicated to the 2,000,000 Jewish Dead of Europe," which harnessed the talents of the German-Jewish refugee composer Kurt Weil; the theatrical producer Billy Rose; the playwright and director Moss Hart; and the actors Edward G. Robinson, Paul Muni, and Sylvia Sydney. "We Will Never Die" played before more than a hundred thousand Americans between its opening in Madison Square Garden on March 9, 1943, and its last, updated performance in the Hollywood Bowl, on July 21, when the tour was forced to close because of opposition by mainstream Jewish organizations. Viewed in retrospect, it seems clear that by March 1943 everything was already in place for the birth of a new genre: Complete support for the war effort mixed with a growing despair over the millions of one's people in European captivity who would never make it through (Baumel 2005, 114–18).

"We Will Never Die" ends by giving those millions a voice: six Jews, "two men, a rabbi, two women and [a] child," emerge out of giant Tablets of the Law to represent "the six million Jews, in German-held lands," of whom "the Germans have said that none shall remain." They are ghostly and gray, in keeping with the narrator's prediction that European Jewry "will have been reduced from a minority to a phantom" (Hecht 1943, 60). Each of the six symbolic voices, each coming from a different then-known point on the Holocaust compass, begins its peroration with the haunting words, "Remember us." As the dead move slowly off stage, the tenor leads the choir in the singing of the kaddish. For all its theatrical excess, overblown props, and cast of hundreds, "We Will Never Die" marked the beginning of a secular liturgy to commemorate the Holocaust.

Somewhere faraway, inside the Jew-Zone, another war was being waged—a war that Jews were losing and, through which, the world was losing a world of Jews. The first response of those who perceived what was happening was to scream. By 1943, when the numberless dead began to demand their due and the full scale of the catastrophe was just beginning to sink in, the second impulse was to remove one's shoes, sit down on the ground, and begin the traditional rites of mourning. Sometimes one family contained both screamers and mourners. Marie Syrkin was a journalist, political activist, and daughter of a prominent Zionist leader. Her husband was the Objectivist poet Charles Reznikoff. Thus, in the Labor-Zionist *Jewish Frontier*, Syrkin published "The Flag on the Ghetto Wall" (1945), marking the start of the Jewish uprising against the Germans, while Reznikoff published his "Kaddish" (1945) for the nameless dead and a prayer for those still living.

There is no one-to-one correlation between what these writers, poets, and public figures knew and how they wrote. But sometimes dates of publication are informative. Bruno Bettelheim was one of hundreds of German Jewish artists and intellectuals who found refuge in the United States. Feeling that his anger about the treatment he had received at the hands of the ss in Buchenwald "might endanger his objectivity," Bettelheim waited nearly three years to publish "Individual and Mass Behavior in Extreme Situations" (1960, 54). The work first appeared in the fall of 1943, when there was finally a chance of defeating the enemy and Bettelheim hoped that by exposing the evils of the concentration camps he would help secure the Allied victory. So the timeline of the war turned even scholarship into a source of activism.

Much of this literature belongs under the rubric of what the Germans call *Exilliteratur*. The German "literature of exile" officially began on the night of May 10, 1933, with the public book burnings carried out by university students across Germany. Those whose books were burned fled the country. Some, like Thomas Mann, became the voice of the anti-Nazi opposition; others, arriving in Hollywood, made their voices heard on screen, in performance, and in public appearances. Addressing the University of California, Los Angeles, Writers' Congress, held on October 1–3, 1943, the celebrated German Jewish novelist Lion Feuchtwanger, who had arrived in the United States only three years before, spoke in English about "The Working Problems of the Writer in Exile." He devoted most of his address to the special plight of writers, who must give up that which is most precious to them—their language—and thus forfeit their economic base. Feuchtwanger's conclusion was surprisingly upbeat, however. "Almost everything that seemed to hamper our work finally contributed to its welfare," he told his audience, seeing as he was now fluent in English (Feuchtwanger 1944, 348). Feuchtwanger also mentioned in passing, without naming names, that "many preferred suicide to the tragicomedy of such an existence" (ibid., 347). Among the names he might have mentioned were Ernst Toller (1893–1939), Walter Benjamin (1895–1940), and Stefan Zweig (1881–1942). A few writers, like Ernst Weichert, went into "internal exile," remaining under Nazi rule without succumbing to its evils.

In the German context, 1938 was the point of no return: the year of *Kristallnacht*; the large-scale, coordinated pogroms throughout Germany that targeted synagogues and Jewish storefronts; the *Kindertransport*, those neatly dressed Jewish children with cardboard numbers around their necks who would survive the war in England but would never see their parents again; and mass arrests and internments in Dachau and Buchenwald. The names of Dachau and Buchenwald were among the first German words to enter the Holocaust lexicon, despite their *ch* sound that is so hard for English speakers to pronounce. What the broken glass, the children's transports, and the German penal colonies had in common is that all were firmly situated on the home front: they were organized, state-sanctioned assaults on a civilian population, and they had nothing whatsoever to do with advancing the war effort. They preceded the outbreak of the Second World War by one critical year.

Exilliteratur is a useful term because it focuses our attention on a large group of individuals who lived in two worlds, as refugees and immigrants. They were among the most responsive to the horrors unfolding in the world they had left behind. Hannah Arendt, for one, was at war with the members of her tribe. In the January 1943 issue of the *Menorah Journal*—her first public appearance in English—she published a merciless group portrait of her fellow refugees, who had lost their homes, occupations, language, and private lives. Schooled to be optimists and idealists, German Jews were ill-equipped to face the new reality, to cope with contemporary history, which, according to Arendt, "has created a new kind of human beings—the kind that are put in concentration camps by their foes and in internment camps by their friends" (2007, 265). "We don't want to be refugees," she summed up her self-indictment, "since we don't want to be Jews" (ibid., 272). The only choices for such Jews, in her view, were total assimilation or suicide.

To arrive at this group portrait, Arendt had only to walk outdoors, since she had settled on the Upper West Side of Manhattan, then popularly known as *Die Klagenmauer* (the wailing wall), because all one heard on the street was German Jews bemoaning their fate. But what of those who came speaking Yiddish? They too underwent a crisis of faith. Until 1943, the politics of Yiddish were aligned with those of the world proletariat, and *Di tsukunft* (The future), the Socialist Yiddish literary monthly published in New York, had been the standard-bearer of enlightenment and in-your-face secularism. Imagine, then, the response of readers when they saw, emblazoned on the cover of the August 1943 issue and within a thick black border, the word "YIZKOR!" (meaning remember, in both Yiddish and Hebrew). More shocking still were the words of Psalms 34:22 reproduced in Hebrew and Yiddish on the inside cover. "Our misfortune is the deathblow of the wicked," it read. "The foes of the righteous shall be ruined." In lieu of an editorial was a full-page reproduction of Marc Chagall's "The Martyr," which depicted a Russian Jew bound to a stake in imitation of Christ on the cross (Roskies 1984, 286–87). Where only months before, ardent Bundists had inveighed against Jewish statehood and upheld the platform of Jewish cultural autonomy in Poland, the same writers were now invited to mourn the destruction of their Polish brethren.

Among the two dozen contributors to the issue was Isaac Bashevis Singer, who had just emerged from a seven-year-long writer's block with both fists flailing (Roskies 1995, 279–93). Asked to evaluate the accomplishments of Polish Yiddish literature between the two world wars, Singer famously pronounced in 1943: *"Zi iz geven getlekh on a got, veltlekh on a velt"* (it was godly without a God, worldly without a world; 1995, 120). To rectify that imbalance, Singer now embarked on a series of densely narrated tales that were designed to reinstate if not God, then at least his demonic Other. Singer called the new series "The Devil's Diary." His radical solution to the crisis of secular Yiddish culture was also his immediate response to the destruction of Yiddish-speaking Jewry: to instantiate the power of evil in a lost world. The answer to exile was to return home—if only in the imagination.

The largest concentration of Jewish refugees and exiles in the world was in the Soviet Union. It was a refuge—as harsh as they come, but a refuge nonetheless—for 250,000 Jews who managed to flee Hitler. The Soviet Union was also the first place to bear the full brunt of the Nazis' Final Solution. With the German invasion on June 22, 1941, the mobile killing units of Operation Barbarossa descended on the dense Jewish populations of Belorussia and Ukraine. To mobilize for the war against fascism, the Soviet regime allowed its Jews a collective voice, and eventually to mourn the incalculable loss of Jewish life.

Here, the problem was not how to combat the apathy and matter-of-factness of one's fellow countrymen. It was either total mobilization or total defeat. Breaking through to public consciousness and finding the appropriate means of expression and performance were matters of state. Founded along with four other outreach organizations to build international support for the Soviet war effort, the Jewish Anti-Fascist Committee held radio rallies in Moscow that were broadcast all over the country and published in the weekly magazine *Eynikayt* (Unity) for both local and foreign consumption. Yiddish writers from Poland—like Chaim Grade, Binem Heller, Rokhl Korn, and Ber Mark, who had fled to the Soviet territories—were also published in its pages. The annihilation of the Jews, a catastrophe demanding its own space within the larger narrative of the global war against Hitler, found its first and most public expression in the Soviet Union (Gorny 2012, 185–202; Redlich 1995, 21–35).

It is easy for Western readers to dismiss the Soviet Jewish response to the destruction of the Jews as propaganda parading as literature. We are repulsed by its strident tones, by a rhetorical register so high that its only useful purpose is declamation. It was in the pages of *Eynikayt*, for example, that Itzik Feffer, a colonel in the Red Army, proclaimed most famously, "I am a Jew!" He said it not once but fourteen times—only twelve times, to be precise, in the *Eynikayt* version but all fourteen times in the uncensored version published in Feffer's *Roytarmeish* (Of the Red Army), which appeared in New York in 1943 with a cover design by his old friend, Marc Chagall (Feffer 1964; Harshav 2004, 524–34). Thousands of Jews actually serving in the Red Army copied and memorized the truncated version—a good thing, because the Soviet censor never again allowed it to be published within the Soviet Union proper (Shmeruk 1964, 802–3).

The war, paradoxically, opened the floodgate. Unlike their Yiddish- or German-speaking brethren in America, Soviet Yiddish writers experienced no crisis of faith. The call to mobilize on all fronts to defeat the Germans and liberate the conquered territories gave them license to consolidate past and present, East and West, their Soviet and Jewish national identities (Murav 2011, 111–49). Peretz Markish was the most respected voice of Soviet Jewry—and the most prolific. In 1943, as soon as cultural production resumed in Moscow, the evacuated capital, Markish published *Far folk un heymland* (For people and homeland), a 125-page collection of his wartime verse. Both the title and patriotic design (the *lamed* and *kuf* of the word *folk* suggesting a hammer and sickle) proclaimed the poet's fierce determination to speak as a Jew and Soviet citizen. In his opening hymn "Dem yidishn shlakhtman" (To the Jewish fighter, 1964a), Markish invoked the Ten Commandments, the Judaic legacy to world civilization, and then recalled with pride the retribution exacted on Shechem by Simeon and Levi for the rape of their sister. By following this precedent exactly, Jews in the Red Army would go straight from Shechem to the sacking of Berlin. Contained in a separate, smaller, section of the volume was a cycle of poems under the Aramaic heading "Ho lakhmo" (This is the bread [of affliction], 1964b). The allusion to the Passover Haggadah with its trajectory from slavery to freedom linked two disparate images: a last klezmer playing for Jews at a shtetl wedding and the same Jews being led to their mass grave.

Suddenly the barriers of Jewish time and space were breached. Overnight, it seemed, the language and imagery of public and poetic discourse were infused with the names of long-forgotten heroes, not as the stuff of legend, not faded under the dust of centuries, but responding directly to the present. Most prominent among this roster of proud names were Samson; David fighting Goliath; the Maccabees; and the last Jewish warrior of antiquity, Bar Kochba. The people of the book had once again been transformed into the people of the sword (Spivak 1946, 24–27).

The call for unity was a call to Jews in the West to financially support the common front. The stated goal was to furnish the Red Army with enough material aid to manufacture 1,000 "Bar Kochba" tanks and 500 war planes. To spearhead the effort, Feffer and Solomon Mikhoels, a famous actor and director, were dispatched on a seven-month mission to the United States, Mexico, Canada, and Britain on behalf of the Jewish Anti-Fascist Committee. The climax came on July 8, 1943, when close to 50,000 people filled the historic Polo Grounds in New York City. It was the largest pro-Soviet rally ever held in the United States. Mikhoels and Feffer were greeted by Mayor Fiorello La Guardia, Sholem Asch, Rabbi Stephen Wise, and many other notables. Closely watched by their Soviet sponsors and the FBI, the two unofficial ambassadors played the role entrusted to them, the role of screamers. They screamed for revenge, and the only avenging angel in sight was the Red Army (Gorny 2012, 188–92; Mikhoels and Feffer 1943).

Jewish photojournalists, poets, and professional writers serving in the Red Army were the first to report and record the discovery of the mass graves and the systematic murder of Eastern European Jewry. The younger generation, city-bred and Russian-speaking, had reaped the rewards of the Soviet system. Never before had they spoken out as Jews. No less important for our story, these discoveries were reported in real time, in the order in which they happened. In a ditch outside the Crimean city of Kerch, Battalion Commissar Ilya Selvinsky discovered seven thousand frozen Jewish corpses at the beginning of January 1942. The Soviets had retaken the city so quickly that the Germans had not had time to cover up the crime. "I Saw It!" was the bold title of Selvinsky's first documentary poem on the subject of mass murder, a phrase that he repeated throughout the work to emphasize his credibility as an eyewitness. It was published immediately, first in the newspaper Bolshevik, then reprinted a month later in the official army newspaper *Red Star* (Murav 2011, 155–59; Shrayer 2012, 67–70). To the description of that horror, Selvinsky admitted in a second documentary poem, "I cannot add even a single word," except to expand on the moment of truth that was to become the haunting memory of the Holocaust:

Kerch . . .
There are cities whose significance lies
Not in their landscape, nor in their culture,
Nor in the aura of their everlasting glory,
But in that lightning bolt of verity,
When the smoldering mystery of the epoch
Would suddenly be revealed, like a ditch in morning fog.
Who were we before our meeting, Kerch? (Shrayer 2013)

Of all the "ditches"—the mass graves filled with Jewish men, women, and children, some clothed and some not—the one in the woods outside of Kiev called Babi Yar (Russian for women's ravine) would enter the Soviet lexicon during wartime, thanks to such Russian Jewish poets as Ilya Ehrenburg (2007) and Lev Ozerov (2007). This happened as the Red Army began its counter-offensive, after the victory at Stalingrad in February 1943, and liberated what was left of the Soviet Jewish heartland. Among the thousand days that the Red Army correspondent Vasily Grossman spent in uniform, what remained forever fixed in his memory was the specter of Ukraine without Jews (2002a)—1.5 million of them had been murdered. A year later, Soviet readers were among the first in the world to learn about "The Hell of Treblinka," from Grossman's eyewitness account (2002b). The war gave Grossman the license and the map to write as a Jew. It turned him from the leading Soviet war correspondent to the first chronicler of the annihilation (Beevor and Vinogradova 2005, 247–61; Garrard and Garrard 1996, 67–194).

The other brave new world that was mobilized—and traumatized—by the war was the Yishuv, the Jewish settlement in Mandatory Palestine. November 2, 1942, was the twenty-fifth anniversary of the day the British government had solemnly declared that it "views with favour the establishment in Palestine of a national home for the Jewish people," a day known throughout the Free Zone as Balfour Day in honor of the British Prime Minister. It was also the day when Field Marshal Bernard Law Montgomery defeated General Erwin Rommel and his Afrika Korps at El Alamein, and the Yishuv, 500,000 strong, scrapped its plans to evacuate the able bodied to Mount Carmel and stage a heroic last stand there, just as the Jews had done against the Romans (Segev 2000, 71). Three weeks later, the Jewish Agency Executive, headed by David Ben-Gurion, devoted an extraordinary session to the fate of European Jewry and made the first public announcement about the systematic extermination of Europe's Jews.

Signing himself "R. B.," standing for Rabbi Binyamin, the Hebrew writer Yehoshua Redler-Feldman issued this proclamation on December 17, 1942:

TO ALL

The "Do Not Be Silent" Group in Jerusalem wishes hereby to inform you that it has begun activities of various kinds; if, for all the hesitations and doubts, there is one chance in a thousand, in ten thousand, to rescue those who are condemned to death, we must use all means at our disposal. Jews of every stripe and in every locale! Organize yourselves at once into active cells! Let us not lose a precious moment in overly cautious delays! We are dispatching messengers and information wherever they are needed. (quoted in Porat 1983, 246)

As its *cri de guerre*, this group of public intellectuals enlisted the Psalmist's appeal to God (Ps. 83:2): *Al domi* (Do not be silent)!

The time had come, the Zionist leader Berl Katzenelson decided, to build a bridge from the war zone to the Jew-Zone. *Min hamoked* (From the fire), a series of war-related books that grew to nineteen volumes and would take five years to produce, was his brainchild (Livneh 2010, 180). For the job of selecting and translating each volume into accessible Hebrew and publishing it in paperback, he chose Bracha Habas, the senior editor at Am Oved, a publishing house in Tel Aviv. Even before Habas knew what it was, she realized that the catastrophe that had befallen the Jews had to be classified, as can be seen from her 1943 prospectus for the series. At this crucial moment of self-definition, of preliminary list making, the documentary and testimonial evidence mattered most; Habas made no plans for volumes containing fiction, poems, or songs, according to a list that appeared on the backs of some of the books:

1. Missives from our brothers who are struggling in their sites of suffering
2. Memoirs of victims of Nazism and fascism
3. Authentic eyewitness accounts from ghettos and concentration camps
4. Testimonies of refugees and survivors
5. Documents from the resistance in the underground
6. Utterances of the fighters
7. The fate of nations in the war
8. The military conduct of the war
9. Discussions of the postwar era

There were already more than enough books from which to choose in order to document the theater of global war—even enough books authored by Jews, like Erwin Bienenstock's *Meanwhile Captivity* and Vasily Grossman's *The*

People Eternal. So translators from German, English, Polish, and Russian were put to work. Yet if Habas wished to inform the Hebrew-reading public about the specific fate and struggle of "our brothers" over the entire expanse of the Jew-Zone, she would have to generate books on this topic on her own.

Mikhtavim min hageta'ot (Letters from the ghettos, 1943) was the third of five anthologies that Habas compiled for the series (Livneh 2010, 180, note 6). It was an old idea: collecting last letters from the war zone as a means of nation building, using the self-sacrifice of the young to forge a collective identity (Natter 1999, 78–121). Instead of soldiers in uniform, Habas drew on the letters of Zionist youth who had made their way to Palestine through neutral channels. The collection was both new and newsworthy. It gave the reader a sense of immediacy, authenticity, and great urgency, as if the war were unfolding in real time. To guard their safety, the names of both sender and addressee were omitted. Only the names of those known to have perished were printed; with each passing day, Habas explained in the preface, more and more of those names could be made public.

Of the 250 letters in the volume, from across the Jew-Zone, the letter of Tosia Altman was the most memorable, because "Tosia" was already a household name in the Yishuv. A leader of the Zionist youth movement, Hashomer Hatzair, she was one of the fighters known (actually, thought) to have perished in the bunker on Mila 18 in the Warsaw ghetto. Her last letter, however, was anything but a battle cry of freedom (Shalev 1992, chap. 5).

"I think you'll agree with me," she wrote to her unidentified addressee in a kibbutz, "that one shouldn't draw strength from a poisoned well. I am trying to control myself not to vent the bitterness that has accumulated against you and your friends for having forgotten us so utterly. I blame you that you didn't help me with a few words at least. But today I don't want to settle my accounts with you. It was the recognition and certainty that we will never see each other again that impelled me to write." Here the tone and substance of the letter changed, as the author described in coded language the systematic murder of the Jews: "But what can be done? This is how things are. I am doing everything to prevent it and to save the person who is most dear to me, but unfortunately there are factors that block the strongest will. Israel is vanishing before my eyes and I wring my hands and I cannot help him. Have you ever tried to smash a wall with your head?" (Habas 1943, 41–43).

Tosia's farewell letter attacked the silent complicity of those living in freedom—and it struck a nerve. The letter was read aloud by the Hebrew poet Yitzhak Lamdan at a meeting of the Al Domi held in Jerusalem in 1943 (Porat 1983, 262). Last letters such as these, which made their first appearance in 1943, rendered the private public. Those living outside the Jew-Zone were given an immediate, terrifying sense of what was really happening inside it.

A significant group of writers and public intellectuals writing in English, German, Yiddish, Russian, and Hebrew took up their pens on behalf of Hitler's most powerless victims. Living as they did between two worlds, these writers were the first to see that one of these worlds faced total destruction. In Britain, the United States, and Mandatory Palestine, the purpose of this literature of mobilization was to rouse public opinion about the plight of European Jewry and to begin mourning the numberless dead. Writers in the Soviet Union, meanwhile, some of them in uniform, tried to place the special fate of the Jewish nation front and center. They issued a biblically mandated cry for revenge. Perhaps because it was already too late to rescue the Jews, this literature has all but been erased from the public memory of the Holocaust.

Three Wartime Parables

In 1943, perhaps by coincidence but perhaps not, three writers in the Free Zone turned to historical fiction, fantasy, and allegory to take the measure of what was happening in the Jew-Zone. One was the Yiddish writer Isaac Bashevis Singer in New York City; the others were the Hebrew writer Shmuel Yosef Agnon, in Jerusalem, and the Spanish writer Jorge Luis Borges, in Buenos Aires. Singer invented an imperious and wickedly clever Jewish devil (the Evil One) to narrate a series of demonic tales, the first of which tracked the downfall of an eminent Talmudic scholar named Zeidel Cohen, who dreamed of becoming "Zeidlus the Pope" (Singer 2004).

Agnon's "The Lady and the Peddler" (1971) was the cautionary tale of a wandering Jewish peddler named Joseph, who took shelter under the roof of a gentile widow named Helen and shared her (unkosher) food and her bed, only to discover, not a moment too soon, that the lady was a vampire. For whom was this cautionary tale intended? It was Agnon's submission to *Basa'ar* (In the storm), a literary miscellany subtitled *"Presented to the Hebrew Soldier Male and Female by the Writers of Eretz Israel."* *Basa'ar* was small enough to fit into their kit bags.

In "The Secret Miracle," as in other tales he wrote in the early 1940s, Borges chose a peripheral participant in the large events of history in order to wrestle with how such events filtered through a single consciousness to challenge accepted notions of time, memory, infinitude, and eternity. Borges's character Jaromír Hladík, a playwright who may have been modeled on Franz Kafka (Stavans 2003, 6), is only marginally a Jew. His story pivots on a sharp divide between the recorded, exterior, public events of the war—which transpire in rapid clock and calendrical time (the date of his execution by firing squad has been set for 9:00 AM on the morning of March 29, 1939)—and the vast planes of agency and engrossment that open up for him a near infinity of interior time (Borges 1998).

In 1943, the forces of evil seemed ubiquitous and inescapable. Singer's Zeidel, for all his learning, fell right into the trap laid for him by the devil, who not only had even more learning but also possessed great psychological acuity, while Agnon's Helen was inscrutable, the only hint of her blood lust being her abstinence from real food. Borges's Nazis were similarly implacable, wanting to "work impersonally and deliberately, as vegetables do, or planets," adopting the ineluctability of the natural world for wholly human and reversible decisions (Borges 1998, 158). Yet all three protagonists were granted a miraculous reprieve. Zeidel experienced a *diabolus ex machina* in the split second before he died, which allowed him to affirm the existence of God. To avoid reciting the bedtime prayer in the presence of a cross, Joseph absented himself from Helen's lodging on the very night she was scheduled to feast on his blood. And God granted Hladík the year he needed to complete his play, that year compressed into the moment between the sergeant's order to fire and the volley of shots. Three master storytellers in three parts of the Free Zone returned to the gothic and fantastical tale to vivify the forces of evil—and to vanquish them through the agency of God.

Storytelling is an ecological art; the storyteller routinely recycles plots and motifs that have been used countless times before. Singer's story has been known since medieval times as "The Jewish Pope," a spectacular "true tale" of Jewish rescue and comeuppance (Sherman 2003). Agnon's Joseph was the lowly, distant offspring of Joseph in Egypt, and Helen was the reincarnation of the pagan temptress. Hladík's story carried an epigraph from the Quran, even as the hero struggled to complete the last act of his verse drama *The Enemies*, which "observed the unities of time, place, and action" (Borges 1998, 159). Much can be gained by breaking down the terrors of history into a story that is at once familiar and very new.

Since the plot is a foregone conclusion (Singer's devil narrator gives it away in the first paragraph), the storyteller's real interest lies elsewhere. What's new is the story's interiority. How exactly does the Evil One tempt the greatest Talmudist in all of Poland to betray his God, his faith, and his pursuit of pure reason? (Dumping his wife takes Zeidel all of one minute.) What are the precise stages in Joseph's downfall, the demonic signs that he willfully disregards, the seductions of the flesh to which he succumbs? Isn't it obvious from his first encounter with Helen that he has sold her the very hunting knife with which she plans to slaughter him? How many dreams and multiple time frames does it take for Hladík to conjure away the fear of his imminent execution and successfully complete his last hexameter?

Where God is an active presence, storytelling is also a conservative art. It is worth comparing the two Jewish storytellers, both affecting an old-fashioned and deeply learned style, with the eclectic religious imagination of Borges. The Jewish God of Singer and Agnon is a stern and skeptical God who keeps His chosen people on a short leash. The Islamic God of Borges is the absolute master of time. All three narrators are omniscient and make it their business to break down the reader's rational mind-set. One promises a miracle and delivers on that promise. But only one is overtly supernatural.

The Evil One (called "the Primeval Snake" and "the Tempter" in other stories) is Singer's first speaker of Jewspeak. All-seeing and all-knowing, he is steeped in Jewish folkways, his use and abuse of Scripture and rabbinic terminology betraying a goodly number of years spent in the infernal yeshiva. Even as he seduces Zeidel to apostasy, the Evil One uses an aggressively anti-Christian style that maintains an absolute distinction between them and us, the sacred and profane (Roskies 1995, 282–91). (Singer waited until his third collection, Short Friday & Other Stories, to make the story available to English readers. By then all possible connection to the war years was irretrievably lost; the translators, meanwhile, systematically neutered the anti-Christian style.) The Evil One performs as if he were a community of one, for his own benefit alone, this being the first entry in what Singer was planning to call Dos gedenk-bukh fun yeytser-hore, (The devil's diary). I blaspheme, therefore I am!

What is gained by restoring these three tales to their original wartime context is a glimpse at the beginning: seeing how great writers grappled with aspects of the Holocaust before such a thing as Holocaust literature existed. Of course they didn't yet know what we know today. What they did know is that sometimes the most direct response to the enormity of a subject is a detour through the distant past, or superimposing the logic of dreams and nightmares on the chronology of evil, self-betrayal, and senseless suffering. Holocaust literature began concurrently throughout the Free Zone—where the imagination roamed free.

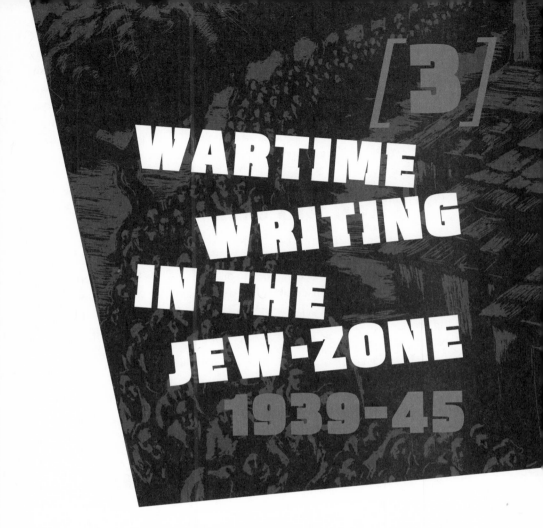

WARTIME WRITING IN THE JEW-ZONE 1939-45

Literature as Resistance

Within the occupied war zone, the counterpoint to mobilization was resistance. As long as there was hope of survival, resistance took one form. When all hope was lost, it took another. Inside the Jew-Zone, therefore, we must proceed year by year. Running through the Jew-Zone is an all-important timeline divided into before and after. The concentration of the Jews within enclosed urban spaces occupies one side of the temporal divide. Their systematic extermination occupies the other. Though so much literary evidence was destroyed, enough has survived that we are able to locate, document, and vicariously experience the moment of truth. By the end, but well before the war was over, the Holocaust became its own archetype.

"Resistance," like "mobilization," keeps the story in the present tense. Resistance preserves the contingency, disbelief, despair, delusion, determination, and descent into the abyss. With Ruth Wisse, we reject the false dichotomy between active and passive forms of resistance, as if the educational, social, cultural, and religious responses of the Jews in captivity were somehow ancillary to the armed revolt. One precedes the other and proceeds from the other. If we define "literature" as the written word, then it is fair to say that "Jewish resistance to Hitler was mounted primarily through literature" (Wisse 2000, 197). Proportionately more paper was saved than human lives.

TIME BEFORE

IN THE NAZI GHETTOS, EVEN COMMEMORATION WAS A FORM OF organized resistance. Thanks to the monumental guide to the Warsaw ghetto edited by Barbara Engelking and Jacek Leociak (2009), we know when, where, how, and by whom Jewish cultural life was organized. We know about the Central Commission for Entertainments, the competing Yiddish and Hebrew cultural organizations YIKOR and Tekumah, the chess tournaments and bridge clubs, the traveling puppet circus, the role of high culture relative to the plethora of light entertainment, and the precise repertoire of performances and the names of all the performers (Engelking 2009). From other sources we know that on September 13, 1941, in a commemoration of the third anniversary of the death of the Polish Yiddish novelist I. M. Weissenberg, the noted Hebrew pedagogue Abraham Lewin used the occasion to express two contradictory— indeed, mutually exclusive—ideas. One was to protest the life-crushing impact of the ghetto, where "death rules in all its majesty, while life hardly glows under a thick layer of ashes," where "the very soul, both in the individual and in the community, seems to have starved and perished, to have dulled and atrophied. There remain only the needs of the body; it leads merely an organic-physiological existence." The second was to celebrate "one of those creative artists who come to us as though by themselves, who grow like a flower in an untilled field." Turning to the young people in the audience, Lewin drew out the analogy of nature in bloom to conjure up the idea of a Jewish cultural renaissance that will "spring up like a hidden source from under the earth," even in a prison such as the ghetto (Lewin 1988, 243–44). Commemoration was never an exercise in nostalgia in the Jew-Zone; the lost heritage was not recalled at a safe remove. Each lecture, performance, contest, and religious rite was happening in the present and—as long as there was a present—was an act of individuation, solidarity, and defiance.

Surrounded by barbed wire and brick walls, by enmity and apathy, Jewish life on the inside was defiantly vibrant. Within their own public sphere, now radically diminished, the Jews sang songs, delivered sermons and eulogies, declaimed poetry, mounted exhibitions, performed plays and cabaret skits, conducted religious services, issued rabbinic *responsa*, organized central libraries, published bulletins and distributed underground journals, attended lectures and concerts, educated the young and fostered their artistic talents, took photographs, administered questionnaires, and—in some ghettos—issued calls to arms. All this happened until curfew, and in the Warsaw ghetto, those who attended programs sponsored by the *hoyf-komitetn*, or house committees, would stay the night. In fact, because of the curfew, performances and social events went on until sunrise (Kassow 2007, 119–28).

For the most part, a cultural life conducted in captivity had a specific, live audience. Scholars estimate the size of that audience in the Warsaw ghetto— those whose souls seemed not "to have starved and perished, to have dulled and atrophied"—at 5–10 percent of the total ghetto population, or about 20,000–40,000 people (Engelking 2009, 531). Some forms of self-expression, like theatrical performances, could be staged only with the support of what the historian Lucy Dawidowicz has termed the "Official Community"—that is, the Judenrat, or Jewish council, under the predatory eyes of the Gestapo and ss (Dawidowicz 1975, chap. 11). Such programmed recitals, lectures, and plays were carefully scripted. No less encrypted were the aboveground publications produced under German auspices by the various Judenräte. When Herman Kruk, the chronicler of the Vilna ghetto, cited the weekly editorials of the official *Geto-yedies* (Ghetto news), he did so with a mixture of sarcasm and scorn. Yet these editorials were the work of a Hebrew pedagogue named Zemach Feldstein, whom the Union of Writers and Artists commissioned, along with Kruk, to write a full-scale history of the ghetto. Reread dispassionately, these same editorials reveal a message of hope with deep roots in Jewish consciousness and culture (Feldstein 1997).

Whether they were located in the Generalgouvernement, within the Reich, or in the newly occupied eastern territories, no two ghettos were alike. In some, the local Judenrat enjoyed the confidence of the ghetto inhabitants and had a leader who convinced the Jews that labor would save them. Some ghettos were "open" while others were "closed," hermetically sealed off from the surrounding populations, with no information going in or coming out. In some ghettos there was a critical mass of writers, intellectuals, and activists to organize a cultural and political life. Yiddish was the lingua franca in some ghettos; Polish and German replaced it in others. A variety of youth movements flourished in some ghettos, together with an active underground press. In some, parallel social service networks competed to save the population from starvation and disease. Some ghettos went down fighting. One lasted almost to the very end.

Numbering over a thousand, the ghettos were starved to death, infected to death, bled to death, and finally deceived to death. Most of the smaller ones were swallowed up—in either an "outsettlement," the euphemism of choice in the Łódź ghetto for the deportations; a series of *Aktionen*, or actions; or an *oyszidlung*, or liquidation—by the end of 1942. When those remaining learned of the demise of the others, new survival strategies were needed: doubling the ghetto's productivity, building underground bunkers, finding safe houses on the Aryan side, or preparing to do battle. The ghettos that kept the most meticulous and multifarious records—Kovno, Łódź-Litzmannstadt, Terezín, Vilna, and Warsaw—are those that are still etched in public memory today. One, where an uprising took place on the eve of the final liquidation, established a new memorial calendar.

Taking the Warsaw ghetto as her template, Dawidowicz subdivided the ghetto into three separate "communities": the Official Community, also known as the Judenrat, forced to carry out German orders; the Alternative Community, with its parallel social service networks; and the Counter-community, where the political underground and youth movements found their home (Dawidowicz 1975, 223–78). Each community kept a different set of records; each had a different stake in the future. In Łódź, the archive operated aboveground as an arm of the Bureau of Statistics, and it almost immediately began to compile an official daily chronicle of events in the ghetto: first in Polish, then in both Polish and German, and after January 1943 exclusively in German (Dobroszycki 1984). Łódź was unique among the major ghettos for the "insettlement" of thousands of German-speaking Jews from Vienna, Frankfurt, and Prague, a meeting of East and West that had disastrous consequence for this refugee population but enriched the annals of the ghetto with an unforgettable mosaic. Łódź was also unique because of the centralization of power in the hands of one man, Mordecai Chaim Rumkowski, the "Eldest of the Jews," who, as all the other ghettos were annihilated in turn, began to fancy himself the ghetto's savior. Added to the unique mix of Yiddish, Polish, and German speakers and the cult of personality were the subversive habits of the chroniclers themselves, who kept a double set of records: one for Rumkowski and another for us.

The underground archive in the Warsaw ghetto—whose code name was Oyneg Shabes, or pleasure of the Sabbath—represented a completely different model. It was the brainchild of the historian Emanuel Ringelblum, a leader of the Jewish Self-Help, the alternative network of social service agencies in the ghetto; and a sworn enemy of the Judenrat, which he saw as a bastion of the Jewish bourgeoisie that, since time immemorial, he maintained, had exploited the poor and the downtrodden (Kassow 2007, 94–95, 135–36). In May 1940, half a year before the Warsaw ghetto was sealed off, Ringelblum began to handpick the staff of his archive. Tabloid journalists, he warned, need not apply. During wartime especially, when each Jew was "a world unto himself" and Jewish life was "so full of tragedy," Ringelblum instructed his staff to avoid "every redundant word, every literary gilding or ornamentation," and to record the sequence of events "as simply and faithfully as possible" (Ringelblum 1989, 387). Unique to the Warsaw ghetto was the presence of 150,000 refugees—most of them expelled from hundreds of surrounding towns that made up a cross section of the Yiddish-speaking heartland—whom Ringelblum hoped would provide him with the laboratory conditions to chronicle the diversity and vitality of Jewish communal life in Poland. He came to view this shtetl project as the single greatest achievement of the Oyneg Shabes (Kassow 2007, 268–78). As the storied center of the Jewish underworld, Warsaw also boasted a robust class of Jewish smugglers. No sooner were the ghetto walls erected than they began to ply their trade.

Vilna and Kovno were much smaller ghettos, each with its pride of place. Going back to the times of Napoleon, Vilna called itself the Jerusalem of Lithuania. To combat apathy and anarchy, the surviving members of the secular intelligentsia tried to recreate the prewar Jewish cultural network; to leverage the future, they laid plans to establish a ghetto museum (complete with a scale model of the seven ghetto streets) and commissioned a detailed history from the two honorary Vilner: Feldstein, from Kovno, and Kruk, a refugee from Warsaw. Kovno, too, had its Jewish pedigree, thanks to the Slobodka Yeshiva, or Talmudic academy; its underground chronicler, Avraham Golub; and (unlike Vilna) a Judenrat chief who was universally revered. Dr. Elchanan Elkes's "Last Will and Testament," written on October 19, 1943, and given to Golub for safekeeping, is the only such document by a chairman of the Judenrat that has survived (Tory 1990, 503–7).

Terezín-Theresienstadt was altogether unique, an isolated garrison town built for a few thousand, to which the Germans deported a hundred thousand Czech, German, Austrian, Dutch, Danish, and Polish Jews in order to deceive the world with a so-called model ghetto, the *Führer's* gift, as a 1944 Nazi propaganda film put it, to the Jews. Among this most literate, prominent, and cosmopolitan group of inmates in all of occupied Europe was a team of dedicated artists who produced work-for-German-hire by day and a graphic chronicle of the true ghetto conditions by night—their slow death through hunger, disease, and overcrowding—even as budding young artists conjured up alternative landscapes in a possible future outside the ghetto.

In some ghettos, writers, artists, and intellectuals were a protected class. It was understood that if the world were ever to learn what happened, it was their testimony that would break the barrier of disbelief. In Vilna, Jacob Gens, a former Lithuanian Army officer turned ghetto chief, issued special rations to thirty-three members of the Cultural Department, whose ranks included Feldstein, Kruk, and Abraham Sutzkever. Crossing ideological lines, they accepted

Gens's invitation to participate in regularly scheduled colloquia that met in his home over a glass of tea in the hours before curfew, where they discussed the history and fate of the Jews (Belis 1964; Roskies 2004). The Union of Writers and Artists established the Tsukunft Publishing House, for which works written in the Vilna ghetto were bought and buried underground, for future publication (Sutzkever 1968, 6). The honoraria, meanwhile, were dignified handouts to the starving writers. In Warsaw, where Rachel Auerbach ran a special soup kitchen for members of the intelligentsia, the latter were solicited for their views on the current and future state of the ghetto (Dawidowicz 1976, 218–25; Kassow 2007, 233–39; Kermish 1986, 717–60). The Jewish National Committee formed in the wake of the great deportation spared no effort to find safe houses on the Aryan side for Jews (Kassow 2007, 348–67). Bereft of his wife and two sons, who had been shipped off to Treblinka, the poet and playwright Yitzhak Katzenelson found shelter among the members of Dror, the Zionist youth movement. In a letter written from the Drancy transit camp, in France, to his cousin in Palestine, Katzenelson (1958) left instructions on how his last writings were to be translated and disseminated after the war. He prayed that his ghetto writings, which had been buried in a bunker, would be discovered by Zionist activists. They were.

Songs of Bereavement

Song, as the most public form of group communication, took the reality of ghetto life and broke it down into ready-made categories: lullaby, love song, work song, cabaret song, ballad, hymn. In the East, everyone sang: the freethinkers and the pious, the young and the old, the women and the men, the prosperous and the dirt poor. In the primitive conditions of the Nazi-ruled ghettos, which seemed a throwback to the Dark Ages, peddlers hawked their wares, urchins begged for handouts, and street singers performed for whatever audiences they could. Their songs were highly topical, rooted in the present. Another way they "spoke" was through their melodies, using set pieces from Yiddish musical theater or borrowing from the standard folk repertory. By matching the brutal lyrics of ghetto life to familiar melodies, street singers stretched the art of popular song to new and terrible limits (Roskies 1984, 185–89; Flam 1992, 49–104).

The parent-child relationship became a universal trope, whether in lullabies (by Shaye Spiegel and Leah Rudnitsky) or in theater songs (by Leyb Rosental and Henryka Lazowert, who wrote in Polish). Spiegel nearly forfeited his life for daring to stage a heart-rending lullaby, *"Makh tsu di eygelekh"* (Close your eyes), written in response to the death of his only daughter. Rumkowski, who sat in the front row with his entourage, thought the song too defeatist

(Flam 1992, 148). In wartime writings, as in life, the child was inducted into a reality too terrifying even for the adult to comprehend, but the very presence of a Jewish child signaled the possibility of regeneration. Rosental called his spunky child protagonist Yisrolik ("little Israel") in the 1942 hit song of that name and cast his own daughter, Khayele, to perform it in the Vilna ghetto (Rosental 1989).

Sutzkever enjoyed an audience in the Vilna ghetto that hung on his every word. He too saw the child as the part that stood for the whole. The artist Rokhl Sutzkever (no relation to the poet) painted an illuminated mural of Abraham's poem "And Thus Shall You Speak to the Orphan," which was put on exhibition (Lisek 2005, 181). Turning to epic verse, a genre he perfected in the ghetto, Sutzkever wrote *"Dos keyver-kind"* (The grave child), the tale of a lone escapee from Ponar who sought refuge in the Jewish cemetery, there to give birth in an empty grave. The poem was awarded first prize for poetry in July 1942 by the Union of Artists and Writers.

Ghetto songs focused on the child: orphaned, abandoned, peddling in the streets, left to fend for itself, the provider, the war's most vulnerable victim, the severed link, Yisrolik the vagabond, the Little Smuggler, the infant born in a grave. Unmanned by hunger, disease, and forced labor, as the deportations and *Aktionen* swallowed up one category of Jew after another, the most a Jewish father could do was prepare his eight-year-old daughter to die with dignity (Shayevitsh, 1989). What Shayevitsh wrote after the deportation of his wife and two children (Blimele, the eight-year-old, and her newborn sister, who had yet to be named) has not survived, though a portrait of him as a father in shock and denial has (Zelkowicz 1989b). To be left behind after the murder of one's wife and children was to confront a meaningless future.

To be left behind after a mother's murder was to confront a luminous past and polluted present. That sudden, brutal loss rendered the bereaved son an orphan at any age; Sutzkever was twenty-eight when it happened. How to bridge the chasm between a son and his beloved mother? When Sutzkever's mother was swept away to "the other shore" where "there is no memory," as he wrote in 1942, he was left on this side, where death had sole dominion (Sutzkever 1991c, 144).

In the winter of 1941 Sutzkever suffered two devastating losses in rapid succession: his newborn son was murdered in the maternity ward of the ghetto by Franz Murer, the deputy for Jewish affairs, and his mother was dragged away to her death, betrayed by a Gestapo agent named Oberhardt (Sutzkever 1945b, 70). To the child he dedicated one muted, encrypted lament, written on the first anniversary of the boy's death (Roskies 1984, 232–38; Sutzkever 1989d), and to the mother he dedicated a cycle of poems, the longest of which he called "Three Roses," one for each of the bullets that pierced her heart

(Sutzkever 1991c). Sutzkever could not forgive himself for being absent when they came to get his mother. "Where was I, / when to the accompaniment of cymbals / you were dragged to the scaffold?" he asks in an eight-part poem called "Mother," originally written in 1942 (Sutzkever 1981, 28). Rushing back to her apartment on the day of her arrest, he found "On the table, a glass of tea / you barely managed to sip. // Fingers still move / on the silver rims" (30). To regain her living presence, he is prepared to rip away the last bodily boundary between them, to cannibalize her, internalize her at any cost—until she cries out to him to stop, for the dead and the living must occupy separate realms, albeit joined by their mutual longing. "If you remain," she assures him,

> I will still be alive
> as the pit of the plum
> contains in itself the tree,
> the nest and the bird
> and all else besides. (31)

Metonymy is the very principle of survival (Wisse 2003, 1236).

Diaries

Certain genres come to the fore under certain historical circumstances, and diaries, we know, are especially prevalent in wartime. "Everyone" wrote diaries, Ringelblum reported in 1943, "journalists, writers, teachers, community activists, young people, even children" (1989, 386). And although most of those written in the Warsaw ghetto were destroyed during the great deportation, a significant number did survive: diaries written on the run, in a safe house, a monastery, an underground bunker, a loft, a pit, a labor camp, a transit camp—diaries in every European language.

Wartime diaries are the most widely read of all Holocaust-specific genres, inspiring plays, movies, memorials, and meticulous research. One whole room in the Museum of the Memorial for the Murdered Jews of Europe in the center of Berlin (just down the block from the Brandenburg Gate and across the street from the American Embassy), is given over to a display of pages carefully selected from an array of diaries and last letters written in every language by victims of every age and both genders. Placed within this sacerdotal setting, they serve to memorialize lost individuals and powerfully evoke the irreplaceable richness of European Jewry. As the most accessible corpus of wartime writing, however, their true literary and artistic merit is revealed only when studied separately, language by language, place by place, and period by period. If today these most private and personal of documents lie at the literal bedrock of public memory of the Holocaust (in the Berlin

Memorial Museum, the scattered rescued pages are displayed on the floor), it is because each diary was produced within a specific collective setting and at a specific interval between birth and death, and represented through its choice of language a specific postwar audience.

To begin with the most celebrated: On March 29, 1944, Anne Frank heard a member of the Dutch government in exile broadcasting from London. After the war, he promised, the Dutch people would document the Nazi occupation by publishing diaries and other firsthand accounts. Anne promptly pulled out her diary and began work on a more polished, literary version (Pressler 1995, v). The war, she knew, rendered the private public. Somewhere off in the imagined future were the diary's distant readers, a target audience already familiar to the writer, for "implicit in the chronicles and diaries is the vision of a posterity resembling the writers'" (Horowitz 1994, 50). Helping the diarist construct that postwar future was the choice of language. Dutch, after all, was Anne Frank's acquired language, and German represented the return of the repressed. "Fine specimens of humanity, those Germans," she protested on October 9, 1942, "and to think I'm actually one of them! No that's not true, Hitler took away our nationality long ago. And besides, there are no greater enemies than the Germans and the Jews" (Frank 1995, 55). What to do, however, if the grownups persisted in speaking German, if sex talk with Peter needed to be couched in technical German terms, if she herself was sometimes at a loss for a Dutch word, and when nothing quite summed up a situation better than a German literary quotation? "I was so upset," she recorded on Saturday, May 20, 1944, "I started speaking German" (ibid., 299).

The most prevalent kind of wartime diary is the durational diary. Exemplified by Frank's, the durational diary begins with some personal or historical landmark but ends abruptly: on the eve of the betrayal, *Aktion*, or deportation order or, in one case, on the day of disembarkation in New York Harbor (Berg 1945). Because diaries kept in real time end *in medias res*, their closure lies outside the work. In these diaries—more than any other genre—the mundane, the frivolous, and the protected realm of one's inner life rubs up against the chronology of mass murder. With every passing day, the gap between survival time and killing time grows ever narrower. Outside the Frank family's Secret Annex, the streets empty out so thoroughly that the sight of a few fugitive Jews is worthy of note. As they write against time, the war may or may not yield up its darkest secret—that Hitler was making good his promise to annihilate the Jews of Europe. At the heart of all Holocaust diaries lies that moment of truth.

The sudden, arbitrary ending endows the last pages of durational diaries with extraordinary significance. How much of the truth did they really know? Because Anne and her confidante, Kitty, are exempted from the moment of

FIGURE 2

Chaim A. Kaplan. *Scroll of Agony: The Warsaw Diary of Chaim A. Kaplan.* New York: Macmillan, 1965. Jacket design by Lawrence Ratzkin.

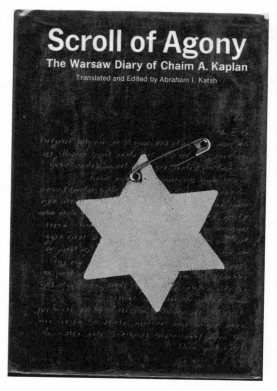

truth, they have come to represent goodness, faith, and innocent sacrifice. Elsewhere in the Jew-Zone, the ghetto often served as a buffer against the truth: ghetto diarists were preoccupied with themselves or their fellow Jews and barely able to account for the behavior of the Germans (Engel 1999). Not so the Hebrew pedagogue Chaim Kaplan, who began keeping a diary in 1933 and renamed it *Megilat yisurin* (in English, *Scroll of Agony*) on July 29, 1940, to signal a shift in perspective from the individual to the sacerdotal. Kaplan consistently reports on German actions, and he consistently employs Scripture to underscore the desecration of God's covenant and the daily degradation of God's chosen. "How has Warsaw, the royal, beautiful, and beloved city become desolate!" he writes on the first day of the Jewish year 5700 (in the Western calendar, September 14, 1939). Biblical analogies eventually fail him, as death itself ceases to have meaning (see A. Goldberg 2005, 409–18), especially after Kaplan introduces a sinister confidant in the person of Reb Hirsch. "My Hirsch cannot be budged from his opinion," Kaplan writes on June 16, 1942. "A catastrophe will befall us at the hands of the Nazis and they will wreak their vengeance on us for their final downfall" (Kaplan 1973, 351). Whether Hirsch was a real person (A. Goldberg 2005, 412, note 68) or a literary invention we will never know. His role, however, is clear: he is Kaplan's alter ego, his naysayer, the speaker of unspeakable truths. Hirsch's prophecy of doom, which proves to be accurate (the great deportation is a month away), anticipates the last, truly eschatological sentence, written in the diarist's own voice: "If my life ends, what will become of my diary?"

Kaplan refused to entrust his diary to the Oyneg Shabes for safekeeping, so zealously did he guard and regard it. Ringelblum, in contrast, judged its historical value by the "ordinariness" of its author (1989, 397); the narrower the lens, as far as he was concerned, the sharper the focus. Ringelblum himself, meanwhile, was one of three individuals (all male) who kept an ongoing "historical diary" for the express purpose of preserving a communal narrative (Kassow 1999). Herman Kruk remained in Vilna in order to keep "a chronicle of the events" of the city (Kruk 2002, 47), and Avraham Golub became both the scribe and keeper of the Kovno ghetto chronicle (Tory 1990).

In the Vilna ghetto, the voice of Zelig Kalmanovitsh—as befitted a founder of the famed YIVO Institute—was that of a public intellectual. In Yiddish, he lectured on Peretz and Ahad Ha'am and delivered an occasional sermon. But Kalmanovitsh kept his diary in Hebrew, replete with scriptural and Talmudic passages to underscore his return to the fold. He believed that history would revere the memory of the people of the ghetto. "Your least utterance will be studied," he prophesied in 1942, "your struggle for man's dignity will inspire poems, your scum and moral degradation will summon and awaken morality" (Kalmanovitsh 1989, 511). Most stunning was the voice of Ringelblum, whose every waking hour was dedicated to preserving the inner Jewish dialogue: between past and present, the elite and the folk, Hebrew and Yiddish. Oblivious to the conditions outside his underground bunker, he completed his most sustained piece of historical research, *Polish-Jewish Relations during the Second World War* (Ringelblum 1992), after Polish Jewry was no more. The work was written in Polish for a Poland that no longer had any Jews.

The Art of Ghetto Reportage

Singers translated the unfolding horror into familiar genres, fitting new lyrics to old melodies. Poets tried to adapt the conventions of the lyric and the epic to contemporary events. Diarists recorded what they experienced, heard, and dreamed. But the reporter's job was to cover every late-breaking development and draconian measure, on a beat where "images succeeded one another with cinematic speed" (Ringelblum 1989, 391). The daily assignment was to write about a whole people *in extremis*, through the prism of the unique social organism that was the ghetto, as if for a deadline sometime in the future, when the war was over, and these writings would see the light of day.

Reportage is a thoroughly modern genre, a child of the newspaper age, a hybrid at once personal and reportorial, factual and full of artifice. A form of engaged journalism, reportage is typically written for a mass of imagined, literate readers. Great effort was expended producing and preserving this body of wartime writing, and great is its value for Holocaust memory, for it plunges the reader into daily life and death, recapitulates the changes in the conditions of ghetto life, and charts the growing awareness of the Final Solution.

In the ghettos in years 1–4, reportage was the bedrock of shared communication. Like song and epic poetry, reportage was not a stand-alone genre designed merely to transcribe or testify or record. It presupposed a collective audience, schooled in a very particular mental curriculum. No subject was too terrible for the reportorial pen, as long as there was room in the horrific present for some reference to a shared past. Reportage was a game of *déjà vécu*, even if the purpose of the analogy, or allusion, was to underscore the irreparable break between the familiar past and the unbearable present.

Peretz Opoczynski (1951) was a seasoned reporter before the war, becoming the scribe of urban poverty and neglect in Warsaw. Working as a letter carrier in the Warsaw ghetto by day—an unnerving and thankless job that he described in one of his finest reportorial fictions—he managed to produce carefully wrought vignettes of ghetto life in the early 1940s by describing a single ghetto courtyard or profession and tracing its changing fortunes and misfortunes over a specific period of time, ranging from one day in the life of ghetto smugglers (1976) to several years in the life of an apartment complex (1989). Welcomed in 1941 by the ghetto population as the first in Poland's history, the Jewish letter carrier eventually must bear witness to the people's despair. Yet in the voices that greet and ridicule him at his debut on the ghetto streets, he picks up on something not heard since the days of the greatest of Jewish humorists, Sholem Aleichem: "A Jewish mailman? Oh, I can't believe my eyes! Tell me, who are you looking for? At what address? We'll show you, you won't have to waste time looking. Jews, will you get a load of this: we've got a Jewish mailman, just exactly as if we were in Palestine!" (Opoczynski 1969, 57).

This sense of living "in Palestine" pervades the writings of many ghetto chroniclers, for whom the analogy is always sardonic. Echoing the monologues of Sholem Aleichem allows Opoczynski to conjure up a shtetl-like environment where Jews are all on intimate terms with one another, then to use this model of solidarity as a foil for unmasking the *shmendrikes*, the self-hating assimilationist Jews, the corruption, and the apathy that takes hold of the ghetto population. Thanks to the modern Yiddish classics, Opoczynski had a rich and adaptable model of the shtetl as collective hero—or antihero—especially in time of crisis (Miron 2000, 1–46; Roskies 1999, 41–66).

In the eyes of Opoczynski, the sight of starving children, beggar children, and dead children on the ghetto streets was an indictment of the community at large (Opoczynski 1970, 99–114). So what did it all add up to? Was the fearful metonymy of the orphaned or abandoned ghetto child—in song, poetry, and reportorial fiction—designed to rouse the conscience of a demoralized body politic, or was its purpose to dramatize the lack of true choices that lay at the heart of the ghetto's darkness? If song, poetry, and reportorial fiction presupposed the presence of a literate readership and a living collective, what would happen when that collective collapsed? The war had been going on for a full two years; how much longer could it last?

Oskar Rosenfeld became a refugee for the second time when, in November 1941, he and five thousand other Jews were deported from Prague to the Polish industrial city of Łódź, which had been renamed Litzmannstadt after a Nazi general on April 11, 1940 (O. Rosenfeld 2002, xviii). Thanks to his credentials and impeccable German, Rosenfeld landed a secure job working on the official ghetto chronicle, but on February 17, 1942, he also began keeping a combination diary and literary journal, of which twenty out of twenty-two notebooks would survive. Three days into his writing—after describing the first public hanging in the ghetto, dutifully recorded by a German film crew—he described the ghetto landscape, a panorama in snow that turned subjective at the mention of the children:

> Bleak and barren roads, partly snowed in and partly covered with mud, stretch between houses dotting the landscape. Stunted trees and bushes extend their meager trembling branches toward the sky. Throngs of children in rags cross the streets, their yellow, weatherworn faces furrowed, weary. At times a fleeting smile appears on one of those faces, sometimes one [pair] of those bloodless lips begins to sing. At times these children throw snowballs like children everywhere in freedom. Nobody can tell what the morrow will bring. What will happen with all of us? What is this all for? Why the ghetto? Is there a tomorrow? A day after tomorrow? Is it worth thinking about it? We are beggars, lepers, pariahs, people without music, without a piece of soil, without a bed, without a world. The likes of this city does not exist anywhere. Come here people over there where workdays and holidays alternate, where there are dreams and purpose and resistance. Come quickly. For when it is all over, our numbers will have been so thinned, so downcast, that we will be unable to enjoy our reunion. . . . And yet, everybody wants to live, "to live it," to know that this life was not completely senseless after all. (Ibid., 29–30)

Life on this barren soil where nothing can grow has already turned adults into innocent children. No one knows what tomorrow will bring, or even if there will be a tomorrow. Only innocent children, "like children everywhere," think there will be a tomorrow. All roads leading out of the ghetto have been destroyed, so there remains only the slimmest hope of communicating with the people who live in freedom. The Jews in the ghetto write to sustain a future that they know will exist—if at all—without them.

Josef Zelkowicz from Łódź also led a double life. His day job, working alongside Rosenfeld, was to report on the productivity of the dizzying array of workshops and makeshift factories in which every able-bodied ghetto Jew was forced to work—and on the social assistance needed by the sick, the old, and the unemployed. Some of these reports are dry as dust, but many have the tone of an omniscient narrator, free to formulate broad, transcendent truths and generalizations and free to pass judgment on the sordid conditions of the ghetto.

When not reporting on the carpenter's strike in the winter of 1941, or the removal of forty-six patients from the psychiatric ward in the ghetto and their subsequent deportation, Zelkowicz penned (literally penned—he did not neatly type and proofread what he had written) the reportage "Twenty-Five Live Chickens and One Dead Document" (Zelkowicz 1989a; see also Web 1988). It was the true story of a murderous guard at the ghetto fence, a man known as "Red-haired Janek," a pure-blooded Christian Pole who passes himself as a *Volksdeutch*, or ethnic German, a veritable VIP. This time, however, Janek's deal to smuggle twenty-five chickens into the ghetto had fallen through, so he plotted revenge against his Jewish partner by shooting and killing twenty-four innocent Jews in reprisal. This could have been just another crime that went unpunished, an event that only an investigative reporter schooled in the complex, deeply divided urban landscape could have exposed and described. But Zelkowicz was more than such a reporter. Schooled in Jewish historical memory, he understood the treacherous workings of memory through time. To signal that knowledge, he framed the story of the live chickens and the dead document within a double frame, the first an epigraph, in Aramaic: "Through a cock and a hen Tur Malka was destroyed ([Babylonian Talmud,] Tractate Gittin 57a)."

"Tur Malka" was another name for Jerusalem, and Zelkowicz expected his readers to remember the rabbinic legend that blamed the catastrophic Jewish rebellion against Rome on a banal incident with a cock and a hen. Roman soldiers had seized these animals from a Jewish wedding procession, the Jews beat the soldiers up, and the emperor thought a rebellion had broken out. Zelkowicz's point is that if such a trivial event could have had such disastrous consequences then, it could happen again. The Germans were no less cruel than the Romans. In the present day, however, history was written on the basis of documents that "either tell us too much," and so hide the nuances from the future, or "tell us too little, so that their story must be enlarged by oral tradition." In the Łódź ghetto archive, Zelkowicz had come across an unsigned, undated, handwritten document that clearly belonged in the latter category and therefore cried out to be "enlarged by oral tradition," provided with both a reportorial and transhistorical context. The analogy to the cock and the hen that had brought down Jerusalem helped Zelkowicz situate Janek's crime, carried out with "murderous German precision," within the covenantal history of the Jews. Wearing two hats—that of the criminal investigator and that of the keeper of Jewish historical memory—Zelkowicz raised the stakes, for if the Łódź ghetto were analogous to Jerusalem, then nothing less than the survival of the Jews as a people was hanging in the balance.

Another ghetto reporter was Leyb Goldin, who had worked as a professional translator of European literature before the war. His sole surviving work from the Warsaw ghetto is the masterful 1941 "Chronicle of a Single Day," in which he breaks himself up into two voices: Arke, the cynical superintellectual and one-time revolutionary, and his stomach. Arke knows about the malleability of time not only from reading *The Magic Mountain* but also from having done time before the war, in solitary confinement. But the war has been going on for two years, "and you've eaten nothing but soup for some four months, and those four months are thousands and thousands of times longer for you than the whole of the previous twenty months—no, longer than your whole life until now" (Goldin 1989, 427). Starvation time is further broken down into three uneven segments: before the single bowl of soup handed out each afternoon at precisely the same hour, during the soup, and after the soup. Ghetto time defies all clockmakers, including those we call writers.

Goldin enlists his full literary and reportorial talent in order to expose what Lewin called the merely "organic-physiological existence" of the living dead. For this proves to be no ordinary day in the lives of Arke and his stomach. On this day not only does Arke receive—by some miracle—a second bowl of soup, which he can afford to eat "graciously," and not only does he find a lost cucumber on the street outside—both of which events together allow him a moment of serious reflection—but also his daily ordeal ends with a moment of existential truth. He happens to walk by a ghetto hospital where he sees a child being operated on. "Our howls are like the cry of jackals," he is forced to admit. "But we are not animals. We operate on our infants. It may be pointless or even criminal. But animals do not operate on their young!" (Goldin 1989, 434). This recollection of time past—the eternal cycle of life and death—will make it possible for Arke to survive another day.

The Search for Historical Meaning

To the Jews of Eastern Europe, schooled in collective memory, the search for ancient analogies always began with the Tanakh, the Hebrew Bible. Faced with a catastrophe of unprecedented scope, both ubiquitous and inescapable, Jewish writers and chroniclers reached into the fund of Jewish collective memory for historical archetypes. Katzenelson organized and presided over public readings of the Hebrew Bible in his own rhymed Yiddish translations, in which he sought to demonstrate that the Prophets had never been more alive, more relevant (Katzenelson 1984, 145–89). The most ambitious publication of the underground press in the Warsaw ghetto was his *Job: A Biblical Tragedy in Three Acts* (ibid., 499–609), of which Dror published about 150 copies on June 22, 1941, the day that Germany declared war on the Soviet Union (ibid., 497). Gracing the cover was Shloyme Nusboym's illustration of Job crouched on the ground, nursing his wounds. While *Job* focused on the existential and erotic struggle of the individual Jew, *By the Waters of Babylon: A Biblical Folk Drama in Four Acts* (ibid., 233–377) described the plight of the nation and ended with a verse translation of Ezekiel's vision of the dry bones.

Working by analogy, trying things on for size, comparing and contrasting present and past—these practices did not always lead to an experience of déjà vu. "The tragedy is tremendous," Rosenfeld recorded in Notebook E, in mid-summer 1942:

Those in the ghetto cannot comprehend it. For it does not bring out any greatness as in the Middle Ages. This tragedy is devoid of heroes. And why tragedy? Because the pain does not reach out to something human, to a strange heart, but is something incomprehensible, colliding with the cosmos, a natural phenomenon like the creation of the world. Creation would have to start anew, with *berajshit* [the first word of the Hebrew Bible]. In the beginning God created the ghetto. (O. Rosenfeld 2002, 105–6)

Ghetto chroniclers were the first to perceive the outlines of something new: the birth of a new archetype of destruction. Was the measure of this new catastrophe the distance, the unbridgeable gap, between the spiritual superiority of prior generations and the demoralization of their own? Perhaps the place to begin was by asking if this was indeed a tragedy devoid of heroes.

Rabbi Shimon Huberband, charged by Ringelblum with the task of documenting Jewish religious life in the Warsaw ghetto, did not believe that German persecution excused Jewish corruption (Kassow 2007, 167). Because Huberband exposed moral lapses in the behavior of Orthodox Jewish women and young Hasidic males, copies of the English translation of his 1969 book would be burned in Brooklyn in the 1980s. More prominent in the work, however, was Huberband's fact sheet of Jewish martyrdom, a compilation of true stories that added up to a new definition of Kiddush Hashem, the sanctification of God's name (Huberband 1987). The fact sheet revealed many instances of Jews who died trying to save or defend their fellow Jews, or to rescue Jewish holy objects. Moreover, if one followed a liberal interpretation of Maimonides's ruling that a martyr was any Jew killed simply for being a Jew, then the Jews of Europe were a nation of martyrs.

Did everyday acts of heroism count as Kiddush Hashem or only as acts of extraordinary self-sacrifice? The ghetto poets were divided on this point, with one school of thought represented by Yitzhak Katzenelson in Warsaw and the other by Abraham Sutzkever in Vilna and Simkhe Bunem Shayevitsh in Łódź. Polish Jewry, Katzenelson resolved in year 4 of the war, was heir to a model of heroism perfected over millennia of exile in which the supreme act of self-sacrifice was performed "with no weapons and no spurs." "And if this Jew spills any blood," he proclaimed, "it is only his own" (quoted in Kassow 2007, 328). A supreme instance of this type of Jew was the rebbe of Radzyn, the scion of an illustrious Hasidic dynasty. In order to bring a trainload of Jews to burial, the Radyzner spurned efforts to buy him safe passage. "The Song of the Radzyner" was the last and longest epic poem that Katzenelson wrote in the ghetto (Katzenelson 1984, 663–706). It was an epic of the old school, about a named figure who was larger than life and who, like Rabbi Akiva and the ten martyred rabbis, turned private defiance into a supremely public act (see also *Berakhot* 1989; Zlotnick 1989). Katzenelson's hero, moreover, was as fearless of death as of the pathos of God—a diminished, powerless God. The Radzyner redefined the meaning of martyrdom as absolute devotion to the people of Israel.

In the Vilna ghetto, even schoolchildren got into the act. The ghetto's history club put Herod on trial in front of an invited audience, and fifteen-year-old Isaac Rudashevski argued the case against him as a criminal, a Roman collaborator, and an agent of assimilation. After heated debate, the court declared Herod guilty (Rudashevski 1973, 109–10). Sutzkever, meanwhile, immortalized the everyday courage of the teacher, Mira Bernshteyn, who plied her trade before an ever-dwindling class (Sutzkever 1991b). The curriculum they were studying, according to Sutzkever, was Peretz's tale of triple martyrdom, "Three Gifts" (2002), which extolled the moral imagination of every man and woman and their courage to go beyond the letter of the law.

Not long after completing this most popular of his epic poems, Sutzkever shifted from the epic to the lyric, with a six-line poem commemorating a unique act of sabotage carried out at the ghetto gate:

A BLIML

Farn veln durkhtrogn a bliml durkhn toyer
hot mayn shokhn zibn shmits batsolt.
Vi tayer iz far im atsind der frilingl der bloyer,—
Dos bliml mitn shvartsapl fun gold!

Mayn shokhn trogt zayn ondenk on badoyer:
Der friling otemt in zayn layb—er hot azoy gevolt . . .
Vilner geto, 29stn may 1943 (Sutzkever 1968, 75)

FLOWER
For wanting to smuggle a flower through the gates
my neighbor paid the price of seven lashes.
Now these blue petals with their nucleus of gold
are such a precious sign of spring returning.
My neighbor bears his scars with no regrets:
Spring breathes through his flesh, with so much yearning.
Vilna ghetto, May 29, 1943 [Translated by Anna Miransky]

Resistance is first and foremost an act of volition: for *wanting* to smuggle a flower into the ghetto, a Jew receives seven lashes but is rewarded for "so much *yearning*" by having his pain transmuted into life-giving breath. Written in honor of spring, this poem ends with the spring coming alive within his neighbor's body, which bears its scars "with no regrets." Resistance is no less an act of the imagination—a spontaneous, creative response to cruelty and horror. Standing in for the precious flower, the standard of beauty that cannot be falsified, is this perfectly crafted poem built on two sets of rhymes: the feminine rhymes *toyer*, *bloyer*, and *badoyer* and the masculine rhymes *batsolt*, *gold*, and *gevolt*. One set is in ethereal, mystical blue and the other in earthly, material gold—two opposing realms yoked together through the mysterious power of rhyme. The "neighbor" remains anonymous because he is Every-Jew, Everypoet, everyone willing to risk all in order to uphold an absolute standard that cannot be breached. Faced with an enemy that defiles and destroys, "these blue petals with their nucleus of gold" represent that which is most precious on earth, as in heaven. Not a Jewish stance, to be sure, but like religious faith, it demands a supreme act of self-transcendence.

Shayevitsh completed the process of defining martyrdom broadly. The mass deportations from the Łódź ghetto resumed on February 22, 1942, and Shayevitsh began writing a 448-line epic poem called "Lekh-lekho" (Go forth), in which God's command to Abraham in Genesis 12 is transformed into an intimate, remarkably muted conversation between a father and his beloved eight-year-old daughter, Blimele (meaning little flower). Shayevitsh was a first-generation secular poet in whose library "lie holy books, / worldly books, my manuscripts. / Isaiah hobnobs with Goethe, / Reb Jonathan Eybeschuetz with Tuwim. // And Yesenin wants to get drunk / and urinate in public, / but suddenly he sees Abraham / leading Isaac to Mount Moriah." The intrusion of that "but suddenly" on the home and hearth of one ghetto family awaiting the expulsion order is the theme of this great poem; the attempt of an otherwise

FIGURE 3

S. Shayevitsh. . . . *Lekh-lekho.*
. . . Łódź, Poland: Tsentrale
yidishe historishe komisye
baym tsentral-komitet fun
poylishe yidn, 1946. This was
the first publication dedicated
to Yiddish literature of the
Central Jewish Historical
Commission at the Central
Committee of Polish Jewry.

powerless father to draw out a semblance of meaning by redefining the biblical covenant in a collapsing universe. As they ascend this new Moriah, where no angel will intercede to stay the knife, the father instructs his daughter to face death with a smile, to defy the enemy with the indomitable spirit of the Jews (Shayevitsh 1989).

Sutzkever's nameless neighbor and the father in Shayevitsh's poem are ordinary people rendered extraordinary by their time in the Jew-Zone. They refuse to be defined by the enemy. They likewise refuse to go by the Book to adhere to the rules prescribed by tradition. Gender roles are now reversed, as daughters must stand in for sons, and although the rabbis of old forbade women from studying Torah, Blimele is given careful instruction in scriptural precedent. Absent the voice of God, her mother will replace Jeremiah on the long road ahead.

Among the young and politically engaged, the search for historical meaning was a search for actual political precedent. The apparently unassuming Mordecai Anielewicz regularly visited the office of Emanuel Ringelblum at the Jewish Self-Help in the Warsaw ghetto to borrow books on Jewish and economic history (Ringelblum 1985, 2:141). Later, Ringelblum gave lectures on historical themes at the underground seminars of the left-leaning Zionist youth, lectures that some would remember as extremely boring. The link between past and future was made explicit by Eliyohu Gutkowski and Antek Zuckerman, leaders of Dror, the Zionist youth movement. The 101-page mimeographed anthology they edited and translated into Yiddish was called *Suffering and Heroism in the Jewish Past in Light of the Present*. It appeared in the summer of 1940, three months before the Warsaw ghetto was officially sealed (Kermish and Bialostocki 1979, 1:44–52). Although the title gave equal weight to both "suffering," or martyrdom, and "heroism," or Jewish self-defense, only one work got double billing: Isaac Lamdan's "Masada," first published in 1927 (Lamdan 1989). Perhaps finding ancient analogies was no more than a mental exercise that fostered inaction. This is certainly what Anielewicz believed when he became the commander of the Jewish Combat Organization, the most respected and feared individual in the ghetto, and told Ringelblum how deeply he regretted the three years in the ghetto that he and the young pioneers had "wasted" on culture and education (Ringelblum 1985, 2:148). To make history, however, these young people had to know history; to break with the past, they first had to unite behind a vision of the future.

Jewish youth movements that covered the entire political spectrum from extreme Left to extreme Right were children of the new age. Founded during the German occupation of Poland in the First World War, they were a revolutionary response to Jewish powerlessness and patriarchy. The youth movements were a true counterculture, obeying their own hierarchy and codes of moral and linguistic behavior. Their members spoke a "modern" Yiddish or Hebrew, or conducted movement business in Polish (Kligsberg 1974). Sooner or later—but too late in the eyes of the young—they adopted the culture of armed resistance in many of the ghettos.

TIME AFTER

"AM I THE LAST POET IN EUROPE?" SUTZKEVER ASKED HIMSELF AT the end of June 1943. "Do I sing for the dead, do I sing for the crows?" The answer he arrived at was a study in realms of opposition forcibly wrenched together: "I am drowning in fire, in swamps, in brine, / Entrapped by yellow badged hours" (1968, 79). There were only two ways to escape from the yellow-badged hours: one was through the coming of spring, the regenerative cycle of nature, which for Sutzkever was always linked to the process of artistic creation; the other was through armed revolt. In his wartime poetry, Sutzkever tracks a paradigm shift that occurred in modern Jewish times. The new Jew, machine gun in hand, fighting as a Jew—the longed-for Jewish army finally fighting under its ancient banner—was born in 1943. From Sutzkever we learn that the labor pains attending that birth were terrible.

"Abrasha" Sutzkever joined the United Partisans' Organization (known as the FPO from its name in Yiddish), under the command of Itsik Vittenberg, soon after its founding. In midwinter 1943, Liza Magun, the FPO's main liaison to the Aryan side of Vilna, was caught and executed by the Gestapo. (Magun was to the resistance movement in Vilna what Tosia Altman and Zivia Lubetkin were to it in Warsaw.) More than a tragic loss and strategic setback, Magun's death made clear to Sutzkever that the FPO was fated to fight alone, because the ghetto population was utterly indifferent. Standing before his fellow partisans, who were gathered legally at a memorial ceremony for Magun, Sutzkever declaimed a thunderous poem of rage, written in the oracular mode of Hayyim Nahman Bialik.

Nowhere is the distance between poet and audience, between the one and the many, more pronounced than here, in "Lid tsu di letste" ("Song for the Last"). The farther apart the prophet is from the people, the greater the tension inside him between rage and sorrow, loathing and lamentation:

I beat my skull on stones to find consolation
for you in the fragments, you, the last,
for I, too, am a letter in your book,
my sun, too, is spring's leprous outcast. (Sutzkever 1989c, 498)

Deeper than the divide between the prophet and the people that refuses to hearken to his word is the gap between the different time zones that the two inhabit. The poetic prophet, alive to the cycles of nature, sees the first signs of spring. Yet just as the natural world is about to be reborn, the ancient cycle of a great and sorely tested people is about to be closed forever. Time has run out on this people, thunders the prophet, because so much of it has been squandered: "Millions at a time you were no one's, / but believed in your individuality." Even "when a thousand years of enmity / has walled the light out completely" (ibid.), it produced no palpable response, no protest, no vision for the future.

The decision to mount an uprising inside the ghetto was born out of that impasse, out of the absolute certainty that there was no tomorrow. But after Vittenberg, FPO's commander, perished in a Gestapo prison and the uprising failed, Sutzkever and his wife, Freydke, left with the second group of fighters to join the Soviet partisans fighting in the Narocz forest. On September 12, 1943, Sutzkever and his compatriots abandoned the ghetto to its fate.

By the end of 1943, year 4 of the war, metonymy became myth for the Jews who remained alive inside the Jew-Zone, most of whom were now alone: hiding alone, dying alone, fighting alone. For the young who took up arms, there were only three choices: go down fighting in a symbolic last stand against the Germans, turning the ghetto into a latter-day Masada; join a Soviet partisan brigade, where Jewish fighters were not always welcome; or forge whatever alliances were possible with the local underground in order to go on fighting as Jews. Mordecai Tenebaum-Tamaroff belonged in the first group. The Sutzkevers belonged in the second. Szymek (Shimshon) and Gusta Draenger belonged in the third. Each group left behind a literary legacy in multiple voices and tonalities. The diary, last letters, and calls to arms issued by Tenebaum-Tamaroff in Warsaw and Białystok were lovingly collected, translated, and published by the surviving members of his Zionist movement (Tenebaum-Tamaroff 1987). Sutzkever continued to date his poetry written in the Narocz forest, even as he edited and augmented his ghetto corpus for eventual publication. The return to the life-giving forest quickened his poetic spirit. "Stretch your hands out," he exulted in perfect rhyme:

> To that whiteness: In its cold and burning
> Veins
> You'll feel returning
> The redeeming life
> It contains. (Sutzkever 1989b)

Yet surrounded at the same time by so much emptiness and enmity, he suddenly perceived the most terrifying of all metonymies:

> And if my people shall remain only a number,
> I adjure it: that from my memory it disappear.
> And may all the graves be buried deeper
> And may no dust remain of the years. (Sutzkever 1968, 108)

The hope and despair of the third group of fighters would be impossible to imagine were it not for the wife-and-husband team of Gusta and Szymek Draenger. Gusta Davidson Draenger, who went by the nom de guerre "Justyna," kept a diary in Polish in which she documented the romance of the resistance. She described in vivid detail the last supper of the Zionist underground, held in the apartment in Kraków that served as the group's refuge and headquarters. She reimagined the event as a combination of a mystical Hasidic Sabbath meal, a Christian communion, and a consecration to arms (Davidson Draenger 1976; 1996, 111–21). Syzmek was the main contributor to and the editor, printer, and distributor of *Hechalutz Halochem* (The fighting pioneer), a publication—in Polish, despite its Hebrew title—that was the official organ of the Combat Organization of Jewish Pioneering Youth, which was active 1942–43. The group had disbanded on the eve of the ghetto's liquidation, and now only the Draengers were left to exhort the Jews in hiding, in the last remaining ghettos, or in labor camps to continue their fight—as Jews. The September 3, 1943, issue contained detailed instructions on how to construct an underground bunker. Draenger also appealed to the Polish peasantry to join forces with the last fighting Jews. A unique feature of this journal was Draenger's weekly editorials, which were based on an extremely well-informed analysis of the geopolitical present and a profound understanding of the past.

"From a personal perspective we are all lost," begins the editorial for August 13, 1943, "and our chances of survival are nil" (Draenger 2006, 61). From a national perspective the prognosis is bleaker still, in Draenger's view, because the healthiest, most vital branch—Polish Jewry—has been utterly destroyed. The Soviet Union represents a physical haven for the Jews but spells their end as a people. Hungarian Jewry's days are numbered, he (correctly) predicts. American Jewry, five million strong, will at best mobilize its philanthropic resources after the fact, leaving the tiny Zionist presence in Palestine as Jewry's only existential hope. It is much easier to die knowing that the dream for Jewish self-liberation will cause the birth of a Jewish state, yet there is nothing in the present to alleviate the loneliness, the burden of being abandoned by the world, which will remain "through the end of time" (ibid., 65). As Draenger's own end draws near, in the issue for September 15, 1943, he turns his analytic mind to the most intractable question of all: how was it that this ancient people lacked the most basic of natural responses—the ability to kill, to avenge, to stand up and fight? "In Praise of the Natural Response" was the most far-reaching critique of Jewish exile and powerlessness written during wartime either inside or outside the Jew-Zone (ibid., 227–30).

The Great Deportation

Metonymy and myth are the two basic means of symbolic shorthand. One is punctual, bare-bones, a world in miniature, which draws on the acute observation of present reality. The other is the punctual rendered transtemporal, a primal plot that recurs again and again, a foundational map of the future. Myth is rooted in collective memory; it is the alphabet used in the grammar of remembrance. What happened inside the Jew-Zone in year 4 of the war is that metonymy became myth. As one ghetto after another was liquidated—the smaller ones first, then the major ones, the "cities and mothers in Israel"—an entire people was reduced to bits and scraps, last letters, a few photographs, and piles of abandoned clothing. As the old, the infirm, the mothers and children were cast into the inferno; and all the strategies for survival failed, those few still left alive cast about for something—anything—that might represent the many, if only as a mnemonic. In the face of total destruction, every memento took on lasting significance.

For Rachel Auerbach, one of Ringelblum's closest associates, the part that stood for the whole had been the soup kitchen at 40 Leszno Street, where writers and intellectuals like Goldin received their daily ration—the kitchen Auerbach ran with selfless devotion and described with scholarly rigor for the Oyneg Shabes (Kassow 2007, 136–43). But of what use was memorializing the social service network in Europe's largest ghetto after its liquidation? In the course of six weeks, 235,741 people were rounded up in one spot, the notorious assembly point called Umschlagplatz, and shipped off in cattle cars to die in a place called Treblinka (Polonsky 1988, 36). A whole city of Jews, a city within a city, masses on masses of people—men, women, and children—were gone. The work of the Oyneg Shabes was temporarily suspended. The only task that remained for the surviving members of the staff was to chronicle the great deportation.

But where should they begin: from the perspective of the dead or that of the living? Each demanded a different lens. Yehoshue Perle renamed his ferocious contemporary chronicle of the great deportation "The Destruction of Warsaw" (1955) the moment he understood it to be a literal reenactment of the original *hurban* (the destruction of the Jerusalem temple). No less fearful was the fate of those still alive, as brilliantly captured by the metonymy of Perle's dog tag, number 4580, issued to the "Chosen-Peoplish" Jews, those 30,000 who survived the great deportation just long enough to work as slave labor. An empty number with no history was all that remained of a lifetime of collective dreams and personal ambitions. Perle's number was, he saw, a sign of the Apocalypse (1989).

The Polish-language poet Władysław Szlengel likewise adopted multiple perspectives. A popular cabaret poet in the ghetto and a one-time member of the Jewish police, Szlengel decided at the beginning of year 4 that it was time to sort through his papers and compose a last will and testament with the sardonic title of "Co czytałem umarłym" ("What I Read to the Dead" 1943). To set the antisentimental tone, Szlengel began by recalling a prewar Soviet film about trapped sailors on a sunken submarine. The last survivor, about to suffocate, had scrawled a final message that affirmed his faith that he was dying for a higher cause. But speaking for the Warsaw Jews, Szlengel could take no such comfort:

> With all my being I feel that I am suffocating as the air in my sunken boat slowly gives out. [Unlike the Soviet sailor] the reasons I am in this boat have nothing to do with heroism. I am here against my will, and without any reason or guilt.
>
> But here I am, in the boat. And although I am no captain, I still think that I should at least write the chronicle of those who have sunk to the bottom. I don't want to leave behind only statistics. Through my poems, sketches and writings I want to enrich (a bad word, I know) the historical record that will be written in the future.

On the wall of my submarine I scrawl my poem-documents. To my companions I, a poet of AD 1943, am reading my scribblings. (Quoted in Kassow 2007, 317)

Among these "poem-documents" is one that recapitulates the methodical murder of Polish Jewry with absolute metonymic precision. "Things" tracks the six stages of the cross—not of one exemplary martyr or of the entire Jewish people, but of their "furniture, tables and chairs, / suitcases and bundles," as the owners are dispossessed and moved to ever more desolate and restricted quarters; forced, by station 4, to move "along a Jewish road / with no big bundles or little bundles, / no furniture or chairs"; reduced to carrying "a small suitcase and a knapsack, / no need for anything else," as they are marched off in even rows of five to the blockhouses reserved for slave labor and finally, to their deaths, leaving behind their "abandoned apartments, / abandoned bundles, / suits and down covers, / and plates and chairs" (Szlengel 2006, 283–85). Aryans will then inherit the spoils in the first of two endings. In their Second Coming, however, the "Jewish things" return in a grand and vengeful procession of *materia mnemonica*, retracing the Via Dolorosa of a martyred people.

Like Szlengel casting about for some disastrous analogue, Auerbach begins her own requiem for the dead in 1943 by recalling a flood she once saw in the mountains. Facing the raging waters from afar, she was close enough to see the gaping mouths of the helpless victims, but not to hear their cries. Just so, standing on the far side of the river of time, she is close enough to recall the catastrophe in every detail, but far enough away to conduct a search for meaning: "And that's how the Jewish masses flowed to their destruction in the time of the deportations. Sinking as helplessly into the deluge of destruction" (Auerbach 1989, 460). To make this leap from a natural to a historical disaster, Auerbach substitutes a "deluge of destruction" for a flood in the mountains to signify the primeval flood. Likening the great deportation to a flood in no way implies that she accepts the biblical belief that an act of God is a sign of divine retribution. On the contrary: the flood analogy means for Auerbach that the evil descended on the Jews from on high like a force of nature, fatally inevitable. The dead were blameless!

Auerbach can make sense of the great deportation only by layering one analogy atop another, like bodies torn loose from their moorings; from the natural realm to the historical, from a flood to the deluge, from Warsaw to Jerusalem. "And if, for even one of the days of my life," she goes on, invoking the famous Psalm of Zion (137), "I should forget how I saw you then, my people, desperate and confused, delivered over to extinction, may all knowledge of me be forgotten and my name be cursed like that of those traitors who are unworthy to share your pain" (Auerbach 1989, 460). The ancient analogies fit the present only contrapuntally and dynamically; the life-and-death struggle of an entire people demands a deeper understanding. Auerbach refuses to see her people as merely passive, or reactive, victims because "every instinct is revealed in the mass—repulsive, tangled":

> All feelings churning, feverish to the core. Lashed by hundreds of whips of unreasoning activity. Hundreds of deceptive or ridiculous schemes of rescue. And at the other pole, a yielding to the inevitable; a gravitation toward mass death that is no [less] substantial than the gravitation toward life. Sometimes the two antipodes followed each other in the same being. (Ibid., 460; emended)

The same people—sometimes the same person—were drawn toward death as powerfully as toward life. Auerbach proceeds to put flesh on the dialectic of destruction by drawing a composite portrait of her people, recalling them group by group: the children and the youth; the women and the men; the idealists and assimilationists; even the underworld, a distinct and especially vital branch of Polish Jewry; the grandmothers and grandfathers; and finally the pietists and the beggars.

Exhausted by the effort to recall each group of Jews individually, despairing of the possibility of ever completing the litany of losses, Auerbach makes her account of the flood more personal—and more gendered. She turns to an incident that happened to her while riding the Warsaw streetcar, the jarring moment that birthed this very work. Sitting opposite her was a Polish Catholic woman, her head thrown back, talking to herself. Seeing and hearing that bereaved mother crying, like one mad or drunk, reminded Auerbach of another woman who seemed drunk or mad with personal grief: Hannah in Shiloh, crying her heart out before God, because she is childless (1 Sam. 1). But as a Jew living on Aryan papers, Auerbach cannot cry in public. What can she do? She can sit down and write her chronicle. She can return to the ancient rite of Jewish mourning, to the recitation of *yizkor*:

> I may neither groan nor weep. I may not draw attention to myself in the street.
>
> And I need to groan. I need to weep. Not four times a year. I feel the need to say Yizkor four times a day. (Auerbach 1989, 464)

Thus the first *yizkor* service for the great deportation, which stands for the Holocaust writ large, was written (scandalously) by a woman. Her composite portrait of the living folk underwrites her personal covenant with a people that now lives only in memory.

The Confessional Diary

A Jew still alive in the Jew-Zone was a statistical error by the fall of 1943. For such a person to take pen in hand at that time was an act of profound self-awareness. At that precise moment, a unique form of confessional diary was born. Time in this diary flows forward and backward; events are both recorded as they happen and reflected on after the fact (Garbarini 2006, 146). The diarists have a terrible secret to confess, forcing them to backtrack to the time of the slaughter. However irrational, they blame themselves for being absent when the roundup occurred, for believing the false promises, for failing to secure a hiding place. They confess to having abdicated their role as father, mother, husband, wife, son, daughter, brother, or sister, their own survival predicated on the death of their loved ones. "Everywhere [I turn]," wrote Grete Holländer on October 31, 1943, "I encounter only dead people. Am I really still alive?" (quoted in ibid., 147). Never far from Holländer's thoughts were her young daughter, Sonja, entrusted to a gentile couple, and "the terrible day" her husband, Marek, was taken from her, not to mention the four hundred women from the Czortków Lager who were taken away before her very eyes. Giving voice to her "unspeakable anger" at their murder, she began keeping a diary in pencil in notebooks typically used by schoolchildren (ibid., 145–48). To write, from that moment on, was for her to work through overwhelming loss and a crushing burden of guilt. In diaries such as hers, time was split in two: time before and time after.

The moment of truth in these confessional diaries was the moment of moral complicity, of radical self-confrontation, which each diarist reached by a different route. In the first days of the great deportation, Abraham Lewin abruptly switched the language in which he kept his ghetto diary from Yiddish to Hebrew. Then, on the day his wife, Luba, was rounded up in Umschlagplatz and shipped off to her death, Lewin began a new calendrical and moral reckoning. Interspersed with the terrible news that reached him hour after hour, which he labored to put into chronological sequence for the sake of future generations, were flashes of self-blame. "The Świeca family has perished," he reported at the end of a lengthy entry dated the eve of Rosh Hashana in 1942:

> He [Mr. Świeca] gave himself up after seeing how his wife and two children were taken. Initially he went with us to Gęsia Street, later he went back, gave himself up and was sent away. I feel a great compassion and admiration for this straightforward person. Strong in mind as well as strong in body. I think that Luba would have done the same, but I didn't have enough strength to die together with her, with the one that I loved so much. (Lewin 1988, 179)

"Where shall I start?" asks Stanisław Adler, hiding on the Aryan side of Warsaw. "There is an overpowering desire burning in me to put in writing as speedily as possible all that has happened to us in these years of war, especially that which I, myself, have been witness to in the last six months. Even now I am terrified that the dangers which threaten me from all sides might prevent me from finishing this manuscript" (1982, 3). Feeding Adler's panic is the knowledge that all his writing thus far "has turned out to be a Penelope's web": the border police burned his diary from the first months of the war; his reconstructed notes were also destroyed when he was interned in the Warsaw ghetto, and everything he wrote inside the ghetto he "had to leave for the wolves to devour" when he escaped to the Aryan side. "Against a logic which I cannot satisfy," he goes on to explain,

> and against a literary tradition which I consciously ignore, I feel almost impelled to start from the end of my story. This is not because it is my intention to begin with the impact of my personal experiences, but because I feel the need to vindicate myself. Instead of an axe or a club I am now holding a pen in my hand. I am alive and living here, and not lying in trenches in an unequal battle or in one of the collective graves of Warsaw Jewry. (Ibid.)

For Dr. Baruch Milch, recapitulated time goes all the way back to the beginning of the war. "On Friday, September 1, 1939," he states in the second paragraph of his diary, "my real life began to end" (2003, 34). As Adler did in his diary, Milch tracks durational time, the hour-by-hour struggle for survival, "hiding in a loft over a stable, in a village, with good people." The date is July 15, 1943: "The risk of death hovers over me, as it does over all Jews these days, and the slightest lapse of vigilance on my part may cost me my life. I desperately need to spill this heavy burden onto paper. Perhaps it will give me a little relief." At the heart of his confession lies an act of self-betrayal: for that terrible crime to be exonerated, he must close the temporal and physical gap between now—his temporary refuge in the loft—and then—the terrible *Aktion* on May 20, 1943, when, trusting the assurances of a friendly Ukrainian, he and his wife left their three-year-old son, Lunek, asleep in the ghetto. It will take many pages to get there, but get there he will, in excruciating detail, and with rage to spare for his Christian neighbors and former patients who did not lift a finger to help (ibid., 118–26). Other revelations are still to come, for in contrast to the murder of Lunek, which he did not witness, when Milch's nephew, also named Lunek, was strangled to death by his father to keep him from screaming and betraying their location to the Germans, Dr. Milch just stood by (ibid., 146–48).

The specter of one's loved ones, be they Lunek or Luba, points to an essential feature of these confessional diaries: they labor to recreate what no longer exists. Their point of departure is when "my real life began to end." On the very day—May 22, 1943—that Yitzhak Katzenelson arrived from Warsaw at the transit camp in Vittel, France, accompanied by his surviving son, seventeen-year-old Zvi, the poet and playwright began to keep a diary (Katzenelson 1964). Instead of bringing him and his son closer together, he recorded, the catastrophe had driven them further apart; both were going mad, in different ways. That distance, in turn, intensified Katzenelson's bereavement for three of the murdered millions, whose names—Hannah, his wife, and Bentsikl and Binyomin, their sons—he repeated like an incantation. Two weeks passed before he wrote another word in the diary. On July 21, the dam burst, with the following day marking the first anniversary, the *yortsayt*, of the start of the great deportation. From then on, Katzenelson backtracked to the slaughter, as if reliving it in real time, back to the liquidation of the Little Ghetto with all its orphans, who had performed the plays he had written for their benefit; back to the discovery that his loved ones had been taken to Treblinka; back to the cellar at Karmelicka 9, on the eve of the first armed resistance; back to finding his works strewn about the abandoned ghetto streets. Each diarist inhabited a private hell. Each labored to reconstruct a paradise lost.

Everything about these diaries was fraught with tension—especially the question of what language to write them in. "*Ikh mit mayn zun Tsvi,*" Katzenelson began his diary in Yiddish. "*Ani im Tsvi beni,*" he translated the words and continued in Hebrew. As simple a phrase as "I and my son Zvi" was for the diarist a statement of faith, because in all the surrounding rooms and apartments, Polish Jews, the last of the last, were making a point of speaking . . . in Polish. What was it that moved both Katzenelson and Lewin to switch from one Jewish language to another? Did writing in Hebrew automatically elevate one's private testimony to a metahistorical plane? Ensure the document's eternality? Render it more conspiratorial? Insert a psychological buffer zone? Or all four? Whatever the reasons, the confusion of languages signaled an attendant confusion of addressee. Who was this document intended to reach? Who was still left to decipher its contents?

"It is May 7, 1943. I am Calel Perechodnik, an engineer of agronomy, a Jew of average intelligence, and I shall try to describe my family's history during the German occupation" was how one diarist began (Perechodnik 1996, xxi). The author ties the work—complete with a prologue and epilogue—up with the following title page:

I dedicate these diaries to
G. S. [German sadism]
P. D. [Polish degradation]

J. T. [the Jewish tragedy]
    Warsaw, 7 May–19 August 1943
    Epilogue: 19 October 1943 (Perechodnik 2004, 7; my translation)

Decipherable only in Polish (we changed the initials to make it work in English), the title page is followed by a "motto" in French, in which Perechodnik provides something of a plot summary:

> *Naître Juif* ce n'est pas une honte,
> c'est un malheur!
> Ma femme bien-aimée *Annie*,
> *seras-tu vengée?*
> Ma petite fille *Athalie*,
> *seras-tu vengée?*
> Les cendres de 3 millions hommes,
> Femmes, enfants juifs, *brulés à Treblinka*,
> *serez-vous vengés?* (Ibid.)

> To be born a Jew is no shame,
> it is a misfortune!
> My beloved wife Annie,
> will you ever be avenged?
> My little daughter Athalie,
> will you ever be avenged?
> The ashes of three million people,
> women, Jewish children, incinerated at Treblinka,
> will you ever be avenged?

How this Polish Jew "of average intelligence" came to learn French we readers of his diary will discover in due course, as we will meet the parents from whom he remains forever estranged. Above all, we will encounter his beloved wife and daughter, who perished nine months before he took pen in hand in order to expiate the crime of having abetted their deaths, instead of protecting them in his capacity as a Jewish policeman during the terrible *Aktion* in the Otwock ghetto, on August 19, 1942. That was the day that tore his life in half, the wound that refused to be sutured, no matter how long he continued living and writing, and no matter what other woman he found to share his bed. What would turn Perechodnik's family chronicle into an X-rated testimony, almost unpublishable, is the depth of his self-loathing, the breadth of his indictment, the baring of his tortured soul. Time does not flow in linear fashion for Perechodnik because the trauma of loss is a regurgitant nightmare, "a black hole in the time continuum" that allows for no redemptive reading

(A. Goldberg 2005, 396–97). When the outside horror penetrates the inner defenses and refuses to let go is when the confessional diary is born.

The Last to Die: The Sonderkommando

In the end the Germans created Auschwitz-Birkenau—the last stop, the final destination. The transport from Luna, which included Zalmen Gradowski and his family, arrived on December 8, 1942. At the beginning of each of his chronicles (Gradowski 1985, 173; 1989, 548) he lists his loved ones who had perished in the gas chambers:

My mother—Sarah	My wife—Sonia
My sister—Liba	My brother-in-law—Raphael
My sister—Esther-Rokhl	My brother-in-law—Wolf

Also included was the address of one of his five uncles living in the United States—"J. Joffe, 27 East Broadway, N.Y." (ibid., 549)—who could supply the details of his biography and a photograph of himself and his wife. Of powerful build, Gradowski had been handpicked for the thousand-member Sonderkommando: men who oversaw the murder of their own people, gave them instructions about where to undress and where to leave their belongings, shaved their heads, and led them to the baths; men whose job it was to pull the dead from the gas chambers, pry open their mouths to extract their gold teeth, and feed the bodies into the ovens; men whose own days were numbered, as he was to number the twenty-two months spent in their company and to mourn their liquidation, counting himself among the last 191 survivors (Gradowski 1977, 109–54). They were quartered in a special block, ate what no one else was allowed to eat, and saw what no one else was allowed to see.

Gradowski was not content merely to chronicle events. He wished also to contextualize them and anticipate the reader's response. Possessed of literary ambitions, with an iterative style and apostrophes to nature that betrayed his debt to Polish romanticism (Wygodski 1977), Gradowski kept circling back to the question of Jewish passivity. To the postwar reader who sat out the war in the Free Zone, Gradowski addressed his "notes" from the underground, whose purpose was to explain how the people of Israel could have vanished so quickly from the soil of Europe. Were they merely casualties of the war? Were they destroyed by some natural disaster? And why did they, each individual and the millions in the aggregate, allow this to happen? As he labored to reconstruct the tortuous journey from ghetto to concentration and death camp, Gradowski dwelt on the myriad ways a person condemned to death could misread the signs (1977, 1985). Of everything he witnessed in those twenty-two months, what stood out in his memory above all else was not the "courageous young man from a Białystok transport [who] had attacked some guards with knives, wounded several of them severely and was shot trying to flee" or the incident of the "Warsaw Transport" before which he bowed his head in deep respect, singling out "the splendid young woman, a dancer from Warsaw, . . . who snatched a revolver from [Walter] Quackernack, the Oberscharfürer of the 'Political Section' in Auschwitz and shot the Referat-führer, the notorious Unterscharführer [Josef] Schillinger" (1989, 549). Rather, it was the fate of the Czech family transport: such intelligent and resourceful Jews, who had been allowed to live together, were duped together, and were gassed together on Purim, March 7, 1944.

To "the Czech Transport" Gradowski dedicated his most sustained work (1989), in which he tried to understand not only the psychology of the murdered, but also the psychology of the mass murderers. His literary means were limited, but his insights were not. The Germans were engaged in a mythic, life-and-death struggle with the demonic *Juden*. The one myth that they were able to make real was the fires of hell—that is, the crematoria ovens—where the members of the Sonderkommando learned which body parts burned more quickly than others (ibid., 563–64). All these crimes would be avenged—of this, Gradowski had no doubt whatsoever. After securing different hiding places for his writings, he led the one-day revolt of the Sonderkommando on October 7, 1944. He was caught, tortured, and publicly hanged (N. Cohen 1994, 523).

Gradowski believed that through his buried chronicles, future historians would understand the psychology of the murderers, the delusionary hope of the victims, and the uniquely tragic fate of the Sonderkommando. Perechodnik believed that millions would someday read his diary and feel deep sorrow for what his beloved Anka had suffered—and thus her memory would live on forever. Kalmanovitsh believed that history would revere the memory of the people of the ghetto. None of these hopes was vindicated. Whatever meaning was salvaged from Auschwitz was constructed by those few who survived, not by those who were the last to die. Perechodnik's diary was anathema to all, his self-blame too painful for anyone to bear. The memory of the ghettos did not inspire generations to study the archival treasures of Warsaw, Łódź, Vilna, Białystok, Kovno, Kraków, and Terezín. Many factors conspired to consign this literary legacy to oblivion. They are the subject of the next chapter.

But the major reason is this: At war's end, the Jews were a nation in defeat, a vanquished people, a bankrupt polity. Hitler had won his war against the Jews of Europe. Their separate civilization on European soil had been destroyed. A literature of the catastrophe written in many languages and manifold genres lay scattered in the ruins. That which was found would be lost yet again.

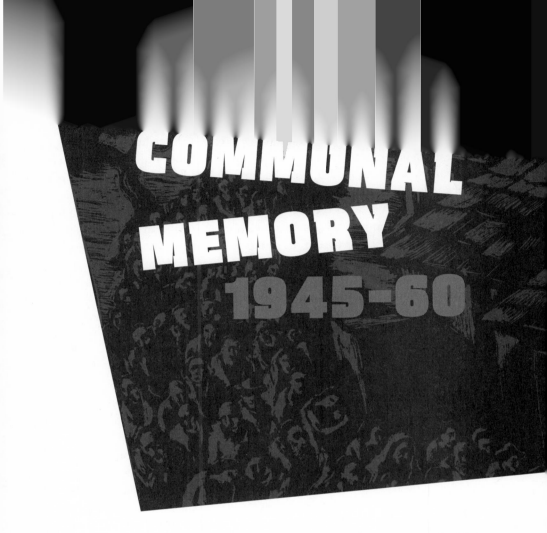

COMMUNAL MEMORY 1945–60

WARTIME WRITING WAS CREATED AT THE CONFLUENCE OF a specific time and place by people variously positioned between the living and the dead. Writing in the immediate aftermath of the war had a similar birth. The response to what had just happened—impossible to comprehend and impossible to forget—needed a habitat, a sanctuary, within which to gestate; it needed the means to produce and disseminate such responses; and it needed, above all, an audience. Communities incubate memory. They foster continuity and provide the grieving individual with a group setting in which to mourn or cry or simply sit in stupefied silence. Communities are also fiercely protective of their turf, impervious to change, susceptible to slogans. They foster intolerance and breed hatred. The sociologist Maurice Halbwachs, a German-French Jew who formulated the concept of "collective memory" (1992), described it as a necessary evil.

In this chapter we shall see the several sides of communal memory: as a unifying and divisive force; as self-critical and sentimental, worldly and otherworldly. At first, we proceed zone by zone, country by country, language by language. When we come up against the Iron Curtain that erected a new divide between East and West, Left and Right, we also encounter fierce public controversies that split one community in two. The medium in this period is the dominant message, and the *yizkor* book becomes the province of sacred memory, while the Yiddish press becomes the main purveyor of living memory. Style is substance, and the sober, plain style, eschewing metaphor and rhetorical excess, becomes the preferred mode of Holocaust writing from Turin to Tel Aviv. "Communal" also means local, occasional, and subject to changing political climates. The best of the published testimonies had the power to challenge a local consensus. In spite of the community, there was also a sporadic movement across lands and languages toward a time beyond time, toward memory as liturgy. But there wasn't much time. The window that opened in 1945 had closed almost everywhere by 1948; cracks made thereafter augured a new opening only in retrospect.

Liberation: The Displaced Person Camps

Communal memory was countermemory, fashioned within weeks and months of the liberation out of rage and thanksgiving, realism and idealism, exile and home.

A mere three weeks after his liberation from Buchenwald, the twenty-four-year-old Mordecai Strigler succeeded in publishing a handwritten, mimeographed newspaper for his fellow survivors called *Tkhiyes-hameysim* (Resurrection; Szeintuch 2006). All six pages were filled with his own writing, a practice that Strigler would continue anonymously and pseudonymously for the next fifty-three years of his prolific career. Other titles that appeared in short order similarly bespoke the dawning of a new era: *Bamidbar* (In the wildnerness, published in Föhrenwald), *Baderekh* (En route, Milan and Rome), *Vidergeburt* (A new life, Munich), *Oyf der fray* (In freedom, Stuttgart; Baker 1990). Among the most ambitious and long-lived publications was *Fun letstn khurbn*, subtitled in English *From the Last Extermination: Journal for the History of the Jewish People during the Nazi Regime*, which was published in Munich from 1946 to 1949. "From the last extermination" yoked together two things that had not been paired before. *Khurbn* was the Yiddish pronunciation of *hurban*, the historical archetype of Jewish catastrophe, the destruction of the Temple in Jerusalem (Mintz 1984). It was an event at once rooted in time and outside of time, both punctual and transtemporal. Like the Exodus, like the Akedah, the binding of

Isaac on Mount Moriah. *Letst* was richly ambiguous, for it could mean "latest" or "the last," the ultimate. If it meant "the latest," then the destruction of European Jewry was a link in a terrible chain. If it meant "the last," then the Holocaust was its own archetype, an end that was also a beginning. Starting from scratch, Israel Kaplan, the publication's tireless editor, collected oral testimony and wartime folklore. For him, the essential units of memory were the annihilated communities (B. Cohen 2010; Schein 2009).

Who were these people, the chroniclers of the catastrophe and the dreamers of a new tomorrow? Liberated from death camps, death marches, and death trains, then quarantined into camps, they were known as displaced persons (DPs for short), a catchall term for deserters, prisoners of war, foreign workers, collaborators, and Wermacht recruits. They were of every nationality, numbering two million in Germany and Austria alone—which had been split into Soviet, British, French, and American zones (Bauer 1970, 43–54). This chapter will focus on those liberated by the US Army and on two tiny groups in particular, who successfully overcame the postwar chaos, squalor, and scarcity of postwar conditions to find civilian lodgings in Munich.

The two groups had much in common. They came from Poland or Lithuania, they had been liberated by the Americans from various German concentration camps, and their day jobs now were to document what had been lost and what could still be salvaged. The Jews, an elite group of intellectuals who were fluent in both Yiddish and Hebrew, were employed by the Historical Commission of the Central Committee of Liberated Jews in Bavaria, established on November 28, 1945 (Lewinsky 2010; Schein 2008). The Christians—led by Anatol Girs, a famous prewar publisher—worked for the Polish Information Center, affiliated with the Polish Red Cross, at 15 Pienzenauerstrasse in Munich, where they also lived. After hours, both groups of survivors worked as it were for themselves, compiling, designing, typesetting, and publishing a new kind of memorial literature.

Both were immensely grateful to their American liberators, a debt of thanks they registered in their first publications designed for wider distribution: a Haggadah and a collection of eyewitness testimonies. In celebration of the first Passover after the war, the Jewish survivors gave thanks by organizing communal seders. The largest such gathering took place at the Deutsches Theatre Restaurant in Munich, where two hundred survivors were joined by a group of Jewish GIs (Touster 2000). "We were slaves to Hitler in Germany," read the English caption to the *Passover Service*, compiled, designed, and partially handwritten by Yosef Dov Sheinson specially for the occasion. This signaled two things to the assembled guests, schooled in Jewish collective memory: first, that in the seamless progression of Jewish catastrophes,

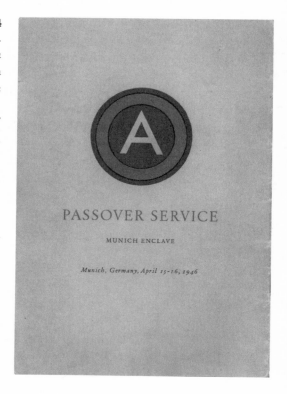

FIGURE 4

Y. D. Sheinson.
*Passover Service: Munich
Enclave*. Printed in Munich
by the Third Army of the
US Army of Occupation, 1946.
Reprinted in *A Survivors'
Haggadah*, edited by Saul
Touster. Philadelphia:
Jewish Publication Society
of America, 2000.

rehearsing the Israelite enslavement in Egypt was the same thing as rehearing the Holocaust; and second, that "we" Jews, whether survivors or soldiers, shared a single historical fate. Of the four zones, only in the American one could the national and religious aspirations of the survivors find open expression. Only there could a US Army chaplain—named Abraham J. Klausner, born in Memphis, Tennessee—conduct the Passover seder service and exhort "the khaki-clad sons of Israel" to continue the universal struggle for justice and freedom (quoted in Sheinson 2000, 8).

The second book was the brainchild of Anatol Girs, a Polish publisher and book designer. Three young men—Janusz Nel Siedlecki, Krystyn Olszewski, and Tadeusz Borowski—had been interned with Girs at a DP camp in Freimann, Germany, where he overheard them swapping stories about Auschwitz. When Girs received permission from the Polish Red Cross Committee in London to establish a family tracing service in Munich and to have the three men work for him, Girs seized the opportunity, encouraging them to prepare a collective volume of documentary tales of their camp experiences, beginning with Auschwitz (Nitecki 2007). The first of Girs's postwar publications with a public mission, it opened with a proud dedication to the

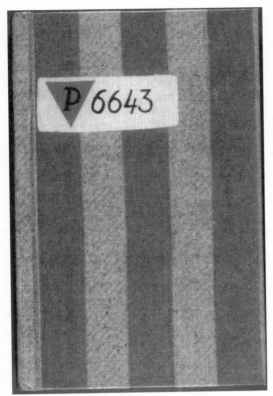

FIGURE 5
Janusz Nel Siedlecki,
Krystyn Olszewski, and
Tadeusz Borowski. *We
Were in Auschwitz*. Edited by
Tadeusz Borowski. New York:
Welcome Rain, 2000. Cover
designed by Anatol Girs,
Munich, 1946.

*VIIth
American Army
which brought us freedom
from concentration camp
Dachau-Allach*

No effort was spared to make these volumes excellent in form as well as content. The *Passover Service* (so-called on its English title page) was richly illustrated with seven woodcuts by the Hungarian Jewish survivor Mikloś Adler, in the best tradition of Central European expressionism, and with elaborate calligraphy and border designs by Sheinson. *Byliśmy w Oświęcimiu* (*We Were in Auschwitz*) was published in an edition of 10,000 numbered copies, some of which were bound in concentration camp stripes cut from original garments (Siedlecki, Olszewski and Borowski 2000).

Both volumes were anthological. Driven by a collective imperative to testify, the authors of *We Were in Auschwitz* gave it the feel of an underground publication. Challenging the notion of individual authorship, each of the chroniclers was identified only by the Auschwitz number tattooed on his arm and then his Christian name. They were listed on the title page in numerical order: 6643, 75817, 119198. Number 6643 was featured on the stark cover as well because in Auschwitz, as the glossary explained, low numbers, denoting old-timers in the camp, were a "source of honor and respect from other old numbers and young numbers, latecomers to the camp, also known as millions" (ibid., 192). So the individual chapters went unsigned, the former slaves speaking with the voice of Everysurvivor.

Sheinson's *Passover Service* combined very different strands of the anthological genre. In ages past, the anthology had been a medium for the transmission, preservation, and creation of tradition. The Jewish classics in this genre were the siddur, or daily prayer book, and the Haggadah for Passover (Stern 2004). Half of Sheinson's work, therefore, was given over to conflations of past and present. The Haggadah's central credo—"In every generation they [the enemies of Israel] rise up against us"—was easy enough to substantiate. Members of the ss were a literal reembodiment of the taskmasters of ancient Egypt, and hauling bricks for Nazi munitions factories was the same as hauling bricks for the building of the pyramids. Similarly, the messianic hope of restoring Zion could be realized in our times only by crossing the waters to a productive Jewish homeland in Palestine.

Sheinson's *Passover Service* also partook of a second, more activist trend, in which the memory of the past was harnessed to call into being a new Jewish culture and community. In Sheinson's imagined community, the only ritual food eaten at the seder was *maror*, the bitter herb.

> *This bitter herb, wherefore do we eat it?*
> Because we were intoxicated by the incense of Exile, because we fled from one exile to another, because we reassured ourselves, saying: Ours will not be the fate that befell our people before us.
> Because we did little on our own behalf to establish our destroyed [national] home and state. (Sheinson 2000, 25; emended translation)

Thus enslavement had taken many forms, not least of which was apathy and bad faith on the part of the slaves themselves. It was the Allies, perish the thought, and not God, who hearkened unto the Jews' cry—and the British who reneged on their sacred promise: "Blessed be He who keeps His promise to Israel [a quotation from the Haggadah], who wrote the White Paper, forbade Aliyah and the purchase of land, and who calculated ways to hasten the end [of the Jewish messianic dream]" (ibid., 41).

Sheinson's *Passover Service* "spoke" most directly through the in-your-face art of countercommentary, first invoking the relevant archetype—reminding God, as it were, of His promise to the people of Israel—then provoking God's response by throwing the present sacrilege in His face (Roskies 1984, 15–52). Blessed be the British, who in mimicking God, made and broke a covenant with Israel. By issuing the infamous White Paper that severely limited Jewish immigration to Palestine, they had retarded the messianic clock. Through such parodic use of Jewish covenantal language, Sheinson expressed the core idea of his Haggadah: the final liberation of the Jews had yet to come, which meant that the signs of their abandonment were manifold and the obstacles that lay ahead were multiple. To wrest meaning from the first postwar celebration of Passover, this communal rite of celebration was reconsecrated to political protest and radical self-confrontation. By reactivating the syntax of Jewish remembrance, during this and other Jewish festivals, Sheinson hoped to mobilize the rescued remnant of Israel (Schein 2009, 128, note 102).

To tell the story the way they wanted to tell it, from within, both survivor groups were painfully aware of the resistance they faced from the very communities they were trying to rejoin and reshape. "False legends are being created around many aspects of this war," Girs warned darkly in his note from the publisher (Girs 2000, 1). "We did not fight for the concept of nation in the camp," Borowski stated emphatically in the unsigned preface, "nor for the inner structuring of man; we fought for a bowl of soup, for a place to sleep, for women, for gold and watches from the transports" (Borowski 2000, 4). The truth-telling chroniclers of Auschwitz refused to recast the war into a narrative of heroic resistance, solidarity, and hope.

Their style was deadpan, stripped of metaphor. They routinely juxtaposed the mundane with the horrific. "With a Baedeker among the Wires," written by a four-year veteran of the camp, was a no-nonsense guide to Auschwitz, as the bitterly ironic title promised. Chief among its tasks was to provide an anatomy of "organizing" as opposed to mere stealing:

> A thief steals a portion of bread under his colleague's head, the organizer steals it from the storeroom, and steals more: loaves of bread, margarine by the carton. A thief steals a piece of cake from a friend's package, the organizer brings gingerbread from the ramp or the crematorium. The ordinary prisoner slowly dies of hunger and writes home for packages; the organizer sends his family assiduously saved banknotes. (Siedlecki, Olszewski, and Borowski 2000, 11)

Just as Auschwitz created a new hierarchy of criminal behavior, it erased the distinction between *Homo sapiens* and other animals, introducing a species known in camp parlance as the *Muselman*. "The muzelman isn't a human being," explained the chronicler matter-of-factly, "he's an animal who is ready to give his life and his freedom for a rotting turnip" (ibid., 17). Much later, when it might have seemed that the chamber of horrors was already filled to capacity, the reader was admitted into the Gypsy family camp, the scene of unbelievable orgies, which gave new meaning to the term "Fire Freezes," the drinking, whoring, and caroling illuminated by the glow of the fire from the crematorium (ibid., 99).

Edited and annotated by Borowski, *We Were in Auschwitz* followed a loose chronology, from the perspective of the lower to the higher numbers. This meant that Borowski's own testimony—four stories that would later become classics—appeared toward the end of the volume; and because Hungarian Jews were not sent to the gas chambers until the spring of 1944, there was always plenty to plunder. "As a rule," said one of the chroniclers of the Hungarian transports, "bracelets were hidden in marmalade, rings in butter, and money in bread" (ibid., 173). The closest kin to *We Were in Auschwitz* was a prewar French novel that Borowski greatly admired—Louis-Ferdinand Céline's *Journey to the End of the Night*—except that never before had the same journey been undertaken by so many and survived by so few (Drewnowski 2007, 325, 353, 355 note 15).

Sheinson reserved his angriest message for the end of his volume, which he set apart from the standard recitation of the Haggadah by means of a different typeface. Speaking now in several voices, he painted a harsh postwar landscape wracked by British perfidy, Christian betrayal, the spiritual kidnapping of Jewish children, and—most painful of all—the poisonous spread of Zionist party politics, which made a mockery of Jewish unity. This last was not addressed to the "khaki-clad sons of Israel," the honored guests from America. Sheinson's *Passover Service* was not written for those who had a home to go back to when their stint in Europe was over. What their own future would be Sheinson's fellow DPs could barely imagine, because the one thing they knew for sure was that they weren't going home.

Communal memory, then, was countermemory, contentious memory, fashioned by those who had suffered side by side and now inhabited the same provisional space, but might just as well have been living on separate planets. The two groups of survivors did not know or wish to know of each other's existence. Each labored alone, battling its own ghosts and conjuring its own future. Girs still dreamed of a free Poland pulsating at the heart of Europe, even while the Soviets were consolidating their territorial gains. How to forget and whom to forget was being decided not in Kraków, Warsaw, or Munich, but in Moscow. The Jewish documentation project in the DP camps, meanwhile— which discovered new creative talent and focused on oral testimony, folklore, the lost communities, and martyrdom—was being challenged from within by professional historians of the Holocaust and from without by Zionist emissaries. How to remember, when to remember, and whom to remember were being decided not in Bergen-Belsen, Föhrenwald, Landsberg, Munich, or Stuttgart, but in Jerusalem (Jockusch 2010; Schein 2009, 121–31).

Before they dispersed, the Jewish DPs did leave a memory trace: not through their publications, soon to be forgotten, and not through their archives, packed up and left unopened for sixty years, but through personal encounters with emissaries from America. In the spring of 1946, the poet H. Leivick and the singer Emma Schaver formed the first cultural mission to the DP camps sponsored by the World Jewish Congress and the United Nations Relief and Works Agency, which then focused on DPs. As the director of the Joint Distribution Committee in the American Zone, the veteran anthologizer Leo W. Schwarz gained intimate knowledge of the plight of the DPs, and the American psychologist David P. Boder arrived in Paris in the summer of 1946 on a one-man mission to record survivor testimonies in their original languages. These were extraordinary acts of intervention, each of which would produce important and pioneering works of Holocaust literature, yet all of these emissaries would see and hear only what they had spent a lifetime training to see and hear.

Leivick, whose experience of Siberian exile had made him the first survivor figure in modern Jewish culture, addressed the themes of martyrdom and messianism throughout his *oeuvre* (Leivick 1940). Armed with a template of redemption through suffering, Leivick found among the DPs what he was looking for: new poetic talents and stark new instantiations of Jewish martyrdom. These he immediately documented in his travelogue *Mit der sheyris hapleyte* (With the saving remnant, 1947) and translated into symbolic form in *Di khasene in Fernvald* (The wedding in Föhrenwald, 1949), possibly the first attempt in any language to place the DPs center stage. Schwarz, a committed Zionist, also found what he was looking for among "the Sheerith Hapletah," to whom he dedicated his superbly edited anthology *The Root and the Bough: The Epic of an Enduring People* (L. Schwarz 1949). Boder's case was more complex. He came to Europe hoping to codify the DPs' stories of physical and mental brutality so as to redefine the concept of "trauma." In light of his extensive interviews—conducted in camps and shelterhouses throughout France, Switzerland, Italy, and Germany—he came to appreciate the DPs' lore and zest for life. *I Did Not Interview the Dead* (1948), his groundbreaking collection of first-person testimonies, made the case that these were uprooted people whose resilience could only be admired (Rosen 2010). Leivick constructed a melodrama of spiritual redemption played against a backdrop of martyrdom and messianic faith. Schwarz constructed a monodrama of national rebirth played against a backdrop of resistance and group solidarity. Boder constructed a psychodrama of individual trauma played against a backdrop of civic courage. Let's call them shadow narratives: survivor testimonies rearranged into coherent scripts that supported the authors' deepest convictions.

Sheinson, meanwhile, did not make aliyah to the Land of Israel. In 1948 he immigrated to Montreal, Canada, where he eked out a living as a Hebrew educator. Instead of returning to Poland, Girs moved to the United States in 1947, where the Girs-Press failed to make it big. Borowski did return to Poland in 1946, was reunited with his fiancée, perfected a new genre of nihilistic prose, and succumbed to despair.

Prime Witnesses: Poland and Her Jews

Poland was and remains to this day the prime witness to the Holocaust. Where Jews, Christian Poles, and Ukrainians had lived side by side for generations stand eight of the most infamous German slaughter sites—Auschwitz-Birkenau, Belżec, Chełmno, Gross-Rosen, Majdanek, Sobibor, Stuthoff, and Treblinka—now part and parcel of the reconfigured boundaries of postwar Poland. Poles, who suffered mightily at the hands of the Germans, never joined special paramilitary units to aid in exterminating the Jews. True, there is a word in Polish—*szmalcownik*—that denotes a professional blackmailer of hidden Jews, but it is a term of opprobrium.

Polish is the first non-Jewish language to find a new name for this unprecedented catastrophe. Normally, historical events are not spelled with capital letters in the Polish language, so when a word was needed to signify the destruction, the extermination of Polish Jewry, *zagłada* was enlisted, so long as *zagłada* obeyed the rules of declension and was paired with a nominal attribute: Whose destruction? Of what or whom? A cadre of Holocaust historians—Rachel Auerbach, Nachman Blumental, Michał Borwicz, Szymon Datner, Philip Friedman, Noah Gris, Maria Hochberg-Mariaęska, Joseph Kermisz, Ber Mark, Henryk Rudnicki, Natan Szternfinkiel, and Isaiah Trunk—began collecting testimonies, issuing guidelines, and publishing rescued manuscripts and preliminary research even while the ruins were still smoldering. Five regional branches of the Central Jewish Historical Commission were already up and running by the beginning of 1945 (Stauber 2009; Tych 2009). Among the first fruits were Friedman's *Zagłada Żydów lwowskisch* (The destruction of the Jews of Lwow) and Gerszon Taffet's *Zagłada Żydostwa polskiego* (The extermination of Polish Jews: an album of pictures), both in 1945; and Datner's *Walka i zagłada bialostockiego getta* (The struggle and destruction of the Białystok Ghetto), Rudnicki's *Martyrologia i zagłada Żydów warszawskich* (The martyrdom and destruction of the Jews of Warsaw), and Szternfinkiel's *Zagłada Żydów Sosnowca* (The destruction of the Jews of Sosnowiec), all in 1946. When the same historians wished to be more inclusive, they adopted the catch-all phrase "under the German Occupation of Poland," but this rubric was also inaccurate because three million Poles had perished during that occupation, and assuming a commonality of fate appeared to presume a commonality of perspective. Why single out the prewar population of three million Jews? Five decades later, and contrary to Polish usage, *Zagłada* (upper case) was finally adopted to signify "Holocaust, Jewish (1939–1945)" (Adamczyk-Garbowska and Duda 2003).

The art of witnessing began with the underground collection of verse *Zotchłani* (From the abyss). Published by the Jewish National Committee in the spring of 1944 (Appenszlak 1945), it brought together surviving members of the Jewish underground like Michał Borwicz, hidden Jews like Mieczysław Jastrun, and Christian Poles like Jan Kott and Czesław Miłosz. Dominating the center of their moral universe was a wall that had once created a terrible divide between victims and witnesses. "Here too as in Jerusalem," wrote Jastrun, "There is a gloomy, wailing wall, / Those who had to face it / Shall see it nevermore" (quoted in Gillon 1965, 29). Standing before that very wall in April 1943, "On that beautiful Warsaw Sunday," something happened to jog Miłosz's historical memory. He was suddenly reminded of Campo dei Fiori, a square in Rome where on February 17, 1600, the Italian philosopher Giordano Bruno was burned at the stake for heresy. Then, as now, the death of the innocent by fire was but a blip in the pursuit of everyday pleasure, the bystanders behaving in Warsaw exactly as they had in Rome, for adjacent to the burning ghetto a merry-go-round had been built, and the Sunday crowds were enjoying life to the fullest. That conjunction of martyrdom on one side of the ghetto wall and mass revelry on the other side made unmistakable "the loneliness of the dying," those "forgotten by the world" (Miłosz 1988, 34). At best, the distant memory of the one would finally kindle rage "at a poet's word" on a new Campo dei Fiori. At worst, the privileged possessor of the redemptive "word" was himself but a passive bystander.

"Campo dei Fiori" and the underground anthology in which it first appeared were the first act in a drama of moral reckoning, of national self-confrontation, that would play out in Poland for decades to come. To bear moral witness meant acknowledging the absolute distinction between the living and the dead.

For Zofia Nałkowska, as for Miłosz, the turning point, the dark epiphany, came in April 1943 with the burning of the Warsaw ghetto. "Nothing of the former world holds true anymore," she recorded in her diary. "Nothing has remained" (quoted in Kuprel 2000, xii). By May of the next year, she was forced to admit that the totality of this catastrophe could never be told. After the war, when Nałkowska confronted the eyewitnesses to these unspeakable horrors, she had to invent a means of transcription. From the depositions she collected immediately after the war, when she agreed to serve on the Commission for the Investigation of Nazi War Crimes, Nałkowska in 1946 crafted a remarkable series of *Medaliony* (*Medallions*; 2000).

With a reportorial style seemingly devoid of affect, Nałkowska allows her informants from all walks of life and ethnic background to somehow articulate their personal experience of atrocity—"somehow," because none of her informants achieves clarity of vision or true self-knowledge. Dwojra (Dvoyre or Deborah) Zielona survived all seven circles of hell with one good eye. Her will to live at all cost was fueled, she reluctantly admits, by the desire "to tell everything just like I'm telling you now." Yet despite that determination to live and bear witness, she joined the transport to Majdanek. "No Jews left," she thought to herself. "If I was going to die, then I preferred to die with the others, not alone" (quoted in Nałkowska 2000, 32). Her eventual liberation by the Soviets neither alleviates her terrible isolation nor restores her to perfect vision. Similar is the tale of a man who had witnessed the mercy killing of a young Jewish woman who jumped from the boxcar headed to the extermination camp "but is unable to understand it" (ibid., 23). What he fails to understand is that he too is an accomplice to the crime. The gaps and silences are left for the reader to fill in. They are what the depositions are all about.

Transformed like Nałkowska by his wartime experience, Adolf Rudnicki rejected previous forms of psychological realism to push the conventions of the genre in order to achieve new levels of factual immediacy and moral urgency. When Rudnicki returned to Warsaw after the liberation (and after fighting in the Warsaw uprising of 1944), he hoped to retrieve his roomful of wartime writings—two novels, diaries, and copious notes. Instead he found a heap of ashes (Shenfeld 1991, 23, 29). Reading backward from that heap, Rudnicki came to view everything that he had written before the war "with anger and disapproval." "My books exude the stuffy atmosphere of papers abandoned in attics," he wrote in 1956:

> The war has already destroyed them, though it has not touched their physical form. The impact of the great conflagration has deprived their pages of readability, deformed them like a bridge into whose trusses a missile has been fired. Life has left them, as it has left the steppes under the crushing weight of the tanks. My art seems to me to be wretched. Wretched! (Quoted in Polonsky and Adamczyk-Garbowska 2001, xvii)

Between past and present lay an abyss that Rudnicki called *epoka pieców*, or the age of crematoria: a world devoid of guideposts, a world in which ordinary men and women were put to the ultimate ethical and psychological tests (Wróbel 1998). In his stories and novellas from the mid-1940s and early 1950s, collected into *The Crystal Stream, Shakespeare, Flight from Jasna Polana*, and *The Dead and the Living Sea and Other Stories* (1957), an all-knowing narrator akin to Rudnicki himself kept a strict moral reckoning. With a descriptive and historical density that turned his fiction into a species of psychological journalism (Polonsky and Adamczyk-Garbowska 2001, xvii), he showed that some of his heroes and heroines were too weak to withstand the inhuman demands that were made of them. Others were condemned for their calculated acts of betrayal. Still others, like Raisa, the heroine of "The Ascension"—his best-known story, first published in 1951—acted courageously on behalf of her brilliant but demented husband, Sebastian, only to survive without him (Rudnicki 2001). Daniel Dzikowski, the eponymous hero of "The Dying Daniel" (Rudnicki 1957, 201–55), survived the liquidation of the Warsaw ghetto not by virtue of his heroism but because of his indecision (Wróbel 1998, 259). For Rudnicki, the war was a test of values and character, in which there was an uneven chance of emerging victorious. Each day, especially each day spent in hiding on the Aryan side, required ordinary people to dissimulate and improvise. "Your face attracts attention," one street-smart Jewish woman instructed her more cloistered friend. "It is drawn with suffering, preoccupied, always feverish: we have no right to faces like that today. You are fair, but our fair complexion is not the same as theirs" (Rudnicki 2001, 110). Rudnicki's novelistic eye, his mix of pathos and lyricism, his "monumental moralism," his heroic views on writing under sentence of death—all this won him a central place in postwar Polish literature. He was admired as the Jeremiah of the Warsaw ghetto (Wróbel 1998, 258–59).

As sympathetic bystander, unnamed investigator, and omniscient narrator, Miłosz, Nałkowska, and Rudnicki positioned themselves as witnesses once removed. Not so Borowski, Auschwitz No. 119198, who saw and was forced to oversee the extermination of Polish Jewry. Assigned his place within the strict camp hierarchy, the speaker in Borowski's stories negotiated freely among the vast collection of nationalities and the Babel of tongues, and with similar ease mixed the mundane with the horrific. But "to strip man of so-called martyrdom" and, more radically still, to demonstrate that "evil was not the work of one side" (Drewnowski 2007, 57–58), the speaker and center of consciousness began with himself, with deputy Kapo *Vorarbeiter* Tadek, an inmate who learned how to rise in the criminal ranks. As a latecomer to Auschwitz, and a Christian Pole no longer in danger of being sent to the gas chamber (Kott 1976, 15), Tadek's privileged position was that of adjacency. Adjacent to the men's camp was the women's camp, where his beloved Maria—with whom he could correspond—was interned. Adjacent to Auschwitz and its satellite camps was the home front, the source of letters and occasional food packages. But adjacent to his punishing work brigade were "The People Who Walked On," the endless transports of the last remaining Jews of Europe (Borowski 1976, 82–97). Never for a moment did Tadek remain unaware of the unique fate of the Jews.

"This Way for the Gas, Ladies and Gentlemen," his most famous story, is a tale of initiation. "All of us walk around naked," it begins, heralding the innocence of Eden or the reality of hell. "The heat is unbearable" (ibid., 29). Everything is recounted in the present tense, as relentless and unstoppable as the technology of mass death, which Tadek is quick to master: "The delousing is finally over and our striped suits are back from the tanks of Cyclone B solution, an efficient killer of lice in clothing and of men in gas chambers." In Auschwitz, Tadek learns next, there is a strict separation of the sexes and an alternative geography, where "Canada" is the place of prosperity and endless booty. Henri, a fat Frenchman, has been around for a while, so he can explain the rules of survival and give Tadek his first exposure to "the cheerful little station" (ibid., 33) that the Germans have built for receiving the Jewish transports with maximum efficiency and deceit: "This is where they load freight for Birkenau: supplies for the construction of the camp, and people for the gas chambers" (ibid., 33–34). All communication, meanwhile, is conducted in "crematorium Esperanto," rendered for the most part without explanation. The ss officers appear, all pomp and circumstance, with "an air of military readiness and agility": "Some stroll majestically on the ramp" (ibid., 35). One particularly efficient and calm officer addresses the mass of Jews from the Sosnowiec-Będzin transport with impeccable manners. *"Meine Herrschaften,"* he says, "this way, ladies and gentlemen, try not to throw your things around, please" (ibid., 38). As trucks loaded with people drive off with their screaming victims, a Red Cross van "transports the gas that will kill these people. The enormous cross on the hood, red as blood, seems to dissolve in the sun." The only poetic similes are those born of Auschwitz itself. Since such infernal signs have never been seen before, the narrator is prompted to break out of the present tense just once, in order to cast an apocalyptic look forward.

> The transports swell into weeks, months, years. When the war is over, they will count up the marks in their notebooks—all four and [a] half million of them. The bloodiest battle of the war, the greatest victory of the strong, united Germany. *Ein Reich, ein Volk, ein Fuhrer*—and four crematoria. (Ibid., 39)

Is there room in this thickest Book of Numbers for individual acts and human interactions? Tadek already knows the camp law: "people going to their death must be deceived to the very end" (ibid., 37). In the name of this "only permissible form of charity," he estranges himself from the Jews and pretends not to speak their language. With cinematic speed, individual vignettes emerge from the Sosnowiec-Będzin transport: the selfless and spontaneous act of compassion of a tall, gray-haired woman; a mother who repudiates her daughter and is contrasted with the behavior of a graceful girl, who goes to the gas "with a shade of proud contempt" (ibid., 44); an elderly German Jew insisting on his right to speak to a supervisor, and the small girl with only one leg. All are thrown indiscriminately into the vans bound for the gas chambers; the good, the bad, the hale, and the infirm. To each of these telescoped encounters Tadek responds differently: once with an attack of self-loathing, once with a total loss of identity. "My God, man," he exclaims to Henri, "I am finished, absolutely finished!" "So soon?" the veteran replies. "After only two transports?" (ibid., 46). By the story's end, the stars are already beginning to pale in the sky, and "great columns of smoke rise from the crematoria"—a sure sign that "the Sosnowiec-Będzin transport is already burning" (ibid., 49).

Not the innocence of Eden, but a meticulously realized hell on earth.

These narratives, twenty in number and appearing in two volumes—the 1947 *Pożegnaniez Marią* (Farewell to Maria) and the 1948 *Kamienny świat* (World of stone)—won Borowski fame and (relative) fortune in the Spartan conditions of postwar Poland. His writing became ever sparer as he adopted the laconic style and airtight structure of Hemingway and other American masters, whom he was busy translating into Polish.

In Poland, Hitler and his helpers had created the laboratory conditions for a new literature of witnessing. The Poles had been conquered, but the Jews still living in their midst were doomed. Could a suffering people compare incomparables? During the war, Polish-language poets confronted the abyss that divided the witnesses from the Jewish victims, coming as close as they could to the ghetto walls. Subjecting a range of eyewitnesses to minute examination, Nałkowska discovered the manifold gaps between testimony and knowledge, while Rudnicki translated the psychological record of the survivors into a moral balance sheet. For Borowski, every eyewitness was by definition an accomplice, for every survivor was a scavenger of the dead. All this literature appeared in under a decade, as if these writers knew that their time for bearing true witness was running out.

The Cold War: Coerced Memory

Communism was the enemy of communal memory. The communal was a vestige of capitalism, something the world proletariat would soon overcome in its struggle for a classless society. Antisemitism, in this scheme, was another such vestige, and the Polish Communist Party campaigned against antisemitism, equating all opposition to its rule with reactionary racial prejudice.

Under Communism, where the dead could not be divided, local pasts were driven underground. The suffering of all Soviet peoples was subsumed under the Great Patriotic War (1941–45). There were no Jewish victims, only generalized, formulaic victims of fascism. In reality, thanks to so-called ethnic cleansing and transfers of whole populations, the various people's democratic republics were nationalist states that belonged to one nation. One catastrophe fit all.

And one style fit all. At first, the Polish Communist Party tolerated Holocaust realism, on the ground that realism liberated literature from the moral impasse of the prewar capitalist system; works not written under Party dictates were co-opted by it, if they were judged to be sincere. But as early as 1947, official Party spokesmen were calling on Polish literary production to liberate itself from war-related themes and to celebrate the future. Optimism was the new watchword; fatalism was evidence of subversion. One writer after another fell into line. In 1949, the Yiddish poet Binem Heller exhorted the Wrocław Conference of Jewish Writers to renounce a "shortsighted naturalism," the breeding ground of fatalism (quoted in Krawczyęska and Wołowiec 2000, 22–23). The Party convened a conference a year later to enforce the primacy of Socialist realism, and Borowski, then in Berlin, answered the call with an hysterical diatribe directed at all so-called Marxist writers for not participating more fully in the life of the masses. He recanted his own "concentration camp complex," bedeviled by "narrow empiricism, behaviorism, and whatnot" (Borowski 2005, 260). When Rudnicki, who was attending the conference, read Borowski's personal attack on him in this article, he tore the issue up and threw it out the window (Drewnowski 2007, 340).

With this act of public suicide, Borowski became "Beta," exhibit B in Miłosz's 1953 exposé, in *The Captive Mind*, of the intellectual under totalitarian rule. "Beta," Miłosz explained, had found in Communism "useful hatred, hatred put to the service of society" (1981, 127). Soon after completing his pitiless portrait of Borowski as "a disappointed lover," Miłosz learned of Borowski's suicide. He had gone home after visiting his newborn daughter in the maternity ward, closed all the windows, and turned on the gas.

The Communist Party was hard at work, not only enforcing the primacy of Socialist realism but also expunging the Jews from the map of collective memory. "Again about the Jews, again about the ghetto, again about suffering?" stormed Jakub Berman, the No. 2 man in the Polish government and a Jew by birth, when Rudnicki presented him with a politically correct novella about the Warsaw ghetto uprising. Denied a venue to publish further tales of Jewish woe, Rudnicki became a highly successful sports writer instead (Shenfeld 1991, 52, 65–66).

In Poland, as in the rest of the Communist bloc, Holocaust memory became a pawn of the Cold War. It fell to Ber Mark, as director of the Jewish Historical Institute in Warsaw—the memory bank of Polish Jewry and the repository of the two surviving parts of the Oyneg Shabes—to become the cold warrior of Holocaust literature. He did this in two ways. First, all the archival sources that he published underwent stringent political censorship—everything from Emanuel Ringelblum's *Notes from the Warsaw Ghetto*, which formed the basis of all subsequent translations into European languages (see,

FIGURE 6

Leyb Olicki, ed. *Tsvishn lebn un toyt*. Warsaw: Yidish bukh, 1955. An edition of Yehoshue Perle's "Khurbn Varshe" appeared in this volume.

for example, Ringelblum 1958) to the fiction and reportorial prose written in the Warsaw ghetto, such as *Tsvishn lebn un toyt* (Between life and death, 1955), which appeared in the series called Literary Creations in the Ghettos and Camps. Second, Mark wrote a Cold War guide to *Di yidishe tragedye in der poylisher literatur* (The Jewish tragedy in Polish literature; 1950). Here, he ranked thirty-odd writers and poets by order of their political correctness. He lavished extravagant praise on Jerzy Andrzejewski's 1945 ecumenical fantasy, *Wielki tydzień* (Holy Week), while summarily dismissing Borowski in three pages for a naturalist style that "distorted reality . . . and essentially leads to fatalism" (ibid., 138–41; my translation). It was not enough to place Poland in the forefront of Holocaust literature. Poland had to be in the forefront of the people's democratic republics.

Then, like a character out of a Cold War novel, Mark recanted. In the privacy of a Paris hotel room in 1956, on the occasion of the official opening of the Centre de Documentation Juif, he confessed his sins before two members of the Israeli delegation, and in exchange for their forgiveness he arranged to have millions of historical documents microfilmed and secretly sent to Israel (Shmeruk 1995). Much later, Mark personally rescued, deciphered, and published (posthumously, with the help of his wife, Esther) the extraordinary writings of the Sonderkommando (Mark 1977, 1985).

The Jewish exodus from Poland began before the new regime established the rule of the big lie. Most surviving Jews left Poland in response to the July 4, 1946, pogrom in Kielce, when ordinary citizens of this central Polish town, together with a few soldiers, murdered forty-two Polish Jews and injured more than a hundred—men, women, and children—in broad daylight (Michlic-Coren 2000, 253–56). The pretext was a blood libel, but the Jewish community understood what had really happened. Once again, as would be the case for decades to come, the Jews were being targeted as the chief threat to the Polish nation, the eternal enemy within (Steinlauf 1997, 23–42).

Among the more than 100,000 Polish Jews who bid final farewell to Poland in the wake of this pogrom was Abraham Sutzkever. Speaking as a proud son of Polish Jewry, Sutzkever allowed that those Christian Poles who had risked their lives to rescue and assist the Jews outweighed the many thousands who had betrayed them. However asymmetrical, he yoked the "saviors" and "traitors" together through the mysterious power of a single rhyme: *reter* and *farréter* (Sutzkever 1968b). Speaking as a proud son of the Polish Republic, however, he refused to forgive the dismal record of Polish self-betrayal. Postwar Poland had betrayed its own humanistic ideals and national aspirations, so poignantly expressed by Juliusz Słowacki, the words of whose stirring hymn punctuated Sutzkever's "To Poland" (Adamczyk-Garbowska 2009). With Adam Mickiewicz, Słowacki was considered a national bard for the role he played in keeping the ideal of Polish nationhood alive during the partitions and political oppression of Poland. Even as he bid a defiant farewell—no longer would his muse be nourished by Polish soil—Sutzkever left open the hope that its poets and poetry would continue to enjoy a place of honor in the country.

Great poetry could not staunch the Jewish exodus from Poland. There remained a loose confederation of writers on the Left composed of Christians like Borowski and Nałkowska and self-identified Jews and Jews still in hiding like Adolf Rudnicki, Artur Sandauer, Antoni Słonimski, Julian Strykowski, and Stanisław Wygodski—writers who still believed that a brave new literature could best be created under progressive patronage. Together, these surviving elites hoped to create a single memorial literature in two languages, Polish and Yiddish. They hoped to fashion a bilingual literature of the catastrophe— *khurbn* in Yiddish, *zagłada* in Polish—under a banner of Jewish stars and concentration camp stripes. Like so many other noble causes in Polish history, this one was doomed.

Heroes and Martyrs, Hebrew and Yiddish

Cast in bronze and set in Swedish granite, the monumental Warsaw Ghetto Memorial by Nathan Rapoport was erected on the ghetto ruins in 1948 (Young

1993, 155–84). There were two sides to the memorial, the first of its kind. The ceremonial side facing the empty plaza was where wreaths were to be laid in front of larger-than-life iconic figures reminiscent of Eugène Delacroix's painting *Liberty Leading the People* that represented Polish insurrections past and present. A muscular figure with one hand bandaged and the other clutching a Molotov cocktail, as befitted the stand-in for Mordecai Anielewicz, once the most feared and respected person in the ghetto, was flanked on the left by the figure of a woman with one breast bared and on the right by a youthful, slightly effeminate fighter reminiscent of Michelangelo's David, with a bearded, Herculean figure below—altogether a defiantly secular, vital, vibrant, and heroic tableau. No matter that the real Anielewicz had been described as slight, pale, and unprepossessing (Ringelblum 1985, 2:141) or that Rachel Auerbach, who represented Jewish womanhood in the memorial, had not taken part in the uprising. (Proud of posing for Rapoport's monument, Auerbach used a headshot of her bronze figure in her ghetto memoir, *Behutsot Varshah* [1954].) The statues stood for the heroes, each of whom would be remembered by name and political affiliation.

The side panel, a bas-relief etched in stone, paid homage to the nameless martyrs. They represented the parochial side of the past, the recurrent specter of Jewish exile, as first depicted in the Arch of Titus and as recently reimagined by Samuel Hirszenberg (Roskies 1984, 276–80). Clutching their children, their few belongings, and a Torah scroll, they were led by a bearded man with the legendary wanderer's staff in his hand—only instead of being presented against a bare, desolate backdrop, they were shown guarded by German soldiers, whose helmets and bayonets protrude from behind the procession. The dark side of the past was patriarchal, pious, and passive.

Rapoport's Warsaw Ghetto Memorial gave public shape to Holocaust memory in the postwar era: the dead were divided between the named heroes and the nameless martyrs; the heroes were rooted in time and place, while the martyrs were but the most recent incarnation of an eternal past. Rapoport exported the same mix of romantic realism to the nascent State of Israel, where the uprising of the doomed was seen as the prelude to the war of national liberation, allowing for a statue of Anielewicz alone to go up at the entrance to Yad Mordechai, the kibbutz built in his memory, and for a desexualized reproduction of the Warsaw Ghetto Memorial to be installed at the entrance to Yad Vashem.

Rapoport successfully negotiated the treacherous postwar terrain by catering to diverse popular tastes. Drawing on familiar Western and Jewish iconography in equal measure, he fashioned a public consensus in two such vastly different settings as Poland and Israel. He also had the advantage of having spent the war in the Soviet zone. For survivors of the Jew-Zone, with a Holocaust-specific story to tell, the odds against going public were much greater, as they encountered linguistic and ideological divisions even within the same postwar community.

Leyb Rochman was among the thousands of survivors and refugees who made their way to Paris and, while en route to permanent homes elsewhere, turned the city into a Yiddish Mecca and a hub of Holocaust memory. Rochman arrived there after a lengthy recuperation in Switzerland with a story to tell, transcribed from the diary that he had kept while in hiding with his wife, his sister-in-law and her husband, and a friend, from February 17, 1942, until their liberation by the Red Army on August 8, 1944. First serialized in the Yiddish press, *Un in dayn blut zolstu lebn* (And in your blood shall you live; 1949) portrayed a world both familiar and utterly strange to its readers. The setting was Minsk Mazowiecki, thirty-five kilometers from Warsaw; the story was the final liquidation of its ghetto on Black Friday, August 21, 1942, and the author's struggle to survive while in hiding among Polish villagers, each Jew armed with Aryan papers and false Polish identities, but essentially living by their wits and on the strength of their relationships with members of the Polish underclass and underworld. Yiddish readers everywhere still remembered these peasants, with their passions, superstitions, and pagan blood lust. No one, however, could remember another time when the Jews had been the hunted and the peasants the hunters, when even children took part in the hunt for Jews; a time when the mewing of a cat, an unstifled cough, or a drunken brawl on the other side of the partition could give you away. And no one had yet divided time in precisely the way it was divided here: survival time in the various hide-outs, each more primitive than the one before; the durational time of the diary, measured with painstaking effort and self-awareness, simultaneous with but opposed to the time of the slaughter, which was broken up into four long episodes and recorded out of sequence—because Black Friday was the heart of darkness that those in hiding tried to keep buried, lest it overwhelm their ability to persevere. Rochman's chronicle, in short, was the first authentic confessional diary to appear after the war, a genre so new that it didn't have a name, and so emotionally wrenching that readers and critics would describe it as "novelistic" (J. Schwarz 2011). Indeed, the partition in Aunty and Felek's cottage was a perfect novelistic device, for it allowed the narrator to be a *roye ve-eyno nir'eh*—a magical unseen seer—and provided a voyeuristic lens through which to view the chamber of horrors. "We don't really count as people," the chronicler explained, "we're just part of the wall" (Rochman 1983, 15).

The diary format made this work perfectly suited for serialization, simultaneously in the New York daily *Der tog* and the Buenos Aires daily *Yidishe tsaytung* (Yiddish was still the universal Jewish language, and the Yiddish press

FIGURE 7

Leyb Rochman. *Un in dayn blut zolstu lebn: togbukh 1943–1944*. Paris: Farlag-komisye bay der gezelshaft "Fraynt fun Minsk-Mazovyetsk" in Pariz, 1949. Cover designed by Bencjon Benn.

was to remain for decades the main disseminator of Holocaust memory). The title, a quotation from Ezekiel 16:6–7, was meant to be understood both metonymically and mythically, for just as the Polish soil was steeped in Jewish blood, the Hebrew words "Bedamayikh hayyi, bedamayikh hayyi!" were the climactic formula of the Jewish circumcision ceremony, proclaiming the blood bond between the God of Israel and those who entered into His covenant. The scriptural reference, in turn, was of a piece with the traditional values shared by those in hiding, which included the fervent hope to return someday to Zion. And finally, because Rochman's personal saga was enmeshed in the destruction of his entire community, the Paris branch of Friends of Minsk Mazowiecki underwrote the book's publication and paid for a modernist cover design by the Białystok-born artist, Bencjon Benn.

Rochman, then, succeeded in producing a Holocaust classic by making fact read like page-turning fiction and by filtering the unassimilable horrors through a Jewish folk sensibility—Rochman being both the last of his generation born in the shtetl and the first to negotiate the Polish landscape with utter fearlessness. The revelatory power of Rochman's wartime diary was widely acknowledged by readers as diverse as the conservative critic Shmuel Niger and the radical nonconformist Isaac Bashevis Singer (J. Schwarz 2011).

In 1950 Rochman immigrated to Israel, where he continued to maintain an international profile through his columns in the New York Yiddish daily *Forward* and his Yiddish broadcasts on Kol Yisrael. Then, one day in 1960—armed with a Hebrew translation of his celebrated work and in the company of his translator—Rochman appeared in the Tel Aviv offices of a young independent publisher named (as usually happens only in a novel) Nathan Rapoport. Like his namesake, this Rapoport believed that he could harness the memory of the Holocaust to negotiate between the New Jew and the Old, so he published a cheap paperback edition of Rochman's work, advertised it in the Israeli press, offered discounts to distributors, and did a mass mailing of fliers complete with blurbs and favorable reviews (Rochman 1961). The result? Most of the 3,000 copies were returned unsold, and Rapoport sustained a considerable loss and swore off Holocaust literature for the remainder of his career (Livneh 2010, 177–78).

If statues could speak, those on the heroic side of the Warsaw Ghetto Memorial would speak to us in Polish-accented Hebrew, and those on the tragic side would speak in Yiddish—authentic, Old World Yiddish. Each language, as it were, claimed opposite sides of the memory bank: resistance on one side, martyrdom on the other. The postwar landscape, as our tale of two Nathan Rapoports teaches us, was fraught with multiple roadblocks, making it almost impossible to cross from one side to the other. Nathan Rapoport the sculptor had to dispense with the martyrs if he wished to export his art to Israel, and despite his outlay of capital, Nathan Rapoport the publisher could not make a chronicle of mere survival marketable to an audience brought up with tales of Jewish resistance. Barely a decade before, Rochman and his fellow survivor refugees had been taunted in the streets of Israel by children yelling *"Sabon! Sabon!"*—based on the belief that the Germans had turned the fat of the Jewish dead into soap; and although the Eichmann trial coincided with the Hebrew publication of Rochman's diary, the work failed to whet readers' appetite for a new kind of narrative. Works of authentic wartime experience could cross over from the Jew-Zone to the Liberated Zone only if they were published in their original languages, in limited editions. The rich and unique body of wartime writing that had survived by dint of extraordinary collective and clandestine effort, and sometimes just by chance, was rooted in different times, places, and circumstances, which often required decoding. Simply put, its natural audience had perished or was too scattered to stand up and be counted. As long as the postwar ruins were divided between East and West, and Left and Right, wartime writing—the bedrock of Holocaust memory, the source for everything that followed—languished in obscurity. What followed, therefore, had to be reinvented.

Two Holocaust Controversies

That reinvention began with a story that the Buenos Aires Yiddish-language newspaper touted as "written especially for" it and that was published on September 25, 1946, in honor of the High Holiday season. Its author was Zvi Kolitz, who happened to be in town as part of his fundraising mission on behalf of the Revisionist Zionist movement. The story was called "Yosl Rakovers vendung tsu got" ("Yosl Rakover's Appeal to God"; 1994). "In one of the ruins of the ghetto of Warsaw," a prefatory note explained, "among piles of charred rubble and human bones, there was found, concealed and stuffed in a small bottle, the following testament, written during the Warsaw Ghetto's last hours by a Jew named Yosl Rakover" (ibid., 362). Apart from the hackneyed device of a found document and the by-now-standard use of the Warsaw Ghetto uprising as the pivotal event of the Holocaust, Kolitz cast a Gerer Hasid in the title role, so as to proclaim his faith in a seemingly absent God on the High Holidays. Rakover, implausibly, was also portrayed as an independent ghetto fighter, in order to propagate the need for armed resistance and the absolute dichotomy between the merciful God of Israel and the merciless God of love. A theologically expurgated version of the story appeared a year later in an English-language collection of Kolitz's work called *Tiger beneath the Skin: Stories and Parables of the Years of Death*, (1947), the changes apparently made by the translator without Kolitz's knowledge (Mallow and van Beeck, 373–74).

Yosl Rakover was a fraudulent figure, a figment of the postwar Jewish imagination that wanted to have it all: a fighter who was also a religious martyr; a model of heroism at once physical and spiritual. The efforts of wartime writers like Huberband, Katzenelson, Shayevitsh, and Sutzkever to distinguish between religious and secular forms of resistance and to define heroism downward were irrelevant to a postwar community hungry to harness the past to further its agenda for the future. Even the survivor community was taken in when, in 1954, an anonymous typescript of the original Yiddish story arrived in the Tel Aviv office of the literary quarterly *Di goldene keyt*, under the editorship of Abraham Sutzkever. "Yosl Rakover redt tsu got" (Yosl Rakover speaks to God), as it was renamed, was published as an authentic document from the Warsaw ghetto, but with stylistic improvements, following Sutzkever's usual practice. Jacob Glatstein, among many others, hailed the newly discovered testament as "a part of our monumental Holocaust literature [*khurbn-literatur*], which will remain for all the generations" (quoted in Borwicz 1955, 199). This caught the eye of the poet, former ghetto fighter, and Holocaust historian Michał Borwicz. Disappointed that Sutzkever gave so poor an explanation of the manuscript's provenance, Borwicz decided to expose the story's manifold historical inaccuracies and obvious literary gildings. In the face of public protest, Borwicz (1955) proclaimed the work a fake and published his findings in a Parisian literary journal.

The public protested because, as Borwicz understood, the need to believe was simply too great. The Yiddish-reading public had responded viscerally to a sacred testament that fully met its expectations and slaked its spiritual thirst. Since the truth of Kolitz's authorship had already come to light by the time Borwicz's exposé was going to press, Borwicz appended an afterword to his article in which he expressed the hope that the public would soon develop a hermeneutics of reading that would distinguish between the literature of the Holocaust and the literature on the Holocaust.

Given the choice, the community of real and vicarious survivors chose the past as mediated through the present, not the past in all its tragic complexity. One more trans-Atlantic controversy, and the die was cast. On March 17, 1952, the New York daily *Der tog* ran a lengthy article in which the poet H. Leivick compared two documents that had recently appeared in scholarly publications. One, an anonymous chronicle of the great deportation from the Warsaw ghetto, Leivick pronounced to be a forgery, a product of the Jew-hating Polish Communist regime. "Love of Israel in the spirit of the Judenrat: a reply to the false accusation of H. Leivick" was the scathing rebuttal of Ber Mark, the document's editor and publisher (Mark 1952). In this case, Mark was armed with facsimiles of the anonymous manuscript in order to substantiate his most sensational claim. The identity of the author had just been discovered to be none other than Yehoshue Perle, a popular and prolific Polish Yiddish novelist, someone whom Leivick and other members of the Yiddish-reading public surely remembered.

Both in form and content, Perle's chronicle was too raw to be admissible evidence of the authentic Jewish response to catastrophe. It was vintage ghetto reportage, just recently unearthed, in fact, from the second part of the Oyneg Shabes. Plunging the reader into the trenches of daily life and death, Perle began in the midst of the daily roundups, first of 6,000 and then of 10,000 victims a day. "Today," he recorded, "August 31, 1942, as I begin writing these lines, drenched in blood and tears, marks the 40th day since the murderous Nazi dogs . . ." (Perle 1955, 100). Even as he tried to give things a name, to define the terminology of mass murder (*iberzidlung*, Umschlagplatz, *aktsye*, shops, numbers) and to place events in chronological order, he interrupted the flow of events to admit the limits of his own moral imagination: "Of Hitler, of this antediluvian beast, it is possible to believe anything. The sadistic methods that he employs surpass all human understanding. No criminal, no matter how great, would ever come up with such bloodthirsty, sophisticated means" (ibid., 103).

Originally, Perle had called his chronicle "*Geyrush Varshe*, the Expulsion from Warsaw." He changed it midway through to "*Khurbn Varshe*, the Destruction of Warsaw," as great a destruction as that of the Temple in Jerusalem, and therein lay the first scandalous act. For Perle, a *khurbn* began with the depths of human depravity. The depraved behavior of the Jewish police was an indictment of the community at large, proof that Jewish solidarity had collapsed and that Jewish agency was bankrupt: "They [the Jewish Police] dragged their tortured victims up from underground and down from the sky; from all the cellars, from all the holes, from all the chimneys. They performed their duty with such zeal, with such self-sacrifice [*mesires-nefesh*] that it is simply impossible to comprehend what kind of wild dybbuk these youngsters were possessed by" (ibid., 125). But *khurbn* also allowed for the heights of human self-sacrifice, and Perle recorded acts of true heroism and altruism, singling out for special praise the orderly procession of Janusz Korczak and his two hundred orphans, described in vivid detail for the first time.

Most scandalous, however, and Leivick's reason for utterly rejecting the legitimacy of this document, was the final indictment that Perle reserved for himself and the whole of Warsaw Jewry. "Three times 100,000 people lacked the courage to say: NO," he raged. "Each of them was out to save himself alone. Each was ready to sacrifice even his own father, his own mother, his own wife and children" (ibid., 140).

At the fault line of postwar memory lay the scandal of self-blame.

Thus, the battle lines were drawn: on one side were those who believed that the way to keep memory alive was by reopening old wounds; on the other side were those for whom the memory of the martyrs was sacred. Fueling the debate over the documents' legitimacy—whether they were authentic or fake—lay a much deeper division over what they should be used for. The debate pitted hard-nosed historians against the guardians of the flock, apocalypse against martyrdom. The historians Borwicz and Mark believed that Holocaust memory began with the unassimilable facts. They were the clear winners in terms of passing judgment on whether these were authentic wartime documents or not. Yet they were the clear losers, too. What ought to have formed the primary canon of Holocaust literature—those novels, short stories, reportage, prose poems, and diaries that miraculously survived—was no longer acceptable to their intended readers now living abroad.

Less than a decade had elapsed between the writing, publication, and rejection of Perle's "Khurbn Varshe" (1955). So much had happened in the interim! Perle's target audience was either preoccupied with reconstructing their postwar lives and so couldn't be bothered, or like Leivick, recoiled from the morally ambiguous landscape of Jews condemned to death.

The *Yizkor* Book: Sacred Memory

What Glatstein had called "our monumental Holocaust literature" was fast becoming Scripture, and the more timeless, the better suited for excerpting, editing, anthologizing, translating, performing, and retranslating. In the major centers of postwar Jewry, Holocaust-specific anthologies became many readers' first exposure to the subject. Thus, in 1948, Niger, the preeminent Yiddish literary critic of his day, published *Kidesh hashem*, whose subtitle could be translated as "A collection of selected, often abbreviated reports, letters, chronicles, testaments, inscriptions, legends, poems, short stories, dramatic scenes, [and] essays, which describe acts of self-sacrifice in our own days and also in days of yore" (Niger 1948). That year, the former Vilna partisan Shmerke Kaczerginski published the definitive edition of *Lider fun di getos un lagern* (Songs of the ghettos and concentration camps): definitive by virtue of size, Leivick's imprimatur, and inspirational chapter headings. Only a handful of these songs were deemed performable at memorial gatherings, but that was enough to establish the genre of Holocaust song as lyrical, communal, sanitized, and vaguely historical (Flam 1992, 4). Emma Schaver returned from the DP camps with a rich repertory of "Songs of the Ghetto" that she later recorded in Israel with an orchestral backup (Schaver 1954). The standard song at such gatherings and performances was "Es brent!" (Fire!) by Mordecai Gebirtig, a stirring hymn written in 1938 in response to a prewar pogrom in Poland that forewarned of a holocaust (Gebirtig 1989).

To sanctify the memory of the dead, the Holocaust was sacralized and read backward in time. Everyone who perished was deemed holy, and everything they had created was rendered holy, too. No effort, therefore, was spared to collect their remains. In New York, Machmadim Art Editions published *Kdoyshim* [Martyrs]: *Poetry of Those Tortured to Death* (1947) on blue-gray stock in a numbered edition, with each selection from the work of a Polish Yiddish poet set to music by the modern composer Henech Kon and illustrated with paintings by Isaac Lichtenstein. In Paris, Hersh Fenster anthologized the artistic legacy of *Undzere farpaynikte kinstler* (Our martyred painters), a folio also issued in a numbered edition that commemorated eighty-four Eastern European Jews who had hoped to become world-class artists in the art capital of the world but perished instead. Introduced by an *hommage* to the martyred artists by Marc Chagall in his own handwriting, this magnificent volume concluded with the names of several hundred Jewish artists murdered in other parts of the Jew-Zone (Fenster 1951). In the Orthodox sector—regrouped and incubating in Brooklyn, New York; Lakewood, New Jersey; and Jerusalem and B'nai B'rak in Israel—the anthological project was led by the indefatigable Moshe Prager, a journalist in Hebrew and Yiddish and a great-grandson of the first Gerer Rebbe. No sooner had Prager escaped from occupied Warsaw and made his way to Palestine than he began documenting the slaughter, producing four Hebrew collections of factual evidence between 1941 and 1945 (Livneh 2010, 180). After the war, he too began sifting through the ruins. With the support of the Conference on Jewish Material Claims against Germany, established in 1951 to underwrite just such projects and still active today, Prager published a 640-page anthology of Yiddish poems, stories and essays written by religious authors, victims of Nazi persecution (M. Prager 1954). To distinguish the authentic voice of religious Jewry from the various attempts of secular Yiddish writers to stylize and satirize the past, Prager defined his subject as *emune-dikhtung*, the poetry of true faith, in the hope of rehabilitating a severed branch of Eastern European Jewry (ibid., 15).

It should be no surprise, then, that the Jewish anthological imagination included Yosl Rakover among the martyrs. He appeared in *Ani ma'amin*, a Hebrew compilation of "Testimonies on the life and death of believers at the time of the Holocaust" (Eliav 1965) and in *Out of the Whirlwind: A Reader of Holocaust Literature*, where an editor's note identified Rakover as a real person whose tragic fate was known to the author (A. Friedlander 1968). Through the art of anthologizing, it was possible to erase the awful divide between the living and the dead, sacralize the lost culture of European Jewry, and harmonize the martyrs with the fighters.

Kolitz seduced his readers into believing that they were privy to an authentic piece of wartime writing rescued from the ruins. In point of fact, little of that corpus made it into the postwar canon of "our monumental Holocaust literature," for what Yiddish and Hebrew readers regarded as Holocaust-specific genres were written or rewritten mostly after the war, with the readers' concerns in mind. Although the Soviet and US Black Book Committees collected direct, eyewitness testimonies from every point on the Holocaust compass, providing evidence of a crime against humanity that had been defined in 1944 as genocide (Ehrenburg and Grossman 2002), the survivors and former residents of the martyred communities turned inward to produce a different kind of testimonial: a comprehensive *yizkor* book in their own collective voice. The first to do so was the United Emergency Relief Committee for the City of Lodz, whose *Lodzer Yiskor Book* (1943) appeared after taking three years to assemble. It opened with a "split-screen" illustration by the Łódź-born artist Artur Szyk that showed a German bayonet thrust through the Łódź municipal coat of arms, above the grieving heads of three Polish Jews: an elderly bearded man, his kerchiefed wife, and their very young son. Then came greetings to

President Roosevelt and former New York State Governor Herbert H. Lehman on behalf of the former residents of Łódź who now lived in America, and whose immediate goal was to bring relief to their coreligionists in the Jew-Zone. Just how great their sufferings were, the American Jews had gleaned from a single source: *Dos blut ruft tsu nekome* (The blood cries out for revenge), a collection of eyewitness accounts of Polish Jewish refugees published in Moscow in 1941. Had the American compilers known about the mass deportations from the ghetto, they probably would have recast the last section of their *yizkor* book—filled with souvenir ads and ending with photographs of Lodzer offspring serving in the us Army, evidently intended to balance remembrance with celebration and fundraising.

There were eventually well over a thousand of these memorial books, the bulk of them appearing long after there was anyone left to rescue, or any desire to exact retribution (Kugelmass and Boyarin 1998). The standard opening was an out-of-scale memory map of the town, drafted in Yiddish or Hebrew to complement an idealized, harmonized image of the Jewish life that was destroyed; the standard ending was a lengthy and terrifying section describing the slaughter. Those volumes produced in Israel sometimes included photographs of the native-born offspring in the uniform of the Israel Defense Forces. The stated purpose of the *yizkor* book was to leave a lasting memorial for future generations. The real purpose was to close the chapter on the tragic past and move on to other concerns, now that the survivors had successfully rebuilt their lives elsewhere. The Book of Lamentations, recent scholarship has argued, was not written in the immediate aftermath of the Temple's destruction but in the midst of its rebuilding (Greenstein 2008).

The most prominent of Holocaust-specific genres in the first decades after the war were memorial volumes compiled by those who had known the dead. Their size and claims of comprehensiveness testified to the staying power of the survivor community. But by the late 1940s, that community was dispersing and dividing. Just as the Jewish deportation community in Paris banded together to commemorate the martyred painters, the writers—most of whom were on the far Left—produced a comprehensive *Yizker-bukh* dedicated *To the Memory of 14 Parisian Yiddish Writers Who Perished* (Spero, Kenig, Shulshteyn, and Shlevin 1946). This volume too opened with a memorial tribute by Chagall, but a unique feature was its bibliographical afterword documenting precisely "How the Manuscripts of the Murdered Writers Were Discovered." (The answer: with great difficulty.) In New York, meanwhile, the surviving members of the Yiddish secular school movement pooled their memories to produce the *Lerer Yizkor Book* (as the English translation of the title appears in the book) an alphabetical lexicon of murdered men and women who had dedicated their lives to raising a proud new generation of Polish Jews (Kazdan 1954).

In Israel, the heroic self-image of the emerging state was greatly enhanced by the visible and vocal presence of survivors who had been active in the Jewish armed resistance (B. Cohen 2003). The means of memorial production, however, were virtually controlled by the kibbutz movements and the political parties of the Left. What got published and by whom was determined by the political affiliation of the fighters, both living and dead (Livneh 2010). Three massive memorial projects resulted from this political alignment: *Sefer milhamot hageta'ot* (1954), which showcased the members of the Zionist underground who had died as ghetto fighters; the 1956 *Sefer Hashomer Hatsa'ir*, which commemorated the Holocaust as an episode in the history of this pro-Soviet Zionist youth movement; and the 1958 two-volume *Sefer hapartizanim hayehudim*, which celebrated as no less heroic and patriotic the Zionist youth who had fought in the forests, either alone or as part of Soviet partisan brigades. Each of these volumes required the mobilization of scarce resources in a difficult period of nation building, and each was published by a different arm of the labor movement. The religious wing of the Zionist movement, meanwhile, had its own publishing house, Mosad Harav Kook, which expended great effort to produce *Arim ve'imahot beYisrael*, a seven-volume work chronicling twenty "Major Jewish Cities . . . Annihilated by the Tyrants and the Impure in the Last World War" that was published between 1946 and 1950—*yizkor* books by any other name (Livneh 2010, 211).

In one massive, meticulously edited and comprehensive volume, *Sefer milhamot hageta'ot* provided readers with the Holocaust Complete, the martyrs all treated as combatants in the "Wars of the Ghettos" and the full sweep of the eastern Jew-Zone—"Between the Walls, in the Camps, in the Forests"—included within its compass (Zuckerman and Basok 1954). Two pull-out maps told the feature story in graphic form: one, titled "The Jewish Underground in Poland, the Ghettos and Camps," used color-coded lines to distinguish between the liaison routes of the underground as a whole and those of the Zionist youth movements in particular; the second, of the Warsaw Ghetto, used similar coding to highlight the battles fought in January and April, 1943. Through testimony, diaries, reportage, last letters, battle bulletins, calls to arm, memoirs, documentary fiction, poetry, and songs from across the eastern Jew-Zone, written by both the living and the dead, the editors Yitzhak Zuckerman and Moshe Basok constructed a heroic master narrative in loose chronological and tight geographical order. Although among the fighters, obvious priority was given to the Zionist underground, the roster of martyrs drew its members from across the social and generational spectrum. Janusz Korczak of Warsaw rubbed shoulders with Reb Mendl of Powianec, and fifteen-year-old Isaac Rudashevski from Vilna with seventy-year-old Hillel Zeitlin from Warsaw. Equally varied was the rich selection of Yiddish, Hebrew,

Polish, and German poetry and prose, much of it translated here for the first time. Whoever studied the work's dense pages—hardly the stuff of leisure reading—came away with the conviction that in the war against the Jews, the Jews had emerged victorious.

A *sefer* was designed for study and for permanence; it was considered holy. Like their editors and publishers, the intended readers of these memorials to the poets and partisans, the teachers and ghetto fighters, the Parisian artists and writers, and Eastern European communities large and small were first-generation rebels from traditional Judaism, removed from the dead by only one degree of separation. During the immediate postwar period, all private memory was communal, for both practical and existential reasons. Without political or institutional backing, no Holocaust testimony or text got published, and in order to go public, Holocaust memory had to obey the habits of the Jewish heart. That heart was now divided between Right and Left, sacred and profane. So the medium of Holocaust memory was key to its message: not only who sponsored its publication, but also where it appeared—whether as a memorial volume created for all eternity or in the daily press; whether enshrined as an emblem of the severed past or enmeshed in the messy, contentious business of creating a new life. Through diverse media and to a different degree in both Jewish languages simultaneously, the two competing sides of Rapoport's memorial were gradually naturalized into the postwar Jewish landscape.

The Yiddish Press: Living Memory

A very different kind of writing flourished in the rough-and-tumble world of the Yiddish press. The Holocaust remained front-page news, what with Nazi killers on the loose, honor courts settling the score with suspected Jewish collaborators, and the scandal of reparations—German blood money—erupting in Israel and spilling over onto the Yiddish-speaking street around the world. Featured in the Yiddish press were the writings of talented young Holocaust survivors in serialized form. The postwar art of reportorial fiction provided just the right mix of history and emotion, Jewish idiom and journalese, the communal and the personal. Written in sound bites, each segment was just long enough to fit into one's favorite (ideologically compatible) daily newspaper.

Mordecai Strigler emerged from the war looking "like a slum-bred thirteen-year-old boy," in the words of the war correspondent Meyer Levin (1950, 241). "He had an intellectual face, widening upward from a delicate chin to a broad forehead; he wore glasses." All his copious wartime notes and manuscripts had been lost, and reconstructing them from memory was neither feasible nor desirable. In order for his experiences in Majdanek; in Factory C., the infamous munitions factory at Skarżysko-Kamienna; and in Buchenwald to reach a wider audience, Strigler decided to adopt a thin fictional cloak, and he defended this decision in a tedious, three-part introduction to his cycle of documentary novels (Strigler 1948, 7–67). Fiction, he argued, would mitigate some of the horror, while a literary approach to his real-life protagonists would help deepen their psychological profile. To ensure that the reader did not mistake this as mere literature, Strigler provided historical documentation to precede and punctuate the story.

Thus the concept of *khurbn-literatur* was born: true tales of the ghettos and camps that employed modes of enhanced reality such as confessions, autobiographies, memoirs, and diaries, lest—as Strigler worried—they be read as mere fiction (see Young 1988). Rochman, Strigler, and others in their cohort each adopted fictional and journalistic techniques to make their stories not only more readable but also more relevant. The most effective way of engaging the reader was through breaks in the narrative, addressing the reader directly through flashes of introspection and voice-over commentaries, punctuated by biblical quotations and rabbinic phrases that together turned the unassimilable record of German atrocity, Christian betrayal, and Jewish cowardice into a species of popular history that Jacob Shatzky described as "written with anger and with bias" (quoted in J. Schwarz 2007a, 185).

Strigler's *Maydanek* opens with the imminent liquidation of his labor camp, located just outside his native town of Zamość. All the inmates, male and female, are headed for Majdanek, to certain death. In an ill-conceived attempt to escape, the narrator tries to leave the barracks, allegedly to take a leak, but he is stopped at gunpoint. "The rifle, clearly, is in no mood to argue," he writes, combining the ss guard and his weapon. "So he throws one word at me that carries with it the warning of all four death penalties meted out by the Beit Din: *Zurück!*" (Strigler 1947, 20–21). In the two seconds that it takes to read this sentence, the reader is expected to see the disjuncture between ancient rabbinic justice, which carried out the death sentence with fear and trembling, and the Nazi penal system, which targeted an entire people for annihilation. All this, compressed into the juxtaposition of the liturgical phrase *arba mises besdin* and the brutal German command *zurück* (get back).

The Yiddish press was—and remains—a school for scandal, so there were no strictures on what aspects of the Holocaust Strigler could describe in its columns. Also serialized was the work of an eyewitness chronicler who was intent on intensifying, not mitigating, the horror by situating the Holocaust within its own geography, representing real personal experience through the veil of hallucination and nightmare, and rendering the historical transtemporal. Enter Ka-Tzetnik 135633, who, when asked his name by his Red Army liberators, replied: "My name was burned along with all those others in the Auschwitz crematorium." Ka-Tzetnik defined himself solely in terms of his experience of absolute extremity. The public would learn only decades later that he was really Yekhiel Fajner-Dinur, an expressionist poet of middling talent, who had emerged from the ranks of Polish Orthodoxy (Miron 2005; Szeintuch 2009).

With literary ambitions even greater than Strigler's, Ka-Tzetnik set out to write *The Chronicles of a Jewish Family in the Twentieth Century.* The first three volumes—*Salamandra,* originally published in 1946 and translated as *Sunrise over Hell* in 1977; *House of Dolls* (1955); and *They Called Him Piepel,* originally published in 1961, in English—concerned the fate of that family in the Holocaust. Ka-Tzetnik invented very little, "Kongressia" being a thinly veiled Łódź; Metropoli based on Sosnowiec, in Upper East Silesia; and Monyek Matroz replacing Moshe Merin, head of the Sosnowiec Judenrat. And the most horrific episodes could be historically corroborated (Szeintuch 2009). Nonetheless, the Gothic style turned reality into nightmare and history into myth. The authorial self was a cipher. The ghetto and *Lager* were a closed system. The branding of Jews—male and especially female—marked a new and demonic covenant, a permanent defilement that could never be eradicated. The world was split between good and evil: Jews versus Germans, Vevke the Saint versus Monyek the Devil, Fella the Survivor versus Daniella the Victim, and so on. When Daniella threw herself on the electrified barbed wire at the conclusion of *House of Dolls,* questions of causality were suspended. Since no human initiative made any difference, her fate was preordained. The train that had whisked her off on her last summer vacation prefigured the train that would transport her to Auschwitz. Pure womanhood defiled became for Ka-Tzetnik the metonym for Auschwitz. Fella the *Feldhure* would never give birth again.

Ka-Tzetnik's Holocaust trilogy was preoccupied with sexual abuse and sadomasochism. He evinced an almost insane obsession with depravity (O. Bartov 1997; Miron 2005). The Nazi guards and their underlings indulged in countless perversions and sexual fantasies. All three of the protagonists were *Prominenten,* or camp functionaries, so they existed outside the pale of humanity. Harry Preleshnik, Ka-Tzetnik's fictional stand-in, began his camp career as a member of the paramedical staff in the camp infirmary but was later inducted into the Sonderkommando. Daniella, his sister, was sterilized (without an anesthetic) before being inducted into the Joy Division, and Moni, their young brother, served as a homosexual sex servant of the Block *Aelteste.*

All this and more, remarkably, was the warp and woof of the Yiddish press. Judenräte, ghettos, *Aktions,* and Umschlagplatz; crematoria, selections, Kapos, and the Sonderkommando; Buchenwald, Sobibor, Treblinka, and Majdanek: within a decade, these Holocaust-specific terms had become standard in the

HOUSE OF DOLLS

by Ka·tzetnik 135633

Daniella Preleshnik, a fourteen-year-old Jewish girl, left her home in Poland one day in 1939 to take a school trip with her classmates and never returned. Based on an authentic diary, House of Dolls is the story of one

(continued on front flap)

FIGURE 8

Ka-Tzetnik 135633. *House of Dolls*. New York: Simon and Schuster, 1955. Jacket design by Sam Fischer.

Yiddish lexicon. In Yiddish, the war-specific lexicon and the terminology of mass destruction never became a thing of the past. In Yiddish alone, moreover, there appeared an extensive popular library whose focus was the civilization of Polish Jewry: its achievements, destruction, and living heritage. Published in Buenos Aires and free of political patronage, Dos poylishe yidntum was an ambitious series of reprints and original works, a kind of portable library of Polish Jewry in exile. Appearing at the rate of almost ten books a year, these black-bound volumes, each with an illustrated jacket and reviews of recent books in the series, were distributed in twenty-two countries, even reaching Holocaust survivors in Poland and the DP camps (J. Schwarz 2007a, 173–74). Among the most prominent titles were Strigler's multivolume *Farloshene shtern* (Extinguished lights), comprising *Maydanek* (1947), *In di fabrikn fun toyt* (In the death factories; 1948), *Werk C* (Factory C; 1950), and *Goyroles* (Destinies; 1952). The youngest author to be included in the Argentinean series was a rookie Yiddish and Hebrew journalist named Eliezer Wiesel. Wiesel's . . . *un di velt hot geshvign* (". . . and the world was silent"; 1956) appeared as volume 117, two after Ka-Tzetnik's *House of Dolls*. Until Wiesel, Hungarian Jewry had not been heard from.

Because the medium was the testimonial message, the same work could assume a different meaning if it appeared in more than one medium. Readers who first encountered Rochman's (1949) chronicle in the Yiddish press responded to it as a work of fiction: they couldn't wait for the next installment. Once enshrined in a book with a covenantal title and striking cover, which memorialized the names of the dead and was sponsored by the home-town society of Minsk Mazowiecki, the work would double as a *yizkor* book until such time as a proper memorial volume appeared (Shedletzky 1977). When stripped of both communal functions, however, and published in a Hebrew translation as a free-standing work of Holocaust literature, Rochman's finely wrought narrative failed to engage new readers. His most lasting impact on Israeli culture would come through his protégé, Aharon Appelfeld (1983).

Documentary fiction of the Holocaust, a species of the new journalism, was produced by survivors who had either just begun their literary careers on the eve of the war and whose wartime experience changed their writing forever, or by those who became writers by virtue of their wartime experience. Ka-Tzetnik, Rochman, Strigler, Wiesel, and their peers introduced Yiddish readers to the landscape and chronology of the Holocaust, differentiated by place and fateful setting, sometimes broken down hour by hour. Together, they established the precise and allowable boundaries of *khurbn-literatur*, grounded in the survivor's lived experience but carefully mediated for a non-survivor audience.

Israel: Intergenerational Memory

Only if Holocaust memory could be brought home to Israel could it speak to a native-born generation with no direct link to the murdered millions. In Israel, theater was the main stage for national identity formation. Original Hebrew productions on contemporary themes were as closely watched as the establishment of each new agricultural settlement and municipality. So who would speak on stage for the destruction of European Jewry? In Leah Goldberg's *Lady of the Castle* (1996), staged at the Cameri Theater in 1955, those who spoke for the war were: (implausibly) a courageous German aristocrat, two emissaries from Palestine, and a Jewish girl rescued from captivity. Drawing on Goldberg's symbolist poetics of indirection, the play was as much about the eclipse of the old Europe as about survivors and rescuers struggling to respond to the eclipse of European Jewry. Since no one on stage was supposed to be really speaking Hebrew, no one spoke with an accent.

A more popular figure by far was Hannah Szenes, a young Hungarian Jewish girl who immigrated to a kibbutz and soon after joined the British army, parachuting into the Jew-Zone with thirty-one others to try to save as many Hungarian Jews as possible (Baumel-Schwartz 2010). Inspired by a recent Hebrew production of George Bernard Shaw's *St. Joan*, in 1958 Aharon Megged created the first Israeli drama about the capture, trial, and execution of this Palestinian Jewish martyr and resistance fighter (Megged 1996; see also Laor 2007). Megged's timing could not have been better, for his play was staged by the prestigious Habimah Theater when the trial, conviction, exoneration, and assassination of another Hungarian Jew, named Rezső or Israel Kasztner, were still very fresh in the public mind. Indeed, Matti Megged, Aharon's brother, had given the Israeli public a choice: either a female Palestinian paratrooper who died heroically, or your typical Diaspora bureaucrat, who saved 1,684 Jews by entering into a pact with Adolf Eichmann, the devil personified. The public resoundingly chose Szenes, with but one dissenting voice—that of the poet Natan Alterman, who rejected the false dichotomy between resistance and negotiation, fighters and collaborators (Alterman 1954; see also Laor 2007).

One way to mitigate the scandal of Jewish passivity and cooperation was to focus on the fate of women and children—especially children. How did one mourn, let alone understand, the murder of 1,500,000 Jewish children? By focusing instead on the narrative of rescue. Thanks to a group known as Anders's Army, 871 children had successfully been rescued from Nazi and Soviet captivity, and their joyous arrival in Jewish Palestine in the summer of 1943 was turned into a pre-state occasion. The so-called Children of Teheran became the stuff of Zionist legend, and their collective fate was followed in perpetuity (Ohad 1977). The fate of those traumatized, brutalized children inside the Jew-Zone who had somehow beaten the odds presented an altogether different challenge. They were *Undzere kinder* (Our children), the name of a Yiddish docudrama filmed on location in Poland with a screenplay written by Rachel Auerbach (Hoberman 1991, 330–31). Here the adults, led by the famous comedians Dzigan and Shumacher, had much to learn from the children before the adults could teach the child-survivors how to laugh.

The way children performed authentic ghetto songs and the way they narrated their own wartime experience would change the course of Holocaust memory, first in Yiddish and Hebrew and later in other languages. Meeting these children face to face and being among the first to collect their eyewitness testimonies, both Noah Gris and Binyamin Tenenbaum were struck by a qualitative difference in word and deed. Gris marveled at the children's seeming indifference to death, their matter-of-fact tone, their "moral equilibrium and stoic calm" (Gris 1947, 57; see also 38–62). Although adults were at a loss to find some analogy to the monomaniacal evil of Nazism and the untrammeled sadism of the German master race, children were emancipated from the need to analogize, so they could describe the atrocities with primitive directness. After collecting testimonies from a thousand children and adolescents throughout Poland and in seventeen DP camps in Germany, Tenenbaum concluded that the young people were free of the self-blame and self-consciousness that bedeviled adult survivors' reconstruction of their lives. The simplicity and directness with which children recalled their wartime experiences reminded him of "an ancient saga or pages of the Hebrew Bible," where events were recounted without elaboration or pathos (Tenenbaum 1948, vi). Gris's *Kinder-martirologye* (The martyrology of the children; 1947) appeared as volume 16 of the Library of Polish Jewry, while Tenenbaum's *Eḥad me'ir ushnayim mimishpaḥa* (One from each city and two from each family; 1948) appeared as part of a series published by the left-wing Sifriat Po'alim devoted to, as the series title put it, The Evil Decrees of 1939–1945. Both anthologies placed the ghettos first and the death camps last, a narrative at once chronological and pedagogical, for the successful rehabilitation of the youngest survivors depended on their being reabsorbed into the Jewish collective. Could one from each city and two from each family ever be reconstituted as a nation?

When, a decade later, the first of these rescued children produced his own unmediated story, he further challenged the communal master narrative under the guise of simplicity. Yurik and his younger brother, Kazik, the two protagonists of *Ḥayalei oferet* (*The Lead Soldiers*, 1980), a 1958 autobiographical novel by Uri Orlev, were just plain children who peed in their pants, screamed in their sleep, and had no idea what a Jew was. The only heroics to speak of were the fantastically elaborate exploits that they invented for themselves. Like Anne Frank, who transformed her Secret Annex into a site of high adventure, fantasy for these children was a means of transmuting reality. Orlev, who went on to become the most celebrated Israeli children's writer, boldly entered the zany, irreverent, capacious mind of his child protagonists, who were capable of turning everything they saw, heard, and suffered into a source of play. They had to, because the reality they entered defied the imagination.

One generation did not beget another. In a short story ironically titled "Yad Vashem" in Hebrew ("The name," in English), Aharon Megged (1950) depicted an intergenerational conflict over the naming of a newborn child after someone who had perished in the Holocaust. The native-born parents refused to burden their son with any relic of the Diaspora or the Holocaust. Neither side of the ghetto monument was of any use to such a constituency, and little if anything of all that had been rescued, recorded, anthologized, translated, and published in Yiddish and Hebrew, as well as little of the quasi-fictions by survivor witnesses.

Out of the entire communal memory bank laboriously regathered in the first fifteen years after liberation, the two figures chiefly responsible for bringing the Holocaust home to the younger generation were neither historians nor poets. They were figures on lurid book jackets: Yosl Rakover, the legendary martyr, fighter, and challenger of God; and Ka-Tzetnik, whose sadomasochistic Nazi women in tight pants and riding boots—not to speak of the virginal Jewish maidens forced into prostitution—provided a whole generation of adolescent readers with forbidden reading material (O. Bartov 1997). It was the old division of the sacred and profane played out against a rarefied and reconfigured Holocaust landscape.

The European Memory Zone

The literature of the Holocaust is a story not of begats but of multiple beginnings. Yet again, therefore, we must start from the top, circling back to the first years of the postwar era, this time with a focus on Western Europe. It is one thing to speak of the communal memory of the *zagłada* or *khurbn* or Shoah taking root in such collectivist societies as Poland, Yiddishland, and the State of Israel. With their mandatory and voluntary forms of affiliation, memory of the war years was structured into their hometown associations, veterans' groups, or political parties. But who would bring the story home to postwar readers in Italy, France, the Netherlands, West Germany, or Austria? All of them were caught awkwardly between past and future. Everywhere was a legacy of betrayal, collaboration, disastrous defeat, and fascism, which the myth of resistance could ease but not erase. Italy had been torn apart by civil war, followed by a humiliating invasion by foreign powers. The surest way to forge a new national identity in the wake of such trauma, in Italy and elsewhere, was to ignore and forget (Consonni 2010, 18–44; Gordon 1999, 51; Woolf 2007, 43).

Could a card-carrying fascist do penance for the past? Indeed he could, winning fame and fortune in the process. *Kaputt* was "a tremendous, ambiguous, and loathed success in Italy" when it appeared in 1944 (Barrett 1952), on the strength of which a superb English translation was published only two years later (Malaparte 1946). The novel was the work of a brilliant journalist, Curzio Malaparte, who claimed that it was a colossal and courageous act of retrieval. As its foreign and provocative title proclaimed, *Kaputt* recounted a latter-day apocalypse. A fascist who had accompanied Mussolini on the march to Rome and a credentialed Italian war correspondent, the intrepid Malaparte had been free to roam the length and breadth of the war zone. Buttressing his claim of authenticity was the overtly Proustian manner in which he reclaimed his lived experience through sensory perceptions and striking imagery, whether reporting from the Finnish front or from the repainted interiors of the Wawel Palace in Kraków, a guest of the self-crowned king of Poland, Hans Frank. Bringing the horror home, *Kaputt* ended with an epiphany of blood in the catacombs of Naples, a spontaneous mass rite whose effect would be to wipe clean the rot of Europe.

For Malaparte, armed with this pan-European perspective, the surest sign of apocalypse was the unique fate of European Jewry: naked Jews being

FIGURE 9

Curzio Malaparte. *Kaputt*.
1st paperback ed. New York:
Avon, 1966. Cover art
by Don Crowley.

marched off to their deaths in the Kraków ghetto; Jewish children shot for sport in the Warsaw ghetto; Jews being butchered to death in Iasi, Romania, by local army and town officials; Jewish girls forced to serve twenty days as prostitutes before being executed on the twenty-first. The problem was that Malaparte had never entered a single ghetto, had never been in Iasi, and had evinced little sympathy for the Jews as long as the Germans seemed to be winning the war (Hofstadter 2005). His readers had no way of knowing that Malaparte had invented his visit to the Warsaw ghetto out of whole cloth. His accounts of the dead laid out on the sidewalks "between Jewish ritual candelabra" as if in a canvas by Chagall, and of his snatches of conversation in French with the squads of young gravediggers, "mostly students from Berlin, Munich and Vienna, . . . cultured young men trained in the best universities" (Malaparte 1946, 93–95) are historically absurd. The business of burial in the Warsaw ghetto lay in the hands of the *Pinkertóvtses*, a den of corruption that only war could breed (Blumental 1981, 239–40). The Jews were dead: therefore, they were emblematic. Inscribing the missing Jews into the postwar memory-scape required a kind of mad calculation and a keen sense of timing.

Malaparte was a unique witness to the Holocaust. His flamboyant manner, effete aestheticism, elective affinity to extremes of human evil and suffering, and his pan-European sweep made *Kaputt* an instant bestseller. He alone crossed the Jew-Zone and war zones with impunity. He alone has not gone out of print. Precisely because it stands alone, *Kaputt* is the perfect counterpoint to the norm that was soon to follow. It was the antithesis of the plain style, whose moral gravity rested on acts of everyday heroism—and betrayal. The plain style, which is thought of today as the gold standard of Holocaust writing, was never a foregone conclusion as long as Holocaust memory remained communally confined.

Each surviving deportee returned with different scars to a different home, speaking a different language and telling a story different enough that it could not be heard beyond his or her own borders. Even if the preferred way of telling such stories was with a sober, plain style and an eye to humanity at large, there was no national or European consensus that remembering the painful past was a universal good, or that publishing such works was either merited or meritorious. Remembrance of the war in these former war zones was communal, which is to say local, occasional, and subject to changing political climates. Discrete, although hardly discreet, the best of these published testimonies needed the power to challenge a local consensus.

The earliest works of testimony were published in limited editions by small publishing houses. Turned down by Einaudi, Turin's vibrant and prestigious publishing house, Primo Levi's *Se questo è un uomo* (If this is a man; 1947) was finally published in an edition of 2,500 copies by a small, leftist publishing house; 1,000 copies remained unsold. Levi's book captured some attention in Turin but otherwise had little impact at the time (Consonni 2010, 30). Liana Millu, who survived alongside Levi in the women's camp at Birkenau, published *Il fumo di Birkenau* (Smoke over Birkenau) in 1947 in her native Pisa, where it languished in obscurity, not translated into English for almost fifty years (Millu 1991).

Nor was anyone particularly interested in the fate of the Jews. To capture what little there was of a French or Italian market, the former inmates and deportees downplayed their Jewish origins. In postwar France there was a discernible tendency "to deny the existence of a Semitic type" and to underscore one's patriotism rather than one's martyrdom as a Jew during the war: "As the *Marseillaise* had marked the departure, so it did the return" (Wieviorka 1994, 147, 143). To judge from French testimonies about the internment camp at Drancy, Christianity was a far more important cultural postwar presence than Judaism. What defined and distinguished the inmates who populated

FIGURE 10

Primo Levi. *Se questo è un uomo*. Turin: De Silva, 1947.

Millu's volume of well-crafted Italian stories was their gender, never their Jewishness. Writing in the pages of *Il Mondo* in 1949, the noted philosopher Benedetto Croce warned the Italian Jews to stop representing themselves as different from everyone else (Consonni 2010, 31). In Italian and French bookstores, the tale of those who had returned from captivity was one of universal and universalist import: Elio Vittorini's *Men and Non-Men* and Carlo Levi's *Christ Stopped at Eboli*, both published in 1945; David Rousset's *A World Apart*, the 1947 translation of his 1946 work (The concentrationary universe); Robert Antelme's *L'espèce humaine*, published in 1947 and eventually translated into English as *The Human Race* (1992); and, of course, Primo Levi's *Se questo è un uomo*. To overcome charges of parochialism, the solution was to adopt the trope of resistance. Rousset and Antelme had both been arrested as members of the French resistance. Their primary identification was with other political prisoners, whether in Buchenwald, Auschwitz, Dachau, or elsewhere. Their cognitive map of the camp experience was governed by Marxist theory and class struggle. This found a receptive audience on the Left Bank of the Seine.

Never had these stories been told before. Although many prisoners of war had published their memoirs, with certain of their exploits celebrated on film—most memorably in Jean Renoir's 1937 antiwar classic, *La grande il-lusion*—and although these works might conveniently be catalogued under a heading such as "World War (1939–45)—personal narratives," there was no known precedent for Auschwitz and Buchenwald, except perhaps by analogy to Dante. *"Hier ist kein warum"* (there is no "why" here), Levi was told angrily by a "large, heavy guard" (1985, 29). Such was the logic of the death camps: first you disoriented and demoralized the prisoner, then you killed him. Terror was the total of prohibition plus irrationality. Assigned numbers that were astronomically high—because they were late in arriving in the camps, and therefore had some chance of survival—the Italians were internally marked as the lowest of the low, fatally unprepared and naïve. *"Alle Franzosen Scheisse"* (all French are shit), the German block leader shouted at the tiny group of Frenchmen who had just arrived in Gandersheim; and in their own estimation, it did indeed seem "that we comprised the lowliest, the bottommost class among the inmates" (Antelme 1992, 11). The camps were the great equalizer. Stripped of name and nationality, all your baggage destroyed when you arrived, the only distinctions that mattered now were the color of your triangle and whether your number was low or high.

Yet these first-generation testimonials were most emphatically not of one piece and did not constitute one literature. As noted above, each author had returned with a different experience, literally speaking a different language. Auschwitz I was not Auschwitz II (Birkenau) nor Auschwitz III (Monowitz-Buna). An extermination camp was not a labor camp. "At Gandersheim," Antelme explained in his preface, "there was no gas chamber, no crematorium" (ibid., 5). The Frenchmen constituted a tiny, homogeneous group that lived together, were evacuated together, and died together. The Kapos lived and ate among the inmates, who even knew what the ss had for supper. So closely intertwined were victim and victimizer that one could watch them changing sides: first Lucien, who turned himself into "a French-speaking auxiliary of those who governed in the German language" (ibid., 126), then Fritz, Ernst, and the other German common criminals with their green triangles, then the Poles. Although Levi could distinguish between one group of Jews and another, between one kind of Jew and another, Antelme knew no Jews at all. In Gandersheim, which produced no *Muselmänner*, hunger did not mean what it meant in Auschwitz.

The message also matched the man—or the woman. For Primo Levi, becoming a *Häftling* (inmate or prisoner) required immediate and total transformation: learning the rules, the camp topography, whom to avoid, and whom to emulate. Otherwise, you didn't survive. Time in Auschwitz did not foster the discovery of self. Time was an instrument of torture. Veteran prisoners laughed when asked: How long? When Levi left the Ka-Be (the *Krankenbau*) at the end of his first course in survival (1985, chaps. 1–4), he was naked, forced to negotiate the whole cycle from the beginning.

With anthropological precision (ibid., chaps. 5–9), Levi demonstrates how what happens in the camps is not the self discovering itself but the self mimicking the Other. Steinlauf convinces him to wash. Alberto "understands everything at once, . . . the rare figure of the strong yet peace-loving man against whom the weapons of night are blunted" (ibid., 57). Elias, the Warsaw tough, models the ground rules of survival. The urbane Henri, with whom Levi seems to share so much intellectual baggage, is finally unmasked as the author's demonic Other, a professional seducer, while the selfless Lorenzo who inhabits the other side of the barbed wire embodies true heroism: the heroism of small acts. The *Lager*, Levi concludes, was preeminently a gigantic biological and social experiment (ibid., 83).

Within this Babel, where Italian is the smallest linguistic group, Levi tries, despite all odds, to salvage a sense of self (ibid., chaps. 10–12), to communicate something, if only one canto about Ulysses from Dante—partially, painstakingly pieced together from memory and translated into French for Jean the Pikolo's benefit after Levi emerges from the underground. There follows (ibid., chaps. 13–16) the winter of their discontent, which begins with a *Selektion* and Levi's condemnation of old Kuhn for praying aloud, thanking God that he has not been chosen, and ends with the futile death cry of "The Last One," the last free man among them. Finally come the ten days of liberation (ibid., chap. 17): each day with its own special character, each act with its own salvific significance. Thus Levi's "ethical uncertainty" and "skeptical humanism" (Cheyette 2007, 67, 72) are borne out by the title and by the way his tightly written stories are ordered, alternating between "The Drowned and the Saved" (Levi 1985, chap. 9).

Levi's low-keyed meditation on the nature of man, his "ethical-cum-ethnological reflection," was by no means unique (Gordon 1999, 52). It resembled the critical sensibility of other European writers who came of age during the Second World War. Antelme's slow-moving, at times ponderous, work was concerned with the human species as a whole. It was a courageous attempt to uphold a worldview of solidarity, to distinguish between the inmates wearing red triangles (the politicals) and those wearing green (the criminals), to argue that "we're still men, and we shall not end otherwise than as men" (1992, 219); to maintain that the ss "can kill a man, but he can't change him into something else" (ibid., 220). So the narrator claimed. As it unfolded, however, the story belied such certainties, and one color bled into another.

Memory as Liturgy

After a decade of latency, scandalous memory gradually and sporadically gave way to sacred memory. When he republished *Se questo è un uomo* in 1958 (with Einaudi, the publishing house that had turned him down the first time), Levi made one significant change: he made his poem "Sh'ma," written in 1946, serve as an epigraph (Levi 1988). Chosen as carefully as the epigraphs to this book, the poem added a liturgical cast to an otherwise secular, almost scientifically sober, memoir. Addressed to those who spent the war safe and warm in their own homes, Levi adjures them to recite his testimony "at home, in the street, / Going to bed, rising"; and to "repeat them to your children" (Levi 1985, 11), as if it were a covenantal narrative recited to God at Mount Sinai. This was the art of sacred parody, of countercommentary, which linked Levi to his fellow survivor, Y. D. Sheinson, who had compiled a counter-Haggadah in the very same year; and, even further back, to the Jewish liturgical poets of the early Middle Ages. If Levi's Auschwitz memoir bore the words of a new, secular covenant, then through this gesture Auschwitz number 174517 wished us to acknowledge his Jewish ancestry. The added epigraph, moreover, encourages a second reading of the memoir itself—especially its opening chapter, which foregrounds Levi's membership in the antifascist resistance and the Jewish people. This chapter ends with a romanticized portrait of traditional Jews experiencing an archetypal grief. To underscore the transformation of *If This Is a Man* into an inspirational work, the American publisher changed the title to *Survival in Auschwitz*.

For the Holocaust to emerge as an archetype, it was not enough to bring it home—to Paris, Pisa, or Turin—with some personal tale of survival. Nor was it enough to map out a separate "concentrationary universe" (Rousset 1982), with Auschwitz and its satellite camps as the mother planet. The Holocaust had to be transformed from a war story, one among many, into an event superficially coterminous with a war, and finally into an indefinably defining event, so that a time-bound catastrophe could be perceived transtemporally. This double transformation was accomplished thanks to the combined effort of poets, playwrights, prose writers, and theologians. It was an effort of writers, thinkers, and artists who were intent on going beyond the facts, who were adepts at allegory and analogy, and whose mastery of ancient paradigms enabled an architecture balancing heaven and earth. Together, they reminded the world that the Jews were a people chosen not only by Hitler but also, once and forever, by God.

Foremost among the poets was Uri Zvi Greenberg. Because of his Revisionist-Zionist views, Greenberg had been ostracized for two decades by both the Hebrew literary establishment and the left-wing kibbutz movement. But

FIGURE 11
Uri Zvi Greenberg.
Rehovot hanahar. Jerusalem:
Schocken, 1951. Cover design
by Jakob Steinhardt.

in 1945, he broke his vow of silence and was immediately acclaimed as "the Jeremiah of our generation," his poems reached a mainstream audience in the influential daily *Ha'aretz*, and a nation in the making hung on to his every word (Miron 2010, 230–37). Only the left-wing kibbutz movement refused to forgive and forget, and Greenberg was conspicuously absent from the thirty poets included in Zuckerman and Basok's *Sefer milḥamot hageta'ot* (1954).

Greenberg was anathema for fundamental reasons as well. In *Reḥovot hana-har* (Streets of the river; 1951), the first and only book of Holocaust poetry designed to be a *sefer*, he discarded all the secular props. He abjured the term "Shoah," which implied a natural disaster unrelated to its root cause—Christian hatred of Jews—and he refused the easy consolation of coupling Shoah with *gevurah*, the martyrs with the fighters. The destruction of a people was a catastrophe of cosmic proportions, requiring a new poetic language—"No Other Instances!" Greenberg proclaimed (1989, 574)—a new accounting with God, a last encounter with the dead, and a final reckoning with the goyim (Miron 2010, 237–46).

Greenberg endowed the murder of Europe's Jews with cosmic and, ultimately, redemptive significance. It was the *sefer ha'iliyot vehakoaḥ* (book of dirges and power), which is to say, a poetry at once bardic, encompassing the sweep of Jewish time and space, and lyric, addressed to the poet's murdered family (Mintz 1984, 181). Speaking throughout in the first person singular, "as one of the many beheaded of father and mother" ("I'll Say to God"), the poet saw a universe riven in two. "A lying poet can poeticize," he said to God in Europe in 1951, "that after entering Your heaven / Your useless shepherd staff will shine, a rainbow in the sky. / Not I—who sees within the vision the divided body of the [sacrificial] bird" (Greenberg 1989, 573). At precisely the moment when Abraham Sutzkever and Paul Celan, still within the Jew-Zone, engaged their murdered mothers in lyric dialogue, Greenberg began imagining hallucinatory encounters with his mother that were so childish, regressive, and raw that they forced Hebrew readers to confront their own loss, guilt, and utter helplessness (Miron 2010, 246). Whatever consolation might yet be won from witnessing "the great palace of power," Greenberg's code for the miracle of Jewish political sovereignty, "the crown-of-the-universal kingdom" in "the returning time of greatness" was predicated on facing an abyss, an unbridgeable divide, which would forever separate Jew from gentile (Greenberg 1989, 572). Little wonder the left-wing kibbutzim wanted no part of his work.

Though written in Hebrew, Greenberg's poetry of personal bereavement and national consolation was of a piece with the response to the Holocaust in Yiddishland. In the wake of the Holocaust, Yiddish had become *loshn-hakdoyshim*, the language of the martyrs, as opposed to Hebrew or Aramaic —*loshn-koydesh*, the holy tongue. The three writers who consolidated the liturgical turn within secular Yiddish culture were Jacob Glatstein, Kadia Molodowski, and Chaim Grade.

With *Shtralndike yidn* (Radiant Jews; 1946), his first postwar collection of poems, Glatstein became a theologian, not merely a poet of the Holocaust. "We accepted the Torah on Sinai," says the poet in the name of the surviving people of Israel, "and in Lublin," in the shadow of the Majdanek death camp, "we gave it back." Quoting Scripture back at God, the poet continues: "The dead don't praise God [Ps. 115:17]— / The Torah was given for Life. / And just as we stood together / At the giving of the Torah, / So indeed did we all die in Lublin" (Glatstein 1993, 92). "O God of Mercy," says Molodowski in 1945, in her first postwar collection of verse, "Choose— / another people. / We are tired of death, tired of corpses, / We have no more prayers" (Molodowski 1988). The "we" of these poems is the Jewish body politic, still grievously wounded. Only when facing off against a diminished, intimate, Yiddish-speaking God does it feel itself empowered.

The chair of the Yiddish Writer's Union in Paris between 1946 and 1948 was Chaim Grade, a different kind of survivor, who had fled eastward into the Soviet Union, abandoning his mother and wife. The crucible of memory, loyalty, and guilt for Grade the poet, essayist, and novelist would henceforth be Vilna—not only its secular Yiddish culture, but also its great Torah sages and radical asceticism. In 1952 he brilliantly pitted these two sides of his personal past against each other in his first work of autobiographical fiction, "My Quarrel with Hersh Rasseyner" (Grade 1999), the lion's share of which takes place in postwar Paris.

Here, in the cradle of the Enlightenment, someone like Chaim Vilner, who broke away from the strictures of Jewish law to embrace the religion of secular humanism, would seem to enjoy a strategic advantage over Hersh Rasseyner, who cut himself off from the secular world and its seductions. Yet Grade keeps the sides evenly matched for these two characters, for Hersh, while an inmate in Auschwitz, dabbled in Western philosophy. The war, he tells Chaim, presented him with such irrefutable proof of the need for Jewish law in the face of barbarism that he is astounded by Chaim's unrepentant humanism. In the end, each side refuses to despair, the one of God, the other of humankind (Wisse 2000, 139), and when Chaim embraces his old adversary, he signals that this internal Jewish dialogue will continue as before—answerable to the past but not crushed by it.

By the early 1950s, readers of Yiddish and Hebrew had two very different literary responses to the Holocaust from which to choose. Enshrined as sacred memory in *yizkor* books, *sefers*, and liturgical volumes of secular verse, the Holocaust became part of a new metanarrative of destruction and rebirth. Through the alchemy of the Jewish anthological imagination, passive martyrs were melded together with armed resisters. One side of Rapoport's monument merged into the other. In order to restore human agency, however, it was necessary to move the brute struggle for survival onto a metahistorical plane. Instead of dwelling on the chronology and terminology of mass murder, one school of prose writers and poets returned to a conceptual vocabulary encoded in the ancient texts. Kolitz, in Yosl Rakover's name, spoke of *hesterpanim*, God's momentary, mysterious lapse. The other approach—newsworthy, raw, and scandalous—focused on the assault to the body. Rochman, Strigler, and Ka-Tzetnik were unsparing in their attention to bodily detail. The men who made it through the first selection in Buchenwald were seen sifting through their own shit to locate the diamonds and precious metals they had swallowed the day before. Oh, how the narrator lamented the loss of his Polish banknotes, which were biodegradable and therefore could not have been salvaged (Strigler 1947, 42–44). In a fairly straightforward, chronological manner, these writers inducted the reader into a new order of reality, centered on brute survival, a world of choiceless choice.

At one pole of response were the liturgists, secular humanists who, in the face of such a catastrophe, become guardians of the sacred flame. Occupy-

FIGURE 12

Eliezer Wiesel. . . . *un di velt hot geshvign*. Buenos Aires: Tsentral-farband fun poylishe yidn in Argentine, 1956. Volume 117 of Dos poylishe yidntum.

ing the other pole were young men raised in traditional homes who for the same reason turned to naturalism, becoming radical realists. These two sides of Every-Jew could no sooner be reconciled than the two sides of every soul, living (as we all do) in the aftermath.

Among the first to make the metamorphic effort outside the Yiddish sphere was the Lithuanian-born philosopher Emmanuel Lévinas. In 1955, he delivered a radio address on "Loving the Torah More Than God," inspired by the recent translation into French of a last will and testament supposedly written by a deeply observant ghetto fighter named Yosl Rakover. Later to appear in the canonical edition of *Yosl Rakover Talks to God*, the meditative essay by Lévinas was an early attempt to wrest theological significance from the extremity of the Holocaust (Kolitz 1999).

Another was the Catholic commentary to the memoir of the young Elie Wiesel, . . . *un di velt hot geshvign* (. . . and the world was silent; 1956), who had just made the shift from Yiddish to French, and from a strictly Jewish to a more ecumenical perspective. In Yiddish, the seeds of Wiesel's youthful activism were readily apparent—from the book's accusatory title to its final pages, where the narrator smashes the mirror hanging on the wall in order to call himself back to life, followed by a warning from the author about the Nazis who remained at large. In Yiddish, the constant shift between showing and telling, reporting and editorializing, linked Wiesel to the journalists turned Holocaust chroniclers who had preceded him (J. Schwarz 2007b, 57). By waiting a decade to break his own silence about the *khurbn*, Wiesel was able to locate his terrible itinerary—from deportation to Birkenau, Auschwitz, and Buna to the death march to Gleiwitz and the death train to Buchenwald, and finally and almost miraculously to liberation—within a larger, scriptural trajectory. The story of Jewish sons, including himself by implication, who were willing to kill their fathers for a crust of bread was nothing less than an anti-*Akedah*, a repudiation of God's covenant with Abraham and Isaac.

Thanks to the intervention of the Catholic theologian François Mauriac, Wiesel's *La Nuit* (*Night*, 1958) became the gospel of a survivor. When appearing before Mauriac as a young foreign journalist, Wiesel identified himself as one of the million and a half Jewish children singled out for slaughter. What Mauriac saw was Lazarus, risen from the dead (Wiesel 2000, xix). Read through a Christian lens, the centerpiece of Wiesel's testimony was not so much the High Holiday services in Buna, where the Orthodox narrator broke with the community of the faithful, but the public hanging of the boy, "the sad-eyed angel" (Wiesel 2000, 64). Since the young Hasidic narrator had as yet no knowledge of Christianity, Wiesel left it to an unnamed witness ("someone behind me was asking") to draw the sacrilegious analogy. The execution was both a literal reembodiment and a grotesque parody of Jesus at Golgotha, crucified between two convicts. Whoever recognized this to be a second crucifixion also understood that there would be no Second Coming.

Definitively and defiantly bringing the Holocaust home to Christian Europe and his fellow Frenchmen was Wiesel's exact contemporary, André Schwarz-Bart. Embracing eight centuries of Jewish life in Europe, the 1959 *Le dernier des justes* (*The Last of the Just*, 1960) exposed the Christian roots of Nazi paganism. Bringing the story closer to home in the concluding chapters, Schwarz-Bart indicted the Vichy regime, recalling the role played by the French police in guarding the infamous transit camp at Drancy. Most outrageously, he dared to penetrate the very heart of darkness—the gas chambers at Auschwitz.

To accomplish these ambitious—indeed, scandalous—ends, Schwarz-Bart chose the family saga as his genre, employing its conventions in both predictable and not-so-predictable ways. To present the expanse of European Jewish history stretching back to 1185, Schwarz-Bart settled on the legendary town of Zemyock, the "Territory of Just Men," focusing on the last three generations—Mordecai and Judith, Benjamin and Fräulein Blumenthal, Ernie and Golda. The weakest link in the chain of tradition was the middle, emancipated generation, relocated to the idyllic German town of Stillenstadt (Quiet Town), setting the stage for the fierce suffering and struggle of the prodigal

FIGURE 13

André Schwarz-Bart. *The Last of the Just.* New York: Atheneum, 1960. Cover design by George Salter.

son, the last of the just. Who were these just men and their wives? None other than the thirty-six Zaddikim, on whom rested the fate of the world (Scholem 1971, 251–56). Though in Yiddish folklore these *lamed-vóvnikes* were hidden or anonymous, Schwarz-Bart endowed them with celebrity, making them into a genealogy of martyrdom, a hereditary chain of exemplary witnesses, chosen receptacles of human suffering—in short, into a family of Christ figures. With one stroke, Schwarz-Bart thrust the Yiddish-speaking Jews, universally reviled, into the center of world history and turned a single dynasty into the touchstone of redemption—and apocalypse. It was a colossal act of chutzpah worthy of the world-renowned Yiddish novelist, Sholem Asch, whose mantle Schwarz-Bart can be said to have inherited.

The Last of the Just also marked the beginning of Holocaust liturgy. Refusing to be reconciled, Schwarz-Bart ended his novel with a sacrilegious kaddish. By alternating the names of the major death and concentration camps with the Hebrew formulas hallowing the name of God, Schwarz-Bart pitted profane history against sacred myth. Through this bold juxtaposition, he argued for an impossible yet necessary linkage between affirmation and negation, covenant and atrocity—a fitting kaddish for a nation of impractical Jews, whose yellow stars became the light of dead stars.

Le dernier des justes was awarded the 1959 Prix Goncourt and was then summarily attacked by every sector of French society in what came to be known as "L'Affaire Schwarz-Bart" (after the infamous Dreyfus affair). The Roman Catholic Church was outraged, for obvious reasons. The professional historians were outraged, accusing Schwarz-Bart of plagiarizing their work. The Left Bank intellectuals were outraged simply because Schwarz-Bart was not one of them (Davison 2004). Transcending the wars of the French, The Last of the Just went on to become the first international bestselling novel on a Holocaust theme. Scandalous memory in one language became sacred in another.

PROVISIONAL MEMORY 1960-85

THE NEXT QUARTER-CENTURY WAS A TIME OF DISCOVERY, of seeing things as if for the first time. Lo, there were survivor witnesses living in our midst, wrote the Hebrew poet, Natan Alterman, whose image, "beyond life and beyond nature," had become indelibly etched into the national pysche (1961, 522). Here they stood, on the witness stand, demanding retribution from their murderers, and revealing a crime of such enormity that it could not have been perpetrated without the complicity of others. Who else was to blame? The survivors bore witness to a war that refused to end, to scars that refused to heal; what they labored to reconstruct had already been destroyed. And since other wars were being fought in the background, some of which targeted the very people who had been targeted before, it seemed as if the annihilation was merely on hold. In every respect, the catastrophe was only provisionally over.

Once the witness survivors assumed a human face, everything changed. What they had experienced may have been "beyond life and beyond nature," but they, as individuals, were not. The earlier division of the dead into heroes or martyrs ceased to be meaningful in the presence of the still living. To be sure, a few were bona fide heroes. But even heroes could mourn, as did Abba Kovner, a former partisan and fighter for Israel's independence, in 1967 when he published a volume of lyric poems dedicated to the memory of *Ahoti ketana* (*My Little Sister and Selected Poems*, 1986). The wars that were being fought in the background also changed everything, because one, the war in Vietnam, was intensely unpopular among the most vocal part of the American population, while the others—the Six-Day War and especially the Yom Kippur War—shifted the perception of the Jewish nation from the heroism to the horrors of war. Each horror had its own grievances, which the state—the nation, the collective—could not redress. Judging by their own writings, at this time just beginning to gain an audience, and from the writings of others who observed them up close, the survivors' life was one of complete alienation. In France, Israel, and the United States, a gallery of ugly survivors reared their heads—Boris D., Raphael Schlemielovitch, Moishe-Genghis Cohn, Bertha, Adam Stein, Sol Nazerman, Artur Sammler, Sophie Zawitowski, Rosa Lublin—and they seemed to be people possessed. Had they wisdom to impart? In what possible sense was their story redemptive?

Presumably silent until now, these witnesses were finding entirely new ways of describing their nightmarish past, in a language at once familiar and strange. "Only with the appearance of Aharon Appelfeld, at the end of the 1950s," the Israeli novelist A. B. Yehoshua recalled two decades later, "did Holocaust literature begin to acquire depth and direction. He brought it out of the ghetto where Hebrew literature had placed it." Yehoshua continued: "I remember Appelfeld reading to us his first stories in his little room in Jerusalem. Instantly we all felt: here is a new artistic code that lets us grasp this experience through its own creative merit. We need not make allowances or accommodate for it; it stands up to artistic criteria like any other true work of creation" (1980, 97).

Appelfeld's "new artistic code" was actually a Hebrew variant of the sober, understated, plain style of the Polish, Italian, and French survivor witnesses who had preceded him but who remained virtually unknown outside of their communal settings. For Holocaust literature to speak anew, every generation of readers had to see itself as the first to bear witness and to feel profoundly scandalized by the presumed silence of those who came before. Giving public voice to this scandal of silence and "ghettoization" was Elie Wiesel. A true response to the Holocaust, he proclaimed, could come about only "One Generation After" (1972), and that generation's time had finally come.

Living Theater: The Eichmann Trial

These were the dramatis personae who were to appear in a makeshift Jerusalem courthouse beginning on April 11, 1961: a balding, bespectacled man in a glass booth named Adolf Eichmann, who was flanked by two armed guards; a fiery Israeli prosecutor and a seasoned German defense attorney; three stern judges, seated under the emblem of the Jewish state; 110 witnesses, mostly recent immigrants to Israel but some brought especially from abroad; anywhere from 450 to 474 journalists, mostly foreign; representatives of forty vitally concerned organizations; some diplomats and VIPs; and members of the general public, for whom the remaining seats had been drastically cut back from 165 to 50 (Yablonka 2004, 60–63). Outside the courtroom, the whole world was reading, watching, or listening, although the news wasn't exactly presented in a state-of-the-art manner. Turning down lucrative offers from every major television network from NBC to the BBC, the Israeli government agency in charge had given the broadcasting concession to a local amateur, with predictable results. (Israel had no networks of its own at that point.) David Grossman, then seven years old, remembers—as do many other Israelis—being glued to the radio every night to hear highlights from the day's proceedings (Herman 2004). In fact, "The Trial Diary" was broadcast only four times a week for a mere twenty-five minutes, with a summary of the "The Week at the Eichmann Trial" aired during prime time (ibid.). Followed around the globe—in Germany, Hungary, the Americas, Israel, and elsewhere—in one medium or another, the trial of Adolf Eichmann revealed the many faces of the Holocaust to a wildly divergent public.

Few faces had been available thus far. To begin with, there was Anne Frank, innocent and childlike on the cover of her *Diary* (1952). A decade later, a dark-haired and dark-eyed young Israelite named Elie Wiesel had appeared before the Catholic theologian François Mauriac (Wiesel 2000); and a year after that appeared another martyr witness named Ernie Levy, the *Last of the Just* (Schwarz-Bart 1960). Those readers who had discovered the writings of Ka-Tzetnik, Primo Levi, or Tadeusz Borowski knew of the *Muselmänner*, the living dead of the concentration camps, who by definition were faceless. Now, for the first time, the witness stand was full to overflowing.

Most familiar, at least to the Israelis in the courtroom, was the iconic survivor as fighter, represented by the vigorous, wrathful, and still youthful Antek Zuckerman, Zivia Lubetkin, and Abba Kovner. Ghetto fighters all, they had gone on to establish kibbutzim in Palestine or Israel and remained very much in the public eye. Then there was the survivor as articulate witness, like George Wellers, a professor whose eyewitness account of the four thousand orphaned children at the Drancy transit camp was devastating in its unalloyed horror.

Ka-Tzetnik, the rare material witness who had seen the accused at the scene of the crime, was forced to reveal his true identity for the first time, causing him to collapse in midtestimony. He had to be carried out on a stretcher. Least familiar, and momentarily uplifting, was the face of the so-called good German, represented at the trial by Father Heinrich Karl Ernst Grüber.

The scripted part of the trial was gripping enough, even though for most of the public the verdict was a foregone conclusion. Seeing the trial as a one-time opportunity to demonstrate the "full extent and unique nature of the destruction of the Jews of Europe" (quoted by Lipstadt 2011, 52), Rachel Auerbach worked behind the scenes with the chief prosecutor Gideon Hausner to find the right witnesses, people who could provide flesh-and-blood descriptions of the five stages of the murder process—*Aktionen* and deportations, death marches, mass shootings, extermination camps, and the mobile killing squads—and others to provide a more general overview. Bureau 06, the Israeli government agency officially charged with preparing the case against Eichmann, poured over thousands of pages of written testimony, looking for the most vivid descriptions and "interesting" style, and with an eye toward covering the whole expanse of the Jew-Zone (Lipstadt 2011, 52–53; Yablonka 2004, 98–99).

It was the unscripted part, however, the part that existed only in the eyes of the beholders, that would live on beyond the trial. Most surprising, if not revelatory, were the ordinary faces of ordinary survivors, who until that point had lacked a collective identity. As more and more witnesses took the stand, one after the other, Alterman saw how "the separate beings of unfamiliar and anonymous people, whom we had passed by countless times, were suddenly joined together." They assumed what he called "an image," "a basic and forceful substance, whose nature and image, and the terror of whose memories are beyond life and beyond nature, and are an ineradicable part of the nature and image of the living nation to which we belong" (quoted in Yablonka 2004, 162). Those who had suffered every inconceivable torture in places heretofore unpronounceable, and who had survived merely by chance, through no particular or collective acts of heroism, were thus inserted into the Israeli mosaic.

For eight months the war hero, poet, and journalist Haim Gouri sat in the press gallery and was transfixed by what he heard. Who was to blame? he asked himself. Representing the native-born Israelis, Gouri felt an overwhelming sense of identification with the ordinary men and women on the witness stand who spoke in Hebrew of what they had suffered. Like Alterman, he felt bound to them by a single, Jewish fate. Hausner's repeated question, "Why didn't you fight back?" was proved to be irrelevant, as their cumulative testimony revealed how the normal rules of behavior had been suspended in that "other planet," as Ka-Tzetnik called it before he fainted. No. If anyone was guilty it was the Yishuv itself, the Jewish polity of Palestine, guilty of silent complicity in the murder of their brothers and sisters in European exile (Gouri 2004). Those who knew and said nothing bore a greater guilt than those who went like sheep to the slaughter (Shapira 2005).

Harry Mulisch, whose father had been a Nazi collaborator, covered the trial for a Dutch daily newspaper before extending his investigation into the mystery of Eichmann and Nazi Germany by traveling to Berlin, Auschwitz, and Majdanek (Shamir-de-Leeuw 2004). Hannah Arendt was present when the trial began and when the defense cross-examined the witness—in German. The rest of her report for the *New Yorker* was based on transcripts (Lipstadt 2011, 178–80). What Arendt witnessed in person made her angry enough. She felt indignant at the chief prosecutor's heavy-handed manner and his less-than-perfect German. What Auerbach and Hausner considered the backbone of the trial, its broad pedagogical purpose, she considered completely irrelevant. The only justification for this trial was to focus exclusively on Eichmann's deeds, not the sufferings of the Jews, not the German people or mankind, not even antisemitism and racism (Lipstadt 2011, 151). At the end of the day, Arendt argued, the root cause of evil was not Eichmann, a mindless, middlebrow bureaucrat, but rather the system that produced him. If anything, the victims themselves were to blame, for actively collaborating with the enemy through the so-called Judenräte, or Jewish councils, like the "Jewish Führer" of Terezín, Rabbi Leo Baeck. (In later English editions of *Eichmann in Jerusalem*, Arendt removed this libelous epithet about the spiritual leader of German Jewry.) Had the Jews been less organized, less compliant, Arendt believed, the Nazis would never have carried out their systematic annihilation.

One woman's lasting legacy to the Eichmann trial was thus the question of complicity, the presumed symmetry that Arendt saw between the Nazis and their victims. Rachel Auerbach left another legacy. She was bitterly disappointed that her day in court was reduced to a mere forty-five minutes. Yet her determination and that of Hausner to base the trial on the story of the Jewish victims as they told it from the witness stand is what gave the survivors a collective presence, being, and voice.

There remained the matter of nomenclature. What subject heading best fit this trial for future reference? A crime against humanity? A war against the Jews? Genocide? After many months of meticulous testimony, it became clear to readers, viewers, listeners, and commentators throughout the world that the subject of the trial required its own name. Why not use the name that official court translators had provided throughout the trial, the name that best rendered the Hebrew term Shoah? And so it was that the capitalized noun "Holocaust" entered the world lexicon (Lipstadt 2011, 188).

Cities of Slaughter:
The Architecture of Personal Identity

The annihilation had rendered the terrestrial extraterrestrial. Real places on a map, difficult to pronounce if you weren't native to the region, were replaced by ruined cities of the mind. Rare indeed was the native son who returned home during this third period of public memory, when Europe was divided between West and East, and the demands of the present trumped the lure of the severed past.

Only where certain languages were still spoken by surviving inhabitants could the covenantal communities of the postwar Jewish mind still be reconstituted. When the great Hebrew writer S. Y. Agnon learned, at some point in 1944, that the Jewish community of his native Buczacz had been annihilated, he sat down to write "Hasiman" ("The Sign"). What would remain of Polish Jewry and its millennia-old civilization? he asked. The name Buczacz, he answered, inscribed into a religious hymn composed by the greatest of medieval Hebrew poets, Solomon ibn Gabirol. Agnon returned to this story in 1962 and expanded it tenfold (1989), even as he began a massive, unfinished project of retelling tales in praise of Buczacz. 'Ir umlo'ah (The city in its fullness) became the first personal *yizkor* book (Agnon 1973).

Between present and past lay an abyss that could be crossed only by those tenacious enough to excavate their place of birth. That is just what the thirty-five-year-old Israeli poet Yehuda Amichai did when he returned to his native Würzburg for the first time since his family had been forced to flee Germany in 1936. In the novel inspired by this visit, *Lo mi'akhshav velo mikan* (*Not of This Time, Not of This Place*, 1968), the double negative says it all: the setting is split between Würzburg (thinly disguised in the book as "Weinburg") and Jerusalem, just as the protagonist is caught between his love for two women, one dead and the other living. Destroyed by Allied bombs, Weinburg's ancient Teutonic monuments were being reconstructed, he discovers, while Jewish Würzburg will survive only in the memories of those who left it. So the narrator vows to write the history of "the covenantal community of Weinburg," which is really the story of all those Jews who perished. Agnon labored to sew Buczacz back together again out of legendary Judaic cloth; Amichai does the same for Würzburg through his longing for the Jewish context of his early life (Gold 2008, 72–73).

Amichai was not a survivor of the Holocaust. A bona fide survivor was someone who had lived through it, in place, or in many terrifying places. In contrast, Amichai was someone who had been forced somewhat earlier to leave everything behind by the pressures building toward the official Holocaust (1939–45). Both he and Agnon lived in a sovereign Jewish state when they set out on their journeys through ruined memoryscapes. In doing so, both reverted back to liturgical modes of commemoration. Did their confrontation with the Holocaust demand that they renounce Zionism's extravagant claim of having put an end to exile, or were they somehow deepening its messianic mandate? A basic Zionist tenet was the biblical dream of *kibbutz galuyot*, the ingathering of the exiles or of the Diasporas, the promise given by Moses to the people of Israel before he died—a promise vividly reimagined by the prophets Jeremiah, Isaiah, and Ezekiel. Although Israel had become the ultimate refuge for Jews from everywhere, a veritable Tower of Babel, who would assume responsibility for those left behind in the mass graves and ash pits of Europe? In order to mourn effectively as Jews, did Israelis have to shed or split their Hebraic identity, or did they need to reach down into its deepest, most ancient strata? As more such Weinburgs appeared on the map, the quest for a concerted personal identity led increasingly in historical, architectural, and graphic directions.

In a visual age, when vicarious pilgrims had to see as well as read about a place, Terezín—the fortress town turned ghetto—became familiar to the English-speaking world, Jews and non-Jews alike, thanks to several remarkable professional and amateur albums of sketches, collages, and watercolors. The State Jewish Museum in Prague published *Children's Drawings and Poems, Terezín, 1942–1944* (Volavková 1959), in which an array of watercolors, collages, and primitive line drawings, both fanciful and mimetic, were matched up with the poetry of Czech Jewish children and young adults, both utterly naïve and extremely prescient. This was followed by two richly illustrated albums: *The Artists of Terezin* (Green 1969) and a facsimile edition of *The Book of Alfred Kantor: Terezín-Auschwitz-Schwarzheide, December 1941–May 1945* (Kantor 1971). This graphic diary, which the young Kantor reconstructed right after the war and completed with quaint English captions, began with the inmates of Terezín trying to domesticate the horror by securing their "privacy," building bunks, and decorating their spartan quarters. But very soon the diary depicted starving people searching the garbage; one toilet for every thousand people; and the grotesque spectacle of the Swiss Red Cross paying a visit to this, the deadliest of all Potemkin villages. The next station was his arrival on the night of December 18, 1943, at "The Hell of Auschwitz," illuminated by spotlights that resembled nothing so much as a movie set. Kantor's primitive, almost childlike drawings were a perfect match for a historical landscape never before depicted: the separation of the still-healthy from those condemned to death, the looting of their abandoned luggage, the roll calls, the tattooing, the omniscient smoke, the burning of bodies in a pit, the endless transports, the "Worlds [*sic*] biggest crematory" (ibid., 54).

As a literary topos, cities of slaughter had an architecture that was more elusive than evocative. Kantor's images yoked together the commonplace and the (almost) unimaginable and gave each city rendered a psychological footing that even the rescued part of Mendel Grossman's photojournal of the Łódź ghetto had not managed (1972). Ever since the first Passover after Liberation, when Yosef Sheinson (2000) discovered the expressionist woodcuts of a fellow survivor from Hungary and fit them to apt passages from the Haggadah, the clash of then and now, here and there, had been set up as the hallmark of Holocaust iconography—and memory.

In this, the third phase of Holocaust memory, the communal and collective ceased to exert moral suasion. Graphic art, rediscovered, tested the boundaries of covenantal space. The ghetto was nothing but a façade, a satanic coverup, from which butterflies were banned. Compared to the Potemkin village of Terezín, Auschwitz was a Hollywood-scale movie set. Many of the writer survivors who made their first appearance in the 1960s and 1970s adopted an anticommunal perspective. The Nazi ghettos—veritable cities of Jews that were once the subject of "thick" and layered reportorial fictions—now became schematic; the ghettos and camps that came ready-made with the classical unities of action, place, and time now remained nameless, more often than not. As actual survivors eschewed chronology and geography to write in nontestamentary ways, they emboldened vicarious survivors to claim the autonomy of art, the particularity of the literary and painterly imagination.

Cities of slaughter, cities of refuge. If they were to exist in the imagination of those born later and perhaps without a genetic, confessional, geographic, or linguistic claim to the map of origins, the locus of identification had to lie elsewhere, in domains that were more personal, psychological, and existential. Here, a city proved to be a city in name only; Badenheim and Weinburg no more locatable on a map than Arad or Miami Beach. More startling and unsettling still, when the map of the catastrophe was redrawn on a new time-space continuum, disassembled into cities of slaughter, fools' towns, and asylums, they were to be reconstructed for the sole purpose of being destroyed. Only one person—the last member of the tribe or family, the last inhabitant of the courtyard—survived to tell the tale.

Ghetto Stories: The Novel of Survival

Edgar Hilsenrath, a child survivor of the ghetto of Moghilov-Podolsk, returns us to the picaresque novel, the rough-and-tumble beginnings of the novel form itself, as if to create the objective correlative of the ghetto as a horrible anachronism. Trapped in some nameless ghetto in Transnistria, Ranek in *Night* (Hilsenrath 1966) will stop at nothing to stay alive. A true picaresque hero, he is thrust into a world of endless night, where he must fight for a place to sleep after curfew and do everything he never knew he could do to survive by day.

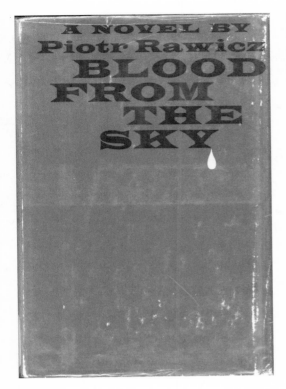

FIGURE 14

Piotr Rawicz. *Blood from the Sky*. New York: Harcourt, Brace and World, 1964.

The ghetto is a closed world of strangers. *Night* begins with Ranek stealing the hat and rags off the dead body of Nathan, his best friend, and ends with some erstwhile friend of Ranek's doing the same thing to him. Ranek fornicates with every woman in sight. We do not shed a tear for his demise, nor are we asked to, even by the saintly, selfless, tearful Deborah. As picaresque journey, the Holocaust can only implode.

Part hallucination, part diary; part diatribe, part elegy—Piotr Rawicz's *Le Sang du Ciel* (*Blood from the Sky*, 2003) established a new sacrilegious norm in 1961. The plot, insofar as it can be pieced together, involves a dissolute, cynical, avant-garde poet named Boris D., whom we meet up with on July 12 in a year in the 1940s, the day of the final liquidation of his unnamed ghetto. Ultimately, he is deported to Auschwitz-Birkenau, which he survives by virtue of an outrageous act of dissimulation. Facing down the anatomical evidence, Boris convinces his captors that he is a full-blooded, Jew-hating Ukrainian nationalist. Boris's tale of survival, therefore, is emphatically, adamantly, astonishingly anticovenantal. Part I of the novel chronicles the cruel implications of "The Tool and the Art of Comparison," in which all Jews bearing the sign of the covenant on their penis are condemned to death; Part III celebrates "The Tool and the Thwarting of Comparison." If the story's narrator adamantly insists at the end that "this book is not a historical record" (ibid., 316), it is because Rawicz insists on a manner of retelling that is fragmentary, paradoxical, and portentous, like latter-day scrolls from the Dead Sea. As in ancient apocalyptic writings, all historical markers are erased or obfuscated. Lemberg-Lwow-Lviv is referred to as an "average-sized town in the Ukraine"; Leyb Landau, the head of the Jewish Self-Help in the ghetto, appears as Leo L., and Salo Greiver, who ran the ghetto workshops, is represented by Garin, the "blood-smeared Golem" (ibid., 8, 38). Standing in for itself, however, is the ancient cemetery, which houses the sacred remains of the Turei Zahav, one of the greatest Polish rabbis, and Boris describes its actual destruction by Jewish slave laborers. The Hebrew letters and iconic images of the smashed, murdered tombstones, Rawicz writes, were set loose into the world "to reorganize themselves into a new community, creating a simple, cruel order, the very opposite of the one that had just been destroyed" (ibid., 58). Even as Boris vows to rescue the old cemetery and preserve it like a black cloak wrapped around his shoulders, his own journey of survival depends on hiding the fact of his Jewishness. *Blood from the Sky* rewrites the Holocaust as a book of broken covenants.

Unlike the major concentration and death camps, which were preserved or turned into national monuments with generalized, formulaic inscriptions, nothing was left of the ghetto walls. Worse yet, an Iron Curtain running down the middle of Europe made it all but impossible for Westerners to gain access to these ghost towns. As humor was a means of collective resistance, so ghetto comedy—the ghetto depicted as a town of fools—could restore some sense of the people still responding as a people. Importing Yiddish humor across the abyss of time was another way to keep the cultural identity of the dead Jews alive, all the more so while writing in German in a humorless police state called the German Democratic Republic, where expressions of parochial grief were strictly forbidden.

Jurek Becker dared to take a comic stab at the Nazi ghetto, where he himself had been incarcerated as a child, by turning Łódź into a latter-day Kasrilevke— this, without any conscious awareness of his elective affinity to the humor of Yiddish-speaking Jews (Schaumann 2004). Sholem Aleichem, the greatest Jewish humorist, had immortalized the jovial paupers of Kasrilevke, their comic antics rooted in the legendary foolstown of Chelm. Kasrilevke and the nameless ghetto of Becker's 1969 novel and screenplay *Jakob der Lügner* (*Jacob the Liar* [1997]) have much in common. Both are crowded urban spaces cut off from the outside world. Both have little access to the news. In Kasrilevke, only one man—Zeydl, the son of Reb Shaye—subscribes to a newspaper, and a Hebrew one at that, while in the ghetto, only one man—Jacob Heym—has access to a radio, or at least he pretends to. In both towns, the Jews do not have enough to eat. Ineffectual though they are in the real world, from which they have been largely excluded, the people of Kasrilevke create an alternative reality, sustaining their faith in a higher truth by using language as a protective shield (Roskies 1984, 163–83; Wisse 1971, 44–57). Stripped of all protection in the real world, from which they have been totally excluded, the people of Becker's ghetto create an alternative reality and resort to lying to save themselves from despair. Lying, indeed, becomes a higher form of truth precisely because the outside world is carrying out a genocidal scheme through its own fantastic web of lies. In both places, humor is the first line of defense, because where real action is impossible—"Not a single righteous shot was fired," says Becker's narrator, a worldly-wise Jewish survivor, "there was never a trace of resistance" (ibid., 80)—reaction becomes the only way a people can define itself. Kasrilevke is ultimately destroyed inadvertently, through fire and flight. A worse fate awaits the ghetto.

Ghetto comedians, true to the art of lying, played fast and loose with historical fact. Since Becker's ghetto remains nameless, it is enough to know that, like the 65,000 Jews who still remained in the Łódź ghetto, its residents came pretty close to surviving the war until, with the Red Army virtually at their doorstep, they were crammed into cattle cars heading to Auschwitz, innocent of the fate that awaited them. *Jacob the Liar* has two endings: one make-believe, mimicking the novel's central theme of lying as a response to despair, in which the Russians liberate the ghetto and Jacob dies a hero, and the other historical, in which the Russians don't save the Jews and Jacob is gassed. The last ghetto comedian is the narrator himself.

In America, where the very idea of a city of Jews was a laughable throwback to the old country, the novelist Leslie Epstein, Becker's contemporary, wrote a ghetto farce called *King of the Jews* (1979). Who were the members of the Judenräte if not the Wise Men of Chelm? Who were the ghettoites if not the offspring of the Chelmites? Who were the European Jews if not a barbershop quintet of comic-sounding names straight out of vaudeville: Luftgas, Sheftelowitz, Klapholtz, Szpilfogel, and that real gas, Philosoff? What was the ghetto if not a Rabelaisian carnival, complete with raw sewage, shit brigades, rotting corpses, all-night cabarets, aging whores, and a stand-up comedian with a hackneyed repertoire of Horowitz jokes? Who was Mordecai Chaim Rumkowski if not king of the Jews? Like his namesake, Jesus, Rumkowski, fancied himself a savior of the children, who—in Epstein's retelling—were the only ghettoites endowed with real agency. The children of Isaiah Chaim Trumpelman's orphanage organized themselves into a gang of smugglers, clandestine photographers, and, finally, ghetto fighters. Like the author, they were orphans in history, one of whose number would survive to tell this grotesquely comic and sadly dated tale.

The Łódź ghetto of the comic imagination was thin on the layered social panorama of a city and thin on a direct depiction of the slaughter. As presentations of Holocaust "lite," Becker's and Epstein's works were enormously popular. *Jacob the Liar* was translated into English in 1975 and 1990 and made into two movies, in 1974 and 1999. Epstein's novel is still in print. To restore both the city and the slaughter, two writers who survived the ghettos of Łódź and Warsaw as children adopted the conventions of the family saga. Chava Rosenfarb, who spent the entire war in the Łódź ghetto, and Bogdan Wojdowski, who survived two years in the Warsaw ghetto, each produced an epic work tracking the lives of multiple families. Rosenfarb's families are spread out over the expanse of the ghetto and its adjacent suburb, and her work requires a map (in the English-language edition) to situate them, while Wojdowski's families share a single courtyard. Rosenfarb's 1972 *Der boym fun lebn*, translated as *The Tree of Life* (1985), is a redemptive narrative; Wojdowski's 1971 *Chleb rzucony umarłym*, translated as *Bread for the Departed* (1997), augurs the end.

Rosenfarb's characters are free agents within their respective age cohorts and social positions. The Yiddish poet Simkhe Bunem Shayevitsh, appearing under the thin disguise of Bunim Berkovitch, his precocious eight-year-old Blimele at his side, debates the ethics of ghetto writing with Rachel, Rosenfarb's fictional stand-in, who blossoms into womanhood and artistic selfhood just as the ghetto faces its end. Rosenfarb endows the poet with special agency because she wrote this trilogy as a testament to Shayevitsh's artistic mentorship and personal devotion (Rosenfarb 1973, 138). As for the villains, they remain true to the familiar outlines of the Yiddish family saga. Rosenberg, the rich Jewish industrialist of Book I, sells his soul to the devil in Book III. Once a greedy capitalist, always a greedy capitalist. Then something unexpected happens. Having followed the fate of these representative families as far as the last transport, the book ends abruptly with the abrogation of language, life, and meaning, in the gas chambers and crematoria of Auschwitz. All the addresses the reader has been tracking end at one place, followed by six blank pages— one page per million dead.

To orchestrate the cacophony of sounds, curses, rhymes, and voices and the daily simultaneity of violence, starvation, and prophetic madness, thirty-nine-year-old Bogdan Wojdowski invited the ghost of James Joyce to help him create a modernist, maximalist epic. As in Joyce's *Ulysses*, Wojdowski's literary palimpsest invoked the foundational myths of the civilization that was home to his formidable cast of characters, even as he parodied, pilloried, and radically recast these myths, from Genesis to Exodus, from creation to apocalypse.

First, Wojdowski introduces us to the family of David Fremde (the last name means foreigner)—his grandfather, father, and uncles—who speak in a mixture of Polish, Yiddish, and Hebrew. Chapter 1 finds them celebrating the festival of Purim, which commemorates the triumph of ancient Jews over those Persians who wished to destroy them. The celebration is interrupted by storm troopers who break into the apartment, smashing everything in sight, destroying the protective mezuzah on the doorpost, and dragging Fremde's aunt away for daring to protest. By the novel's end, most of the major Jewish festivals will be described—and desecrated. As in Joyce, there are elements of the bildungsroman, including David's formal education at the hands of Dr. Baum and his induction into Barukh Oks's gang of ghetto smugglers. As in Joyce, there are forays into forbidden realms (the Aryan side of Warsaw), nighttime reveries and a motley assortment of nightmares, all held together by ancient practices, motifs, and scripts. The same mezuzah that a German officer rips out of the wall and desecrates in the opening chapter becomes a talisman for the young smugglers in the middle chapter, then a conduit for secret messages in the closing chapter. But it is the struggle for daily bread, the cries of the beggars and peddlers for bread, the changing currency of bread, the dream of bread, the criminal acts for bread, and the sanctification of bread that pull all the disparate strands together.

Wojdowski's novel is completely anomalous in this period of anticommunal Holocaust narrative because its center of consciousness, David Fremde, is inducted into the ineluctable fate of his people, even as he alone is fated to carry on. Yet whose school of interpretation is David to follow: Grandfather's, who believes that Scripture is a prophecy about the future, or Professor Baum's, who argues that the Holy Bible conceals astronomical observations? David reflects: "People say that someone is following his star; the Jews, too, were following their star until they reached the Promised Land, and there's no doubt about that. He closed his eyes tight, making a great effort to imagine his own star, but the words from the letter forced their way into his thoughts and something terrible and suffocating fell onto his face" (Wojdowski 1997, 204).

In the contest between Grandfather's covenantal reading of history prodded by miracle and Dr. Baum's scientific reading of the universe, Grandfather will be proved right, because the end of Polish Jewry—so vividly and scrupulously recorded by the boy David, whose lone star will continue to shine—is prefigured by its scriptural beginning. At every turn, on every street, in every encounter, the terms of the covenant are invoked only to be defied and defiled, in the writing of a new and more terrible Bible. The people of David's book are "Leibush with the fish scales on his skin; Roizele, dragging her swollen foot in the dust; Long Itzhok, Moishe the Crip, Henio the Herring." "How many of them were there?" he asks. "Living dead," he answers. "They surround him relentlessly, watch him greedily, with pained attention, as if he were a piece of bread that had been thrown to them." Their loyal scribe, "he sits over a piece of paper with nothing on it, where to the left of the equal sign a steep fraction, bristling with difficulties, piles up, and on the right side is a long product of squared parentheses linked to each other like freight cars. Is he sleeping? In his delirium, the faint, repulsed figures move about, circling timidly, hanging over him, and he feels they are poised to punch his neck" (ibid., 208–9).

Hunger consumes him as he falls asleep, and hunger serves as a metaphor for his art, executed with mathematical precision ("to the left of the equal sign a steep fraction"), as befits a disciple of Dr. Baum's, for it falls to David to chronicle how each person perishes, whether from hunger or a well-aimed bullet fired by Bloody Hands, the German policeman who zealously guards the ghetto gate, or in the great deportation, which is described here in excruciating, unparalleled detail. As the last Jews of David's courtyard are rounded up, someone from a neighboring street warns them not to go to Umschlagplatz, because everyone is being led to the slaughter in a demonic substantiation of the Exodus: "The smoke rises to the sky; the smoke can be seen everywhere. . . . *Loy yamish amud he'onon yomam ve'amud ho'eysh layla lifney ha'om.* Jews, remember!" (ibid., 374). Among the last sights of the little ghetto that David records, before being marched off to an unknown future, are enormous, bloated gray rats feeding on the carcasses of Jews shot during the last and most terrible roundup, "aggressive rats that seemed to want to reach the faces of the living" (ibid., 389). Nowhere was the Final Solution more final than this.

Once the whole habitation and all who lived therein have been destroyed, what is the tally sheet of survival? For both Hilsenrath and Rawicz, it is a tale of survival at any price. Deborah presumably survives Ranek, though Hilsenrath's pitiless narrative is assuredly not hers. Boris's "tool" is literally incomparable, other than as the emblem of a new and terrible anticovenant. Endlessly in transit, fleeing himself and the fate that awaits him, his survival is as arbitrary as the story he tells. Becker and Epstein turn survival into the stuff of dark comedy. Jacob Heym, whose surname means "home" and who makes his home in a world of fantasy and deception, dies either as a hero or a martyr; the narrator survives, in order to give the reader a choice. One of Trumpelman's orphans survives the carnage, and as children are wont to see adult behavior as laughable, their world as caricature, so too does he. Rosenfarb and Wojdowski are the great exceptions. Rosenfarb's focus is on the tree, not the individual branch. Her novel makes real the abstract idea of the ghetto as a social organism. Having come of age in a city of Jews whose total destruction was hers to witness, Rachel constructs a linear narrative of group survival, prolonged death, and six blank pages, which ends with precious, precarious rebirth: she spots a cherry tree outside her tenement apartment in postwar Brussels. Wojdowski witnessed almost the same trajectory, only David's account is resolutely cyclical, fusing the mythic beginning of the people of Israel with a minutely realized account of their end, an apocalypse that refuses to end.

The Ugly Survivor

In biblical times, a person guilty of involuntary manslaughter could seek protection in one of six cities of refuge, three of which were east of the Jordan, and three were to the west. In modern times, a survivor of the mass slaughter could seek refuge from the pain of the past on the Left or Right Bank of Paris or in any one of New York City's five boroughs. On the most basic level, Yiddish writers during the 1950s were desperate to find cities of refuge where their fictional characters could feel at home speaking in their murdered mother tongue, which is how Chaim Vilner and Hersh Rasseyner, still locked in fierce debate, moved from prewar Białystok to Vilna in the Free Zone and then to postwar Paris (Grade 1999); how I. B. Singer's circle of misfits ended up in Hertz Dovid Makover's smoke-filled living room on New York's Upper West Side in the mid-1950s (Singer 1998), and how his "Last Demon," in the story of that name originally published in 1959, found shelter in an attic in the *Juden-* and Devil-*rein* shtetl of Tishevitz (Singer 1983b). Even "The Cafeteria" on Broadway would do, for close Yiddish encounters of the demonic kind (Singer 1983a). A few Jews talking was the sum total of what remained from a nation of arguers and kibitzers.

But it turns out that there was no good place to hide: neither on the Left Bank, where the unnamed narrator of *Blood from the Sky* owned a café, nor on the storied Place de l'Etoile, where Raphael Schlemielovitch—a white slaver, thief, fraud, cheat, usurer, and murderer—ruled the roost (Modiano 1968); neither in Sol Nazerman's pawnshop in Harlem (Wallant 1961) nor on Artur Sammler's usual beat on New York's Upper West Side, where African American pickpockets plied their trade in the open (Bellow 1970). Just as Sophie Zawitowski failed to escape her Polish past in a Brooklyn boardinghouse in the arms of her demented Jewish lover (Styron 1979), so did Rosa Lublin, the madwoman and scavenger, after smashing up her store in New York and moving to Miami (Ozick 1983). The Holocaust survivor Herman Broder may have had a wife or lover in Coney Island, the Bronx, and the Lower East Side, but each woman, like Broder, was a victim twice over, inhabiting a haunted landscape (Singer 1972). The perpetrators were also pursued by their dybbuks, like Hans Helmut Schatz, the police chief of a small town called Licht, who was inhabited by the spirit of Moishe "Genghis" Cohn, a one-time Yiddish comedian (Gary 1968).

West of the Jordan lay the State of Israel, home to the largest concentration of Holocaust survivors on earth. Now middle-aged men and women who spoke with accents of varying heaviness, who made up the rank and file of the Labor Party, and who were busy creating new families (Yablonka 2004, 155–71), these "unfamiliar and anonymous people" had assumed for the old-timers and Sabras an essential "image" ever since the Eichmann trial. In Hebrew—as in French and American—works of the literary imagination, however, came to represent a counterreality, a wound that could not be healed. As opposed to the survivors in fact, the survivors in fiction began to be fitted with the armbands of the outsider, the alienated, uprooted individual who was far from home.

Their chief spokesman was Aharon Appelfeld, whose protected childhood as the only child of assimilated German-speaking Jews ended in 1941, when the Romanian and German forces seized control of his native Bukovina, murdered his mother and grandmother, and incarcerated him and his father in the Czernowitz ghetto. The Romanians then sent them to do forced labor in Transnistria. Escaping alone from a labor camp at the age of nine, Appelfeld lived on the run for the next three years, until he met up with the Red Army and got work as a kitchen boy. More wanderings followed, through Yugoslavia and Italy, alone and with other refugees, until Youth Aliyah, on the lookout for orphans like himself, discovered him on the crowded beaches of Naples and arranged to have him smuggled into Palestine, where he landed once more in a camp, this time under British guard (Sokoloff 2004). Like the brothers Orlowski-Orlev before him, young Appelfeld was soon absorbed into the agricultural and communal life of a nation aborning. He changed his first name from Erwin to the Hebrew Aharon and set out to master Hebrew. Unlike the brothers Orlev, who had been immersed in Polish language and culture, Appelfeld brought no real language with him, only a mishmash of German, Romanian, Ukrainian, and some Yiddish picked up from fellow refugees along the way. Just as Jerzy Kosinski (1965) adopted the trope of muteness to render the essential condition of the Jew in hiding, the haunted—and hunted—bird, Appelfeld created a gallery of Holocaust survivors whose essential condition was defined by their very transience, the poverty of their speech, and the failure of Zionism to rescue them from their oedipal struggle (Hever 1999, 63, 66–67).

Appelfeld established his name as a teller of spare and spooky tales, in volumes whose titles bespoke a symbolic landscape outside of time: *Ashan* (Smoke; 1963), *Begai haporeh* (In the fertile valley; 1965), and *Kefor 'al ha'arets* (Frost on the earth; 1965). The characters he brought to life had technically survived, though all were still trapped. The physical setting—the smoke, the valley, the forest, the frost, the wilderness, the desert, the road—signified a world of impossible moral choices, of estrangement, enmity, and self-blame. Grounded in a historical reality never mentioned by name, these stories were set either before or after, like all allegory. It was an all-Jewish landscape devoid of Jews.

"Bertha," from his inaugural collection of 1963, exemplifies Appelfeld's method. Fifteen years have passed since Max and Bertha escaped the slaughter. He had received her in the dead of winter "during the big escape when the others couldn't take her" (Appelfeld 1999, 20). She is now his helpless charge in Jerusalem, to all the world an overgrown autistic child, who spends her days "knitting for Maxie" and unraveling her knitting by nightfall. He—a productive member of society—works at a bottling plant somewhere so far to the north that it requires his absence for long periods at a time. She is immobile and fixed; he comes and goes as he pleases. Both, in fact, are fragmented, just as their story is so difficult to piece together. She is ageless and insulated; registering no visible change, she lives in a fantasy world of eternal light. Has Bertha perhaps enchanted him, and that is why he cannot leave her for Mitzi and start a normal, married life? Or is Bertha Max's dybbuk, his haunted past, and therefore—try as he might over the course of this story—he cannot be rid of her? Passive on the surface, both female characters reveal themselves to be the active partners: Mitzi refuses to join Max in institutionalizing Bertha, and Bertha herself unexpectedly blossoms during his last absence. It is as if, the world having betrayed her, Bertha no longer depends on the world for validation or a sense of self.

Appelfeld's characters are wound tight, not within any cycle of natural time (Max works for a man named Frost) but within mythic time, where the loyal Penelope, awaiting the return of her beloved husband, is forever weaving a shroud by day and tearing it apart by night. A deep melancholy suffuses the lives of all his characters, as well as the narrator's voice.

A generation of the wilderness, these writer survivors were in search of a language in which to write and of the literary means to displace the historical. Even those who continued to write in their native language sought refuge among speakers of a foreign tongue, never fully at home. Edgar Hilsenrath met the German-Jewish writer Jakov Lind in Israel, when the two of them were hoping to find a day job in construction. Abandoning their Zionist dreams and the project of nation building (Lind had served in the military police and as an air traffic controller), and moving to a new country that wasn't German-speaking, both adopted a brutal, dispassionate, sometimes parodic style. Hilsenrath wrote the second draft of *Night* (1966) on the Upper West Side of New York. Lind wrote *Eine Seele aus Holz: Erzählungen* (*Soul of Wood*, 1964) in London. Hilsenrath's portrayal of Jewish depravity proved so repugnant to his German (especially German Jewish) audience that, having sold a mere 791 copies, his publisher pulled it from the market (Klingenstein 2004).

Some, like Henryk Grynberg and Arnošt Lustig, became political exiles, choosing never to return. Liberated from Communist Poland by an invitation to study in the United States, twenty-four-year-old Jerzy Kosinski embarked on a double life. Using ghost translators and editors, he established his reputation as an expert on communism. Then came his electrifying first novel, *The*

FIGURE 15
Aharon Appelfeld.
Badenheim 1939.
Boston: Godine, 1980.
Jacket illustration by
Nancy Lawton.

Badenheim 1939

a novel by
Aharon Appelfeld

Painted Bird (1965), which he claimed to have written in English himself and to be a true account of his horrific childhood experiences as a hunted child. An international bestseller that redefined the genre of the Holocaust memoir, it was condemned by his fellow Poles as a slander against the Polish people. The intellectual circles of New York, meanwhile, were more forgiving of his duplicity, especially after Kosinski publicly acknowledged his Jewishness in 1968 (Adamczyk-Garbowska 1999; Lilly 2004). But when his celebrity plummeted and he had run out of life stories to reinvent, Kosinski took his own life.

Perhaps there really was no place of refuge, neither in the postwar present nor in the reimagined past. If the theme was entrapment, then the literary vehicle could be anything at all. Only a bus ride away from the Jerusalem hospital where Appelfeld's Bertha died during Max's absence was Mrs. Seitzling's Institute for Rehabilitation and Therapy in Arad, where Yarom Kaniuk's (1971) Adam Stein, a circus clown and concentration camp comedian, is sent away to be healed. And only one time-trip away from Appelfeld's Jerusalem in the early 1960s is the Austrian resort town of Badenheim in the last summer before the war (Appelfeld 1980). The work's rich and representative cast of characters serve as the vehicle for a community arbitrarily assembled and doomed to disaster.

Cast ashore in their New Worlds, fictional landed immigrants cut a grotesque figure: Adam Stein chooses madness for as long as it suits him. What drives Rosa Lublin is her implacable anger. Artur Sammler's daughter, Shula, is emotionally crippled by her experiences; his son-in-law, Eisen, is a brutalized man of iron; Bruch, a survivor of Buchenwald, is appropriately named Hernia; and Artur himself—named after Schopenhauer, the philosopher of nihilism, who preached that the sex organs are the seat of the will—is the collector, anthropologist, observer, his one good eye a symbol of suffering and survival—leaving him one blind eye to look inward. All told, they are ugly survivors, studies in alienation.

The Survivor as Time Traveler

Unhinged from its source languages, its geography, the constraints of testimony, and the need to forge a consistent group narrative, the literature on the Holocaust experienced something remarkable in this third period of its development: it became temporally displaced as well. Try though the Library of Congress might to delimit the temporal scope of the "Holocaust, Jewish" to the years of the Second World War, the writer survivors had plans of their own. One of those writers was Dan Pagis, an Israeli poet and scholar of medieval Hebrew poetry. In 1970, he published this six-line poem, destined to become, along with Celan's "Todesfuge," a poem of almost scriptural authority:

KATUV BE'IPARON BAKARON HEHATUM
kan bamishloah hazeh
ani Hava
im Hevel beni
im tir'u et beni hagadol
Kayin ben Adam
tagidu lo she'ani

WRITTEN IN PENCIL IN THE SEALED RAILWAY CAR
here in this carload
I am eve
with abel my son
if you see my other son
cain son of man
tell him that I (Pagis 1981, 23)

With absolute precision, Pagis displaces space into time. The universal reach of the Nazi genocide is immediately apprehendable because the graffiti discovered (by whom?) inside the sealed railway car, of the kind that transported

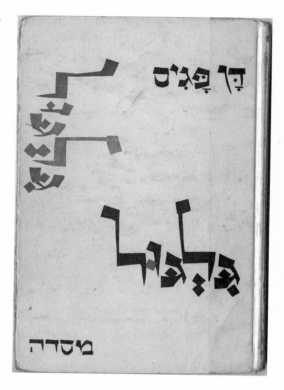

FIGURE 16

Dan Pagis, *Gilgul: shirim.*
Ramat-Gan, Israel: Massada,
1970. The poem "Katuv
be'iparon bakaron heḥatum"
originally appeared in
this volume.

millions of Jews to their deaths, is addressed to Cain, the world's first murderer—related, through a brilliant pun, to Ezekiel, the prophet of the resurrection, the only "Son of Man [ben Adam]" in the Hebrew Bible. And what is
this writing? Is it a memorial, an act of defiance, an apocalyptic warning, akin
to Daniel's writing on the wall; an amulet, perhaps, an invocation of God's
name designed to guard its bearer against evil? Why, then, have a mother and
son been shipped off to their death, which is far worse than "just" a brother killing his own brother, for in this carload something has happened that eclipses
everything that happened before—although as in Genesis, only Cain is left
on earth, which suggests that every reader of this poem is a member of the
Cain-anite race, carrying the curse of perpetual wandering and murder. Every
survivor is Cain, and Cain is every survivor, which in turn suggests that this
poem too was "published" (for someone had to provide the title) out of guilt,
his brother's blood crying out to the poet publisher and, by extension, to each
one of us. The first generation used biblical and historical referents that merge
and coexist with the present. Pagis uses the present to disfigure the past.

Like Appelfeld, Pagis uses Hebrew against the grain, a language at once
colloquial and strange—like the Holocaust survivor in our midst, like the

memory of the dead. As Sidra Ezrahi has noted, Pagis relinquished "the mimetic project in his poetry," renounced chronology, dispensed with "the available strategies for structuring experience through the myths . . . by which a community remembers," and—finally, in the most courageous act of all—"surrendered the 'privileged' status of the survivor" (1994, 126).

Pagis's response to the Holocaust was temporally "displaced" in two other senses: between his arrival on the shores of British Mandatory Palestine as a sixteen-year-old refugee from Romania, ignorant of Hebrew, and the 1970 publication of *Gilgul* (Metamorphosis), where his first Holocaust poetry appeared, nearly a quarter-century had passed. So thoroughly in the interim had Pagis assimilated the rich classical tradition of the language that in his scholarly work he became the foremost living authority on the poetics of Hebrew literature in the high Middle Ages and the Renaissance. Israeli readers knew him primarily as a writer of children's literature. But from 1970 onward, Pagis's "poetry of displacement" (Alter 1981) became the sanctioned way of writing about the Holocaust in a language and landscape at once familiar and strange. Today, his six-line poem is engraved in Hebrew, English, and Polish in the Bełżec Victims' Memorial.

Charlotte Delbo returned to Paris from Buenos Aires in 1941 to rejoin her husband, who was working with the Communist underground. She was caught by the Gestapo, who shipped her off to Auschwitz-Birkenau in a woman's transport, then on to Ravensbrück. She was among the 49 women who survived from that original transport of 230. Auschwitz became the subject of *Aucun de nous ne reviendra* (*None of Us Will Return*), a series of unusual prose poems, which would eventually form the first volume of a trilogy. Invented by one French poet, Aloysius Bertrand, in 1842 and popularized by another, Charles Baudelaire, the prose poem aimed at discerning or revealing something that was inaccessible through the more restrictive conventions of verse. Indeed, the essential distinction between looking and not looking became the moral and experiential nexus of Delbo's poem. In order to communicate the incommunicable, she mixed up time as she did her prose and poetry. In "Arrivals, Departures," the opening canto, Auschwitz is described as the largest railroad station in the world, where the new arrivals "expect the worst—not the unthinkable" (Delbo 1995, 4). All things coexist: ordinary arrivals and departures elsewhere in Europe or somewhere in one's past with these dead-end ones; picturesque train stations with Station Auschwitz; documented travelers with numberless, anonymous arrivals. Here all of Europe meets, in the most cosmopolitan station in the world. A mother slaps her child for misbehaving. She doesn't know it's their last moment together. She doesn't know that it makes no difference. Here all of Europe ends, the end of the road simultaneous with the end of the poem, except for those accursed few who entered the

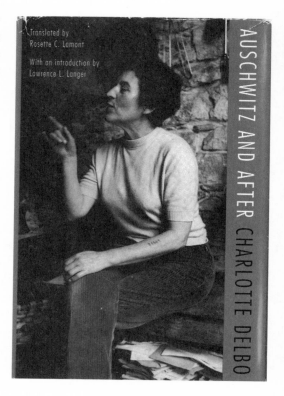

FIGURE 17

Charlotte Delbo. *Auschwitz
and After*. New Haven: Yale
University Press, 1995. Jacket
photo by Eric Schwab.

camp and "tell themselves it would have been far better never to have entered, never to have found out" (ibid., 9). There follow cantos titled "One Day," "The Next Day," "The Same Day," and even "Sunday," but time in Auschwitz will have no relationship to anything familiar. The poet ends the first book of her Auschwitz trilogy in "Springtime," a place of remembrance "outside of time" (ibid., 112).

None of Us Will Return is a journey from life to death, which is written in a mélange of poetry and prose that allows Delbo, Auschwitz No. 31569, to strip away the multiple layers of memory. The first—though chronologically the last—is survivor time in the present: Delbo is sitting in a Parisian café as she writes these lines. Frozen just beneath the present surface lies terror time—standing motionless in the snow during roll call. Roll Call is both punctual and never ending. But to allow one to look, really look, at the core of that collective experience, the prisoner (and reader) must arrive at trauma time—one's first death experience, the deepest level of personal memory.

"This night will never end," says the guy from Saumur, the leitmotif of Jorge Semprún's 1963 symphonic novel *Le long voyage* (*The Long Voyage*, 1964). This awareness is the one familiar signpost that accompanies the transport of prisoners all the way to the gates of death—and will accompany some fortunate few on their journey home. Like Delbo, Semprún entered the war as a member of the Communist underground, all of whose heroic exploits and acts of betrayal were suddenly derailed the moment he was caught and found himself bound for some unknown destination in the East. Like Delbo, he somehow survived, and as he struggles to recover the unreality of that prolonged nightmare, he too must dispense with linearity. As a twenty-year-old, he traveled light. "I'm twenty," he writes, as if still living in the present, "I don't give a damn about memory" (ibid., 29). Fifteen or twenty years later, he discovers, the personal and group memory of that journey will weigh heavier still, not only because the experience of the concentration camps lies so far beyond the quotidian, but also because "this night will never end." Punctuating the initial journey of 1943 is his return to the camp two years later, when, accompanied by "two incredible girls," he registers the "real shock" of seeing it from the outside, as if for the first time. Keen to experience the horror after the fact, the "poor girls" suddenly realize that the kitchen they're standing in is not a kitchen but a crematorium (ibid., 68, 72, 76). Even for the visitor, let alone the former inmate, atrocity does not remain safely buried in the past.

In 1943, Semprún's personal life, like that of Delbo and Levi, was cut in half. All three had entered the war eager to play a part in the narrative of resistance. War's end found each of them cast ashore on the other side of time. Defying psychic vertigo, Delbo produced her first sequence of prose poems in 1946, then put them away in her desk drawer. The time was not yet ripe, certainly not on the Left Bank of Paris, for something quite so artful, gendered, and apolitical. She waited until a new period of public memory, ushered in by the critical acclaim of Semprún's *The Long Voyage* and major defections from the ranks of the French Communist Party, which allowed her to publish and augment her cycle of prose poems. Written in 1970 mostly in prosaic form, *The Measure of Our Days*, the last volume of her trilogy, tracks the survivor's journey home and shows the impossibility of picking up again where she left off.

The passage of time made ever greater artistic and psychological demands on the survivor and witness. Semprún's journey from life to death and back again was not communicable as a linear voyage within fixed points. To render the simultaneity of life and death and the actual experience of thirst—what it tastes like in your dreams and thoughts, not only on your lips—Delbo adopted the hybrid form of the prose poem, invented in more innocent times to capture an already conflated act of remembering. The narrative of survival in Auschwitz, which Primo Levi was able in 1946 to lay out in a sequential sequence of analytically concise short stories, reappeared in a 1975 later collection of twenty-one short stories as embedded within *The Periodic Table* (1984). This chemical taxonomy of existence (as we described it in our Guide to the

First Hundred Books), which by definition can never be complete, includes Levi's experience in Auschwitz as but one basic building block of a life that challenges the very idea of coherence and continuity. After Auschwitz, the concept and formal properties of autobiography must change, too.

No one understood this better than Abraham Sutzkever. Still in wartime, the creative—and moral—focus of Sutzkever's poetry began to shift from chronicling the here and now to engaging the greater enemy, time itself. "Look out at the snow," he wrote on his joyful reunion with nature, his first and beloved home: "In memory's art / Is expected / Radiance, and in / The speeches of the heart, / You yourself are / Resurrected" (Sutzkever 1989b). Yet when the heat of a Moscow summer suddenly recalled "in fields of snow, / frozen Jews, row on row," the impossible juxtaposition of ice and fire, of marbled beauty and absolute horror, drove the survivor to the edge of insanity (Sutzkever 1991a). And what were the "Epitaphs" over which he labored for three years, in the Vilna ghetto, Moscow, and Łódź, if not a desperate attempt to leave something behind, by giving voice to the dead (Sutzkever 1988b)?

Sutzkever engaged time in solitary combat, so as not to allow living memory to recede or become dulled over time. When poetry proved insufficient, he turned, like Delbo, to the prose poem, the gift of the French poets to the survivor journeying through multiple time zones. Calling his 1955 cycle of prose poems "Green Aquarium" (1982), Sutzkever stated that his purpose was to "see the dead," to recapture momentary glimpses of certain persons and events, despite the barrier of intervening time (Sutzkever 1991d, 357–69). Written in highly charged figurative language and a syncopated rhythm, the poems follow a loose chronology from the first *Aktionen* in the Vilna ghetto to the day of liberation. Thanks to this new medium, Sutzkever turned himself into the prism through which the past would be briefly rendered (Wisse 1982, 95).

Sutzkever's response to the Holocaust unfolded both backward and forward: backward, as he published previously unknown work; forward, as he produced new work of ever greater subtlety. In 1979 it all came together. In that year Sutzkever, under his own imprimatur, published a tiny volume called *Di ershte nakht in geto: lider, lidvariantn, fragmentn, geshribn in di khurbn-yorn 1941–1944* (The first night in the ghetto: poems, poem-variants, fragments, written during the Holocaust 1941–1944). What was so special about these "variants" and "fragments" that they warranted separate publication? What did they contain that could not be published before? They contained censored memories, overtly confessional poems, and antiheroic stanzas that he now felt free to make public, with appropriate drawings commissioned from the Vilna-born artist Samuel Bak (Sutzkever 1979a).

Enlisting the services of another Vilna-bred artist, Yonia Fain, more grotesque and minimalist than Bak, Sutzkever published *Dortn vu es nekhtikn di*

PLATE 1] Janusz Nel Siedlecki, Krystyn Olszewski, and Tadeusz Borowski. *We Were in Auschwitz*. Edited by Tadeusz Borowski. New York: Welcome Rain, 2000. Cover designed by Anatol Girs, Munich, 1946.

PLATE 2] Eliezer Wiesel. . . . *un di velt hot geshvign.* Buenos Aires: Tsentral-farband fun poylishe yidn in Argentine, 1956. Volume 117 of Dos poylishe yidntum.

(opposite)
PLATE 3] Curzio Malaparte. *Kaputt.* 1st paperback ed. New York: Avon, 1966. Cover art by Don Crowley.

AVON / N135 / 95¢

OVER 1½ MILLION COPIES SOLD

KAPUTT

CURZIO MALAPARTE

author of THE SKIN

**The turbulent epic of a
ravished continent in the throes of decadence,
debauchery and unspeakable crimes**

PLATE 4] André Schwarz-Bart. *The Last of the Just*. New York: Atheneum, 1960. Cover design by George Salter.

PLATE 5] Piotr Rawicz. *Blood from the Sky*. New York:
Harcourt, Brace and World, 1964.

Scroll of Agony
The Warsaw Diary of Chaim A. Kaplan
Translated and Edited by Abraham I. Katsh

PLATE 6] Chaim A. Kaplan. *Scroll of Agony: The Warsaw Diary of Chaim A. Kaplan.* New York: Macmillan, 1965. Jacket design by Lawrence Ratzkin.

דויד גרוסמן

עיין ערך: 'אהבה'

PLATE 7] David Grossman. *'Ayyen 'erekh: 'ahava.'* Tel Aviv: Hakibbutz Hameuchad, 1986. Cover art by Jean Dubuffet.

PLATE 8] Art Spiegelman. *Maus: A Survivor's Tale.* New York: Pantheon, 1986.
Cover art by Art Spiegelman.

FIGURE 18

Abraham Sutzkever.
Di ershte nakht in geto: lider,
lidvariantn, fragmentn, geshribn
in di khurbn-yorn 1941–1944.
Tel Aviv: Di goldene keyt,
1979. Cover design and
illustrations by Samuel Bak.

אבֿרהם סוצקעווער
די ערשטע נאַכט אין געטאָ

shtern (Where the stars spend the night; Sutzkever 1979b). These truly fantasti-cal tales render a deranged reality, in which cloistered present—the survivor as Yiddish writer living on the top floor of an apartment building in upscale Tel Aviv—encounters severed past, unexpected visitations that suddenly ac-quire the status of broken-down myths (ibid.; see also 1991d, 373–422). The visitations happen in random order, weaving in and out of the various sta-tions in the poet's life. Most occur in the Vilna ghetto during the "time of the slaughter-knife": "Lupus," "Where the Stars Spend the Night," "Faithful Needles" and "Glikele." One horrific tale, "The Boot and the Crown," revisits the Narocz forest, where Sutzkever fought with the Soviet partisans; and the last, "The Coin from Heaven," returns us to his childhood in Siberia. Because the poet takes precedence over the chronicler and the stories are populated by the dead who are alive, they yield biographical information only to someone who already knows the poet's life story.

In the sixth and seventh decades of his life, Sutzkever redefined the auto-biographical project. *Poems from My Diary*, written in the period 1974–85 and universally recognized as his crowning poetic achievement, is an exercise in time travel. The poems share with a diary the use of the first-person singular; are ordered chronologically; and are full of names, places, and occurrences. Sutzkever's diary, however, is not governed by the course of biographical or historical events, is self-reflexive without being the least bit confessional, and is not addressed to a physical reader. Its direction is a time beyond time.

Of two poems that deal directly with the Holocaust, one is dedicated to the memory of Yanova Bartoszewicz, the Polish Christian peasant who hid Sutzkever in her cellar and brought food to his family in the ghetto; and the second is about a tiny memento that arrives from present-day Vilna, now known as Vilnius (Sutzkever 1988a). Master of metonymy, Sutzkever has found the tiniest possible part to stand for the catastrophic whole. Although nearly half a century has elapsed, Sutzkever's memory is nurtured by the same habitat as before: the bounty and beauty of nature.

In 1943 the emblem of resistance was a "Flower," a flower with blue petals and a nucleus of gold that the poet's nameless "neighbor" tried to smuggle past the ghetto gate—and paid for that deed with seven lashes to his body (Sutzkever 1968, 75). In "1981" it is but a single blade of grass from somewhere far away, smuggled into a letter by someone from a former life: a natural artifact from the farthest reaches of time and place. The flower was physically rescued by a man. The blade of grass was plucked and delivered by a woman. In between, the natural and human habitat were ground to ashes.

Well along in years now, the poet receives a letter from the town of his birth. Written by a woman he once loved, the letter contains a touching memento: a blade of grass. True, the contents of the letter are probably more complicated, for the memento is enclosed in *"ir libshaft un ir tsar"* ("between torment and fondness"). That wrenching of opposites is ever present in Sutzkever's poetry, never more so than during the war. In any event, the aging, distant lover ends the poem by swearing never to part with his blade of grass and pledges to take it with him to the grave—a typical poetic gesture. Each of the poem's four stanzas ends with a ballad-like refrain about the blade of grass.

The odd word out is *Ponar*, and the full line reads: "a blade of grass from Ponar" (Sutzkever 1988a). Once upon a time, lovers picnicked in Ponar, and its flora and fauna were the subject of botanical study. Then came the Germans, and they and their willing Lithuanian helpers turned Ponar into the killing field of Vilna Jewry. So "a blade of grass from Ponar" is the ultimate metonymy. Once a stand-in for the life-giving cycle of nature and young love, it now represents the slaughter, the tsunami that destroyed everything in its path. "A blade of grass from Ponar" is also the perfect combination of opposites, yoking together as it does two irreconcilable realms. Plucked from its natural habitat, the blade of grass takes on a life of its own, uniting the living present with the dead past.

There, in the past, under a "moribund cloud," the poet "kindled the alpha-bet" and became the bard of destruction (ibid.). Thinking that he is safe in his "snug little world" of the present, in the "doll's house" of his mind, suddenly he hears "children play fiddles in rows as they burn." Perhaps they are being lined up to be shot, or perhaps their dead bodies are laid out in rows, the better to be burned in a huge pyre. Ponar, after all, is a place for all seasons. And orchestrating this slaughter, the ruler over present and past, is the "maestro," death, waving the blade of grass from Ponar. Can there be a more fitting gift than this to bring to the Lord as his "oblation at last"? The good earth in which he longs to be buried, says the poet in the final stanza, will make room for him as well as his precious gift.

Just as Ponar is both a picnic site and a funeral pyre, the blade of grass is both a memento of nature and love and a metonymy of mass death and horror. To put it differently, the Holocaust has rendered an innocent blade of grass from Ponar self-contradictory, yoking two opposite realms together. No wonder the aged lover refuses to part with his memento. It embodies both his method and his meaning. Combining opposites is not merely his preferred poetic mode; it is the essential post-Holocaust condition. As a gift, the blade of grass carries multiple meanings: precious memories; love that is still fragrant and fresh; the wellspring of poetic inspiration that comes from heaven and earth; and the metaphysical gift that connects the human realm to the divine. This gift the poet will take to his grave, where a person is stripped of all illusion.

To the Yiddish ear, any improvised, personal gift, or *matóne*, that is "brought to the Lord" is of a kind with the "Three Gifts" of the master storyteller I. L. Peretz (2002). Whatever Peretz's allegorical intention had been, in the Vilna ghetto, the work was understood to be a story extolling ultimate self-sacrifice. That is why the Teacher Mira had included Peretz's story in her curriculum. Now it was Sutzkever's turn. This fourth gift would not prove Israel's merit in the eyes of heaven. It would redeem no wandering soul that had lost its way between heaven and hell. The blade of grass plucked from the scorched earth of Ponar would express the abiding rage of a poet survivor against a God who watched as His innocent children, the creative life force of the future, were turned to ashes.

Sutzkever's late blossoming as a modern metaphysical poet represents the survivors' journey before time, in time, and against time.

The Survivor in America: One Generation After

Making the calculation that one generation had elapsed since the Liberation, Elie Wiesel used the occasion to issue a manifesto on behalf of all survivors. An indifferent, disbelieving, and hostile world had cowed the survivors into silence, he proclaimed: "They were afraid of saying what must not be said, of attempting to communicate with language what eludes language, of falling into the trap of easy half-truths." "One generation after," these survivors had finally come of age, as would their offspring in due course, so that "from here on," there would be a change: "From now on, one will speak differently about the holocaust. Or not at all" (Wiesel 1972, 13, 17). Through the trope of unspeakability, Wiesel empowered the next generation to see itself as the first to bear witness, and to feel profound outrage at the presumed silence of the prior generation.

Thanks in large measure to Wiesel's efforts, the Holocaust crossed the three great divides—from then to now, from them to us, and from there to here.

FROM THEN TO NOW

On September 27, 1979, the President's Commission on the Holocaust, chaired by Wiesel, presented its report to President Jimmy Carter. *The Report of the President's Commission on the Holocaust* is a remarkable document. Theoretical positions on the meaning and root causes of the Holocaust, which until then had been the province of specialists, appear on its pages as national policy. Emil Fackenheim's "614th commandment" not to grant Hitler a posthumous victory is presented to Carter as an article of faith. So, too, is the shame of President Franklin D. Roosevelt's America, for not doing more to make people believe that the Holocaust was happening "or to translate information into effective action" (President's Commission on the Holocaust 1979, 11; see also iii)—by no means a commonplace in American historiography then—and so, too, are Raul Hilberg's and Richard Rubenstein's analyses of Nazism as "a thoroughly modern expression of bureaucratic organization" (ibid., 4–5). The report contains veiled references to Watergate and openly criticizes the Soviet Union and the Communist bloc in general for having effaced the particular fate of the Jews. "The universality of the Holocaust," writes Wiesel in his oracular mode, "lies in its uniqueness: the Event is essentially Jewish, yet its interpretation is universal" (ibid., iii). (Note that for Wiesel, like the Ineffable Name of God, the Holocaust is best referred to as the "Event.") Consistent with his own manifesto of 1970 is Wiesel's definition of the survivor "as a messenger and guardian of secrets entrusted by the dead" (ibid., iv).

The report enshrined the Holocaust within the civil religion of the United States of America. Beyond the wildest dreams of Rabbi Irving Greenberg when he created the Zakhor Holocaust Resource Center in 1975, the President's Commission on the Holocaust now called for Days of Remembrance of Victims of the Holocaust to be proclaimed in perpetuity and to be held annually. Later called Holocaust Remembrance Week, the date would be fixed each year in accordance with the Jewish calendar. To complete the transformation of the Holocaust into a second Sinai, the source of a new ecumenical revelation, the commission recommended the establishment of a national Holocaust museum in the nation's capital.

FROM THEM TO US

When the first "encounter groups" of children of Holocaust survivors, led by Eva Fogelman and Bella Savran, began to meet in private homes in Boston in the spring of 1976, out came a dirty secret. Beneath the façade of new lives, new families, and new prospects, theirs was a story of unending trauma (Fogelman and Savran 1979). Wanting to protect their children from the past, fearful of bonding with those closest to them lest those people (too) be taken away, the survivors experienced a fear of loving, repressed mourning, and psychic closures—all of which had engendered a powerful sense of identification with suffering on the part of their children, but also rage, depression, and self-loathing. A series of publications brought the problems to light. The first, from Bloch Publishing and therefore not widely known, was *Living after the Holocaust: Reflections by the Post-War Generation in America*, edited by Lucy Steinitz and David Szonyi (1976). There followed an article titled "Heirs of the Holocaust" by Helen Epstein, which appeared in the *New York Times Magazine* on June 19, 1977, and then her influential book, *Children of the Holocaust: Conversations with Sons and Daughters of Survivors* (H. Epstein 1979). Just as the parents had banded together to find and support one another, so too did their children, who founded an International Network of Children of Holocaust Survivors. What had begun as group therapy quickly burgeoned into a movement that was very much in the public eye. Thus was born a second generation unlike any seen before.

Singled out from among their cohort by a historical experience not their own, the residue of the terror experienced by their parents—what the Kabbalists called the *reshimu*—clung to the offspring, marking them for life. Because the catastrophic damage of the Holocaust was felt most profoundly in the psychic realm, working through the trauma could not be accomplished by means of memorializing the lost culture, seeking meaning through analogies and archetypes, or by calling for vengeance—not, in short, by any of the sanctioned means perfected over millennia. Rather, the solution involved psychosocial therapeutic means, facilitated in a group setting.

What bound the children to their parents most powerfully was the myth of suppression. Wiesel's manifesto of 1970 became the rallying cry not just of one generation, but of two. If an indifferent, disbelieving, and hostile world had cowed the survivors into silence because "they were afraid of saying what must not be said, of attempting to communicate with language what eludes language" (Wiesel 1972, 13), and if, "one generation after," these survivors and their offspring had finally come of age, then by banding together to break the silence, they would now force the world to listen. This mandate was doubly liberating, because it turned former victims and their disaffected children into a formidable revolutionary cohort, and it started the memory clock all over again with yet another generation of survivors. Who spoke for the Holocaust were all those who bore its psychic scars and were now prepared to bare them.

FROM THERE TO HERE

America became the global arbiter of Holocaust memory because it was by this time the main purveyor of movies. Increasingly, the real business of public memory was conducted not in smoke-free offices, not in academic seminars, but in popular culture, which increasingly meant on the big and little screens. Even the briefest survey of the feature and documentary films made about the Holocaust reveals a powerful synergy between literature and film. The vaudevillian shtick of Chaplin's 1940 *The Great Dictator* situates it ever so firmly within wartime memory. The high-mindedness of Alexander Ford's 1948 *Border Street*, Alain Resnais and Jean Cayrol's 1955 documentary *Night and Fog*, and Stanley Kramer's 1961 *Judgment at Nuremberg* is the mark of their "communal" aesthetics. The period of provisional memory witnessed a series of daring art films, including Sidney Lumet's *The Pawnbroker* and Andrzej Munk's unfinished masterpiece, *The Passenger*, both from 1963; Jurek Becker's original screenplay for *Jacob the Liar*, written in 1967 and finally filmed in 1974; the heady New Wave of Czech cinema, which brought us Ján Kadár's 1966 *The Shop on Main Street*; Vittorio de Sica's lush 1970 production of *The Garden of the Finzi-Continis*; and Max Ophuls's fiercely polemical *The Sorrow and the Pity*, also from 1970. As was the case with writers, the filmmakers were divided: some believed that the way to keep memory alive was by reopening old wounds (Lumet, Munk, and Ophuls), while for others the memory of the martyrs and fighters, the lovers and losers, was sacred (Ford, Kadár, de Sica, and Becker).

Against this backdrop, Gerald Green's 1978 television miniseries, *Holocaust*, may seem like a giant step backward. Wiesel and other crusaders were predictably outraged at what they saw as a Holocaust soap opera. But 220 million viewers in the United States and Europe watched it, including half of all adults in West Germany (Flanzbaum 2003). Certainly they would remember the portrayal of ss officer Erik Dorf as anything but banal.

Such things are difficult to document, but seeing the Weiss and Dorf families—the one Jewish, and therefore good; the other German, and therefore morally ambiguous—in the privacy of one's own home, with or without commercial interruption, may have broken the last taboo associated with the destruction of European Jewry. This was, after all, in the wake of the Vietnam War, when Americans and audiences worldwide had the experience of viewing death and destruction up close as an everyday event. The same audience could now approach another terrible subject on the small screen with something like familiarity. Once the Holocaust became normalized and standardized, it became possible—indeed, mandatory—to teach it to one's children. In the 1980s, Holocaust curricula were introduced into state schools in the United States, Germany, France, and elsewhere.

Having crossed the three great divides—from then to now, from them to us, and from there to here—the Holocaust was positioned to enter public memory forever, aided and abetted by the cultural power of America. The writer who most successfully harnessed the autonomous power of literature to breach the borders of time and space was Philip Roth.

With the publication of *The Ghost Writer* (1979), Roth signaled several things at once. To begin with, he dedicated the novel to the exiled Czech writer Milan Kundera, thus reserving a special place for those writers who honed their craft in the face of the twentieth century's worst disasters. Then he introduced a writerly alter ego named Nathan Zuckerman, free to mimic the life and literary career of Philip Roth in order to challenge the sensibilities and literalism of his readers from the strategic vantage point of art. Nathan is a wannabe writer, just starting off, and an avid reader of the stories of Isaac Babel—purged by Stalin. Faced with accusations of betraying his own tribe, Roth-Zuckerman finds the perfect defense: he falls in love with the most tragic figure from the hallowed Jewish past—Anne Frank, supposedly reincarnated as Amy Bellette.

Is twenty-six-year-old Amy Bellette "really" a reincarnation of Anne Frank? A close reading of the novel reveals Nathan Zuckerman's love affair to be pure fantasy. Roth has arrayed his characters in two generational camps: the parent's generation, for whom the Holocaust remains a species of minority discourse, a flag under which to rally the troops, faces off against the writers in the next generation—E. I. Lonoff, Amy Bellette, and Nathan Zuckerman—who are totally dedicated to their craft, and for whom the ultimate truth is the truth of fiction. However else *The Ghost Writer* is read (its Library of Congress classification is "Men authors—Fiction"), it is a novel about the central role that the Holocaust has come to play in the making and unmaking of cultural meaning in America.

Roth's dedication to Kundera is unambiguous, however, and consistent with his effort to promote the work of neglected fellow writers. Roth was not the only author to capitalize on his fame to do so—for instance, Piotr Rawicz in France nominated Adolf Rudnicki for the Nobel Prize in Literature (Rudolf 2004, 280)—but it was Roth's remarkable paperback series dedicated to "Writers from the Other Europe" that introduced American readers to Polish, Czech, Hungarian, and Serbo-Croatian prose masters with barely pronounceable names. Thanks to Roth's intervention, Tadeusz Borowski got a new lease on literary life. The republication of two collections of short stories by Bruno Schulz, sometimes called the Polish Kafka, turned Schulz into the most famous literary victim of the Holocaust; his native Drohobycz into a paradise lost; and his lost masterpiece, "The Messiah," into a source of endless fascination for such diverse writers as David Grossman and Cynthia Ozick (Sokoloff 1988). Thanks to Roth, Jiří Weil's *Life with a Star* (1989) appeared in English, forty years after its publication in Czech. It was Roth who was to interview Aharon Appelfeld in 1988 for the *New York Times Book Review* (Appelfeld 1994) and whose "conversation" with Primo Levi would be appended to the popular English-language edition of *Survival in Auschwitz* (Levi 1996). Finally, having interviewed and befriended Appelfeld, Roth accorded him the highest accolade: Appelfeld appeared alongside such luminaries as "Philip Roth"; his wife, Claire Bloom; and the war criminal John Demjanjuk in Roth's 1993 *Operation Shylock*.

It was one thing for Elie Wiesel, Romanian-born and Jewish-bred, to speak of and for the Holocaust, and something else again for Philip Roth, US-born and American-bred, to do the same. Roth's novels, library of Writers from the Other Europe, interviews, citations, and fictional appropriations gave the Holocaust a permanent home in the American literary imagination. It validated Holocaust literature as a self-conscious and self-referential genre. Amy Bellette was more than an imaginary trophy bride for the wannabe writer Nathan Zuckerman. In the logic of literature, she was the survivor as proxy victim and witness of the Holocaust, akin to Rosa Lublin, Artur Sammler, and Sophie Zawitowski, whom American fiction writers of the 1970s and 1980s enlisted in order to break the generational silence.

Once the survivors had made their presence known in the United States, once English became the main purveyor of Holocaust writing, and once Holocaust literature took on a life of its own, the provisional phase of Holocaust memory was over.

AUTHORIZED MEMORY

1985–PRESENT

ENGLISH, MERELY A MEDIATOR UNTIL NOW, BECAME THE authorized language of Holocaust memory—with a German accent if spoken by British survivors, and a Polish Yiddish accent if spoken by naturalized American citizens. This marked a fundamental shift from the languages in which the Holocaust was lived to the languages in which it was relived. The survivors, an ambiguous presence until now, became the sacred vessels of Holocaust memory. Their children, who had nursed their wounds in private until now, became the second generation, a memory force to be reckoned with. The Germans—until now, sadistic storm troopers, goose-stepping auto-matons, or mindless bureaucrats—become individualized men and women of conscience, victims in their own right. And the East, out of bounds until now, became a place of pilgrimage, revealing chamber after chamber of new horrors.

Self-positioning, in this phase of Holocaust memory—the phase in which we live today—is a search for personal identity in a vertiginous time and silenced space. It has become impossible to separate the archeology of place from the archeology of self. Nor is it possible to predetermine in which direction the search will go, from place to self or from self to place. When it comes to the memory of the Holocaust, moreover, the quest for resolution can occupy the whole of one's life—or bring an end to one's life.

The Holocaust as Pilgrimage

"That place, Mr. President, is not your place," Elie Wiesel pleaded at a special memorial gathering held in Washington. "I . . . implore you to do something else, to find another way, another site" (Wiesel 1986, 243). The contested site was the Kolmeshöhe Cemetery in Bitburg, West Germany, where President Ronald Reagan was scheduled to lay a wreath to mark the fortieth anniversary of VE Day. What sparked the protest was the embarrassing discovery that among the war dead were members of the Waffen SS. To add insult to injury, Reagan insisted that most of the dead were teenagers inducted into the German army in the last months of the war, who "were victims, just as surely as the victims in the concentration camps" (Reagan 1986, 240). Reagan, raised on an older American narrative in which the annihilation of the Jews was subsumed into the Second World War, had not been briefed that by 1985 the two could no longer be conflated. The consummate politician, Reagan ended up spending all of eight minutes in Bitburg, proceeding to a longer (and quite moving) ceremony at the Bergen-Belsen concentration camp.

The memory of the Holocaust had become normative, its memorial mandate so compelling that it now brought world leaders to their knees: West German Chancellor Willy Brandt knelt before the Warsaw Ghetto Memorial on December 7, 1970, as did Pope John Paul II in 1983 (Young 1993, 180–81). The very evolution of these memorials testified to the profound changes taking place in the tenor of public memory of the Holocaust. In the beginning had been the monumental, socialist realistic art of Nathan Rapoport, whose Warsaw Ghetto Memorial stood on the site of the former ghetto. In the beginning had been the names and dates of 77,297 Jewish victims of the Holocaust from Bohemia and Moravia inscribed on the walls of the main nave and adjoining areas of the Pinkas Synagogue in Prague, designed and executed by the painters Václav Boštík and Jiří John between 1954 and 1959—the first window of opportunity after the death of Stalin. But by the next period, the purpose of memorial art was to embody a metaphysical state of brokenness, an absence and a presence—be it Franciszek Duszenko's and Adam Haupt's 1964 Treblinka Memorial, an abstract design constructed out of thousands of scattered stones and one huge obelisk, or Tadeusz Augustynek's 1984 memorial to the murdered Jews of Kazimierz-Dolny, made from the carved limestone fragments of desecrated Jewish tombs and reset in mortar (ibid., 200–201). With the help of two Polish Jews who could read Hebrew, Augustynek placed men's tombstones on the right, women's to the left, but what first struck the passerby was the sight of a massive wall unequally split in two, with a jagged break large enough for a person to walk through: the irreparable break in the history of Polish Jewry.

Then the unanticipated happened: the Berlin Wall was torn down, the "Evil Empire" (in Reagan's memorable phrase) met its end, the map of Europe was redrawn, and Holocaust memory was reterritorialized. Not only was the real, physical landscape readmitted as evidence of the crime; it was also evidence of efforts at the complete erasure of the crime. Since the early postwar period, the theme of return has figured prominently in works of the literary imagination—not only the physical return of Levi and Bassani to Turin and Ferrara; Antelme and Delbo to Paris; Alfred Kantor to Prague; Imre Kertész to Budapest, in remembrance of the forgotten fact that Hungary was "the Eastern European country where the greatest proportion of surviving Jews decided to stay after the war instead of emigrating" (Varga and Nolden 2008, 161); but also the spiritual return of Amichai to "Weinburg," Agnon to Buczacz, and Singer's Last Demon to Tishevitz. The return of the native sons and daughters now gave way to personal odysseys, quests, and pilgrimages undertaken by those who had never been there before, except in the dreams and nightmares of their parents and grandparents. A place called the shtetl—heretofore inaccessible, irrelevant, or a source of shtick—became the anchor of mourning and memory.

Until the early 1990s it might have seemed that Holocaust memory could move in only one direction, from East to West. From the perspective of North America, the East became irrelevant once the United States had taken over the means of memorial production. The new sense of landedness would challenge that hegemony. Alongside the psychic landscape, with its map of repressed and surrogate memories, there was now a foreign, physical landscape crying out to be negotiated, confronted, and internalized.

There is much to delight the eye and challenge the mind in the US Holocaust Memorial Museum, which opened in 1993. Most visually arresting and thought-provoking is Yaffa Eliach's Tower of Faces, a three-story tower within the building, which is lined with close to a thousand photographs of everyday life in her Lithuanian shtetl of Eyshishok (the present-day Eisiskes). The photographs of family groups, weddings, picnics, swimming parties, sporting events, holiday celebrations, gardening, bicycling, and other aspects of daily life provide a composite portrait of a Jewish market town in a time of rapid modernization. It looks like a place that any visitor would want to call home.

After visiting a Holocaust museum in Europe, a person with means could arrange a visit to the abandoned or reinhabited homestead. So could a person of no means, when the government of a united Germany paid all expenses and rolled out the red carpet. Jewish high-school seniors from across the globe began to take part in what is called the March of the Living, carefully orchestrated so that all groups met at the entrance to the Auschwitz *Stammlager* and marched together to Birkenau (Feldman 2001). Failing that, one's European roots could be traced via the Internet, where everyone was free to create a virtual *landsmanshaft* (hometown association). A grass-roots movement sprang up, its mission to translate all *yizkor* books into English.

For second- and third-generation offspring of Polish Jewry, the search now begins at home, in the present, in Melbourne, London, or Long Island. It proceeds either from a surfeit of family memories or (more typically) from ignorance of the past, but for the one precocious and especially intrepid son or grandson, it becomes all-consuming, a veritable odyssey across continents and time zones that eventually will lead the traveler back in time to the very scenes of the crime. None of these explorers is a child of Holocaust survivors, but each has likely grown up with a memorial volume to the martyred home. Other memory-enhancing objects are also strewn about the house—mostly photographs, but also letters and newspaper clippings. Two of them travel alone. A third prefers the company of his brother or former PhD adviser. But only the officially designated pilgrim writes it all down, to become Orpheus, or Dante, descending into Sheol.

Arnold—whose first name honors his maternal grandfather, Reb Aaron Yankev Probutski, and whose family name, Zabludowski, was Anglicized to Zable in 1946, a year before his birth—is the lucky one. He speaks and reads Yiddish, has attended memorial gatherings from an early age, and has a father who is a font of epigrammatic and oracular wisdom. "'Beware of sentimentality' the old man has often warned, 'That is why I have lived so long.'" "Do not be overly idealistic. Revolutions and wars come and go, but our inner drives and obsessions remain the same" (Zable 1994, 33, 86). Armed with little more than his father's handwritten life story and some primitive maps, Arnold at age thirty-nine is ready to abandon armchairs for a seat on the trans-Siberian railroad to his ancestral home in Poland. A grown-up now, he is painfully aware of his presumptive position in the broken memory chain. "We were born in the wake of the Annihilation," or so he sees his life, always in the first-person plural. "We were children of dreams and shadows, yet raised in the vast spaces of the New World. . . . 'You cannot imagine what it was like,' our elders insisted. 'You were not there.' Their messages were always ambiguous, tinged with menace, double-edged. 'You cannot understand, yet you must. You should not delve too deeply, yet you should. But even if you do, my child, you will never understand. You were not there'" (ibid., 163). There is no ambiguity, however, in the timetable of destruction, in what Zable calls the "grim folklore" unique to his family of origin:

Red Friday—June 27, 1941
Martyr's Thursday—July 3, 1941
Black Sabbath—July 12, 1941 (ibid., 121)

He continues: "an epitaph for each day of the week, dates for future generations to absorb and be condemned to remember, and mass graves that would one day draw grandchildren to them to clarify their confused dreams" (ibid.).

Zable writes beautiful English prose. He makes his particular experience yield universal significance with seeming effortlessness. A vicarious native son returns to the city of Białystok—its Polish national landmarks rebuilt, its Jewish cultural landmarks utterly neglected—yet he could be any child of refugees trying to piece together the fragments and shreds, the *Jewels and Ashes* of his title, into a coherent journey to the lost patrimony and back again.

Although technically of the same generation as Zable, the British-born author and documentary filmmaker Theo Richmond began his odyssey long after the death of his Polish-born parents, and some two decades after he came into possession of the *Konin Memorial Book*, whose contents he could not then read. But there they were, in the alphabetical list of murdered townsfolk, the names of the Ryczke clan of Konin, those who were never Anglicized to Richmond and therefore had shriveled to a thin line of names. Theo resolved to write a personalized *yizkor* book, "a book that would interweave past and present, that would be a confluence of two rivers, the Thames and the Warta" (1995, xix–xx). It was to be an odyssey of self-discovery, to something beyond the self.

"The more I knew, the more I became aware of what I did not know," Richmond wrote (ibid., 131). He had not anticipated how difficult it would be to flesh out the censored memories, reconcile partisan perspectives, negotiate among psychopathologies. Wanting to witness the surviving Koniner on almost-native ground, he attended a memorial meeting of the Ladies' and Men's Society of Konin on the Lower East Side of Manhattan. Seeing them as a group, in all their contentiousness, our second-generation Koniner reasserted his British abhorrence for "undisciplined" and "petty" behavior (ibid., 151). Until then he had not known how much easier it is to love the dead Jews than the living. Nor had the dead Jews been living in paradise, either. "In the heat of the summer the reek of human excrement rose to a peak" in Konin (ibid., 176); in addition to a lending library, which foregrounded the Jews as a spiritual aristocracy, Konin concealed within its backstreets at least one resident whore.

Richmond did not know what Zable had already discovered. The last stop, Konin proper, would prove the least satisfying, not only because Richmond was rushed through town by an overeager guide, but also because—this was the moment of truth—Konin was *Judenrein*. The stupefied pilgrim underscored the screaming silence of present-day Konin by saving for last the most terrible text in the most terrible tongue: a Polish "Protokol" of the Konin killing fields. Nothing has prepared the reader for the unmediated horror of this document, taken straight out of the *Konin Memorial Book*. Yet for all that, there are still two more chapters to go, wherein the Warta flows back into the Thames.

Daniel Mendelsohn was the unlucky one. He had little more to go on than an uncanny resemblance to a lost uncle. He was born into a dysfunctional family. And Long Island was such a long way from Belechow. Yet never was a Holocaust memoir written with such an unremitting teleology as this; every stray comment, salvaged letter, photograph, phone call, interview, itinerary, false lead, insult, even the scenery and scholarly digressions—all 503 densely printed pages of transcript are dedicated to finding *The Lost: A Search for Six of Six Million* (2006). Indeed, it reads like a thriller. Our three detectives, Daniel, Matt, and Froma, uncover the betrayal and violent death of six members of the Jäger family of Belechow (present-day Bolekhiv, Ukraine) during and after the final liquidation of the ghetto. Detailed and documented in real time, this is conclusive evidence that the Holocaust is the story to end all stories. The fact that Mendelsohn's tireless quest turned him into a biblical exegete—his close, interpolated readings of select passages from Genesis, the family saga of the Hebrew Bible, are set in italics—proves that in contemporary America, the personal memory of the Holocaust is sacred memory.

The Lost can be read as three family sagas in one: those of the Mendelsohns, the Jägers, and the Adam-to-Abraham family. Virtually no detail in the family dynamic and pathology of the Mendelsohns is withheld from the reader. Thankfully, by the saga's end the two estranged brothers are reconciled, and Matt's dark portrait of Daniel graces the inside jacket flap. The Jägers, too, are restored to the fullness of their prewar lives and wartime deaths, but not beyond the family circle. Belechow as a shtetl, a covenantal community in its own right, remains a cipher. Shmiel Jäger, we learn on page 322, was one-time president of the Yad Charuzim of Bolechow, but what social services the Hand of the Diligent Society provided is of no concern to the nephew. That Yitzhak Jäger left Bolechow for Palestine because he was caught selling unkosher meat goes a long way toward undermining the Zionist family narrative. About Zionist or anti-Zionist activity in town we learn nothing. It is a third family—the families of Adam, Cain and Abel, Abraham, Hagar and Sarah—that drives the metanarrative and firmly connects the end to the beginning, apocalypse to genesis.

Three travelers set out on a reverse journey—from present to severed past and from New World to Old. Zable discovers that life is a palimpsest of losses. The refugee parents never recover from the expulsion. The sons and daughters who are forced to witness their old age also assume the burden of commemorating the annihilation, to which from the very outset they have been denied access. Richmond's quest for personal identity is less tragic, relying as it does on the confluence of two rivers, and premised as it is on reimagining the dead in the fullness of their lives. Mendelsohn's route is open to only the most fearless, tireless, and literate traveler, for to approach the unimaginable death of six million one must exorcise the last family demons. Tailoring Scripture to fit the length and girth of one's family provides the only spiritual relief in this death-defined odyssey.

The riveting climax of Mendelsohn's book restores the real, physical landscape as evidence to the crime. There is no room here for displacement, evasion, allegory, symbolism, analogy, metonymy, myth, or elaborate exegesis. No more is this a matter of individual empowerment, personal odyssey, and identity formation. No more are we concerned with popes, presidents, and chancellors being brought to their knees. Just the thing itself: who did what to whom, where, when, how, and—possibly—why. This is the place of no return, and it takes years and miles and megabytes to get there.

The Last Survivors and Their Testimony

Nothing has changed so dramatically, so fundamentally, in the course of sixty years as the status of the Holocaust survivor. In Primo Levi's first iteration, to have survived at all was a source of profound existential shame. As the Red Army pushed westward, in October 1944, the members of the Sonderkommando in Birkenau blew up one of the crematoria, and all who took part in the uprising perished. One of the plotters was caught and publicly hanged to serve as a warning. The inmates were forced to witness his "solitary death," preceded by a German speech, "which nobody understood." "But everyone heard the cry of the doomed man, it pierced through the old thick barriers of inertia and submissiveness, it struck the living core of man in each of us: '*Kamaraden, ich bin der Letzte!*' (Comrades, I am the last one!)" This man was the last to resist as an individual, to have a voice and to be heard. Yet those who bore witness failed to respond. "The Russians can come now," Levi summed up the dark epiphany, "there are no longer any strong men among us, the last one is now hanging above our heads." Even as he honored the resistance, the survivor confessed to his own abject state (1985, 149).

Flash forward to 2009, when a chief custodian of Holocaust memory in the United States issued this anguished warning: the last survivors were soon to pass from this earth, each endowed with personal charisma, each a model of communal leadership and philanthropic largesse. Most important, in a time of cynicism, anomie, and generational rupture, the survivors were an unimpeachable residuum of moral authority (Berenbaum 2009). In the beginning, "the last of the just" referred to those whom Hitler had annihilated. In the end, those who still survived assumed a mantle of sainthood. At Auschwitz, the cry of the last free man was a cry in the wilderness. At the USC Shoah Foundation for Visual History and Education (formerly Steven Spielberg's Survivors of the Shoah Visual History Foundation), over 50,000 survivors have deposited the videotaped stories of their survival.

Between points A and B, between the survivor as broken vessel and the survivor as last keeper of the flame, came the age of the witness, when "the individual and the individual alone became the public embodiment of history" (Wieviorka 2006, 97). The Eichmann trial had endowed the voices of the victims and the witnesses with radical ethical force. A generation later, when a global network of Holocaust survivors organized their first widely publicized gatherings in Jerusalem and New York, the chaos and pathos of private memory were being turned into a coherent story in the public domain. Willy-nilly, survivors began to perform according to an emotional script that evoked a horror that was never so great as to be nihilistic. Whatever they said, their testimonies and the testimony of their lives insured that the moral order was immediately restored: good is good, and bad is bad. Overexposure, even to the inexpressible, generated a melancholic pleasure. Familiarity bred contentment. The historian Amos Goldberg calls this the "melodramatic mode," which produces pleasurable identification with human suffering (2009, 228). This is all the more so when projected onto a silver screen, or replayed on one's iPad: those whom the camera has individualized are rescued from Auschwitz, while hidden from sight are all the named and anonymous victims consigned to the gas chambers (Horowitz 1997, 135–36).

"Ich bin der Letzte!," as Levi wished us to hear it, is a voice radically different from our own, in a language we barely comprehend, whose experience shatters our moral equilibrium. *"Ich bin der Letzte!"* returns us to an aesthetic of the tragic. It is the voice of scandalous memory, an act of witnessing that swallows everything in its wake and everything that came before; that focuses us on the violence wrought by Hitler's war against the Jews and against humanity, on the Nazi murder machine and those who kept it running, on the desperate and debilitating struggle of one family to survive—a story so radically different from our own that it must be branded in a foreign tongue: *Shoah, Maus.*

Interviewing Holocaust survivors on film was not new. The Holocaust Survivors' Film Project, begun as a grass-roots archive and deposited at Yale University in 1981, became the core collection of the Fortunoff Video Archive for Holocaust Testimony. The English literary critic, Geoffrey Hartman, who had been evacuated from Germany on the *Kindertransport*, was a driving force behind this archive. At Yale, one person (or at most two) sat in a bare room (or living room), staring at a camera and talking to a total stranger in accented English.

Claude Lanzmann, the former French resistance fighter and Left Bank intellectual, was a far cry from Hartman, the genteel English professor. The interviews that made up his nine-and-half-hour-long documentary, *Shoah* (1985), were carefully staged against a specific backdrop: the present, bucolic site of the former Chełmno extermination camp, a marketplace in Grabow, the living room of a former ss officer, a barbershop in Tel Aviv, and on board a freight train heading for Treblinka. The verisimilitude lay in close-ups and skillful editing. A catch in the voice, eyes momentarily averted from the screen, groping for the right word—these signaled that some deep psychic wound had just been opened. The verisimilitude lay in the witnesses speaking in their native languages, even when the subtitles did not always do them justice. The verisimilitude lay, paradoxically, in the studied absence of documentary film footage. Everything the eye beheld was a reenactment in the ever-present.

Lanzmann christened the Holocaust with a new name because, for him, the Shoah was incomparable. Subtitled *An Oral History of the Holocaust* when it appeared in book form (Lanzmann 1985), the documentary was history as followed through a single lens. Lanzmann enlisted his willing and unwilling informants to testify to the Nazi terror, not to their own lives, either before or after (Kushner 2006, 290). Believing that Auschwitz cannot be explained nor can it be visualized, he declared a biblical ban on its representation. The explicit representation of Holocaust horrors, Lanzmann maintained, diminished their atrocity (Rothberg 2000, 5, 126–27, 233). Instead, their ritual rewording before an all-seeing camera would echo the ineffable, the incomprehensible, annihilation.

In the absence of a real crime scene, the burden of the retelling is on those former victims, perpetrators, and bystanders who have never before been asked so straightforwardly, so directly, to summon up a world lost to anything other than word. Only one expert witness, the historian Raul Hilberg, is called on to testify, surrounded by his books. "Without exception," Naomi Diamant comments in our Guide to the First Hundred Books, "the perpetrators and bystanders claim not to remember the details, while the survivors have forgotten nothing. 'If you could lick my heart,' [Antek] Zuckerman tells Lanzmann, 'it would poison you.'" Lanzmann can accomplish in nine and a half relentless hours what the hands-off, genteel approach of the Hartman or Spielberg archives cannot: turn metonymy into myth; the minute scheduling and bureaucratic thoroughness of the German murder machine into trains of the apocalypse; the faces of the architects, barbers, conductors, and couriers (such as the courageous Jan Karski)—the ABCs of an atrocity buried for half a century under foliage, forgetfulness, and lies—into Shoah.

The story of the Holocaust is not over until the last survivor community has borne witness. After half a century of memorial production, unprecedented in the annals of historical catastrophe, the visible and vocal presence of Holocaust survivors is what defines a Diaspora community as Jewish. Consider the shock that the literary scholar Ilán Stavans experienced during a visit to Spielberg's Survivors of the Shoah Visual History Foundation in Los Angeles, when he began comparing notes with a group of fellow academics. Every self-respecting Western country had its celebrated survivors, he realized, yet in the whole Spanish- and Portuguese-speaking world, he could cite only a handful of titles by survivors originally written in these languages (Stavans 2004, xi). If such books did not yet exist, then they had to be constructed. Stavans did just that with *Unbroken*, a survivor testimony written in fits and starts by Charles Papiernik (2004) over the course of fifty-six years in French and Spanish, with a rich sprinkling of "English, Polish, Yiddish, German and Hebrew words" (Sadow 2004, ix) that were to bedevil the English translator. Although told countless times before, the cultural significance of Papiernik's story lay in its subtitle: *From Auschwitz to Buenos Aires*. No matter that Buenos Aires was for over two decades the main venue of Holocaust literature worldwide, the Library of Polish Jewry alone introducing the likes of Nachman Blumental, Michał Borwicz, Yehuda Elberg, Chaim Grade, Mordecai Strigler, Jonas Turkow, and Eliezer Wiesel—all with title pages translated into Spanish. To qualify as authentically South American and to speak to a new generation of readers, a Holocaust testimony had to be written or rewritten in Spanish or Portuguese, with South America as the survivor's final destination. Alternatively, given the dearth of authentic South American survivor testimony, the solution was to seek the help of a native speaker, which is what the Romanian-born Salomon Isacovici did with *A7393: Hombre de cenizas* (1990). That work's publication was marred by the threat of a lawsuit from an Ecuadorian priest-turned-professor named Juan Manuel Rodríguez, who claimed the manuscript to be his own invention. An English translation, *Man of Ashes* (1999), was published after Isacovici's death with both names appearing as coauthors (Franklin 2011, 179–82; Stavans 2001, 37–42).

The survivors, if blessed with longevity, mobility, and the means of production, were privileged to impose a narrative structure on the miracle or accident of their survival, and herein lies the real interest in Isacovici's collaborative memoir. *Man of Ashes* is framed by a meditation on death: mass death at the hands of those (Germans, Hungarians, and Ukrainians) for whom "killing is their daily work" (Isacovici and Rodríguez 1999, 1) and the individual encounter with possible death at the hands of a heart surgeon in Massachusetts General Hospital. So many years have elapsed since the annihilation that the only way for Isacovici to begin is from a moment of extreme danger in the present that jolts his mind into one last heroic effort to remember. Isacovici, it turns out, was never a stranger to death. One of seven strapping brothers, Salomon—or Sanyi, as he was called in the old country—began his career as a smuggler early on and took part in a revenge killing as soon as Romania ceded his native Sighet to the Hungarians. Sanyi's Sighet, moreover, bears but slight resemblance to that of another local teenager, named Eliezer Wiesel. "Whenever I'd go into town," Sanyi recalls, "I'd run into a wretched old man who seemed to have gone crazy. He would talk to passers-by about the horrors committed in Galicia. Though no one wanted to believe him, his words seemed to touch raw nerves" (ibid., 44). This is the famous Moishe the Beadle from *Night*, the prototype of Wiesel's many beggars and madmen, but without the mystical overlay. It is from Isacovici that we learn about Rabbi Samuel Danzig, the spiritual leader of Sighet's Sephardic Jews, and about his heroic behavior during the deportation (ibid., 57). From Isacovici we learn about the futility of wreaking revenge for the crime to end all crimes. Death is the frame, not the eschatology.

For Isacovici, postwar existence takes up half the book. After the war, he returns to the river, fields, forests, caves, and homestead of his childhood and youth—the land and landscape that remain most vivid in his memory—in a desperate, atavistic, and doomed attempt to rebuild, replant, and reseed after surviving the death camps and the death marches. "In 1948," he writes, breaking up the chronology with the second of two flashes forward, "I left Europe forever, and suddenly I found myself living in one of the most beautiful countries of South America: Ecuador" (ibid., 36). Yet the natural splendor of "this Andean country" did not erase the Holocaust from his mind, because "the expressionless faces of the Indians, . . . whose daily lives are nothing more than pain and suffering," were a constant reminder of the camps; so much so that he was forced to move to the nearest big city to escape "those faces tortured with hunger and slavery." Sanyi's failure to secure his former home and Salomon's failure to escape from the past through his adopted homeland signal new ways of plotting survival that continuously challenge the reader's expectations of a linear, redemptive narrative from hell to new home.

For longevity can also be a curse. When it comes to the memory of the Holocaust, the futile and unattainable quest for resolution can occupy the whole of one's life—and can bring an end to one's life. Suicide, an aberrant response until now—who could forget Tadeusz Borowski's death by gas in 1951?—became almost normative for survivor witnesses in the 1980s and 1990s. Jean Améry wrote *Hand an Sich Legen* (*On Suicide: A Discourse on Voluntary Death*,

1999) in 1976 before taking his own life two years later, at the age of sixty-six. *Hand an Sich Legen* may be read as a requiem to his fellow survivors, who also "laid a hand on themselves," in that elegant German phrase: Paul Celan in 1970, Piotr Rawicz in 1982, Primo Levi in 1987, Bruno Bettelheim in 1990, Jerzy Kosinski in 1991, and Bogdan Wojdowski in 1994. Sarah Kofman (1996) took her own life after completing her autobiography, in 1994. Celan at fifty was the youngest among them; Bettelheim at eighty-seven the oldest.

Haunted Children: The Second Generation

Achieving closure was no less elusive for Art Spiegelman, who grew up the child of survivors. Could a child become the repository of his parents' suppressed and unknowable past? Could their experience be imagined, reenacted, and transfigured? Spiegelman subtitled both parts of *Maus* (1986 and 1991) *A Survivor's Tale*. But whose tale was it? Whence came its sanction and authority—did it derive from the father or the son; from the paranoid, fanatically parsimonious, and narcissistic first-generation survivor or from his emotionally scarred son, whose artistry helped him work through his mother's suicide?

Among other possibilities, *Maus* can be seen as a species of oral history, in which the son graduates from taking notes longhand to interviewing his reluctant and sometimes hostile chief informant with a tape recorder. Artie's authority is clearly embedded in the experience of his parents. At the same time, *Maus* is very much an autobiography (Mikics 2003), for the parents "bleed history" into their children. Not directly—what can these children possibly understand?—but through the denial of love and emotional overload, through silence and cryptic signals, which the child struggles to decipher. From its opening panels in "Rego Park, N.Y.C. 1958"—when Artie, the young artist, was ten or eleven, and he tried in vain to get his father to fix the child's world—the reader is thrust into a fraught domestic drama. The domestic battlefield, with its fierce parent-child conflict and deep psychic wounds, is littered with the bodies of Hitler's most vulnerable victims: the survivor parents and their children.

Maus is part fable, part animal Haggadah (an archetypal tale that must be continually retold and illustrated), part political allegory (along the lines of *Animal Farm*), part spoof on the American cartoon (at one point, his father confuses Artie with Mickey Mouse [Spiegelman 1986, 133]), and several parts avant garde comics. The iconography of *Maus* is designed to bridge the generations. Spiegelman's cartoon images of "Mauschwitz," human mice being exterminated by human cats, and Jew-mice parading as Polack-pigs are both familiar and strange. So simple, even a child can read them. So terrifying, even an adult cannot fathom them.

In its domestic, psychoanalytic focus and its feminism; in its iconography,

FIGURE 19

Art Spiegelman. *Maus: A Survivor's Tale*. New York: Pantheon, 1986. Cover art by Art Spiegelman.

comedy, ethnicity, and politics, *Maus* is an American tale. Part II opens with an epigraph from Adolf Hitler, calling on German youth to repudiate "the dirty and filthy-covered vermin, the greatest bacteria-carrier in the animal kingdom" (Spiegelman 1991)—that is, the Jews and their American trademark, Mickey Mouse. The rabid racism of Nazi ideology led in two directions: to the extermination of a people refigured as vermin and, through the figure of Mickey Mouse, to a direct attack on American values. Vladek, unlike Sol Nazerman, the antihero of Edward Lewis Wallant's *The Pawnbroker* (1961), learns nothing about Jews in relation to other victims of exclusion and racism. "How can you, of all people," Françoise protests after they drop off a black hitchhiker, "be such a racist! You talk about Blacks the way the Nazis talked about the Jews!" "Ach!" says Vladek in reply. "It's not even to COMPARE the Shvartsers and the Jews!" (Spiegelman 1991, 99). Vladek's suffering has hardened his heart toward the suffering of others. His bigotry does not allow for "multidimensional memory," the use of the Holocaust as a template for the present (Rothberg 2009). Real Americans, in contrast and by implication—be they the native-born, like Artie, or those who have absorbed American values, like Françoise—are capable of responding to multiple traumatic pasts.

The evolution of Spiegelman's *Maus* also allows us to see precisely how provisional memory became authorized. The first part contains the Ur-text of *Maus*, "Prisoner on the Hell Planet," written in 1973, and created in the heyday of avant-garde comics in a hyperrealistic, expressionist style (Spiegelman 1986, 100–103). Artie is quite literally a prisoner, wearing prison stripes, as if that were standard issue in the mental hospital from which he has just been released; and he is figuratively a prisoner of the mind, overwhelmed with a burden of guilt for having "caused" his mother's suicide. His grief is unassimilable, like the black borders in the binding. Spiegelman conveys the sense of being branded for life.

Maus, written between 1980 and 1986, is a different work entirely, not only because the private has been rendered public through recourse to animal allegory, but also because Spiegelman has chosen a safer venue by shifting from his mother's story to his father's. Ever since Wiesel's *Night*, the master narrative of Holocaust literature has been the drama of fathers and sons, hearkening back to the Christian myth of the Father and Son and farther back to the Judaic myth of Abraham and Isaac. Embedded within a Judeo-Christian narrative of sacrifice and renewal, Artie and Vladek Spiegelman are authorized to enact the terrible drama of survival after Auschwitz.

Like *Shoah*, *Maus* is written in the tragic mode. The earlier Judeo-Christian narrative, in which the Holocaust represented the triumph of good over evil, hope over adversity, is here replaced by an "existential extremism" (Mikics 2003, 21). Yet some of that old-time religion must be present in order to authorize the memory of the Holocaust. Midway through the "Prisoner on the Hell Planet" sequence, we see a grief-stricken Vladek intone the Hebrew-Aramaic kaddish, the memorial prayer, at Anja's coffin. The opening lines appear in Hebrew lettering, courtesy of the visible hand of the son, acting the role of a scribe (Rosen 2005, 166–67). If Vladek himself survived the hell planet, it was in no small measure due to his sense of election, having been nominated for survival—first by his rabbi grandfather, who came to him in a dream, and then by the priest in Auschwitz. Perhaps some of these blessings will be passed on to his rebellious son when, just before quitting this sorrowful life, Vladek the patriarch mistakenly calls Artie by the name of his martyred brother, Richieu (Mikics 2003, 21–24).

Even as they struggled for their own stories to emerge, a whole generation of sons and daughters assumed the role of family historian, reopening the old wounds for all the world to see. Gila Almagor, Israel's leading actress, not only wrote but also starred in her quasi-autobiographical *Hakayits shel Avia* (The summer of Avia, published in 1985 and filmed 1989) and its upbeat sequel, *Ets hadomim tafus* (Under the domim tree, written in 1992 and filmed in 1994). "Quasi-autobiographical" does not do justice to the shock of seeing a star of stage and screen portray not herself, the wannabe Sabra, but her clini-cally schizophrenic survivor mother. In Israel, where the personal is always political, the second generation went public in 1988, when the director Orna Ben-Dor Niv released her film *Biglal hamilḥama hahi* (Because of that war), the very title signifying a dramatic shift in national perspective: from Israel's War of Independence to "that" unmentionable war. On screen, for the first time, parents spoke openly to their children of their fears; two survivors of Ausch-witz, one from Warsaw and the other from Salonika, compared horrors; and two of Israel's most popular performers, Yehudah Poliker and Ya'acov Gilad, discovered that, beyond their love of music, what drew them together was the wartime experience of their parents. To celebrate that bond, they perform rock music composed about the camps, the first songs written about the Ho-locaust in Hebrew since the 1940s.

The second generation now took over the means of memorial production. Two exceptionally fine works of Holocaust fiction appeared in 1986, both written from the perspective of an only child of survivors and both by an author practiced in a fantastical genre—one in comics, the other in children's literature. Both were immediately recognized as a watershed: the first part of *Maus* and the four-part experimental novel *'Ayyen 'erekh: 'ahava'* (*See Under: Love*), by David Grossman (translated in 1989). With Spiegelman and Gross-man, not just the manner and the generational perspective but the very sound of the narration changed—in a shift from the languages in which the Holo-caust was lived to the languages in which it was relived.

Learning to Speak Jewspeak

See Under: Love ends with a "Glossary: The Language of 'Over There'" that contains all manner of Yiddish and Polish words and expressions. "Over There" itself a code name adopted by the nine-year-old Shlomo (Momik) Neu-man (the "new man"), who serves as the novel's chief protagonist, already so prescient and wise beyond his years that he is affectionately known as *alter kop* (old head). That is presumably so familiar an appellation that it doesn't even appear in the glossary, and in fact huge chunks of this madcap postmodern novel are written in Jewspeak.

Jewspeak—so late in the day to be introducing a new term of art—is not a real language of social intercourse. It exists only in performance on stage or screen and in works of the imagination, serving to identify the speaker as a community of one: here, the lone survivor displaced from a home to which there is no return. It used to be, in the days before hatred of the Jews turned genocidal, that Jewspeak mimicked the way Jews in real life tried to pass as proper Germans or native-born Poles. In that case their comic speech patterns

FIGURE 20

David Grossman. *'Ayyen 'erekh: 'ahava.'* Tel Aviv: Hakibbutz Hameuchad, 1986. Cover art by Jean Dubuffet.

were known as *Mauschlen* (talking like Mosche, Moses) or *Żydlowanie* (from *Żyd*, Polish for Jew), and they quickly became vehicles for Jewish self-hatred as well as Christian hatred of the Jew (Gilman 1986). After the Holocaust, that kind of racial humor was no longer funny, which is why it has been so difficult since then to render *Ost-Juden* on the German or Polish stage (Bern 2004), and why American English and modern Hebrew enjoy a strategic advantage. The Holocaust scholar Alan Rosen has provided a remarkable linguistic guide to English-speaking survivors, from the babble of Philip Roth's "Eli, the Fanatic" and the eradication of accent (and memory) from the speech of Sol Nazerman, to the celebration of English as the language of survival in *Maus* (Rosen 2005). Jewspeak Lite is the language spoken by lovable losers, like Woody Allen in his various guises; it is a humorous mix of intonation, topicalization ("problems, I don't need"), with a sprinkling of kitchen Yiddish. The main character in Bernard Malamud's 1963 story "The Jewbird" (1997), fittingly enough, is fluent in Jewspeak, seeing as the poor thing must battle the enemy within (Jewish self-hatred) and the enemy without (antisemitism), as must his fantastical cousin, I. B. Singer's "The Last Demon" (1983b), who loses nothing in translation.

Momik can be said to speak juvenile Jewspeak, which grows thicker and more idiomatic after the release of his long-lost grandfather, Anshel Wasserman, from the insane asylum in Bat Yam. This sets Momik on a desperate search for the Nazi Beast that is hiding, he believes with the literalism of a child, in the cellar. In Part III, Wasserman takes over, speaking both to Shleimeleh [the Yiddish diminutive of Shlomo], his now-adult grandson, and to Auschwitz Camp Commander Obersturmbannführer Neigel, in a Jewspeak so dense that it often eludes the English-language translator and, presumably, her readers, too. Still, it can be heard loud and clear because Wasserman's monologue is bracketed by the neutral prose of Shleimeleh and the clipped, humorless *Nazi Deutsch* of Herr Neigel: "Neigel leans back and plays with a small ruler. 'I understand nothing about literature, *Scheissemeister*.' And Wassermann blurts, 'Nu, to each his own, your honor.' And blanches with fear" (Grossman 1989, 195).

Created by Sholem Aleichem, Jewspeak is the language of the hapless underdog whose psychic survival depends on achieving an ironic balance between high and low, inside and out (Wisse 1971, 41–57). Grossman learned to say "Nu, to each his own" from reading Sholem Aleichem in Hebrew translation. *Scheissemeister* he may have learned from reading Primo Levi, not yet available in Hebrew.

Those who speak the language of "Over There" with heavy accents (Vladek Spiegelman and Momik's parents, grandfather, and neighbors) are authentic survivors. Those who learn to orchestrate the languages, dialects, and stylistic registers of the whole cast of Holocaust characters—living and dead, good and evil—are the sons and daughters in the second generation, authorized to speak in the name of the survivors. Like the violation of standard English in Spiegelman's *Maus* and the polyphony of languages in Wojdowski's *Bread for the Departed* (1997), Grossman's Hebrew in *See Under: Love* is the sum of all languages, dialects, and literary styles. But only Grossman provides his novel with a "Complete Encyclopedia (First Edition)" of the life of his most fantastical character, an encyclopedia that, even in translation, follows the order of the Hebrew alphabet, from Aleph "(AHAVA. LOVE. *See under*: SEX)" to Taf "(TEFILLA. PRAYER)."

Amir Gutfreund's 2001 *Shoah shelanu* (*Our Holocaust*, 2006) reads like a parody of Grossman. Instead of just one foreign-born grandfather, the children of Katzenelson Street in Kiryat Hayim (north of Haifa) grow up with a whole slew of acquired grandparents, uncles, and aunts, based on the so-called Law of Compression invented by the first generation of the Holocaust, who survived without close family members and therefore "had done away with the requirement for precision" (ibid., 4). Grandfathers are in especially short supply, and so just about anyone can qualify, even someone like Grandpa

Lolek who isn't strictly speaking a Holocaust survivor since he fled to Russia, where he joined the volunteer army of the Polish General Anders—and who, in light of the terrible losses sustained in battle and the horrific conditions on the battlefield, makes light of the monotonous suffering of the survivors. Instead of Grossman's Anshel Wasserman, the speaker of authentic Jewspeak in Gutfreund's adoptive family is Grandpa Yosef, related through the bonds of literature to Tevye the dairyman. The sadistic, pathological Untersturmführer Kurt Franz, known in Treblinka as *Lyalke*—"The Doll looked out at us. I am the *Shoah of Shoahs*, he seemed to be saying" (ibid., 121)—is none other than Grossman's Sturmbannführer Siegfried Staukeh, Neigel's adjutant; and both narrators have an only son named Yariv, who represents the third generation. A significant number of survivors in both novels are certifiably crazy.

Anxiety of influence? Plagiarism? An inside joke? By mimicking Grossman and covering much of the same ground, Gutfreund is offering the reader a very different model of custodianship, one that does not lavish exclusive attention on the creative writer, be he named Anshel Wasserman-Scheherazade, the martyred Polish-Jewish fabulist Bruno Schulz, Herr Neigel ("A Nazi could never be a good writer. They don't feel anything. Am I right, Scheherazade?" [D. Grossman 1989, 197]), or Momik-Shleimeleh-Shlomo. Neither precious nor precocious, Gutfreund's protagonists are an ordinary bunch of kids who happened to grow up on the same street. *Our Holocaust* is the first communal bildungsroman in Holocaust literature.

The children of Katzenelson Street—parody of parodies—are the real-life counterpart to characters in the Children of the Heart, Anshel Wasserman's celebrated series of adventure stories, so famous that even Herr Neigel read them as a child. A streetful of Momiks, or Tom Sawyers, grow up on complicated "non-linear" stories (Gutfreund 2006, 62), which—by dint of sleuthing, scheming, and prodding—they try to reorder into a consecutive Holocaust narrative, although they are constantly being told they're not old enough. Knowledge of the Holocaust unfolds over a lifetime in fits and starts, and at no stage is it age appropriate. For the unruly preteens, it is a peep show; what Levertov fails to reveal about the Doll's atrocities at Treblinka can be gleaned by reading Ka-Tzetnik, although Grandpa Yosef manages to traverse their entire childhood "without giving away too much" (ibid., 190). The children of Katzenelson Street (which they insist on renaming after the "real" Katzenelson—not the Labor Zionist leader, but the martyred poet) augment their knowledge through official rites of commemoration, as through their life experience, until they are finally old enough. Then they go to Poland with Dad to see his stories made real and are shocked to discover that, as opposed to the "conspiratorial reality" of their childhood and adolescence that had seemed so scandalous, the lane Dad zigzagged through—the one he had been taught by *his* father "to always run in zigzags when shots were being fired"—is part of a luminous, layered landscape to which they too someday will add shades of color "in the alleys of Gaza, in Khan-Younis" (ibid., 191). Discovering the Holocaust is a lifetime project, punctuated by timeouts to get married, have kids, and dodge bullets in their own wars. Being old enough means that one of them, the narrator, becomes the designated scribe, and after scrupulously transcribing Grandpa Yosef's travels (which take up a third of the book), he turns his attention to "the other people in the family and in the neighborhood. The stories. The Big Bang" (ibid., 325). Being old enough means it is time to pass some of these stories on to Yariv. It means learning everything there is to know about villainous Jewish collaborators. It means realizing that Crazy Hirsch wasn't so crazy after all when he kept screaming, again and again, "Only saints were gassed?" (ibid.). It means acknowledging that ordinary Germans were also singled out for special treatment of a different kind, and that this nonlinear, endlessly complicated story goes well beyond the borders of Katzenelson Street and its inhabitants.

Somewhat awkwardly, Gutfreund breaks the spell with an afterword, where he reveals that most of what we've just read is pure invention and provides chapter and verse to show how he transgressed the historical truth in order to enliven the dead. Like Grossman, then, Gutfreund believes that only art can bring the dead back to life. But too much art can also distract from the moral imperative to record the killers' names with absolute precision (Kurt Franz is the Doll's real name) and the obscenely light sentences they received for their crimes, a tally sheet of ignominy that Gutfreund entrusted to "Attorney Perl," whose real-life prototype actually lived in the house at 7 Leonarda Street in the Bochnia ghetto, with the author's family, but never made it to Katzenelson Street because he perished in Belżec.

So much to learn, reconnoiter, reorder, and memorize. If you're a time traveler, you must learn the contents of the memorial book, a vast amount of background material, followed by the itinerary, topography, and names and addresses of your informants and tour guides. If you're taking testimony, you learn how not to take no for an answer. If you're a child of survivors, it's how to draw, sing, act, transcribe, imagine, invent, inventory, and keep your marriage from falling apart. If you're any of the above, it's how to communicate in foreign tongues and perform in a vernacular no longer spoken among the living.

Haunted Children: The Marranos

"The last survivors," writes Michael Berenbaum with a hint of disparagement, "will be children of the Holocaust who most often avoided the camps and found refuge in hiding—either openly, by pretending to be non-Jews, or in secret, in attics, basements and barns." "They will be around for another 20 years," he predicts, "but their direct memories will be more limited because they experienced the events known as the Holocaust as very young children" (Berenbaum 2009). Full-bodied survivors, by implication, survived the real Holocaust—the concentration camps and death marches—and were fully formed by the time of their liberation. Their testimony is therefore more complete and reliable. From the perspective of literature and the arts in general, however, Berenbaum has it all wrong. As a group, a cohort, these Marrano children, precisely by cutting the Holocaust down to manageable size and struggling to make sense of their fragmented memories, have made certain that the latest period of Holocaust memory will not be the last.

Nomenclature is important. To call them Marrano children instead of "hidden children" is not to blur the boundaries between the sixteenth century and the twentieth but to return, again and yet again, to our point of departure: Holocaust, Jewish (1939–45). To survive, a Jewish child was taught "to become someone without qualities, the most ordinary of the ordinary" (Głowiński 2005, 83); to know that it was the Jew who killed Jesus; to knock on the door not like a Jew; to remain calm when accosted by a *szmalcownik*, or professional blackmailer; never to acknowledge the presence of another Jew on the street; and to continue to live in hiding even after the Liberation. To survive, in short, Marrano children had to hide everything, deny everything, renounce everything. Let's be blunt: they had to un-Jew themselves.

This last cohort of child survivors hearkens back to the first. The polyglot manuals of concentration camp survival, we recall, focused relentlessly on the raw self, on a landscape in which culture and religious values were the detritus of a world best forgotten. These chronicles of the camps are of a piece with the survival tales of lone Jewish children, in style as well as substance. Louis Begley, Sarah Kofman, and Michał Głowiński return us to the spare, unsentimental style of Borowski, Antelme, and Levi; to the thingness of things, as children typically are able to experience them or as *Ka-tzets* (concentration camp inmates) are, rendered childlike by absolute extremity: a spoon, a bowl of soup, a lead soldier.

The art of survival for *Lager* inmate as for Marrano child was a return to radical nakedness and constant fear, yet the younger cohort of writer survivors needed to find a new way to retrieve this parallel universe. As Berenbaum cautioned, the direct memories of the latter were indeed more limited because they experienced the events known as the Holocaust as very young children. For them, the events were more limited, more fragmented, and inevitably more filtered through a screen of psychological defenses and a wealth of cultural associations accumulated over a lifetime. Returning to the scene of the crime after half a century, a successful New York attorney, a famous French philosopher, and a pathbreaking Polish literary theorist created a "collage of two voices"—those of the child protagonist and the adult narrator (Shore 2005, xi). On a split screen, these fully acculturated and highly accomplished adults had the courage to confront their terrified, Jewish, child doubles.

Oddly, both Kofman in *Rue Ordener, Rue Labat* (1996) and Głowiński in *The Black Seasons* (2005), break up their story into sound bites, which follow a loose and unpredictable chronology. Of the two, Kofman affects a more straightforward style, as if for the purpose of telling this confessional tale she has left her post-Freudian and skeptical hermeneutics far behind her. But she has not (Stanislawski 2004, 139–74). The two streets of the book's title are the two sides of her wartime identity—Orthodox, Yiddish-speaking Sarah versus French Catholic Suzanne—and the homes of the two adult women warring for her affection. It is obvious that the woman who rescued her wins over the woman who bore her, even if the burgeoning love between Suzanne and "Mémé" dare not speak its name.

It doesn't matter that the witness was a mere child. What matters is the historical weight of what she witnessed relative to the larger wartime narrative. Kofman's father, the rabbi of a small synagogue in the eighteenth *arrondissement* of Paris, was among the 12,884 French Jews who were arrested on July 16, 1942, transported to the Drancy detention camp, and from there shipped off to Auschwitz, where he perished. This was the Vélodrome d'hiver roundup, the blackest day in the history of modern France. It is enough to mention that date (which Kofman does twice) for every French reader to understand why the fountain pen that Rabbi Kofman left behind becomes a sacred relic for his daughter, and why his patriarchal presence would loom so large in her memory so many years later. The child just barely remembers, but the adult sets the memory in stone.

Głowiński's collage begins with the central act in the tragedy of modern Poland: the great deportation from the Warsaw ghetto in the same summer of 1942, which he refers to as "the season of great dying" (2005, 11). The author was eight years old at the time, so all he can remember are "Fragments from the Ghetto," but he will return to the *Aktion* in which his family was dragged off to Umschlagplatz in harrowing detail. *The Black Seasons* is a masterful blend of showing and telling and a primer in Holocaust memory at all levels. As the child experiences traumatic flashes, the adult interrogates these disparate memory traces—a word, a color, a knock on the window—to seek corroboration, ponder the vagaries of the human mind, and penetrate the motives of other actors.

And just when you think that the worst is over, when our little boy has found refuge in Turkowice under the care of courageous nuns—"On a Sunday Morning," of all times—comes the most terrifying encounter of all, when the three brothers Z. decide to denounce him as a Jew. "There's no way to describe this most basic fear," says the adult narrator, "a fear so thoroughly piercing that it belongs to those experiences evading language, laying bare the flatness, the inadequacy, and the incommensurability of words" (Głowiński 2005, 116). What about the brothers? What was their motive, seeing as how there was no monetary gain to be had and the consequence of their action would be certain death for their victim? "Wholly unreflective hatred," comes the answer, "bound up with the spirit of the times or emanating from it," for "not only was Jewish life cheap, it was of no consequence. It had become dispossessed of any value" (ibid., 118). There are many such passages punctuating Głowiński's book, in which the reader can profitably exchange Armenian, Cambodian, or Tutsi for Jewish to gain deeper appreciation of the author's moral intelligence. Yet let there be no mistake. Half a century has not dulled the perception of the child vis-à-vis the killers. "Even today," when most people prefer to blame the Nazis, Głowiński insists on using the word "German" for those who conceived and carried out the Final Solution (ibid., 172), a practice that we too have adopted throughout this book. "Germans were those who annihilated Jews consistently, programmatically and mercilessly, and in essence existed in order to torment, torture, and kill, at first one by one or in fairly small groups, and later . . . en masse," writes Głowiński (ibid., 173–74). On the issue of moral responsibility, he does not distinguish between first- and second-generation Germans. The adult refuses to issue blanket absolution to the German people for the crimes committed against the child.

Good Germans

When President Reagan maintained in 1985 that teenagers inducted into the German army in the last months of the war "were victims, just as surely as the victims in the concentration camps," he spoke out of line, and was censured for doing so. But Hollywood, his prior world, was listening. Less than a decade later, Oskar Schindler became the Hollywood icon of the good German.

In *Schindler's Ark*, a 1982 book by the prolific Australian novelist and playwright Thomas Keneally, Steven Spielberg found a true story that pitted good against evil, mixed Germans and Jews, and had a happy end. Spielberg underscored the seriousness and authenticity of his 1993 *Schindler's List* by filming it in black and white and by paying meticulous attention to historical and geographical detail. The street-by-street blockade of the Kraków ghetto was a tour de force of documentary realism (even though the actual ghetto was situated on the other side of town): never again would a filmgoer confuse ghetto, labor camp, and concentration camp. At the same time, however, the perspective of Keneally's novel was rooted in the author's Catholicism, which

Spielberg exploited by turning the (rather dissolute) life of Oskar Schindler into a Christian parable of sin, death, and resurrection, complete with a full-color, true-life pilgrimage to his shrine in Jerusalem. Politically, too, the film came at an auspicious moment. It consolidated the prototype of the good German for a Germany only recently reunited. The premiere of the German-language version, *Schindler's Liste*, in March 1994 was a state occasion, allowing East Germans the same national catharsis that West Germany had experienced fifteen years earlier in response to the television miniseries *Holocaust* (Weissberg 1997). Small wonder that *Schindler's List* tours are now a staple of the Polish tourist trade, a made-for-Hollywood pilgrimage site, which includes the rebuilt factory.

Another good German who won posthumous glory was Captain Wilm Hosenfeld, the man responsible for saving the Polish Jewish pianist and composer Władysław Szpilman. Disguised as a good Austrian for reasons of political correctness (Biermann 1999, 221), Hosenfeld made a cameo appearance toward the climactic end of Szpilman's 1946 survivor testimony, *Śmierć Miasta* (Death of a city). And there his memory rested, as long as Holocaust writing was still only for local consumption. But after the reunification of Germany and feeling the need for reconciliation among all victims of the Holocaust, Andrzej Szpilman, the author's son who was by then a resident of Germany, arranged for the memoir to be translated first into German and then into English, with one slight addition: excerpts from the wartime diary of Captain Hosenfeld. That unprecedented combination of a German wartime diary, a postwar Jewish memoir, and the story of a man whose passion was music and whose masterpiece was survival, as the tagline put it, caught the eye of Roman Polanski, the Polish Jewish filmmaker. *The Pianist*, released in 2003, won three Oscars, and the Szpilman-Hosenfeld memoir and diary was reissued as a mass market paperback (Szpilman 1999).

The good German as rescuer was made for the screen. The good German as narrator was made for literature. A scholar and purveyor of Holocaust memory, the Anglo-German writer W. G. Sebald brought that narrative voice to perfection. As a scholar, he produced insightful essays about Levi and Améry, while as a public intellectual he attacked the German literati for their twenty-five-year-long failure to admit their suppression of the Holocaust and their lack of empathy for its victims (B. Prager 2005, 85–86). Even as a child, Sebald grew up feeling that "something had been withheld"—at home, in school, and also by the German writers whose books he read in the hope of being able to find out more about "the enormity in the background" of his own life (quoted in Franklin 2011, 185). With Lanzmann, whose work he greatly admired, Sebald considered that "enormity" to be unrepresentable; refusing recourse to the imagination, Sebald chose to go only through textual

and visual quotation from other sources. For him, the purpose of all literature was the excavation of a secret history. Breaking one taboo, Sebald broke
another shortly before his untimely death, being among the first to break the
silence on German suffering during the Second World War (Franklin 2011, 186,
193; B. Prager 2005, 77–81).

A melancholy constantly pervades the voice of the narrator in Sebald's 1992
Die Ausgewanderten (*The Emigrants*, 1996) and its 2001 sequel, *Austerlitz*, as well
as the lost souls whom he excavates and the landscapes in which they live. It
is hard not to be seduced by Sebald's style, his Proustian ability to render the
passage of time, and his painterly attention to shades of gray. If there is pleasure to be had from human suffering, then reading Sebald on states of inner
Jewish exile is where it can be found. Everything becomes an emblem of loss:
the landscape, the shuttered lives, and—most hauntingly—the visual relics in
the form of blurry, nondescript, black-and-white photographs, which seem at
once punctual and timeless. The good German, a voluntary émigré who has
wandered off into self-exile, has taken on a kind of penance, dedicating his life
to piecing together what can never be fixed.

Were Sebald's informants, living incognito, the last locatable victims of Hitler? If *Fragments: Memories of a Wartime Childhood* (1996) were a true story, as
the world was led to believe, then its author, Riga-born Binjamin Wilkomirski,
would occupy a place alongside Begley, Głowiński, and Kofman as the youngest survivor to "remember" the concentration camp experience, fully half a
century after the Liberation.Because the story is fabricated out of whole cloth,
we must consider the real author, Bruno Dössekker, as an aberrant species of
the good Swiss, so overidentified with the Jewish victims that he reinvented
himself as his Holocaust double. Yet there is much to be learned from Dössekker's act of "identity theft," in Ruth Franklin's felicitous phrase (2011, 215–34).
With the Holocaust experience now understood as a trademarked species of
individual psychic trauma, Wilkomirski has turned every abused child into
a concentration camp victim in miniature. The very fragmentariness of his
specious autobiography reveals how tortuous is the process of retrieving lost
memories, of recovering one's lost identity. Were it not for the masquerade,
Fragments could be read as a novel about the struggle to reclaim a battered
self. Instead, it becomes a school for scandal, where our Holocaust is exposed
to ridicule: our reading habits, our expectations, our revisioning of the past
through the monocle of the present. As such, *Fragments* is most certainly not
the last word, for the power of the Holocaust to scandalize is what has kept its
memory ever present, always on the razor's edge. Every generation must be
scandalized anew by the Holocaust.

Re-covery: How the Holocaust Book Was Made

What goes on the cover? As I write these words, the book you are holding in your hands does not yet have a cover design. This book, like any other, must follow the requisite steps and pass the usual checkpoints, from writing, revising, vetting, revising yet again, copy-editing, producing galleys, and proofreading to printing and binding, and the cover art usually falls into place when there is a place on the bookshelf about to be occupied. The most important decision—what goes on the cover—is usually left for last.

So let us try to imagine what the editors, authors, publishers, and publicists were thinking when they chose the cover art for the twenty covers that lie scattered throughout this volume in black-and-white, some of which also appear in a beautiful full-color insert in the middle. Those who brought Holocaust literature to the light of day did not yet know what we know: that these covers, which cover the years 1946–95, would mimic the movement from the communal to provisional to authorized memory of the Holocaust. Rather, each was working in the present, hoping to find a mnemonic for the past and a link to the future.

Some things change, and others remain constant. The choice of style is always made with a specific audience in mind. Whether the graphic style be mimetic or symbolic, commercial or high modern, will depend on the wished-for audience. Is this awesome subject intended only for readers with a genetic, confessional, geographic, or linguistic claim to the map of origins, or should the locus of identification lie elsewhere, in domains more personal, psychological, and existential? Who and what stands in for the Holocaust? A mother and child, a husband and wife, or only the child, alone? A ghetto or a concentration camp, or will a hiding place be sufficient to inspire terror and awe? Barbed wire or a crematorium, or will a brick wall do? A number, a letter, or a yellow star? The fire, the smoke, or the sun?

What does change is that a switch occurs when Holocaust literature comes into its own. This is the famous and "inevitable 'cultural lag' between the emergence of the new and the development of a vocabulary—be it conceptual or artistic—to describe it" (N. Levi and Rothberg 2003a, 6). At a certain point in time, which can now be located with precision, Holocaust literature becomes a self-conscious genre, and the cover designs illuminate the way. There comes a time when a Holocaust book can be judged by its cover.

COMMUNAL MEMORY: THE ABC OF DESTRUCTION

Gracing the 1946 cover of *Byliśmy w Oświęcimiu* (*We Were in Auschwitz*) is Janusz Nel Siedlecki's Auschwitz number, P6643—and nothing else (see plate 1; also fig. 5). A concentration camp number affixed to a striped uniform (some copies had actual uniform pieces on the cover) was an icon never seen before. The utter anonymity of the cover is already the message; only once inside the book's pages does the reader learn that the red triangle indicated a political prisoner, "P" stood for Polish, and the "low numbers" were a sign of distinction. Three things prevented this Auschwitz anthology from reaching its natural readership, the Polish-reading folks back home, despite an astonishing initial press run of 10,000 copies: the chaos of postwar Europe; the decision of Anatol Girs, the book's designer and publisher, to start a new life in the West; and, not least, the content. Auschwitz numbers P6643, 75817, and 119198 insisted on implicating everyone in the crime.

Less stark, though no less startling, was the huge *A* printed on the cover of the *Passover Service*, edited by Yosef Sheinson in Munich in 1946 (fig. 4). That letter was the insignia of the Third Army of the US Army of Occupation. For the survivors and American Jewish GIs assembled at the first postwar communal seder, the letter by itself signified the Liberation. So both these anthological projects used salvaged materials—the numbers and ABCs of war-torn Europe—at once as a utilitarian gesture and a sign of the new world order. P6643 was a sign of the apocalypse, the *A* a portent of redemption.

Publishers in the first postwar period, whether Jewish or gentile, presented the unprecedented as something already familiar. The iconography was chosen with a very specific reader in mind. Every survivor who picked up the first publication of the Central Jewish Historical Commission at the Central Committee of Polish Jewry dedicated to Yiddish literature (fig. 3) recognized the cover photo. It was taken at the time of the *Szpere*, the great deportation of 1942 in the Łódź ghetto. A mother in the foreground has her worldly belongings strapped to her body, while her daughter, all bundled up, walks by her side. The carriage wheels visible in the background are apparently not meant for them, headed as they are for the deportation on foot. Every reader capable of deciphering the Hebrew title, *Lekh-lekho* (go forth), the biblical command to Abraham that lays out the itinerary for God's Chosen People, can also draw the analogy to the (graphically enhanced) Jewish stars affixed to the fronts of the coats of the departing ghetto Jews (cf. the original photograph reproduced in Adelson and Lapides 1989, 252). Only the most discerning reader, however, would notice that the two Hebrew words are flanked by ellipses, to signify an ancient charge that echoes across the boundaries of time.

What of the black, tortured body (fig. 10) splayed across the cover of Primo Levi's *Se questo è un uomo* (If this is a man; 1947)? Its contours and bodily contortion are reminiscent of Goya. Whoever he was, the unmarked and unidentifiable black body offset by the red typeface was not a Jew. Levi's humanist title—how else could a work of Holocaust testimony by a Jewish survivor writing in a non-Jewish language reach out to a broader audience?—was an appeal to conscience on behalf of the victims of fascism. For all that, the small Turin publishing house of De Silva agreed to publish the manuscript only after two interested parties intervened on Levi's behalf (Consonni 2010, 30). Levi's time had not yet come.

Communal cover art used an in-group symbolic language to signal intent. With the financial support of the "Friends of Minsk-Mazowiecki," the Parisian-based artist Bencjon Benn was commissioned to do the cover art for Leyb Rochman's searing diary and chronicle of survival (fig. 7). Benn produced a serene and symmetrical design. The Yiddish title, *Un in dayn blut zolstu lebn* (And in your blood shall you live), contained three letters *lamed*, the first of which Benn elongated into a speck of light surrounded by the sun. How did Benn come up with such a hopeful icon? From Rochman's first diary entry, in which the captive Jews "scoured every part of the partition and finally found a tiny speck of light high above it." Benn wished to convey the idea that the five Jews in hiding were sustained and ultimately rescued by this "message from the sun" (Rochman 1983, 11).

One hardly notices that the sun is shining in Jakob Steinhardt's expressionist cover art for Uri Zvi Greenberg's *Reḥovot hanahar* (fig. 11) because the sun's rays are offset by the flames and smoke coming from the rustic-looking crematorium. Steinhardt, one of the most celebrated European-born artists in Israel, literalized the poet's metaphor of "streets of the river" by portraying an endless procession of Jews flowing to their deaths—the river, as it were, hugging the banks of the crematorium. In keeping with Greenberg's metahistorical view, Steinhardt renders the destruction of European Jewry as a cosmic event, attended by the heavens above and the crematorium fire below. The Hebrew lettering is in the distinctive font reserved for books published by the prestigious publisher Schocken. So the source of consolation is encoded thus: as early as 1951, a Jewish national artist illustrated a jeremiad by a Hebrew national poet that was issued under a transnational imprimatur.

There was only one state-sanctioned Yiddish publishing house in Communist Poland. Working within the strictures of political censorship, Ber Mark published a series called Literary Creations in the Ghettos and Camps, choosing a consistent cover design for the novels, short stories, reportage, prose poems, and diaries that he wished to place at the forefront of Holocaust literature. *Tsvishn lebn un toyt* (Between life and death; 1955) was the fourth in this series and included a number of masterpieces: prose poems by Josef Kirman; Leyb Goldin's study in starvation, "Chronicle of a Single Day"; a memorial address by Abraham Lewin; and the last surviving works of the major Polish Yiddish novelist, Yehoshue Perle (fig. 6). Barbed wire atop a brick wall was a fitting symbol, both of the Nazi ghettos and of the impenetrable wall that had arisen between East and West at the height of the Cold War. Perle's chronicle of the great deportation, we recall, had already been the subject of a ferocious trans-Atlantic debate between Mark and the revered American Yiddish poet H. Leivick, as a result of which this and everything else in the series was rejected by its intended readers living in the West. The cardboard covers and cheap paper literally crumble today at one's touch.

The cover of Elie Wiesel's . . . *un di velt hot geshvign* (. . . and the world was silent; 1956) depicts a German concentration camp enclosed by a primitive barbed wire fence, with smoke rising out of the barracks' chimneys into a reddish sky (see plate 2; also fig. 12). The only human presence is that of two helmeted soldiers armed with bayonets, who are guarding the camp perimeter. There is little to suggest that the barrack in the foreground might be a crematorium. The cover art is middlebrow and unexceptional, in keeping with a popular library dedicated to works about the legacy and destruction of Polish Jewry that had been appearing in Buenos Aires since 1946. Bound in black, each volume had a thin paper jacket, a title page in Yiddish and Spanish, and was printed in an easy-to-read font; selected reviews of recent volumes and an up-to-date list of titles in the series rounded out the volume (J. Schwarz 2007a). Intended for every Jewish home, the cover art for Wiesel's memoir, volume 117 in the series, domesticates the concentrationary landscape and downplays the activist, accusatory tone of the title.

Another way of mainstreaming the Holocaust was to market it as pornography. The first English edition of Ka-Tzetnik's *House of Dolls* (1955) was still pretty soft core; later editions were more sexually explicit. Sam Fischer's jacket design (fig. 8) depicts the helpless, white-clad heroine as if she were literally a doll. Still, it takes two strapping Nazi soldiers to subdue her. This jacket art also illustrates the (inaccurate) plot summary, showing the relics of the school trip from which she presumably never returned, and perhaps the allegedly authentic diary on which this novel is apparently based. The jacket art and copy are designed to recast Ka-Tzetnik's adolescent victim as another Anne Frank, reincarnated as a sex slave. Pornography has its own code, taking the complexity of human relations and reducing it to a formula.

PROVISIONAL MEMORY:
BLOOD, SKY, AND SAFETY PINS

Then came the paperback revolution. Curzio Malaparte's 1944 *Kaputt* resurfaced after his death as pulp fiction (1966), with an appropriately racy cover (see plate 3; also fig. 9), having already sold "over 1½ million copies." Immediately translated into English, this sensational reportage on war-torn Europe had won Malaparte fame and fortune, even though as a card-carrying member of the Italian Fascist Party, he had covered the war from the wrong side. The purple prose accompanying Don Crowley's cover art of a headless statue

(European civilization gone kaput?) and the promise of easy sex for our boys in uniform helped promote this work as a best-selling war story. The sexual exploitation of Jewish women described halfway through the book delivered on that promise. Neither the first nor the second edition of *Kaputt* made any visible gesture toward "Holocaust, Jewish."

From 1960 on, a Holocaust book could be accurately judged by its cover, and American publishers were chiefly responsible for setting the course. The new aesthetic norm was exemplified by the English-language editions of André Schwarz-Bart and Piotr Rawicz. With its rich palette, the cover of *The Last of the Just* bespoke a work of broad historical symbolism (see plate 4; also fig. 13). George Salter's design moved from the fiery red of the auto-da-fé below to the sky blue above, where a nation of *luftmentshn* was turned into *luft*. The white drop of blood against an all-red backdrop in *Blood from the Sky* (see plate 5; also fig. 14), in marked contrast, augured an apocalypse. These covers placed horror and beauty in tense juxtaposition. Not so the yellow star that the cover artist Lawrence Ratzkin affixed to a page from the Hebrew manuscript of Chaim Kaplan's *Scroll of Agony* (see plate 6; also fig. 2). Hebrew script plus Jewish star would have bestowed scriptural authority on this major work of Holocaust testimony—were it not for the absurd and anachronistic presence of a safety pin. Never mind that there were no safety pins in the Warsaw ghetto. The safety pin invited the American reader to imagine that being a Jew inside the Jew-Zone was a matter of contingency. Why, the Jewish star could come right off, without even leaving a trace. Never mind that Kaplan's diary was an anatomy of Jewish fate—inexorable, gratuitous, and horrifying.

Provisionally sacred, provisionally scandalous: that was the status of Holocaust literature in the 1960s and 1970s. In France, the medium of the cover for Jean-François Steiner's *Treblinka* (1967) was also the book's message. Highbrow, serious works of French literature were produced with austere, white covers; you needed a knife to cut the pages. *Pour épatér* just about everyone, the cover for the first French edition of *Treblinka* (fig. 1) was a species of tabloid journalism. The in-your-face image of a Jewish child wearing a striped concentration camp cap was meant to memorialize the adolescent boys who, according to Steiner, had helped prepare the uprising in the Treblinka death camp. Steiner's American publisher, burned by a threatened lawsuit and steering clear of the culture war that the French edition of *Treblinka* had provoked, produced a simple, unadorned book jacket, featuring the single, iconic word "Treblinka."

There was by now a substantial body of Holocaust poetry that demanded a special graphic design—or did it? Nothing on the cover of Dan Pagis's *Gil-gul: shirim* (Metamorphosis: poems; 1970) suggested that a unique corpus of the poet's belated response to the Holocaust was contained therein (fig. 16), save for a sentence in the jacket copy on the back. Nor could anyone have predicted the canonical status that these eight poems would someday achieve. Then again, Pagis belonged to the school of understated and minor-key poets that arose in rebellion against the pathos of Greenberg and the other pre-State Hebrew poets, so perhaps precisely by not calling attention to itself, this collection of poems was quintessentially Israeli.

Like Schwarz-Bart's and Rawicz's covers, then, and like the title *Gilgul*, the new cover art of Holocaust literature was rapidly moving away from the deportees, barbed wire, and crematoria into ever more symbolic and extraterrestrial spaces. Abraham Sutzkever asked Samuel Bak, whom he had discovered as a child prodigy back in the Vilna ghetto, to do the cover of and illustrate a tiny volume of Sutzkever's wartime poetry that had remained in manuscript; the cover art for *Di ershte nakht in geto* (The first night in the ghetto; 1979) is highly evocative indeed (fig. 18). Bearing down on the archway of the old Jewish quarter of Vilna is a crushing pillar of smoke, as massive as rocks or snow from an avalanche. The streets are deserted, and the pavement is cracking, as if from an earthquake. The destruction is coming from above and below. This is not one of the gates to the Nazi ghetto, however, which both Bak and Sutzkever would never forget, but the gateway to the fabled ghetto of Vilna lore, the icon of Jerusalem of Lithuania, the temple of Eastern European Jewry.

Aharon Appelfeld's entire *oeuvre* is set in the wilderness, amid smoke, in the fertile valley, where even the most innocent setting is a gateway to destruction. Nancy Lawton's jacket illustration for *Badenheim 1939* (fig. 15) renders a Middle European spa as a doll house. It was commissioned by the Boston-based publisher D. R. Godine, which specializes in beautiful books and has a particular interest in the Holocaust. Readers who are equipped to "read" the Holocaust will know to beware of the façade of innocence. The studied naïveté of the cover art reveals Badenheim to be a city of false refuge.

AUTHORIZED MEMORY:
SYMBOL, ARTIFACT, AND SURVIVOR

In our own day, Holocaust literature is marked by a tremendous diversity of styles and is truly international in scope. If we judge by the cover art, the turning point came in 1986, with the simultaneous publication of two masterpieces, both written from the perspective of the second generation. Published in the most prestigious and cutting-edge series dedicated to new Israeli fiction, David Grossman's *'Ayyen 'erekh: 'ahava'* (*See Under: Love*; 1986) is appropriately avant-garde (see plate 7; also fig. 20). Were it not for the fact that the French painter Jean Dubuffet had died in 1985, it might have seemed that he personally knew Grossman's nine-year-old protagonist, Momik, and painted him in suspended animation. At a time when Israeli literature was experiencing a novel "boom" (Mintz 1997), attaching Holocaust literature to the aesthetic of high modernism was a powerful means of rescuing it for a new generation of readers.

So too the alchemy of American-born Art Spiegelman, who turned the tale of his survivor father into the homegrown iconography of *Maus* (see plate 8; also fig. 19). A Hitler-cat emblazoned over a swastika serves as the backdrop to Vladek and Anja as mice, huddled in the foreground. In the brilliant economy of Spiegelman's comic book art, the fact that Vladek's tail is showing, at the very moment when Anja seeks protection in his firm embrace, is evidence of his extreme, "Jewish" vulnerability.

One way, then, that the memory of the Holocaust has been authorized is by means of a graphic design (in Spiegelman's case, created by the author himself) that transposes the reimagined Jew-Zone into a symbolic system completely emancipated from the landscape or languages of the Jew-Zone itself. Through such acts of translation or displacement, all readers everywhere are free to appropriate the memory of the Holocaust as they see fit. The DNA of Holocaust memory mutates exponentially.

A second way is by marketing all manner of Holocaust literature as a precious relic. Exhibit A is none other than Malaparte, revealed in our own century to be the first in a long line of Holocaust fabricators. Only with its third English edition (Malaparte 2005) does *Kaputt* come to occupy its rightful place under the rubric of "Holocaust, Jewish, 1939–45." Dignified with a scholarly afterword and new cover featuring a set of decaying, demonic dentures, *Kaputt* will never again be mistaken for a bodice-ripper.

We Were in Auschwitz and Sheinson's *Passover Service* are exhibits B and C. These works are known today because they have finally been translated into English; the anthology in 2000, by a small house called Welcome Rain, and *Passover Service* in a limited facsimile edition by the American Jewish Historical Society in 1998 and as a handsome coffee table book by the Jewish Publication Society of America in 2000. Rebranded as *A Survivor's Haggadah*, the latter required a different cover. The original *A* was replaced by one of seven superb woodcuts by the Hungarian Jewish expressionist artist Miklós Adler that were originally chosen by Sheinson to serve as a visual countercommentary to the ancient text. Few American Jewish readers, however, possessed the mental curriculum demanded of Sheinson's *Passover Service*, so besides the translation of the classical citations from the Haggadah and of Sheinson's supplementary readings in Hebrew and Yiddish, the editor added a considerable scholarly apparatus: an introduction, a running commentary, references, and notes (Sheinson 2000). These adjustments and additions justified a list price of $50.00. Imported from Munich to the United States, both anthologies made the quantum leap from communal to authorized memory, but only as precious artifacts, as then books with a historical, distant claim on the now.

What commands attention in the here and now is the voice and visage of the living survivor. The memorable portrait of Charlotte Delbo that graces the cover of her trilogy, *Auschwitz and After*, can serve as icon of the survivor's moral stature at the present time (fig. 17). The photographer Eric Schwab has captured the author at the hearth of a French country home, surrounded by manuscripts and cooking utensils. Each arm tells a different story. While Delbo's right arm is pointing with confidence at an invisible interlocutor, the tattooed number on her left arm is legible, but unexceptional. Note that the survivor in our midst is a non-Jewish woman. To the extent that women were victims, they were also Jews. To the extent that all Jews were victims, all Jews figuratively were also women.

Can any of these covers be seen as truly iconic? Can a singular cover, to cover all possible meanings past, present, and future, even exist? This brings us back to our point of departure. To answer the question "What is Holocaust literature?" we needed to revisit two separate war zones, track four messy but distinct stages of development, eavesdrop on a conversation in twelve languages, gain familiarity with a variety of genres, and meet a huge cast of characters. The same holds true for the covers. It is pointless to look for one graphic symbol or visual mnemonic for all seasons. Each presupposes a different mental curriculum. Each is enmeshed within a different web of associations, like memory itself.

My copy of Shayevitsh's *Lekh-lekho*, its cover reproduced here, was pristine when I found it in a pile of remaindered Yiddish books some thirty-five years ago. If now it resembles a *genizah* fragment rescued from some ancient ruin, it is because my attempt to make meaning out of historical catastrophe began with hearing this work read aloud. Over the years, I read (and photocopied) this flimsy booklet to pieces. From cover to cover, in marked contrast, Uri Zvi Greenberg's *Streets of the River* was made to last forever. Designed to be a *sefer*, it was meant to serve as a spiritual anchor, to be savored, pondered, and—above all—never to be thrown out. But Holocaust literature, as we have seen, is also a species of pornography, so by making the experience of atrocity irresistibly seductive, the graphic designers Sam Fischer (for Ka-Tzetnik) and Don Crowley (for Malaparte) were doing their job. (The children of Katzenelson Street didn't need to be seduced by the cover of Ka-Tzetnik's *House of Dolls*, their initiation into sexual depravity. So it was for me: the first Yiddish novel I read on my own, far from my mother's ever-watchful eye.) At one end of the iconic spectrum is Auschwitz number P6643 against a blue-and-gray striped background. At the other is a richly-plumed bird ascending or escaping heavenward from the sacrificial pyre below, a phoenix rising from the ashes. Holocaust literature belongs at both ends of the spectrum, and everywhere in between.

GUIDE TO THE FIRST HUNDRED BOOKS

This list includes only longer pieces. Single poems, short works of fiction, and essays are not included unless as part of a larger anthology. Books are presented in order of writing or completion, not necessarily by date of first publication. "DGR" indicates material by David G. Roskies, "ND" material by Naomi Diamant.

Wartime Writing, 1938–45

Communal Memory, 1945–60

Provisional Memory, 1960–85

Authorized Memory: 1985–Present

Wartime Writing, 1938–45

[1940]

Jacob Glatstein. *Emil and Karl.* Translated from the Yiddish with a preface
   and afterword by Jeffrey Shandler. New Milford, CT: Roaring Brook, 2006.
   First published as *Emil un Karl*, by Yankev Glatshteyn.

Parents who raised their children speaking Yiddish spoke to them about the
Holocaust. The conversation that began in 1938 has never ended. It went on
everywhere, from Buenos Aires to the Bronx, from Melbourne and Mexico
City to Montreal. Dedicating this book to his three children, the poet, novelist,
critic, and journalist Jacob Glatstein wrote what is probably the first action-
adventure story on the Holocaust designed for young readers. It was originally
published in New York in February 1940.

   Emil and Karl is the story of two boys—one Christian, the other Jewish—
who are orphaned in the immediate wake of the Anschluss, after which their
fates become one. It is also the story of how a few are able to withstand the
tyranny of the many. "Only good people have a face," the two boys learn
early on, but the others all look the same, wearing the same uniform. These
boys are nine years old; they cry in the dark, and they miss their mommies.
The good Christians are either Socialists or belong to the working class, but
there are shades of gray and many surprises. Of the two boys, Karl, the son of
Socialists, is by far the more active, and it is through his eyes that the (secular)
reader learns about the practice of the Jewish religion. The boys' life together
is a crash course in mass hysteria, sadism, and schadenfreude, all directed
against the Jewish population of their native Vienna. Bullying and violence
begin at school and carry over into the streets. On Sundays, people come out
to the park to make sport of the Jews.

   "What makes them do it?" Karl asks again and again. The boys will get no
adequate response. They too are briefly caught in the net of Jew hatred and
are forced to scrub the sidewalks with their bare hands. "I was also treated like
a Jew," Karl will state proudly. They meet a wonderful cast of characters, but
the adult world is rapidly imploding, and ultimately their sole route of escape
is to leave with the *Kindertransport.*

   In *Emil and Karl,* the crisis of German Austrian Jewry was refracted through
a double lens. One was the lens of Yiddish. Karl's first Yiddish word is *Zeyde,*
the name that Emil remembers calling his (Eastern European) grandfather,
and it is from the same surrogate grandfather that Karl learns a Yiddish mel-
ody, which he will rehearse when the going gets rough. Yiddish is about joy
and survival. The other was the lens of America, where parents did not disap-
pear into the night, where the persecution of minorities never has the blessing

of the state, and where putative enemies were not yet placed in concentration camps. America is about freedom and civil liberty. The date was February 1940, and America was not to enter the war for another twenty-one months. When it finally did, the Yiddish-speaking kids knew why. (DGR)

[1942]

Shimon Huberband. *Kiddush Hashem: Jewish Religious and Cultural Life in Poland during the Holocaust.* Edited by Jeffrey S. Gurock and Robert S. Hirt. Translated from the Yiddish by David E. Fishman. Hoboken, NJ: Ktav, 1987. First published in Hebrew as *Kiddush hashem: ketavim miyemei hasho'ah.* Edited by Nachman Blumental. Tel Aviv: Zakhor, 1969.

Orthodox Hasidic rabbis did not write their autobiographies, record current events, or conduct interviews, let alone collect jokes and expose the moral failings of their flock to the harsh light of the future. How did this Judaic scholar and member of the Hasidic elite become a beloved public servant, the first to chronicle Polish Orthodoxy in the Holocaust and to redefine the meaning of Jewish martyrdom? Rabbi Shimon Huberband assumed these roles because Emanuel Ringelblum recruited him to work for the Jewish Self-Help by day and to write for the underground Oyneg Shabes by night. What survived were these clustered notes and chapters, each one following the directives laid down by Ringelblum and his staff.

Ringelblum feared that with events changing "with cinematic speed," no one would remember how it all started. Huberband, then thirty years old, was not likely to forget, because his wife and child had been killed in the first weeks of the war, and he blamed himself for the tragedy. His first-person chronicle of the life of "a Jewish civilian" during the first months of the war was hardly confessional, however. The closer he stood to an event, the more traditional his lens. "I couldn't stop thinking of the historical Naomi and Ruth, in whose situation we now found ourselves," he wrote. "Now, after eight days, we were returning without all of our belongings, and with deeply wounded hearts." The farther he stood, as when documenting "The Extortion of Money from Jews by Jews," the sharper his contemporary focus. "What Became of the Hasidic Youths?" he asked. He reported that "a considerable part of" the young men who were supposed to be spending their days in Torah study "left the straight and narrow path during the war, and ceased being observant Hasidim." He named the "harsh" youthful followers of the Gerer Rebbe by name, an offense that the Hasidim who regrouped in Brooklyn would not forgive.

This was history writ small, the way Ringelblum wanted it: a section devoted to jokes and messianic signs; a photo gallery of the ghetto; all aspects of banned religious observance—from Jewish dress to prayer, from wedding and divorce to the kosher slaughter of poultry and cattle. This was everyday heroism: the rabbinic concept of Kiddush Hashem, the sanctification of the name of God, instantiated by well-known religious figures as well as by ordinary people, by the pious as well as the godless. For two millennia, men of Huberband's rabbinic caste had adopted a hermetic and elitist mode of writing, and they had written in Hebrew to preserve the unbroken chain of tradition. Huberband adopted new and secular modes of self-expression, and he wrote in the spoken vernacular, Yiddish, to produce a documented, impersonal, panoramic, and transparently honest record, at once reportorial and inspirational. (DGR)

Chaim A. Kaplan. *Scroll of Agony: The Warsaw Diary of Chaim A. Kaplan.* Edited and translated from the Hebrew by Abraham I. Katsh. 2nd rev. ed. New York: Colliers, 1973. First published as *Megilat yesurin: yoman geto Varsha*, 1966. For an alternative translation by Jeffrey M. Green, see *The Literature of Destruction: Jewish Responses to Catastrophe*, edited by David G. Roskies (Philadelphia: Jewish Publication Society of America, 1989), 435–49.

There are many wartime diaries from which to choose. From the Warsaw ghetto alone, we have the published and translated diaries of such leading personalities as Adam Czerniakow, Janusz Korczak, and Emanuel Ringelblum, who by virtue of their public roles knew everyone and everything that it was possible to know; a former Jewish policeman (Stanisław Adler); a Jewish educator (Abraham Lewin); and an adolescent (Mary Berg). Then there is Chaim Kaplan, the sedentary scholar, a man of extraordinary intelligence, who sat at home caring for his ailing wife even while he made daily entries in the Hebrew diary that he had begun keeping in 1933. Whereas Czerniakow's or Ringelblum's personalities rarely come through in their diaries, and you need copious notes to follow the course of events, to read and remember Kaplan, all you need is a Hebrew Bible.

Events unfold on three temporal planes at once. Kaplan registers his changing moods, the ebb and flow of his own "divine inspiration." Just as dutifully, he speaks in the first person plural to register the fate, the fears, and the growing demoralization of the Jewish collective. "Poet of the people, where art thou?" he bursts out on November 30, 1939. Who is there to immortalize the pain, as in the days of the great national bard, Hayyim Nahman Bialik? And then there is Scripture, the prayer book, the cycle of the festivals and fast days. "But He who sits in heaven laughs," he records on October 24, 1940, when Jews and Poles protest the Nazi establishment of a closed ghetto. On November 13, 1940, on the day the closing of the ghetto is decreed, Kaplan is "reminded" of Nebuchadnezzar, the king of Babylon who "came and confounded the world."

Moving deftly from one plane to the next, Kaplan tries to separate fact from rumor, the precedented from the unprecedented. On July 29, 1940 (four months before the ghetto was established), he gives the diary a name, *Scroll of Agony*, to signal a fundamental shift in perspective from the personal to the sacerdotal. On April 7, 1942, learning about the liquidation of Jewish Lublin, "the city of scholars and writers, of learning and piety, . . . an entire community of 44,000 Jews," he acknowledges that reality has "surpassed imagination by far." And on May 30, he begins arguing with his friend—or alter ego—Hirsch, a very clever Jew, who fears the worst. Hirsch is the prophet of doom, whose strident voice has invaded the private space and battered spirit of the chronicler. A month later the great deportation begins, and in the evening hours of August 4 (the second entry for the day), Kaplan's diary ends—his death presaging the end of Warsaw Jewry. (DGR)

Irène Némirovsky. *Suite Française*. Translated from the French by Sandra
    Smith; with appendices and preface to the French edition. New York:
    Alfred A. Knopf, 2006. First published in French in 2004.

Suite Française burst onto the literary scene more than sixty years after it was written. It is a fragment of a much longer work that was never completed. The book is divided into two sections: "Before the Storm," an account of the panicked French flight from Paris in June, 1940, ahead of the Nazi invasion, and "Dolce," set in a small, rural village in the provinces, which chronicles the town's occupation by German cavalry. None of the characters—or, indeed, the writer—has the luxury of retrospection. No one knows what will happen. Much of the time, no one really knows what has already taken place. This makes for pages so unsettling that the novel sits uncomfortably within the corpus of Holocaust literature as conventionally defined.

Why include a novel with no Jewish characters or any reference to the Jewish experience in a collection of Holocaust literature? By 1940, Nazi antisemitism was clear, but the great deportations and concentration camps were yet to come. The book is situated squarely in the present time of occupation, where the German occupiers appear morally superior and no one except a disgruntled farmer, Benoît, is interested in any direct form of resistance. Age-old battles continue between the petite bourgeoisie and the haute bourgeoisie, between farmers and townspeople. Liberation in this context is from the constraints of social existence, whether it is the boys from the Paris orphanage who break into the château and murder the priest who is their chaperone, or the daughter-in-law—Lucille Perin, whose husband is in a POW camp—

who falls in love with the German officer billeted in her mother-in-law's house.

Suite Française is a work of social observation, an unsparing look at the revealing minutiae of daily life. If the period were not so terrifying, and the ultimate fate of the writer not so devastating, the novel would qualify as a comedy of manners set during wartime. In this regard, it carries with it overtones of the first part of Tolstoy's *War and Peace*, Proust, and even Anthony Trollope's social comedy—portraying the upper classes so that they indict and convict themselves. All these approaches serve to delineate the world of what historians have called *la France profonde* (the deep, unchanging, authentic France), daily life with all its repetitiveness and mean dramas.

Framed by increasingly desperate letters from the author to her publisher, as well as a brief biographical note, the book has to be read within the larger context of the author's life and death. We know that Némirovsky died in Auschwitz in 1942, yet without its ancillary materials, the book reads like a work of collaboration more than resistance. In that respect, it is probably much closer to the contemporary public experience of the French defeat and Nazi occupation than any of the French works of the period (usually associated with the resistance) that have come to dominate the French account of the Second World War.

Suite Française is a book that cannot be read except through multiple lenses, and in this respect it calls on the reader to be self-conscious about what he or she is bringing to the reading of the text: knowledge of the course of the Second World War, an understanding of both the shame of collaboration and the savagery that the occupation and deportations released within this most self-consciously cultured society. (ND)

Simkhe Bunem Shayevitsh. . . . *Lekh-lekho* . . . (Go forth). Edited by Nachman Blumental. Łódź, Poland: Tsentrale yidishe historishe komisye baym tsentral-komitet fun poylishe yidn, 1946. "Lekh-lekho," translated from the Yiddish by Leah Robinson, in *The Literature of Destruction: Jewish Responses to Catastrophe*, edited by David G. Roskies (Philadelphia: Jewish Publication Society of America, 1989), 520–30; "Spring 1942," translated from the Yiddish by Chana Mlotek, in *Lodz Ghetto: Inside a Community under Siege*, edited by Alan Adelson and Robert Lapides (New York: Viking, 1989), 250–62.

Both of Shayevitsh's surviving poems from the Łódź ghetto are addressed to a child. Shayevitsh's muse is his eight-year-old daughter, Blimele, the apple of his eye. Both poems are suffused with religious symbolism. "Look," he says halfway though his dramatic monologue, as father and daughter are setting out into the unknown, "I'm packing the *tallis* / And the *kitl* and the shroud / And also the small red Bible." These he will need both for prayer and for burial. And one thing more: "And Leivick's poems for a time of rest." To strengthen the daughter's resolve, the father rehearses all past instances of Jewish martyrdom, beginning with Isaac on Mount Moriah and ending with "our uncle's stride on Siberian roads," a reference to Leivick's travails as a revolutionary in exile. Thus, the first expulsion of 10,000 Jews, January 16–29, 1942, is an echo of *lekh-lekho* (go forth), the biblical command to Abraham, and a link in an unbroken chain of heroic response to suffering.

In the spring of 1942, the mass deportations entered a second phase, affecting 34,000 victims. It now became clear to the poet that the ghetto was a city of slaughter, designed not for survival but for death. In light of this, he composed a parodic ode to spring, which he dated according to the Jewish calendar. Shayevitsh did not have to look far for an exact analogy. Once again, God called up the slaughter and the spring together, exactly as had happened in 1903, during the Kishinev pogrom: "God with a mild hand / Also presented us with twins, / A death expulsion and a spring." Exactly as in Kishinev, the bloodletting coincided with the celebration of the seder.

Like Bialik, the prophet and bard of Kishinev, Shayevitsh surveys the human wreckage of the ghetto, focusing on the plight of one seventeen-year-old girl in particular. But when at last Shayevitsh summons Bialik from the grave, it is only after all past analogies have been judged inadequate. The Spanish expulsion of the Jews? Mere "child's play when compared to today." Then Bialik the person is subjected to a point-by-point rebuttal. He stands convicted of lack of empathy, lack of historical imagination, and—most of all—the hubris of a Romantic poet, who allowed his own agonized voice to drown out the cries of the victims and the echoes from the hallowed past. This Passover, the speaker's sense of eternal pasts is especially keen. Now addressing Blimele directly at the seder table, the father instructs his daughter to recite the litany of curses, "Pour Out Thy Wrath," glossing every ferocious Hebrew phrase into Yiddish. Within Shayevitsh's two surviving poems is a curriculum of Jewish responses to catastrophe, so essential that even a child must learn it. (DGR)

Josef Zelkowicz. *In Those Terrible Days: Writings from the Lodz Ghetto.* Edited by Michal Unger. Translated from the Hebrew by Naftali Greenwood. Jerusalem: Yad Vashem, 2002. First published as *In yene koshmarne teg.* Translations by Joachim Neugroschel from the Yiddish original are scattered throughout *Lodz Ghetto: Inside a Community under Siege*, edited by Alan Adelson and Robert Lapides (New York: Viking, 1989).

As an employee of the Łódź Ghetto Archive, Josef Zelkowicz had free access to every ghetto tenement, institution, workplace, Judenrat office, and official document. As a seasoned journalist, ethnographer, and amateur historian, his favored medium remained reportage, through which he as a Yiddish writer could speak directly to the people in their own language. But the Łódź ghetto had neither a free nor an underground press, all work on the official *Chronicle* was conducted in Polish or German, and what Zelkowicz found most compelling as a Jewish reporter was impossible to make public. So he adapted to the new reality and each week typed up his hidden transcripts for postwar publication.

Zelkowicz is the connoisseur of official documents, whose main purpose is to cover up human tragedy and duplicity. But since it's lonely to collect data on the living conditions of ghetto dwellers, he takes along a female traveling companion, named Ryva Bramson. Ryva is his great invention; fastidious, acculturated, never getting a word in edgewise, she is shocked and dismayed by the squalor and depravity that stare her in the face. She is also the perfect foil, because much like the postwar reader, Ryva has little knowledge of this exotic population, is unable to distinguish between its members, cannot comprehend their language. Furthermore, she is overtly sentimental, and seems to accumulate no wisdom. Here it is, the twenty-sixth apartment they've visited together, questionnaires in hand, and still she must be told: "Next time Ryva, when you enter a room where the smoke from the small oven stops your breath and stings your lovely eyes, do not pamper yourself by demanding fresh ghetto air. It is high time, Ryva, for your eyes and nose to stop thinking in prewar terms." Her guide, in contrast, can take the measure of how much has changed, though he too is stunned by what he hears.

What he hears is a people speaking in multiple voices—plaintive, manipulative, despairing, naïve, hallucinatory—Jewspeak in the raw—for which there is no place in the official ghetto *Chronicle*. When reporting on the carpenters' strike of January 1941, which Rumkowski ultimately puts down by force, Zelkowicz alone becomes an advocate for the truth, because he alone allows all sides to speak in their own voices.

But who can speak for the *Szpere*, the violent lockdown and mass deportations of September 1942? How to signal that the ghetto population has entered archetypal time? By addressing his 345-page handwritten chronicle to the "Son of man," instructing him to "go out into the streets" and behold what no human eye has ever seen before. When Rumkowski addresses the crowd and urges them to give up their children and elderly parents in order to save what can still be saved, Zelkowicz includes their hysterical cries.

This is reportage as apocalypse. (DGR)

Gusta Davidson Draenger. *Justyna's Narrative*. Edited with an introduction
by Eli Pfefferkorn and David H. Hirsch. Translated from the Polish by
Roslyn Hirsch and David H. Hirsch. Amherst: University of Massachusetts
Press, 1996. First published as *Pamiętnik Justyny*, by Gusta Dawidsohn-
Draengerowa. Kraków, 1946.

"I would like to write the epic of my life and death," Gusta Davidson Draenger
confided to a fellow fighter, "which will come soon"—whereupon she gave
herself up to the Gestapo in order to be under the same roof as her beloved
husband, Szymek (Shimshon). This was the second time that she had joined
him in captivity. The first was at the beginning of the war, when Szymek was
interned in a concentration camp for his anti-German activity. Now, by February 1943, as founding members of the Jewish Combat Organization in the
Kraków ghetto, both Gusta and Szymek Draenger had indeed become the
heroes of a modern epic.

Gusta refers to herself in the third person as "Justyna," her nom de guerre.
Dictated to her cellmates over a three-month period, this document could easily
fall into the wrong hands, as Gusta well knew. It is a narrative of extraordinary
heroism and overwhelming loss told from a woman's perspective, by someone
schooled in Polish Romanticism and the pioneering spirit of Zionist youth.

Her narrative frame is paradise lost. The work opens on a bucolic scene at
an agricultural colony near Kraków, with our young, muscular, suntanned heroes returning from the field to celebrate the Sabbath. Their nine-month idyll
is about to end, because "Marek" (Szymek), the movement's chief ideologue,
has just returned from the city with horrifying news. The Germans are intent
on annihilating the entire Jewish people. At best, a few will survive. Not only is
the movement itself doomed, but its ideals of nonviolence and cultural work
are bankrupt. In whatever time remains, the surviving revolutionary youth
must erase the shame of their people by avenging their deaths. What follows,
after their return to Kraków, is a dramatized chronicle of how dreamers and
farmers turned themselves into a fighting underground and kept fighting as
their members were killed in action or swept up in the deportations. The climax of their self-transformation comes when the last major *Aktion* severs all
parental and communal ties, setting them free—but no longer to engage the
enemy as a unified band of brothers and sisters. As the narrative began, so it
draws to a close with a celebratory Sabbath meal in their urban commune,
their Last Supper.

There are many melodic lines, as Gusta puts it, to the story. One is the
unrequited love of a beautiful, caring, intuitive woman for her fanatically
single-minded, cerebral husband, whose skill as a forger keeps the underground

financed and whose fearless intelligence keeps it absolutely focused on the armed struggle. Another is the collective portrait of a generation that wanted above all to serve its people and discovered that in order to fight effectively, it had to mask every part of itself. (DGR)

Jacob Glatstein. *Gedenklider* (Poems of remembrance). New York: Yidisher kemfer, 1943. Selections translated from the Yiddish in *American Yiddish Poetry: A Bilingual Anthology*, edited by Benjamin Harshav and Barbara Harshav (Berkeley: University of California Press, 1986); Jacob Glatstein, *Selected Poems of Yankev Glatshteyn*, translated and edited, with an introduction, by Richard J. Fein (Philadelphia: Jewish Publication Society of America, 1987); Jacob Glatstein, *I Keep Recalling: The Holocaust Poems of Jacob Glatstein*, introduction by Emanuel S. Goldsmith, translated by Barnett Zumoff (Hoboken, NJ: Ktav, 1993).

"With proud stride / I decide—: / I am going back to the ghetto." With these defiant words, Jacob Glatstein changed the direction of Yiddish secular culture in April 1938. He intended this call of return to be a paradoxical rallying cry of self-liberation; not forward toward the future, where millions of poor and disenfranchised Eastern European immigrants were heading when they began a new life in the New World, but "back to the ghetto": "Back to my kerosene, tallowed shadows, / eternal October, minute stars, / to my warped streets and hunchbacked lanterns, / my worn-out pages of the Prophets"—that is, back to the cultural habitus that the Jews had created in their own sphere. This was Moses leading his people in reverse, even as he railed against the enemies from without and false prophets from within. Exposing the desperate state of his people, Glatstein asked whether this dark and depleted place called "ghetto" could ever again be a living landscape. His resounding answer was this book of poems, the first significant poetic response to the Holocaust to be published in the Free Zone.

Glatstein's answer became the answer of Yiddish culture as a whole: to translate space into time. The contracting physical universe of the Jews, and the enmity, hypocrisy, and indifference that surrounded them on all sides, could be countered only by cracking open the barriers of time. This Glatstein did by adopting the persona of Rabbi Nahman of Braslav, whom he recast as the first speaker of Jewspeak, a richly idiomatic, down-to-earth, yet profoundly introspective religious thinker. A dramatic folk monologue in free verse, "The Braslaver to His Scribe," begun in 1943, inspired Glatstein's efforts for decades to come. He invented a poetic language replete with neologisms that would defy the best efforts of his translators ("Kleine Nacht Musik"). And by returning to the lullaby ("Ghetto Song") and the liturgy. And by taking pity on his diminished God ("God Is a Sad Maharal"). And by openly defying the Christian world ("On the Butcher Block"). And yes, by also turning his back on America and its anemic Judaism ("In a Chapel").

The dividing line between a Jew-Zone of the mind and the real Jew-Zone was time itself, as unnatural as it was native. To distinguish between the two, Glatstein provided precise dates, from April 1938 to June 1939, for the poems he wrote before the war began. After September 1, 1939, again after real ghettos were established in Eastern and Central Europe, and again once the dead numbered in the millions, the poet was forced to admit: "I have never been here before." As the "now" shifted, the "here" almost disappeared.

Because these poems affected an idiom at once folksy, conversational, confessional, and liturgical, they helped shape a shared response among the helpless bystanders living almost halfway across the globe. As the partial list of translations testifies, Glatstein's poetic and prescient response to the annihilation also became a bridge across the generations. There was the here of the here and now. (DGR)

Yitzhak Katzenelson. *Vittel Diary [22.5.43–16.9.43]*. Translated from the
    Hebrew by Myer Cohen. Israel: Ghetto Fighters' House, 1964. First
    published as *Ketavim aharonim* (Last writings) in 1947. First complete
    edition published as *Ktavim aharonim: begeto Varsha uvemahane Vitel*,
    vol. 5, *Ktavim*, edited by Menahem Dorman. Tel Aviv: Beit Lohamei
    Hageta'ot and Hakibbutz Hameuchad, 1988.

From the moment he found refuge in Warsaw, in mid-November 1939, the poet Yitzhak Katzenelson was a man with a mission: he was active in both the Yiddish and Hebrew cultural societies, always declaiming his verse before live audiences, marking literary anniversaries, writing plays for children and grown-ups, and responding to events throughout the Jew-Zone by redefining the meaning of martyrdom. Now it was all over. Katzenelson arrived in Vittel, the German transit camp in France, with Zvi, his one surviving son, after Bentsikl and Yomke, his younger sons, had perished in Treblinka along with their mother, Hannah. What lay before him was a void. What lay behind was a calendar overwritten with deaths. The date was May 22, 1943, and it was all he could do to jot something down in a diary. Beginning in Yiddish, he continued in Hebrew and then stopped writing, overwhelmed by his losses. When he picked up again two months later, it was with a newfound twofold purpose: to mourn his personal losses and the destruction of his people; and in their name and his own to demand a moral reckoning from the Germans, the Poles, his fellow Jews, and the free world. The next day marked the first anniversary of the start of the great deportation.

The confessional wartime diary finds its fullest iteration here, in Katzenelson's *Vittel Diary*, which has held up much better than his poetry or plays. Like Calel Perechodnik's diary, it could not be published as is: Katzenelson spared no one, least of all his long-standing foes on the political Left and religious Right, some of whom were still alive in 1964 when this translation appeared. The *Diary* is a fiercely Zionist reading of the Holocaust—past, present, and future.

As a Zionist, Katzenelson must preserve some past and future vision of the Jewish people capable of striving for self-determination. During the great deportation, there was one group—the Jewish police—that through its behavior cut itself off from the matrix of Jewish fate. Katzenelson now writes them out with a vengeance, casting them all as non-native, self-hating intellectuals. As a bereaved father and spouse, Katzenelson must come to terms with the murder of his loved ones, which he does by describing Treblinka in great detail. As a survivor, he must try to relive the slaughter, especially the last two days of the deportations, which he spent hiding in a cellar in Karmelicka 9. What happened to him in that cellar, his encounters with people both real and imaginary, and his reveries and fantasies of revenge are a masterpiece of Holocaust testimony.

Writing this Hebrew diary allowed Katzenelson to work through the trauma. Three weeks after making his last entry, he began to compose his Yiddish epic poem, *The Song of the Murdered Jewish People* (1980), which took him six months to complete. The poem was dedicated to the memory of Hannah, his muse, the only source of meaning now that the heavens, in whose poetic mission he had once believed, were silent. (DGR)

Dawid Sierakowiak. *The Diary of Dawid Sierakowiak: Five Notebooks from the Łódź Ghetto.* Foreword by Lawrence L. Langer. Edited by Alan Adelson. Translated from the Polish by Kamil Turowski. New York: Oxford University Press, 1996. First published as *Dziennik Dawida Sierakowiaka*, with an afterword by Adolf Rudnicki, 1960.

Dawid Sierakowiak was a New Polish Jew. When we first meet him, he is attending a Zionist summer camp and enjoying treks in the Polish mountains. There he meets up with Jewish Scouts, less ideologically committed but fun to be with nonetheless. He writes and performs skits in modern Hebrew and attends an all-boy Polish-Jewish *gymnasium*, which goes co-ed when the war begins. He is at odds with his irascible Orthodox father but adores his mother. The German occupation and the "present social conditions" awaken in him a keen interest in Marx, and he joins the Communist underground the moment the ghetto is established. By joining—and changing—political movements, tens of thousands of Jewish youth across Poland and the Baltic countries had hoped to create a counterculture that would combat Jewish patriarchy and passivity. They were encouraged by the YIVO Institute for Jewish Research to keep diaries and write their autobiographies—in Polish, Yiddish, or Hebrew (Shandler 2002).

Dawid's five notebooks from the Łódź ghetto lead us to the dead end of such youthful aspirations. Instead of liberating himself from his father's Orthodoxy and tyranny, he finds himself trapped inside an imploding, dysfunctional family. More resourceful than either of his parents, it is he who must forage for food and try to pull strings to find some form of employment for them. Instead of mobilizing the masses, he watches helplessly as numbers of his brethren are resettled in and resettled out, and watches those who remain work as forced laborers until they drop dead of starvation and disease. Instead of helping to cultivate a new cadre of Jewish leaders, he must deal with the power that lies in the hands of one man—Mordecai Chaim Rumkowski, who is called the Eldest of the Jews but who seems to grow more youthful each month that the ghetto grows more fatal.

As the circles contract, so too do Dawid's hopes for survival. He decides not to dedicate his life to the revolutionary underground; nonetheless, he continues to seek out his erstwhile cell leader, Niutek, and dutifully records all changes on the political front. His thirst for knowledge continues unabated after he graduates from *gymnasium*; he just grows too weak to hold a book in his hands. The approach of death begins to take its daily toll in myriad forms: from toothaches, illnesses, and fevers to famine, which reduces his diet to potato peels. The instances when his father hoards the bread ration grow ever more frequent and rancorous. When the mass deportations of September 1942 sweep up his beloved mother, already emaciated from hunger, all efforts to exempt her as a working body are futile. In comparison, he barely notes his father's death from starvation.

Youth was supposed to be the vanguard of the future. Rumkowski had staked everything on rescuing the young and able-bodied. Dawid's journal ends on the eve of Passover 1943, with the certainty that "there is really no way out of this for us." (DGR)

[1944]

Anne Frank. *The Diary of a Young Girl.* Definitive ed. Edited by Otto H. Frank and Mirjam Pressler. Translated from the Dutch by Susan Massotty. New York: Doubleday, 1995. First published as *Het achterhuis: dagboekbrieven van 12 juni 1942–1 augustus 1944,* 1947. Movie version, *The Diary of Anne Frank,* directed by George Stevens (United States, 1959).

The Anne Frank enshrined in postwar memory is a trusting, fun-loving child. To project this image, her father and Dutch editors cut and pasted from the two extant versions of her diary: one that she wrote for herself alone, and one that she began to rewrite in March 1944 for postwar publication, after hearing a Dutch radio broadcast from London. Published on the fiftieth anniversary of the Liberation, the definitive edition re-presents Anne Frank as an assertive, sexually aware young woman, bursting with literary ambition. Occupying center stage here are the oedipal conflict with her parents, her burgeoning love for Peter but eventual disenchantment with him, and her growing sense of herself as a citizen of Europe.

"I'm young and strong," Anne proclaims, "and living through a big adventure." This literary self-awareness adds a second dimension to the drama of "The Secret Annex." From reading *Rin Tin Tin* and *Daisy Goes to the Mountains*, she graduates to arguing with Dussel, her middle-aged roommate, about male psychology and discussing sexual nitty-gritty with Peter. Marking the rapid pace of her education is her own commentary (printed in italics) as she rereads the pages of her diary every now and then and is highly critical of what she wrote.

The role of "Kitty," the imaginary addressee, remains constant throughout. Kitty is prudish, naïve, discreet, and ever patient. Best of all, she isn't Jewish. She knows nothing about how Jews celebrate or about their special disabilities. Kitty is an amalgam of some heroine from an adventure story and the Dutch Christian classmates whom Anne had just begun to befriend before she was forced to enroll in the Jewish Lyceum. Thus, Kitty is privy to some of Anne's best writing: a detailed list of items from an imaginary shopping trip to Switzerland; a mock-serious "Guide to the Secret Annex"; lively and exquisitely differentiated dialogue; and the introduction of strangers to the Annex as a way of underscoring the absurdity of the whole situation. Although based on her diary, *The Secret Annex* she was planning to publish would have been closer to a novel of manners than a riveting drama about these trapped individuals unfolding in real time. Kitty might not have appeared there at all.

The almost unspoken Holocaust narrative provides the third dimension. Anne knows the net is closing: Holland is becoming *Judenrein*, and those interned at Westerbork never come back; the million Hungarian Jews now under Nazi occupation are effectively doomed. But even as the catastrophe makes Dussel, Peter, and her older sister, Margot, more assertively Jewish, "at a time when ideals are being shattered and destroyed, when the worst side of human nature predominates, when everyone has come to doubt truth, justice, and God," Anne asserts her primary allegiance to Holland, Europe, the humanizing mission of the Jews, and an ideal of universal humanity. Read in this light, *The Diary of a Young Girl* is a manifesto of Jewish emancipation. (DGR)

Etty Hillesum. *Letters from Westerbork*. Introduction and notes by Jan G. Gaarlandt. Translated from the Dutch by Arnold J. Pomerans. New York: Pantheon, 1986. First published as *Het denkende hart van de barak: brieven*, 1982.

In *Survival in Auschwitz* (1985), Primo Levi reserves some of his most savage comments for the men who put Emilia Levi—a bright, curious two-year-old unrelated to the author—on the transport from Milan. Jorge Semprún (1964) turns the train journey to Buchenwald into an intricate novel of delirium. The train ride itself, then, is a common motif, but the Western European assembly camps of Drancy, Fossoli, and Westerbork are in general absent from the literature. They are points of passage, temporary in the extreme, their inhabitants already among the lost if they only knew it.

Etty Hillesum's letters from the Dutch deportation camp of Westerbork present a compelling series of snapshots of people in the full throes of social adaptation. As a staff member attached to the camp's Jewish Council, she has certain privileges relative to the larger group and tries to use them to ameliorate other people's living conditions. She conducts an extensive correspondence with friends in Amsterdam, receives packages, requests basics—bread, butter, sugar—and provides news about members of the community who have "come through."

At twenty-seven, Etty has an insistently positive voice. Through her correspondence, we watch her developing a philosophy of acceptance, seeking validation in the moment, and trying hard not to judge others too harshly. As one reads, with the knowledge that she died at Auschwitz in November 1943, it is hard not to be critical of what appears to be her blind optimism. Surely, one feels, she must know what awaits all the thousands who have passed through Westerbork. The great image of the letters is the train whose tracks literally cut the camp in half and that ships out victims and brings in their replacements. As the letters continue, and their tone darkens, Etty communicates the details of deportation to the outside world: paper "mattresses" placed on the floors of the cattle cars for the sick, but no food and water for them. She describes her work in comforting the ill, how she tries to ease their physical and spiritual condition as they await their summons from week to week, and how she is forced to work feverishly off-loading new trainloads of Jews and getting them squared away.

This is deportation *in medias res*. Erudition and talent is a valueless commodity. But others have inner resources to meet the external pressures, and Etty describes both the people and their resources. She writes about the stress of not knowing if her parents will be on the next transport; her contempt for the soldiers and guards; the horse-trading in lives that goes on in the camp. At the same time, she has deeply moving conversations about faith and philosophy with friends in the camp. She is buoyed by seeing a beautiful rainbow. Hers is less an unseeing optimism than a willed philosophical position.

In the end, as she expects, she and her family are deported, but in separate carriages. Typical of Etty, she gets caught up in a different part of the train because she was looking for a friend. Etty passes briefly before us, and forces us to recognize the cost of an individual life cut short. In the moment, as events converge, people have only their own inner resources on which to draw, resources in which Etty Hillesum was particularly rich.

The volume from which the *Letters* are drawn is called *An Interrupted Life* (Hillesum 1983). That title might well apply to the literature of the Holocaust *toute entière*. In Hillesum's case, one feels the impact of the interruption and a sense of personal regret at not having met, in other circumstances, this woman filled with light and love. (ND)

Joseph Kermish, ed. *To Live with Honor and Die with Honor: Selected Documents from the Warsaw Ghetto Underground Archives "O.S." (Oneg Shabbath)*. Jerusalem: Yad Vashem, 1986.

It takes more than a "Glossary of Unfamiliar Terms" to negotiate the 790 densely printed pages of this anthology, and more than training in the social sciences to sound its depths. The work's encyclopedic scope is staggering, so the best place to begin is with Emanuel Ringelblum's retrospective essay on the goals, achievements, and interrupted life of his underground archive, whose code name, Oneg Shabbath, means pleasure of the Sabbath. Its guiding principles were these: to be objective and comprehensive; to provide multiple perspectives on every aspect of ghetto and wartime life, as experienced by young and old, men and women, natives and refugees, freethinkers and the God-fearing, the underworld and the law-abiding; to be of the people, for the people.

This anthology surveys a wide range of testamentary and documentary genres: reports, memoranda, bulletins, letters, diaries, wills, eulogies, prayers, street songs, jokes, reportorial prose, and a Jew-Zone genre unique to the Warsaw ghetto—answers by leading prewar intellectuals to a questionnaire about the present and future. These answers range from wildly optimistic (H. Rosen, Shoel Stupnitski) to profoundly pessimistic and prescient (Yehoshue Perle, Israel Milejkowski, Hillel Zeitlin). No less revealing are the various questionnaires in the archives, along with outlines and research plans, including a twelve-point outline on "The Street," a twenty-one-point outline of religious life, and a statistical breakdown of the whole ghetto in 1941. Of the three communities within the ghetto, the focus here is on the "alternative community" of the Jewish Self-Help, with its network of house committees, soup kitchens, schools, orphanages, refugee gathering points, and cultural activities. Ringelblum, ever the Marxist, saw the Judenrat as an arm of the self-serving Jewish bourgeoisie and failed to preserve its archive. The underground press, the voice of the "countercommunity," is preserved elsewhere.

As the addressee changes, so too does the nature of the archive. Most of the documents are intended for internal use only, or to serve future historians as the authentic core of wartime memory. These documents are factual, straightforward, and extremely polished. Everything written during or after the great deportation has a sense of urgency and agency; it reads like the last testament of those who know that all trains leaving the Umschlagplatz are headed to Treblinka. Although the Oyneg Shabes ceased operation in 1943, the last document included in Kermish's anthology is dated March 1, 1944. It is both a summation and a farewell addressed to the surviving Yiddish writers and cultural leaders in New York, written by Ringelblum and Adolf Berman "at a time when 95% of the Jews of Poland have already perished." The book's heroic title comes from that last letter.

Literature of and on the Holocaust is ordinarily animated by the culture of selfhood—the self asserting itself in the face of all that negates it. This anthology is not that. It is a testament to collective self-help and self-study as a revolutionary response to political powerlessness and genocide. (DGR)

Lucjan Dobroszycki, ed. *The Chronicle of the Łódź Ghetto 1941–1944*. Translated from the Polish by Richard Lourie and from the German by Joachim Neugroschel et al. New Haven: Yale University Press, 1984. First published as *Kronika getta Łódzkiego*, 2 vols., 1965–66.

Two narratives shadow this remarkable chronicle: the one benign, the other sinister. The positive idea that brought this work into being was the community as a collective hero, a *kehillah*—the Hebrew and Yiddish name the Jews of Łódź called themselves from the beginning of the nineteenth century until October 1939, when the prewar *kehillah* was disbanded by the German occupier. This famously industrious city was worthy of its own narrative, all the more so in the difficult circumstances of wartime and for the sake of future historians. The other shadow was cast by the authorities, their Gestapo offices located inside the ghetto, so menacing a presence that they could not even be mentioned in Jewish code as Ashkenazim. The existence of this chronicle was kept secret from the Germans, but anything could happen. Every sentence was so worded that the chief perpetrators, predators, and criminals were never named.

The keepers of this so-called community chronicle were a group of seven writers and scholars, only one of whom was a native of Łódź. Coming as they did from far and near, and speaking different languages, their voices merged into a polyphonic choir. The official language of the chronicle shifted from Polish to German, and the more linguistically transparent it became to the authorities, the more the writers needed to watch every word. As in *U.S.A.* by John Dos Passos, statistics, weather reports, and new bulletins were interspersed with reportorial writing from a specific point of view, yet at no point was that perspective at odds with the Judenrat or its megalomaniacal ruler, Chaim Rumkowski. The most discordant element of the chronicle derived instead from the screaming contradictions of ghetto life itself. Even as the chroniclers took careful note of the ghetto's rising productivity, the network of schools and orphanages, the fight against crime, and the concerts and religious celebrations, the chroniclers themselves were succumbing to hunger and disease. More and more, the good news was giving way to reports of suicide and a rising death toll from starvation, to rumors and to the radical shrinkage of the ghetto population through "resettlement." What was built and created at the outset of the chronicle was being dismantled and depleted as the end approached.

For the ultimate shadow was the shadow of death. Following the September 1942 *Szpere*, the Łódź ghetto equivalent of the great deportation in Warsaw, the last vestige of ersatz autonomy was removed, and the ghetto functioned as a forced labor camp. The simplest statistics spoke volumes. On July 1, 1943, the chroniclers noted: "Deaths: Nineteen. Births: None." Then came the end of the chroniclers themselves, who were on the last transports to Auschwitz, an ending so sudden that the archive was simply abandoned.

Two people, both survivors of the ghetto, were responsible for its rescue: Nachman Zonabend for its physical rescue, and Lucjan Dobroszycki for its publication. Almost alone among postwar editors, Dobroszycki did not add a shadow narrative of his own. (DGR)

Herman Kruk. *The Last Days of the Jerusalem of Lithuania: Chronicles from the Vilna Ghetto and the Camps, 1939–1944.* Edited by Benjamin Harshav. Translated from the Yiddish by Barbara Harshav. New Haven: Yale University Press, 2002. First published as *Togbukh fun vilner geto*, edited by Mordecai Bernshteyn, 1961.

Herman Kruk fled Warsaw at the outbreak of the war and sought refuge in Vilna (also known as Wilno and Vilnius), where he was joined by thousands of other Jewish refugees in the months and years that followed, as the city changed hands several times. Two days prior to the German conquest, on June 23, 1941, Kruk decided to stay put in order "to write a chronicle of the events of Vilna." He knew that sooner or later the Germans would establish a ghetto, as they had done throughout the occupied territories. He did not know that Vilna would be the first Jewish community to feel the full brunt of Operation Barbarossa or that only 20,000 Jews would be left to inhabit the tiny ghetto after two-thirds of the prewar population was murdered in nearby Ponar.

So Kruk, a card-carrying Jewish Socialist and professional librarian, set out to keep an historical, as opposed to a personal, diary and—by dint of his optimism, energy, and moral authority—established a new library, which he turned into the cultural center of the ghetto. There, every day, he dictated the diary to his secretary, who typed it up in three copies. One almost complete copy survived (Kassow 1999).

Compressed within its pages is the push and pull among three competing notions of time: future time, or how the surviving elite rebuilt a whole network of social and cultural activities while the Judenrat labored to increase productivity; extermination time, or how the Germans and willing Lithuanians carried out *Aktionen* that they continued to cover up; and resistance time, or how the United Partisan Organization planned for an uprising that had to be aborted. Populating its pages are a gallery of party activists, poets, artists, songwriters, Jewish police, and Jewish partisans, with cameo appearances by the authorities, who come to plunder, murder, and deceive. Kruk, who moved with relative ease throughout the city, also portrays the attitudes of Poles, Lithuanians, and ordinary Germans. Animating its pages is the mystique of a place that had been known since Napoleonic times as the Jerusalem of Lithuania and since modern times as the cradle of the Jewish Labor Bund and of Yiddish secular culture. How long that mystique could be sustained as time imploded is the underlying plot of Kruk's diary.

The diary can also be read as a lesson in radical metonymy: how a community of 60,000 was reduced to 20,000; how that saving remnant conspired to survive for as long as possible; how its members in turn were deported to slave labor camps; and how the last of the survivors managed to scribble a last entry on the day before the camp was liberated. Information on how Kruk perished in Klooga—a row of bodies and a row of logs—is on view at the entrance to the Yad Vashem Museum, in Jerusalem. (DGR)

Curzio Malaparte. *Kaputt*. Afterword by Dan Hofstadter. Translated from the Italian by Cesare Foligno. New York: New York Review of Books, 2005. First published as *Kaputt*. Napoli: Casella, 1944. First English edition New York: Dutton, 1946; second, paperback edition 1966. Movie version of chapter 6 ("The Rats of Jassy"), *Călătoria lui Gruber* (Gruber's journey) directed by Radu Gabrea (Romania, 2008).

Kaputt blurs the line between fact and fiction; it is a combination of memoir, journalistic account, and commentary. The narrator is an Italian journalist with diplomatic connections and socially impeccable credentials, a critic and an aesthete, a connoisseur of vulgarity and a sophisticated observer of atrocity. The form of the book forces readers into active roles as arbiters, continually uncertain as we are about Malaparte's position vis-à-vis his material. This uncertainty is accentuated by the book's odd tone—a mélange of high-mindedness, gaiety, and unsparing rawness of detail.

Malaparte signals from the very beginning that this book breathes in the gap between journalism and fiction. Every part of it is infused with a kind of self-consciousness that makes the author the main character for a work in which war is described as destiny, Jews as rats, and Russians as dogs (a gesture that Art Spiegelman would use some fifty years later to great effect). Part I begins with a chapter titled "Du côté de Guermantes," echoing the celebrated third volume of Marcel Proust's great novel *A la recherche du temps perdu*, a work devoted to the recovery of memory through art itself. These are not insignificant ambitions for a man constructing an account of the Second World War.

Throughout the book, the narrator's sympathies shift. He claims to despise and dislike the Germans, intimating that he is forced into sycophancy by the tenuousness of his position. Yet it is his choice to write about war as social comedy, and he enjoys the remnants of the aristocratic way of life. Malaparte is of course an immensely privileged observer to the theater of atrocity. He has immunity as a member of the diplomatic community and, as an Italian, is viewed by the Nazis as an ally. The book is redolent with the language of social class and class judgments with regard to aesthetics. In the section about Hans Frank, the governor general of Poland, and his court, Malaparte's judgments are fiercest about the philistinism and crudity of the environment, as if atrocity were a consequence of poor social skills. Similarly, his compassion seems reserved more for the young German officers on General Dietl's staff than for the "rats" of Jassy—that is, the Jews who are experiencing the full savagery of the times. It is the young Germans who are Christlike, Malaparte tells us, used up by atrocity. But they are still alive.

Further investigation (well presented in Dan Hofstadter's afterword) points to the ways in which Malaparte's account is unreliable and self-serving. For example, Malaparte never visited the Warsaw ghetto, was never in Jassy, and certainly never witnessed the pogrom that he describes in such detail. And it is equally troubling to discover that the book was able to garner an English-language audience much sooner than most Holocaust writing by survivors was available to a broad audience (a benefit, one supposes, of an aristocratic background). Despite the repellent aspects of the book, *Kaputt* forces the reader to think carefully about how history is propagated, how claims of witness can be abused, and how (or whether) high culture can retain its moral authority. In Malaparte's hands, high culture as a frame of reference is complicit; it distorts moral choice. It renders atrocity banal and sinister. It sabotages the possibility that an educated sensibility must be the undergirding for an ethical, sustainable response to the catastrophes of history. In this context, the book's title suggests that not only is the Third Reich kaput—that is, broken or destroyed—but also that the culture behind which the narrator hides is fractured beyond repair. (ND)

Calel Perechodnik. *Am I a Murderer? Testament of a Jewish Ghetto Policeman.* Edited and translated from the censored Polish edition of 1993 by Frank Fox. Boulder, CO: Westview, 1996. First complete Polish edition *Spowiedź: dzieje rodziny żydowskiej podczas okupacji hitlerowskiej w Polsce.* Revised and edited by David Engel. Warsaw: Ośrodek Karta, 2004.

This is the most scandalous work in the literature of the Holocaust. It is almost unbearable to read. The author holds nothing back. Everyone stands accused in this confessional diary: the Christian Poles, for their deep-seated hatred of the Jews; the Jewish religion, for inculcating "a psychology of distinctiveness"; the Jewish political parties of the Left and the religious Right. German cruelty and sadism the author takes as a given. Above all, he blames himself, with unsparing candor born of the certainty that he will not survive. The two most salient points in Perechodnik's biography are these: the happiest years of his life were those he spent studying agronomy in Toulouse; and as a member of the Jewish police, he unwittingly led his wife, Anka, and two-year-old daughter, Athalie, to their deaths. This diary, which he completed on the first anniversary of her death, he dedicated to Anka. The book would be their second child, an eternal surviving monument to her sacred memory.

Although he introduces himself as a Jew of average intelligence, Perechodnik is anything but ordinary. A man for whom Polish is both medium and message, he writes about Polish behavior as an equal. This sense of equality, which ran afoul of his first editor, he acquired abroad, his life in France providing him with a competing model of self-worth, loyalty, and civility, all of which he is able to signal through a generous sprinkling of French words. To read about *"l'air du pays"* in the context of a dead landscape bounded by the Otwock ghetto and the Umschlagplatz is deeply ironic. When Perechodnik cries out to avenge the deaths of his wife and daughter, whose names he invokes again and again, he does so in French. Subverting the narrative itself—the story of his life, his abiding love, the liquidation of the Otwock ghetto, his stratagems to survive in Warsaw, his hatred for his father—is the overwhelming burden of guilt.

Perechodnik's life collapsed on Wednesday, August 19, 1942. Every detail of that day, the height of the *Aktion* in the Otwock ghetto—which, as a member of the Jewish police, he was forced to observe and oversee—every desperate decision, every German order and deception, he relives and redies. More than that. He accompanies his beloved Anka into the fourth cattle car from the locomotive . . . all the way to Treblinka. The diary is only a third over when she and Athalie reach their final destination, and there is still a whole year to go before the first anniversary of their deaths.

By diary's end, Perechodnik is a different man. This, their second child, he vows in his last letter to Anka, will avenge her death when his diary will be read by millions. Yet he cannot withhold from her the fact that he has found solace in the bed of another woman, that he does not love his parents, that he will never again believe in God. Her memory alone is what enables him to hope that the name of Calel Perechodnik may someday be readmitted into the community of humankind. (DGR)

Oskar Rosenfeld. *In the Beginning Was the Ghetto*. Edited and with an
    introduction by Hanno Loewy. Translated from the German by Brigitte
    M. Goldstein. Evanston, IL: Northwestern University Press, 2002. First
    published as *Wozu noch Welt: Aufzeichnungen aus dem Getto Lodz*, 1994.

This could almost be a travelogue. An urbane Middle European—a novelist, theater critic, journalist, scholar of Romanticism, and translator—arrives for a lengthy sojourn in an exotic outpost called Litzmannstadt, so renamed in honor of some German general. He is separated from his wife, Henriette, who has made it to London and whom he misses terribly. Technically, he is a refugee twice over, since he and Henriette fled from Vienna to Prague in 1938, but now, in November 1941, he is on his own. A city within a city, Litzmannstadt is strange to him, but the native, Yiddish-speaking people are not, since our traveler has long evinced a fascination for their language and culture and has even translated their modern classics. The Nazi ghetto of Litzmannstadt proves to be so rich, so full of tragic contradictions, that on February 17, 1942, he begins keeping a combination diary and literary journal—containing short stories, sketches, poems, and copious notes for a novel and a screenplay. Cut and pasted from the twenty notebooks that survived, this English-language edition has the feel of a postmodern novel.

With the eyes and ears of a novelist, filmmaker, and participant observer, Rosenfeld records the grotesque sights and cacophony of the Łódź ghetto. He is especially attuned to the weakest groups, the children and the German-speaking refugees. (He considers the Jews from Prague to be a heartier sort.) Rosenfeld conveys the passage of time by dwelling on the signs of transformation—the debilitating effect of hunger, filth, and boredom; the deportations into and out of the ghetto, accompanied by paralyzing fear and still greater hunger and punctuated by concerts and theatrical revues (until the cultural club is closed) and by the celebration of the Jewish festivals (until the very end). Rosenfeld also sees things through a seasoned literary eye, carrying in his head works such as Hamsun's *Hunger*, Kubin's *The Other Side*, Zola's *The Belly of Paris*, Carlyle's *The French Revolution*, Maurois's *Disraeli*, and Dostoevsky's *Crime and Punishment*. After trying these classics on for size, he reaches the conclusion that the Nazi ghetto is a city unlike any other, and that the mass deportations portend a catastrophe unprecedented in either fiction or history. As for himself, writing for the desk drawer, he admits on one page that "suddenly all Eastern Jews are strangers to me" and on the other, "I feel good. I suddenly belong to them all, the so-called Eastern Jews." As the final liquidation of the ghetto approaches, Rosenfeld's sense of unreality grows: "life writes fiction." His last entry of July 28, 1944, for a series of sketches he calls *Little Ghetto Mirror* comes under the heading "Apocalypse or Redemption." West and East, European and Jewish culture, the personal and reportorial, and sight and sound meet in these notebooks as nowhere else in wartime writing. (DGR)

The Scrolls of Auschwitz. Edited by Ber Mark. Translated from the Hebrew
   by Sharon Neemani. Adapted from the original Yiddish text. Tel Aviv:
   Am Oved, 1985. First published as *Megiles Oyshvits*, 1977.

The last to die were the Sonderkommando, after they finished processing, plundering, and burning the dead. No other genocide produced such a precise hierarchy of death, where a random selection of very strong men presided over an inner sanctum of death: the gas chambers and crematoria. They were the last to touch and to speak with the victims in life and to observe the behavior of the killers at the scene of the crime. Three such men, knowing that they were the last, left a record for posterity.

All three—Zalmen Gradowski, Zalmen Loewenthal, and Dayan (the title for a judge in a rabbinical court) Leyb Langfus—came from the heartland of Polish Jewish piety, and all three had a hand in the one-day uprising in Crematorium IV. In addition to burying their writings throughout Birkenau, they also scattered thousands of teeth, as evidence of the millions of murdered victims (N. Cohen 1994, 525). When Loewenthal arrived in Birkenau on December 10, 1942, "there were only a few buildings here and there"; by the time he completed his detailed chronicle of the world's greatest death factory, on October 10, 1944, the Hungarian transports had already been incinerated and the uprising had been quashed.

It is possible that the three men coordinated their writing, for one chronicle completes the other. Langfus describes life in the ghetto on the eve of its liquidation. Gradowski, the most self-consciously literary of the three, takes his reader of the postwar future on a detailed antijourney from the liquidated ghetto to the gas chambers—and beyond. As Gradowski dwells at length on the minds of the victims, who hang onto every shred of hope even unto the last, Loewenthal labors to explain the psychology of adaptation on the part of their brethren, whose job it was to plunder and burn their bodies. As Loewenthal praises Langfus for refusing to "adapt," to participate in the cremations, Langfus records the last protests and prayers of the victims who are undressing for the gas. Gradowski goes one step further by entering into the thoughts of the German master race as they eliminate the Jewish vermin from the face of the earth.

The world as seen from the inner circle of hell looks something like this. First there are "the dogs walking on two legs" who organize the mass murder "with the help of dogs walking on four legs." Some are identified by name. Then there are the millions of unnamed Jewish victims whose death is unstoppable because they are unable or unwilling to resist. Then there are the Christian Poles, who surrounded the Jews with enmity, rejoiced at their downfall, tried to prevent their revolt inside the camp, and will falsify the record after the war. And finally there is the indifferent, or actively disbelieving, world outside. All this is written in the present or simple past tense because the fires of hell are still burning, night and day. Killing time in these chronicles seems to last forever. (DGR)

[1945]

Abraham Sutzkever. *Di festung: lider un poemes geshribn in vilner geto un in vald 1941–1944* (The fortress: poems written in the Vilna Ghetto and in the forest 1941–1944). Edited with a foreword by Nachman Mayzel. New York: YKUF, 1945. Most of the poems are translated in *A. Sutzkever: Selected Poetry and Prose*, introduction by Benjamin Harshav and translated by Barbara and Benjamin Harshav (Berkeley: University of California Press, 1991), 122–82.

The thirty-nine poems in this poorly edited volume, followed by another twenty published three months later, introduced the wartime poetry of Abraham Sutzkever to the West. The poet was still living in Moscow, and the Soviet Union was at the height of its prestige; publication by a Communist-affiliated press added considerable value to the work for all freedom-loving people. For the average Yiddish reader, the mere fact of Sutzkever's survival was miracle enough.

The poems do not yet tell a coherent story, since their present order lacks rhyme or reason, and some exceptionally important ones, like "On the Anniversary of the Ghetto Theater" and "Song for the Last," will not appear for another twenty years. But the range of Sutzkever's wartime verse, from lyric to epic and from confessional to high rhetorical, is clearly in evidence.

Of this tentative corpus, three narrative poems entered Jewish collective memory. The first is the ballad-like "A Wagon of Shoes," with its haunting refrain, "And the heels go tapping, / With a clatter and a din, / From our old Vilna streets / They drive us to Berlin" (my translation), which tells of the poet discovering his mother's shoes in a wagonload of plundered shoes. The second is the heroic ballad of Mira Bernshteyn, "The Teacher Mira," who imparts the values of Yiddish secular culture to her young charges even as their numbers dwindle from 130 to 7. The third is the mini-epic "Lead Plates at the Rom Press" (Sutzkever 1988c).

The truth claims of Holocaust poetry can be tested against this twenty-four-line poem. The story line is pure legend: young fighters in need of bullets steal into the building of the Rom Press one night, in order to melt down the lead plates of the Vilna Talmud, that towering cultural achievement of Eastern European Jewry. This in turn recalls a still more ancient exploit, that of the Maccabees, whose pouring of oil into the candelabra of the Jerusalem Temple is akin to the lead of Hebrew letters being poured into bullet molds. And the alchemy succeeds: in the last stanza, the Jewish soldiers are now armed, the uprising has happened, and the ghetto in its final hours is likened to Jerusalem under siege. But none of this is true! The lead plates had been plundered by the Germans much earlier, the uprising was aborted through tragic circumstances, and the central conceit of the poem is just that.

Reread from the perspective of today, Sutzkever was not lying. He described not the uprising but its ancient precedent. "We dreamers must now become soldiers!," proclaimed the poet turned partisan. The ability of the young to make history, to take up arms, and to fight as Jews derived from their ability to refine the voices of the past. That spiritual alchemy was the meaning of the poem, the truth claim that no one could gainsay. (DGR)

Communal Memory, 1945–60

[**1945**]

Alfred Kantor. *The Book of Alfred Kantor: Terezín-Auschwitz-Schwarzheide, December 1941–May 1945*. Preface by John Wykert. New York: McGraw-Hill, 1971.

Like Art Spiegelman's *Maus* (1986), *The Book of Alfred Kantor* defies classification. Is it the first graphic diary in Holocaust literature? This handsome facsimile edition certainly has the feel of an authentic wartime record of Kantor's three incarcerations—two years in the fortress town of Terezín, six months in Auschwitz-Birkenau, and ten months in a forced labor camp at Schwarzheide, near Dresden—culminating in a death march and liberation. Yet at the same time it has all the trappings of a survivor memoir, with a sequential, clearly marked narrative and happy end. Or perhaps it belongs among the coffee table books of Holocaust art that were just beginning to appear in the early 1970s, each watercolor accompanied by two explanations—a handwritten English caption with quaint mistakes and an incisive historical note—plus an auto-biographical and biographical preface. *The Book of Alfred Kantor*, in short, is the perfectly imperfect segue from one phase of Holocaust memory to another.

Kantor's apprenticeship as an artist happened in the field. He has an unerr-ing eye for objects—buildings, barracks, bunks, latrines, and barbed wire—but his humans look like stick figures, even before the survivors of mass extermination are reduced to such through hunger, disease, and torture. The only portraits included in the 127 numbered pages of his original album are of three men whom Auschwitz has rendered subhuman: a thirty-year-old pris-oner turned into a living skeleton "after a few weeks in camp," a robust Kapo, and a vicious camp leader, who still has the profile of a professional murderer. In contrast, objects take on a life of their own.

Kantor begins the book with the well-dressed Jews of Prague getting off trolley No. 17 in front of the Fair Building in the early hours of December 1, 1941, each person carrying at least one suitcase. A mere two pages later, this luggage is the sole means of securing "privacy" in Terezín, where 70,000 pris-oners of all ages occupy a space built to accommodate 3,000 soldiers. Within moments of their arrival in Auschwitz, however, all the newcomers' baggage and worldly possessions are ordered thrown into the dust as they are herded into the waiting trucks, and on page 36, ss men are already supervising the plunder of the abandoned luggage.

Kantor's primitive style and meticulous attention to physical detail convey a surreal landscape: the elaborate façade of a café, promenade, barber shop, outdoor posters, and sports arena to cover up the extreme human degrada-tion in Terezín; miles of barracks lying "peacefully" on a clear night in Aus-chwitz, disturbed only by "a bright flame shooting out of a low smokestack" a thousand feet or so away; and finally the smokescreens that fail to hide the German chemical plant from Allied bombers. Is this any less surreal than the final tableau of well-wishers surrounding a prisoner still wearing his stripes on the streets of a liberated city, where flags are flying and the trolley is about to pull up? (DGR)

Der Nister. *Regrowth: Seven Tales of Jewish Life before, during, and after Nazi Occupation.* Translated from the Yiddish with an afterword by Erik Butler. Evanston, IL: Northwestern University Press, 2011. First published as *Vidervuks.*

Soviet Jews, cut off from their brethren in the east by the Polish-Soviet border, were reunited with them physically (through the Soviet annexation of the easternmost part of Poland in 1939) and spiritually (through the influx of a quarter-million Jewish refugees thereafter). As early as 1943, the great Yiddish prose master who hid behind the name of Der Nister (the hidden one) produced a volume of reportorial fiction called *Korbones* ([Sacrificial] victims), based on eyewitness accounts of individual "cases in occupied Poland of today." Then, in early March 1944, came the miraculous airlift to Moscow of the "partisan poet" Abraham Sutzkever, made famous in the pages of *Pravda* by the master of Soviet propaganda, Ilya Ehrenburg (Novershtern 1983, 50). Der Nister was keen to learn from Sutzkever about the fate of Lithuanian Jewry in general and Vilna in particular. Sutzkever told me in 2004 that Der Nister burst into tears when Sutzkever read him the opening cantos of *Secret City,* his epic poem about the last survivors of the Vilna ghetto. Out of his encounters with Sutzkever came "Meylekh Magnus," the longest of Der Nister's literary responses to the Holocaust.

"There is no need, now, to mention what happened there," writes the biographer of Meylekh Magnus, his late master and teacher, in Der Nister's story. Magnus, the father, and his seventeen-year-old son have been driven into the ghetto by the power that "ruled the Polish lands," a euphemism for the Germans. "The witnesses who survived and escaped have given us such rich material—both orally and in writing—and we, the present generation, have torn our hair out over it (and later generations, too, will have cause to do the same—if they want to . . .)." Der Nister's stories on and from the war abound in such passages of self-reflection, which signal the author's intent. Read them not for mere documentary evidence of Jewish suffering and self-sacrifice. Read them rather as memory manuals, in which the parent-child—and, by extension, the teacher-student—bond is the basic conduit of cultural transmission, even when that bond is physically severed and when the raw data of the eyewitness must pass through multiple refinements before it yields its hidden meaning.

Meylekh Magnus—a reclusive and stubborn scholar of antiquity and "graduate of the class of '05," the failed Russian revolution of 1905—is loosely based on the figure of Zelig Kalmanovitsh. The twenty-six-year-old secretary of the Jewish Council who inducts Magnus's son into the underground and comforts Magnus when the son is shot trying to smuggle arms into the ghetto is a composite of Jacob Gens and Itsik Vittenberg. The astonishingly positive portrayal of the secretary, inspired perhaps by Sutzkever's account of the regular meetings of Jewish intellectuals that took place in Gens's home, is of a piece with Der Nister's defiance of all the binary oppositions that will soon be set in stone: between passive and active forms of resistance, the Judenrat and the underground, the pious and the politically engaged, and even, most provocatively, between the merchant class and the proletariat. Der Nister conjures up a reality that is subversively open-ended and subject to human desire, passion, mendacity, loyalty, and spontaneous bursts of extraordinary courage. The successful businessman Boris Grosbaytl (the surname means fat wallet) becomes responsible for providing Magnus with an almost-secure underground bunker. Then the sedentary scholar discovers within himself the hidden wellspring of defiance. For the secret of Magnus's life and death is also the secret of the best Holocaust literature. It is the method of "'sublimation'—that is, the ability to channel feelings and thoughts that beset one at a given moment into entirely different directions." Der Nister, alone among Soviet Yiddish writers, continued to practice the art of sublimation, until he perished four years later, in the Gulag. (DGR)

Zvi Kolitz. *Yosl Rakover Talks to God*. Afterwords by Emmanuel Lévinas and Leon Wieseltier. Edited by Paul Badde. Translated from the German by Carol Brown Janeway. New York: Pantheon, 1999. First published as *Yosl Rakovers vending tsu got*.

Yosl Rakover Talks to God was the first work of Holocaust theology to achieve worldwide currency. It has been translated into Hebrew, French, German, and Spanish, and into English three times. What accounts for its renown and longevity? Like Chaim Grade's "My Quarrel with Hersh Rasseyner," first published in 1952 (Grade 1999), it was written by someone schooled in Jewish piety who found the literary means to appeal to a secular reader. Inspired by Dostoevsky, Grade turned his theological concerns into a passionate debate between two articulate survivors, while Kolitz, appealing to a mass audience, adopted the familiar form of a testament, or ethical will, and turned his eponymous hero into a ghetto fighter. *Yosl Rakover Talks to God* was theology dramatized as Jewspeak and the Holocaust turned into tidy melodrama.

The Warsaw ghetto uprising is no less idealized than the patriarchal figure of Rakover. "Gasoline-filled bottles" prevail against German tanks, and everyone is fighting side by side: the freethinkers and the faithful, the children and the grown-ups. Although the ghetto is in its final throes, Rakover has the presence of mind to succinctly summarize the fate of his family and folk before proceeding to the real business at hand, his argument with God. Not since the Hasidic master Reb Levi Yitzhak of Berdichev has any Yiddish-speaking Jew challenged God so eloquently.

What has changed in the wake of the Holocaust? It is impossible to explain the catastrophe, states Rakover unequivocally, as a punishment for one's sins. Through its suffering, Israel stands purified before the Lord. Rather, it is to the mystical doctrine of *hester-panim*—God's momentary, mysterious lapse; God's countenance-veiling indifference—that one must now turn. Never have God's Chosen People been more certain of their special relationship to God than now, when their suffering has exceeded anything known before. Yet never has the individual man of faith been more empowered than now, for the only way to affirm God in the midst and wake of this annihilation is through enormous inner struggle. A lover of God, he proclaims, is not a blind amen sayer.

What Kolitz has attempted to salvage, by inventing a courageous ghetto fighter and equally fearless man of faith, is the sacred triad of God, Torah, and Israel. Once it was the Lord who could be counted on as the most stable partner in the triad. Now it is the Torah that is inviolable, together with those few who are still alive to uphold it. And when Rakover talks, does God listen or respond? Or is this really a monologue hoping to be a dialogue? (DGR)

Y. D. Sheinson. *A Survivor's Haggadah.* Edited with an introduction by Saul Touster; translated by Yaron Peleg, Robert Szulkin, and Marc Samuels. Philadelphia: Jewish Publication Society of America, 2000. First published as *Passover Service.*

Liberation began with the reclamation of time. This is why Primo Levi ends *Survival in Auschwitz* with "The Story of Ten Days," and why the celebration of Christian festivals looms so large in the first postwar chronicles of the camps. A unique document in Holocaust literature is this "Supplement" to the first Passover since the Liberation, a seder different from any other before or since. No effort was spared to make it speak to the moment and to speak for all 200 survivors crammed into the Deutsches Theatre Restaurant in Munich, as well as the American Jewish GIs who were their invited guests.

Behind this effort with his calligraphy, religious imagination, and ideological zeal was a Hebrew pedagogue from Kovno named Y. D. Sheinson. Providing the logistical base was a Tennessee-born chaplain named Abraham J. Klausner, and finally, there was a Hungarian-born survivor named Miklós Adler, who would never know that his expressionist woodcuts of the labor and concentration camps were inserted into the Haggadah to provide a visual commentary.

Each of the four languages used in this Haggadah added another voice and provided a different message. Klausner, addressing the "khaki-clad sons of

Israel" in English, spoke about the universal struggle for justice and freedom. (Klausner later collected and published lists of Holocaust survivors in volumes called *Sharit ha-Platah* [Surviving remnant] and composed a book about them called *A Letter to My Children, From the Edge of the Holocaust.*)

Citations from the Haggadah in ancient Hebrew rehearsed the particular fate of the Jews and echoed their call for divine retribution. Most powerfully, Sheinson used the Haggadah against itself, turning the joyous song of "Dayyenu" into a litany of destruction from ancient times until the Nazis, and praising the Allies—instead of the Lord—for hearkening unto our cry. Less effectively, Sheinson used *Ivrit*—modern Hebrew—to castigate the Righteous of the Nations for having abandoned the Jews and for their continued abuse of the rescued children, saving his harshest words for the emissaries from Palestine, who were imposing their divisive ideological agendas on the survivor community. Since that community for the most part was Yiddish-speaking, Sheinson ended the Haggadah with long citations in Yiddish from the (Hebrew) writings of mainstream Zionist thinkers. As the designer and editor, Sheinson distinguished among these languages by means of different fonts or calligraphic styles.

How was this seder night different from any other? On this night, the Egyptian taskmasters were reborn as the ss, the death of the firstborn anticipated the crematoria, and the story of the Exodus was a foreshadowing of the near-total extermination of European Jewry. On this night, the true liberation of the stateless Jews of Europe was still a distant dream, for the gates to the Promised Land were blocked by the British. And on this night, there was not a single child present to ask the four questions. (DGR)

Janusz Nel Siedlecki, Krystyn Olszewski, and Tadeusz Borowski. *We Were in Auschwitz.* [Edited by Tadeusz Borowski.] Translated from the Polish by Alicia Nitecki. New York: Welcome Rain, 2000. First published as *Byliśmy w Oświęcimiu.*

Before Primo Levi's skeptical humanism, before Robert Antelme and Charlotte Delbo challenged and championed the notion of human solidarity in the camps, before Ka-Tzetnik's "other planet," there was Tadeusz Borowski, the editor, annotator, and coauthor of *We Were in Auschwitz*, a place where everyone was complicit in crime. Before there were single-authored works with a clearly individuated style and a reconstituted sense of self—Levi's *Survival in Auschwitz* (1985) ends with the bedridden survivors crying out his name—there was this anthology, in which the authors were listed in Auschwitz-numerical order and their work appeared anonymously. Before Holocaust writing was classifiable as one thing or another, there was reportage, the fictional art of unadulterated, unassimilable truth.

To help the reader negotiate Auschwitz, Borowski appended a glossary of fifty-seven "Auschwitz Terms." Some—like Appel, Kapo, Kommando, Krankenbau, Lager, Muselman, Sonderkommando, and Zyklon—were obviously of German provenance, while others were idiolects, innocent enough terms in any other context: Block, Canada, Chimney, Old Number, Organizing, Selection, Stripes, Ziguener (which means the gypsy camp). Situated "At the Juncture of the Sola and the Vistula," Oświęcim was created as an extermination camp only for Poles, but the purpose of this anthology was to chronicle "Auschwitz's fantastic career," when an "internal" Polish camp known to nobody changed "into an enormous international extermination camp for many millions of European Jews." This all-European and multicultural landscape demanded its own vocabulary and spatial coordinates. 6643, the lowest number among the authors, with four years' experience in the camp, opened the volume with a "Baedeker among the Wires."

The power of this anthology lies in the "showing," narrated in a bitterly ironic, deadpan style. The "telling" is mostly confined to Borowski's unsigned preface. "It was defeat," he writes categorically, "the almost immediate abandonment of ideological principles." Them's fighting words, and Borowski's two collaborators share his fierce determination to counter all notions of heroism, agency, and solidarity. Every new transport brings with it a faith in a quick and immediate end to the war, but there is no end in sight, no room for heroics. Tadek (not to be confused with Borowski), who manages to escape, was just like the others. He thrived in the camp by gulling the living Jews and robbing the dead.

"Telling" also happens in Borowski's prefatory remarks to his own narratives and those of the others. "Iodine and Phenol" is Siedlecki's harrowing description of the Auschwitz clinic. Borowski informs the reader that the doctors and nurses bear part of the blame for killing the patients, though their fault "is as a drop in the ocean compared to the crimes of the ss." Sometimes, he corrects what the others say—there was no washroom on the Block in the period Siedlecki described, and as a preface to his own inaugural tale, "A Day at Harmenz," Borowski writes that "the real Becker worked in the Kommando, but didn't come from Poznan, he was a Jew from France and, out of hunger, ate raw frogs." Guardian of the moral and factual truth, Borowski is also the consummate storyteller, and *We Were in Auschwitz* marks the beginning of his brilliant and tragically brief career. (DGR)

Robert Antelme. *The Human Race*. Homage to Robert Antelme by Edgar
   Morin. Translated from the French by Jeffrey Haight and Annie Mahler.
   Marlboro, VT: Marlboro, 1992. First published as *L'espèce humaine*.

Robert Antelme was arrested by the Gestapo and deported in 1944 to a small
concentration camp called Gandersheim, one of the satellite camps in the
Buchenwald system. Antelme was a political prisoner and a Frenchman. Although his book interrogates the nature of the human species as a whole,
there are hardly any Jews in it. They are not within the world experienced by
Antelme, and therefore they do not enter into his analysis. Whereas Levi's
social laboratory focuses on the various categories of prisoners in Auschwitz
Monowitz, Antelme focuses on the breakdown of political and national solidarity in a much smaller and more homogeneous camp, which is a metonym
for the commonality of humankind. For Antelme, the camp is the test case
for ideological commitment. If you are a communist and believe in the socialist international, then what does your behavior mean when your drive for
survival overwhelms political engagement? What is the value of the political
identity if it cannot withstand the Nazi assault on humanity? As Antelme ob-
serves human behavior, a different vocabulary of words and gestures emerges:
the German supervisor who whispers "Monsieur," acknowledging an identity
for the prisoner beyond the destitute inmate. The "man with buttocks" is the
traitor to the human race: he has fattened himself up sufficiently to have an
arse, and that has to have been at the cost of his fellow prisoners.

The feast days of Christianity—Christmas, Easter, and Sunday—are both
acknowledged and distorted by the subhuman lives of the prisoners. What
is the value of the symbolic in a world where only the concrete—the potato
skin, the rutabaga—has true substance? Is there a role for language to describe
these experiences, the shared humiliations, betrayals, and shame of this particular group of people?

Antelme's preface is a critical document in the construction of Holocaust
memory. His is the quiet, humdrum atrocity, with no drama or flames shooting
out of chimneys—just destitution, abysmal hunger, and the loss, loosening,
or destruction of the self. That destruction does not end with the Liberation,
because although the speaker may wish to speak, he does not have the audience that is prepared—linguistically, emotionally, psychologically—to listen.

In this respect, Antelme's writing is continuous with that of authors like
Levi, whose use of the plain style makes no concession to an audience that
can engage with atrocity only when assured of its exceptional, inexpressible
nature, and then presented with survivors as icons of the unbelievable having
been overcome.

For Antelme, however, this perspective is exactly wrong. Atrocity is ordinary in the sense that ordinary people commit atrocities on each other, stealing from the dying, betraying the sick, abandoning the faithful. Yes, there are moments of solidarity, but not anywhere near enough, even for a political man or woman, to count against the magnitude of the rest of the time. In the end, the Liberation passes Antelme by. It happens, but in the struggle for existence it is not a marker that can be engaged by anything other than utter exhaustion.

A book that galvanized the prewar generation, André Malraux's great 1933 novel, *La condition humaine*, had celebrated the political and glorified sacrifice in its name. As if in counterpoint, Antelme's book, written for an audience unable or unwilling to listen, explodes the solidarity of ideology. What remains of the human species must be painfully restored through language, even as the account documents a species that appears to be beyond recuperation. (ND)

Hans Keilson. *Comedy in a Minor Key*. Translated from the German by
   Damion Searls. New York: Farrar, Straus and Giroux, 2010. First published
   as *Komödie in Moll*.

At about the time that Anne Frank's *Diary* was being prepared for publication, Hans Keilson was writing this novella about a young Dutch couple who take in a Jew and hide him in their house for a year. The refugee dies, and the couple dispose of the body by leaving it in a park, so that it will be discovered and buried. But then the wife remembers that she had lent him a pair of her husband's monogrammed pajamas and, even worse, that the clothes had a laundry mark leading directly back to them. The young couple is rushed into hiding, comfortably, in a rooming house, where several days pass before they learn that the policeman assigned to the case destroyed the incriminating evidence, and that they may safely return to their home.

The novella is like a small Dutch genre painting, within whose small frame one finds a multitude of important and far-reaching details. The writer uses the most delicate brushstrokes to delineate the internal forces that cause ordinary people to behave morally in situations where others would fail the test. Keilson maps the delicate shifts between curiosity and privacy, how much the couple asks about their lodger, how much he is willing to confide in them. After he dies, the wife goes through his things and finds a package of American cigarettes hidden away in his room. At first, she feels affronted—wondering how could he not have shared his cigarettes with Wim, her husband, who would so have appreciated a hard-to-find, high-quality cigarette. But then, in an effort of empathy, she is able to understand that the cigarettes represented a point of connection to the fugitive's past, as well as a tiny space of privacy in an existence that had been largely ripped apart.

Just under the gentle surface are the real risks and fears that come with resistance. It later turns out that everyone in the story is connected to the underground resistance, but treachery and betrayal are so common that no one is willing to entrust that knowledge to anyone else.

The structuring irony in the novella is the role reversal that Wim and Marie experience when they are forced into hiding. Suddenly on the run themselves, they get a taste of the inner resources needed to withstand solitude, the grind of constant fear, the loss of self that comes with losing familiar places and habits. Yet once they return to their house after a mere four days, the armature of habit contains them again, and they revert to the mundane with a sense of relief that they prefer to leave unexplored.

Altruism is a big word for a series of small actions with very big consequences. Keilson's accomplishment is to shape his narrative to the scale of the action, and to leave the reader to draw whatever larger conclusions he or she chooses. (ND)

Primo Levi. *Survival in Auschwitz: The Nazi Assault on Humanity*. Including "A Conversation with Primo Levi," by Philip Roth. Translated from the Italian by Stuart Woolf. New York: Touchstone, 1996. First published as *Se questo è un uomo*. Turin: De Silva, 1947. First published in English in 1958.

Survival in Auschwitz is one of the handful of truly indispensable works to emerge from the misery of the Nazi concentration camps. A chemist by training, Levi presents his memoir as the study of what he calls a "social laboratory." He is supremely interested in the naming of things. After the initial chapter, in which he describes his capture, Levi focuses on taxonomies. He describes the stratification of the camp—the criminals, the homosexuals, and the Jews and their relative status. He creates new categories of discrimination: What does it mean to have well-fitting shoes? The difference between life and death. What does it mean to understand a language? Once again, the difference between life and death. He describes hunger with the focus and clarity of a man attempting to describe the deepest human impulses, such as love, hate, and greed. Because he positions each word so carefully, the reader cannot but become more aware of the significance of naming the components of the concentration camp a "laboratory." The laboratory contains the "pitiless process of natural selection." Even a reader who may have read about natural selection countless times will be brought to a standstill by the weight of the adjective "pitiless."

Beyond the laboratory, in Levi's hands, existence at Auschwitz is essentially about systems of exchange. What can a man lose and still survive? What goods, exchanging hands, assure profit to one and survival, perhaps, to the other? The goods are not necessarily concrete. In a chapter that might serve as a bookend to Hamlet's soliloquy "What a piece of work is man," Levi tries to teach a fellow inmate Italian by quoting from Dante's "Canto of Ulysses." But where Hamlet's speech asserts the wonder of human aspiration and potential, Levi as protagonist struggles to remember the words, aches to fill in the gaps, and ultimately cannot communicate with his French-speaking interlocutor. The power of thick language to sustain the self collides with the thin vocabulary of survival—cabbage and turnips, the sum total of a day's meal.

Transparency is one of the greatest accomplishments of the memoirist. In Levi's hands, language in its plainness is the means of confronting the depths to which human beings have brought each other. Yet in *Survival in Auschwitz*, there is a clear line between passion and sentimentality. All men feel. But to translate that feeling into language requires an extraordinary restraint.

That restraint holds up even under the barely controlled anger with which Levi describes the academic examination by a German chemist of a filthy concentration camp prisoner who may be needed to perform laboratory work. Unforgettable is the clash between the amorality of a man conducting a standard oral exam when the potential colleague standing across from him is emaciated, filthy, and reduced in circumstances, brought to this state precisely by this man and his fellows. Equally unforgettable is Levi's even voice, recounting the exam questions put to him, feverishly trying to remember facts that come to him as from a different life. And it becomes the basis for uncompromising moral judgment on Levi's part.

It is tempting to construct *Survival in Auschwitz* into a triumphal narrative that celebrates the power and resilience of the human spirit. But that interpretation does not emerge from the book itself. The book itself is more accurately described by the English translation of the original Italian title, "if this is a man." It is not a given that humanity is salvaged by the fact of survival. The motif of "the drowned and the saved" runs throughout Levi's *oeuvre*, culminating in his last book, which uses this phrase as its title. Survival is a provisional achievement—a victory that is, on some level, a profound defeat. That is what the social laboratory of the *Lager* has wrought. (ND)

Zofia Nałkowska. *Medallions*. Translated from the Polish with an introduction by Diana Kuprel. Evanston, IL: Northwestern University Press, 2000. First published as *Medaliony*.

Through almost imperceptible staging, accurate transcription, and the most minimal commentary, Zofia Nałkowska helped established the new norm of Holocaust realism. The factual basis of her tiny book of eight brief chapters was incontrovertible. In February 1945, this eminent Polish writer was chosen to preside over the Commission for the Investigation of War Crimes in Auschwitz, making her the first civilian to systematically visit and study the camp. She followed this with other interviews of people who had been in the camp, conducted in an empty apartment, a hotel room, or a cemetery. One witness appeared still wearing her camp gray-and-navy-striped gabardine and matching cap. All had lived so long in a state of evil, or had been so brutalized by their experiences in the camps, that their speech was robbed of affect. Some could no longer distinguish between right and wrong, cruelty and pity, victim and perpetrator. Others were crippled and partially blind. "Why me, I don't know," protested the student from Gdańsk who faithfully served in Professor Spanner's Anatomy Institute, which perfected a formula for turning human fat into soap. "I don't have an aversion to Jews," said the survivor with the beautiful smile and sparkling brown eyes. "Just like I don't have an aversion to ants or mice." This self-hating Jew had effectively cut herself off from all feeling. *Medallions* marked the beginning of Holocaust testimony as art form, which was to achieve its fullest expression in Claude Lanzmann's *Shoah* and Henryk Grynberg's *Drohobycz, Drohobycz and Other Stories* (2002).

Except for the last summary chapter, each of the eight in Nałkowska's book is a performative speech act, rendered with psychological precision. But this is speech punctuated by silence, fatigue, and evasion, or interrupted by workers coming in to fix the sink. Dwojra (Dvoyre or Deborah) Zielona accompanies her testimony with hand motions: "With her one eye, she peers through the chinks between her fingers." As in *Shoah*, the performance is enacted within a carefully chosen frame, each setting or close-up designed to dramatize the story being told. Nature is in bloom as the Cemetery Lady, surrounded by elaborately inscribed tombstones, rehearses her favorite story about the husband who disinterred his wife. This is but a distraction from the real story, of the Jews jumping from the burning balconies of the ghetto, the sound of their shrieks and cries, and the thwack, thwack of their falling bodies hitting the ground. Unaware as she is of the discrepancy of "ordinary, private death next to the immensity of collective death," she is deaf to the rabidly antisemitic slogans that she accepts as true. So too the student from Gdańsk, who sees everything from behind a purple curtain, and the rather lovely gray-haired woman with the delicate, shapeless hands, who will tell of cannibalism and of women going mad in the transport from Ravensbrück. In Nałkowska's retelling, speech, testimony, and bearing witness yield no catharsis, no deeper understanding, no poetic closure. This is a book of speech through silence, which ends as it begins, with one truth: "People dealt this fate to other people." (DGR)

Nelly Sachs. *In the Habitations of Death*. Selections in *O the Chimneys: Selected Poems, Including the Verse Play, Eli*. Translated from the German by Michael Hamburger. New York: Farrar, Straus and Giroux, 1967. First published as *In den Wohnungen des Todes*.

The two major German-language poets on the Holocaust are Nelly Sachs and Paul Celan. They are very different, just as Abraham Sutzkever differs from Jacob Glatstein in Yiddish and Uri Zvi Greenberg differs from Dan Pagis in Hebrew. The former are more rhetorical and old-fashioned, the latter more understated and self-consciously modernist. The former have traveled poorly outside of their native languages; the latter are universally studied and revered. To read Holocaust literature in chronological order is to recover the surprise of first encounter.

Nelly Sachs escaped in May 1940 on the last flight from Berlin to Stockholm, but it was not until 1943, year 4 of the war, that knowledge of the Final Solution changed her from a poet of German exile (*Exilliteratur*) to a poet of Jewish catastrophe. *In den Wohnungen des Todes* was her first book of poems, and it established her reputation as "the poetess of Jewish fate" (Bower 2003, 1068). The "ingeniously devised habitations of death" are the crematoria, their chimneys reaching heavenward to describe a "Freedomway for Jeremiah and Job's dust." The destruction of Europe's Jews, to judge from these poems, especially the million-and-a-half Jewish children, informs and transforms the universe, endowing every object—sand, stones, shoes—with ultimate significance. These are liturgical poems, the chorus of the rescued, the orphans, the shadows, the stones, the stars, and the unborn, culminating (as in the prayer book) in the redemptive voice of the Holy Land. The suffering and saintliness of the victims are their divine merit. Via her love affair with Hasidism, which acculturated German Jews of her generation saw as an expression of the exotic East, Sachs arrived at a mystical understanding of the unity of all things. Souls flow into stones, caterpillars are transformed into butterflies, Jews become smoke, and Jewish smoke ascends to heaven. These are lyrical poems, which disassemble the catastrophe into tiny, manageable parts. "If I only knew / On what your last look rested. / Was it a stone that had drunk / So many last looks that they fell / Blindly upon its blindness?"

Sachs's career path as a poet of the Holocaust did not happen in a vacuum. In 1957, she began corresponding with Paul Celan, her fellow exile; and in 1966, almost twenty years after the appearance of her inaugural volume of Holocaust poetry, she split the Nobel Prize for Literature with S. Y. Agnon, both writers celebrated for representing the fate of the Jews. Her sudden fame stimulated a flurry of translations, such as this 1967 English-language collection that has never been superseded. Just as quickly, her reputation became fixed in stone.

Where poetry no longer serves liturgical ends, the suffering of the victims, their traffic with angels and prophets, and their essential, timeless Jewishness arouses no passion and provokes no discussion. (DGR)

Isaiah Spiegel. *Ghetto Kingdom: Tales of the Łódź Ghetto*. Translated by David H. Hirsch and Roslyn Hirsch. Evanston, IL: Northwestern University Press, 1998. First published as *Malkhes geto: noveln*. Łódź: Dos naye lebn, 1947.

Isaiah (Shaye) Spiegel's stories hearken back to a time of innocence. A musician from Germany appears in a Yiddish-speaking courtyard, and there's an aura of mystery to him, as if he were I. L. Peretz's magician ("The Sorcerer"). A little boy climbs the roof so that he can look down with envy into his neighbor's garden, an exact replay of Sholem Aleichem's *Motl the Cantor's Son* ("Blossoms"). And an intellectual narrates a bizarre tale without an ending about an undelivered letter, as if he too had stepped out of a monologue by the same master of dark comedy ("In a Death Alley"). Prostitutes and pimps steal from old ladies, as in the satires of Mendele the Book Peddler. What's more, it isn't only the narrator who invokes those better times, through his figurative language. All the characters—whether old or young, male or female, once rich or always dirt poor—do the same. To escape from their present reality, they routinely fall into reveries, escape into dreams, or succumb to madness.

The remembrance of things past is set in the Łódź ghetto, where Spiegel's stories were first written, between 1940 and 1944. His storied ghetto is a kingdom of starvation, disease, and death. Here "the ghetto wind always hears a sighing lamentation at night, like the sobbing of dying children," and by day "an exhausted sun sags limply in the narrow streets." The palette of ghetto colors are the hues of yellow, as hunger and dysentery ravage the body. To provide the dead with shrouds and prepare their bodies for burial requires a supreme act of courage ("Enchanted Fruit"). The workbench going back generations in a family of weavers (Łódź was to Poland what Manchester was to England) is recycled as a funeral board ("The Workbench").

The best example of Spiegel's method is the story "Bread." The theme is familiar to readers of Peretz: the gender reversal in the traditional Jewish family, where the father spends his days in prayer and study, while the mother is out foraging for food. Shimele, having replicated the same family structure in the ghetto, abdicates his parental role altogether when, in a moment of inner collapse, he steals the entire bread ration. Their hovel borders the ghetto gate; within, however, is a tiny room redolent of the past. Here pigeons used to come and roost, and Shimele's two children, Umele and Pearl, have discovered two cracks in the wall that give them a line of sight to their objects of desire:

loaves of bread and fresh rolls in the bakery on the Aryan side. For the children reverie is real, both sustaining and devastating. The family is finally reconstituted when Shimele is caught in a deportation and there's finally enough bread to go around.

Spiegel's lyrical prose about the slow death of Polish Jewry drew on the best traditions of modern Yiddish literature. His was the last all-Jewish kingdom on European soil. (DGR)

[1948]

Eleanor Mlotek and Malke Gottlieb, comps. 1983. *Mir zaynen do: lider fun di getos un lagern; We Are Here: Songs of the Holocaust.* Foreword by Elie Wiesel. Singable translations by Roslyn Bresnick-Perry. Illustrated by Tsirl Waletzky. New York: Educational Department of the Workmen's Circle and Hippocrene Books. Based largely on *Lider fun di getos un lagern,* compiled by Shmerke Kaczerginski and edited by H. Leivick (New York: CYCO, 1948).

The Jewish liturgy is suffused with themes of redemption and destruction, retribution and mourning. Not all is love of God and personal salvation. These habits of the Jewish heart carried over from the synagogue to the street, from the street to the ghettos and camps, and from there—in less than a decade—to Holocaust memorial services everywhere. Of the many hundreds of songs that were collected and recorded after the war, only a handful were deemed appropriate for public gatherings: those that were not too topical, satiric, gritty, despairing, or narrowly ideological. Once Yiddish was no longer the spoken vernacular of a living people and became the *loshn-hakdoyshim* (the language of the martyrs), what vanished from the repertoire were songs that mixed in too many Slavic words and songs that were altogether in Polish, Russian, or German (from Terezín, for example). Of the many ghettos, only Warsaw, Łódź, Kraków, Vilna, Kovno, and Białystok remained etched in public memory. Of the many killing fields, only Babi Yar and Ponar. Of the many death camps, only Auschwitz and Treblinka. A process of coding and conflating catastrophes that had evolved over millennia was recapitulated in less than a decade.

What is called a "Holocaust song" is not merely a song written or sung during the Holocaust but a song that evokes the right commemorative mood. Eleanor Mlotek and Malke Gottlieb culled the forty songs of their anthology from sixteen songbooks and arranged them in a single volume to tell a story that begins with a lost home, proceeds to life and death in ghettos and camps, dwells on the tragic fate of the child, and ends with songs of hope and armed resistance. Fully eighteen of the forty were written by a handful of professional songwriters in the Vilna ghetto. Three are by the beloved Yiddish folk bard Mordecai Gebirtig: his stirring hymn, "Es brent!" (Fire!), written in 1938; his defiant "Moments of Hope," written in the Kraków ghetto; and a third song set to music after the war. Those few that adhere to the traditional four-line stanza of the Yiddish folksong are among the most affecting: the lullabies "Drowsing Birds," "Babi Yar," and "No More Raisins, No More Almonds"; and Hirsh Glik's "Still the Night." The anthology accurately reflects the "new" Yiddish theater song, born in the 1880s, each with a story to tell in a recitative style and with a complicated rhyme scheme, punctuated by a catchy, singalong refrain. A surprising number are set to tango rhythms. The last section features the newest sound: hymns of ghetto fighters and partisans set to marching tunes, some of Soviet provenance, like Glik's "Partisans' Hymn."

Thanks to the international klezmer revival in recent years, the Holocaust song has gained a more secular venue for the performance of a darker, raunchier, multilingual repertoire. The time has come for a much more comprehensive Holocaust songbook with singable translations in the new vernacular. (DGR)

Tadeusz Borowski. *This Way for the Gas, Ladies and Gentlemen*. Introduction by Jan Kott. Translated from the Polish by Barbara Vedder; introduction translated by Michael Kandel. Harmondsworth, England: Penguin, 1976. First published as *Kamienny świat*. First English edition 1967. Movie based on this collection of stories, *Krajobraz po bitwie* (Landscape after the battle), directed by Andrzej Wajda (Poland, 1970).

Tadeusz Borowski was arrested in Warsaw in 1943, imprisoned for two months in a prison abutting the Warsaw ghetto and then deported to Auschwitz. After an initial stint digging holes for telegraph poles—back-breaking labor that all but guaranteed the death of the prisoner—he was transferred to work as a *Vorarbeiter* (foreman), a comparatively privileged position, and then as an orderly in the Auschwitz hospital. This narrator has ample food, so much that he doesn't need the daily soup ration. He receives food parcels from home. He is able to send letters out of the camp to his fiancée and beyond. He does not live in fear of the gas chamber. He is a participant in and observer of mass murder, and he appreciates that he is fatally compromised as a result.

These stories, published between 1945 and 1948, are characterized by an economy of means, a protagonist who reports events as he sees them and also realizes that he is colluding with murder on an industrial scale. Borowski's short stories are savage in their judgments (including the narrator's of his own conduct). In a world where survival is the goal, anyone will do anything, will sacrifice anyone or anything, in order to live. That is the fundamental principle of all human behavior, from the Nazi camp commander to the lowliest *Muselman*.

Reading Borowski is a vertiginous experience. His stories take familiar forms and words and turn them into containers for the unbearable, vicious, and absurd. In Borowski's hands, defamiliarization—the term that the Russian formalists coined to describe how the poetic could emerge from ordinary language—turns into an essential tool. Only it is the ordinary, normal, morally acceptable that is defamiliarized because in the concentration camp what is irrevocably familiar is atrocity. What deviates from the norm is generosity, compassion, and anger. These are the dangerous emotions, and when the autobiographical narrator, Tadek, describes instances of this behavior, they are never without cost—sometimes to the giver, sometimes to the recipient, sometimes to both. In the longest piece, "Auschwitz, Our Home," the writer is composing a letter home, taking advantage of a seminar given for medical orderlies. "What delightful days," he writes, and describes a series of atrocious experiences. Yet in the world of Auschwitz, a day without physical labor, with enough food to eat, and without physical violence is, indeed, a delightful day. The irony is built into the collision of ordinary language with the mundane of the concentration camp.

One engages with the narrator because of one's own heightened awareness of the unacceptable nature of survival and privilege. In "The People Who Walked On," Borowski describes a transport of Jews entering the Auschwitz station and walking into the gas chambers, between two throw-ins at the soccer game that is taking place at the same time in another part of the camp. This is not like D. M. Thomas's *White Hotel*, where the boundary between dream world and reality is blurred. These are two sets of concrete behavior occurring in the single time and place that the narrator describes. Both reflect a very traditional notion of narrative, a way of transcribing the ordinary into a story. Yet when they are juxtaposed, the two sets of actions are absurd and hideous.

Borowski's writing reflects a deep commitment to the speakability of atrocity. His stories are perhaps the most successful articulations of Levi's "human laboratory of Auschwitz"—what it was, what it meant, and what it continues to mean. (ND)

[1949]

Leyb Rochman. *The Pit and the Trap: A Chronicle of Survival*. Introduction by Aharon Appelfeld. Edited by Sheila Friedling. Translated from the Yiddish by Moshe Kohn and Sheila Friedling. New York: Holocaust Library, 1983. First published as *Un in dayn blut zolstu lebn: togbukh 1943–1944*. Paris: Farlag-komisye bay der gezelshaft "Fraynt fun Minsk-Mazovyetsk" in Pariz, 1949.

When Leyb Rochman's chronicle begins, on February 17, 1943, his entire world has already been destroyed. The Red Army is still 1,800 kilometers away. But he is not alone. With the help of Auntie, an old Christian whore, Leyb has secured a hiding place for himself and four others, including his bride, Esther. It will be two years before they meet another living Jew, a boy with nine lives who goes by the name of Konyak. The five people in hiding also have assumed names and Aryan papers, though with their Jewish looks and accents, the three men don't stand much of a chance living on the run. Nor have they run very far. Auntie has rescued them from the ghetto of Mińsk Mazowieck and the adjacent labor camp of Kopernik, and outside their hiding place, the hunt for Jews continues unabated. In a few months, they will overhear the peasants talking about a Jewish uprising in the Warsaw ghetto and of the flames from the burning ghetto that can be seen on the horizon at night. Leyb's field of vision, in contrast, is tiny. From one spot inside their hiding place, he can just glimpse a speck of sunlight. *The Pit and the Trap* conveys a sense of entrapment in space and time that has no parallel in Holocaust literature.

Leyb lives in three times. One is ad hoc and open-ended until the moment they are discovered, when it will end. That is survival time, rendered in days or, when the hunt is on, compressed into minutes. Another is Black Friday, August 21, 1942, the time of the slaughter, and the Jews' harrowing escape from the ghetto and work camp—suppressed memories that burst into Leyb's consciousness out of sequence, whenever there is a reprieve from the daily struggle for survival. But there is a third dimension of time that is unique to this chronicle: the five Jews seem to be trapped sometime in the hoary past. For they have been captured by an old witch and imprisoned in a Polish village still governed by pagan blood lust, rivalry, vengeance, greed, theft, superstition, and the hatred of the Jews that has lasted for millennia. Yet they are rescued from the margins of this peasant society by selfless and spontaneous acts of courage. The five adults and their young sidekick survive the war thanks to an old whore, a notorious robber named Felek, and a loyal dog named Morwa.

For two millennia, Jews of the Diaspora believed that there was safety in numbers. They lived mostly in cities and small towns. From 1943 onward, Leyb and his group discovered that there were better chances of survival hiding in a remote village among strangers and surrounded by hatred, fear, and betrayal than among tens of thousands of their fellow Jews. They were saved thanks to a speck of sunlight up above and acts of elemental empathy down below. (DGR)

Jiří Weil. *Life with a Star*. Preface by Philip Roth. Translated from the Czech by Rita Klímová with Roslyn Schloss. New York: Farrar, Straus and Giroux, 1989. First published as *Život s hvězdou*.

As the books in this Guide indicate, different authors use abstraction in different ways to communicate the depths of humiliation and desperation experienced by Nazi victims. Spiegelman uses the devices of the comic book to make Nazi metaphors into reality. Patrick Modiano, a generation earlier, uses the device of the star as the mechanism for a grotesque parody of antisemitism, so extreme that it insists on its opposite. Aharon Appelfeld uses the metaphor of the holiday spa. Jiří Weil's book does not name the occupier (the Nazis), the victims (the Jews), or the city it is set in (Prague). The destinations of the transports to the East (Auschwitz) and the fortress town (Theresienstadt) are also unnamed. The book relies on the reader to understand and fill in the context. One can imagine a reader a century from now who is ignorant of the historical context reading Weil's book as a cognate perhaps of the tales of Borges. Those readers who do understand the allusions to the star are able to fill in all the details, becoming as a result deeply implicated, because understanding this world leaves the reader tainted by that knowledge.

In the world of *Life with a Star*, the narrative hovers between metaphor and myth. Life and death exchange places—the living, whether they are willing to accept it or not, are already dead. The dead live vibrant lives. Symbol of life and energy, the circus becomes the place where victims are rounded up for deportation. Those who have nothing are the freest of all. The safest place to work is in the cemetery because there is never a shortage of dead people. (ND)

[1950]

John Hersey. *The Wall*. New York: Knopf, 1950.

John Hersey is best known for *Hiroshima*, an article that took up the whole of the August 31, 1946, issue of the *New Yorker*. The article traced the consequences of the first atom bomb exploded as an act of war through the eyes of six Japanese characters. Later published in book form, the novel was awarded the Pulitzer Prize.

Hersey adopted the same literary technique for *The Wall*, an account of the creation, existence, and destruction of the Warsaw ghetto that was published in 1950. A journalist stationed in Moscow at the end of the Second World War, Hersey had visited some of the Nazi concentration camps very soon after Liberation, as the Eastern Front advanced. As a journalist, he was deeply concerned with translating the scope of historical events on a more human scale, so in his story of the ghetto, he creates a cluster, a "family" brought together not by blood but by overwhelming circumstance.

Although we know from the editor's introduction that all but one of the characters dies, the characterization is sufficient for the reader to empathize with the choices facing the characters, who are forced to make decisions without benefit of hindsight and with the severely limited information at their disposal. One sees the development—indeed, the erosion—of morality in times of crisis and, perhaps most touching, the ways in which people under extreme stress still seek to make sense of their lives and to find ways of creating meaning for themselves, even in the most dangerous and temporary of circumstances. Some people rise to the challenges, others don't. Heroism is a fungible category. People change, grow, and develop over the course of the novel. For some—for example, the archivist, Noah Levinson—the ghetto enables an experience of human connection that he had never before experienced.

Elsewhere in this volume, we have discussed Emanuel Ringelblum's massive Oyneg Shabes. Ringelblum's enterprise was at the basis of Hersey's undertaking. He hired Lucy Dawidowicz as a translator and described in later articles the process of acquiring a knowledge of the archive not just through the texts she translated but through the translator's narrative interpolations.

Hersey was an early exponent of what would be called the New Journalism, in which a journalist draws on the resources of fiction in terms of pace, plot, and characterization while recounting an historical event. In comparison to the richness of Ringelblum's archive, Hersey's novel pales, but it remains an important work because it is still broadly accessible today. Well before such seminal works as Raul Hilberg's *The Destruction of European Jews* and novels such as Elie Wiesel's *Night* (1960), Hersey was trying to foreground the ghetto as a critically important source of historical and artistic materials. Without engaging with the history, archives, art, and social structures of the ghetto, an understanding of the Holocaust would be impossible.

Hersey's novel proved to be a massive bestseller throughout the 1950s, but its time passed once the conventions of unspeakability took hold. The fact that his attempt was only partially successful should not outweigh the book's value as a document of the early development of Holocaust literature in languages other than Hebrew and Yiddish. (ND)

[1952]

Paul Celan. *Mohn und Gedächtnis* (Poppy and memory). Selections in *Selected Poems and Prose of Paul Celan*, translated from the German by John Felstiner (New York: W. W. Norton, 2001); *Poems of Paul Celan*, translated from the German by Michael Hamburger, rev. and expanded ed. (New York: Persea, 2002). Both are bilingual editions.

Paul Celan's "Todesfuge" (Death fugue) is a stand-alone poem. It is also a stand-alone chapter at the dead center of his inaugural volume, *Mohn und Gedächtnis*, which is made up of fifty-six lyric poems. Only in this poem does

Celan specifically mention *Deutschland*, or Germany (Felstiner 1995, 36), repeating the name half a dozen times, the last four in the chilling refrain "death is a master from Deutschland." In contrast to his private lyrics, which are written in a radically condensed and hermetic style, this poem in the first person plural tells a story, with named characters—villains and victims—in a landscape both extraterrestrial and absolutely real. Just as the poet immortalizes Germany as the homeland of death, here alone he builds up to an incantation of apocalyptic rage. It is the most quoted poem in all of Holocaust literature and has been set to music by more composers than any other.

"Todesfuge" is set within a rich mosaic of associations. Celan's poetic landscape in this volume ranges from "Akra" and Egypt to Paris; from desert sands and seascapes to forests and parks. Much of the volume is given over to scenes of love and lovemaking, to mementos of loss and the recollection of the luxurious hair (even "harsh pubic hair") of his several unnamed lovers. There is much talk of God, both personal and Christ-like, but nothing explicitly Jewish save for the exclamatory "Ruth! Naomi! Miriam!"—generic lovers, all ("In Egypt"). Amid the lovers, however, who are very much alive, several poems invoke the memory of his mother, murdered in the Ukraine: "Aspen Tree," with its song-like symmetry between the natural and human realms; "The Travel Companion," in which "mother" is repeated in every line; and the closing poem, "Count Up the Almonds," where she is not explicitly mentioned, but the almonds resonate with the "Raisins and Almonds" of Yiddish folksong. Mother, fair-haired and soft-voiced, lives on in her son's memory; even in death she remains his essential muse: "This word is your mother's ward."

Against this highly poeticized and private landscape, "Todesfuge" stands out with its ferocity and almost pornographic explicitness. The impossible pairing of black with milk; music with death; and the ashen-haired, biblical Shulamith with Margareta, she of the golden hair, symbol of German womanhood, makes surreal sense in one place and one place alone. There the personification of death in *Deutschland* is the commandant, who steps out of his house, "whistles his hounds to stay close / he whistles his Jews into rows has them shovel a grave in the ground," even as he commands the band to "play up for the dance." Day and night, the "we" of this poem drink the black milk of the gas chambers as the smoke from the crematoria inscribes "graves in the air."

With this signature poem, Celan made the Nazi concentration camp the proper subject for poetry, the matrix of personal and communal memory, and the touchstone of metaphor. (DGR)

Ka-Tzetnik 135633. *House of Dolls*. Translated from the Hebrew by Moshe M. Kohn. New York: Simon and Schuster, 1955. First published as *Dos hoyz fun di lyalkes*.

House of Dolls was read by over five million readers in eleven languages. For publishers, it was soft-core pornography, which told of sadistic and sadomasochistic German guards and officers, aided and abetted by doctors and nurses, who indulged in countless types of perversion and sexual fantasy. For adolescents, it underscored the dirtiness of the Holocaust secret.

House of Dolls, the middle volume of Ka-Tzetnik's Chronicle of a Jewish Family in the Twentieth Century, follows the brutal coming of age of Daniella Preleshnik, turned into a *Feld-Hure*—a sex slave of the Germans—in Auschwitz. Her older brother, Harry, the author's fictional stand-in, works as a member of the paramedical staff in the Auschwitz infirmary, and in the third and final volume, the 1961 *Piepel*, their young brother, Moni, will serve as homosexual sex servant of Block *Aelteste*. Less obvious is the fact that most of the male characters—Haim-Yidl, Vevke, and Zanvl Lubliner—are young, traditional Jews forced, like the author himself, to confront limitless evil. *House of Dolls* tracks their fate from the ghetto of Metropoli to the Dulag (the transit camp) to Auschwitz.

In the novel's opening scene, Daniella and her friends sort through huge piles of plundered clothing, the sheer volume and diversity of which gradually bringing home to them the methodical nature of the Nazi design and the commodification of death. When the ghetto is liquidated and they reach the Dulag, Daniella finds a sea of names and inscriptions on the walls, all that remains of those thousands who passed through here; and when she arrives in Auschwitz, after all her clothes are thrown into the same kind of heap from which she once worked in the ghetto, she is issued the very shoes that she was once forced to produce herself. Desperately, she tries to hold onto her locket, for if all that remains of people is their clothing, how can the still-living preserve their individuality?

In the "other planet," as Ka-Tzetnik famously described Auschwitz during his brief testimony at the Eichmann trial, the Germans completed their work of branding the Jews. Shlamek's father, in the first weeks of the German occupation, had "JUDE" carved into his forehead, and all Jews, in short order, were forced to mark their clothing with a Star of David. Once, when leaving the ghetto, Harry and Danielle ripped off their yellow stars, "but the spot where the star had been stood out, unfaded." On her arrival in Auschwitz, as part of a special female transport handpicked by Monyek Matroz, the Judenrat chief,

Daniella had "Feld-Hure A13653" branded between her breasts. This was a new covenant, never to be eradicated.

As the first and most accessible novelist of atrocity, Ka-Tzetnik's influence was enormous. In an unacknowledged tribute, Joshua Sobol opened his play *Geto* with a scene of the Jews sorting through the plundered clothing of the dead (Sobol 1992, 1995). (DGR)

[1956]

Uri Orlev. *The Lead Soldiers*. Translated from the Hebrew by Hillel Halkin.
New York: Taplinger, 1980. First published as *Ḥayalei oferet*.

Yurik (Uri) and his young brother, Kazik, are two pampered boys circumcised against their parents' wishes. They belong to a new generation of thoroughly acculturated Polish Jews. The two of them were imprisoned in the Warsaw ghetto, survived the great deportation and various periods in hiding on the Aryan side, were caught in the Hotel Polski affair, and sent to Bergen-Belsen, finally reaching Palestine where they were successfully absorbed into a socialist, Hebrew-speaking kibbutz. Their life story is unbelievable, no less action-filled and fantastical, in fact, than children's make-believe, their favorite works of juvenile fiction, or Aunt Stella's séances and dreams. Seeing as they are still children when they arrive in Palestine—a photograph of them leaving the Atlit Detention Camp appears on the book's back cover—what better way to render their true experience than as a never-ending game, which gets ever fiercer, ever more eclectic and elaborate?

Make-believe and play are a means of both escaping and transmuting reality. That reality is the Jew-Zone, here described as a place of ubiquitous hatred of Jews, both overt and covert, spoken and unspoken; of Jewish self-hatred; and of growing terror, with incredible rumors of mass annihilation culminating in the victims' being hunted down in their own homes. When the hunt for Jews is in full swing, the only recourse is either to go into hiding or to jump into the air like angels—which Sofia, the children's lifelong caretaker, does. Reality itself becomes utterly phantasmagorical, exceeding all adventure stories ever written. What the children of all ages discover is that the untrammeled human imagination may be the only possible response to the annihilation of a whole world.

As with so many works in our Guide, Orlev's true story of Marrano children operates on more than one level and has more than one ending. From the sobering epilogue, we learn that the boys' father, a Polish officer who survived the war in Russian captivity, remarried and severed all ties with his sons; that their guardians, Stella and Finkel, became slave owners in South Africa; that the boys received reparation money from the Germans—a ferociously controversial subject in the 1950s—and that Mr. G.—the novel's most evil character—rose to fame and fortune in Haifa. Then there are the startling intrusions scattered throughout the book, in which the adult narrator tries to interfere with and change what happens to his characters. Like the epilogue, these authorial intrusions guard the reader against an excess of sentimentality. "Don't read your emotions into him," warns the author at a particularly poignant moment in Yurik's story. "He wasn't at all upset. He was sure that this was how it was supposed to be." Through this and similar interpolations, Orlev signals that *The Lead Soldiers* is to be read also as fiction: the work of an adult impersonating a child; an Israeli impersonating a Polish boy; and a survivor impersonating the dead. (DGR)

[1958]

Arnošt Lustig. *Night and Hope*. Translated from the Czech by George
  Theiner. New York: Dutton, 1962. First published as *Noc a naděje*. Movie
  version, *Transport Z Raje* (Transport from paradise), directed by Zbynek
  Brynych (Czechoslovakia, 1962).

The six stories that make up this collection by Arnošt Lustig are set in Theresienstadt, a camp in Bohemia that served as both a transshipment point for Jews from points West to Auschwitz and as a ghetto for very important Jews, such as Leo Baeck, the former chief rabbi of Berlin. Theresienstadt was also used as a showplace, a Potemkin village for the Red Cross and other agencies whose goodwill the Nazis sought. Whatever its uses, the facts show that of the 144,000 Jews who passed through Theresienstadt, there were 12,500 survivors at war's end. The rest were transported or died from starvation and disease. Lustig's characters are the still-living. It is a parlous condition, however, because it makes them vulnerable to illusion and hope, states of being as dangerous as typhus and tuberculosis.

For Lustig, the larger collective exists only insofar as the individual feels the anguish of being alone. In the first story, Tausig leaves the relative safety of his hiding place in order to escape the anxieties associated with the constant anticipation of disaster. Smuggling himself into a transport of Jews, he feels a sense of relief. He no longer has to worry about being caught. Like Cousin David in Ida Fink's short story, Tausig is one of the impatient ones.

Lustig's characters are lodged in the everyday, and that is the power of the book. Children play pranks, as usual, but these pranks involve stealing food and carry a death sentence. A woman works in a store, where a man beats her half to death. Another man does a good deed and gives her a luxury item—a tin of sardines. A woman dies as a result. Another man conspires to advance his career. His wife doesn't get the social tone right enough to impress his boss. Her husband wants to kill her but kills a Jew instead. A boy and a girl meet and fall instantly in love. They kiss. The next day the boy looks for his girl. She was transported to Auschwitz during the night. It's a scorching hot day, which puts people into a bad mood. Kids are singing jazz—outrageous! Someone else dies.

The longest story is devoted to Murmelstaub, a thinly disguised version of Benjamin Murmelstein, the ghetto elder, known by the inmates as Murmelschwein. One of the cruelest attacks on the Jews of Europe made by their brethren in Palestine and then Israel was the accusation that they had gone like lambs to the slaughter; that they had not resisted.

In this story, Lustig delineates the toxic combination of ego, social climbing, survival instinct, and choicelessness that led the leaders of the Jewish community to help in their own community's destruction, all the while postponing the inevitable moment of their own execution. (Lustig's forthrightness about the Jewish communal leadership does not remove an iota of responsibility from the Nazis, the true wielders of power in this situation.) It is a brilliant portrait of moral vacuity that rivals in its own way such great depictions as Marcel Proust's Bloch, the Jewish schoolmate of the narrator of *A la recherche du temps perdu*. Murmelstaub's close companion is the Jew described by Primo Levi who prays in thanks when his bunkmate—and not he—is selected for the gas chamber.

Night and Hope makes the reader participate in the quotidian, which is perhaps the most disturbing role for the reader to adopt. There is no place to hide. The facts alone are sufficient indictment; everyone is a co-conspirator; and no one can plead the Fifth. (ND)

Elie Wiesel. *Night*. Foreword by François Mauriac. Translated from the French by Stella Rodway. New York: Hill and Wang, 1960. Published in a new translation by Marion Wiesel with a new preface by the author (New York: Hill and Wang, 2000). First published as *La Nuit*.

No discussion of Holocaust literature in its postwar afterlife can occur without mentioning Wiesel's *Night*, not because it is the greatest literary work in the literature but because the book and Wiesel's role as survivor par excellence have done so much to shape the discourse of Holocaust literature. *Night* is a dystopian bildungsroman, the story of a young boy leaving home and growing into an adult refracted through the ghastly lens of the concentration camp, where adulthood means betrayal, survival reflects permanently compromised moral standing, and the compass points of existence—compassion, morality, and human engagement—are systematically inverted.

The book begins with the prelapsarian past: a small town, religious community life, a timeless existence. Then there is the harbinger, Moche the Beadle, who returns to tell a story that no one believes. Then come the roundup, the transport, the selection, hunger, the struggle for existence, the son's betrayal of the father, and, finally, liberation without joy. Wiesel's concentration camp has very few characters in it—the father, a relative, and one or two Kapos. The tight focus keeps the book a coming-of-age tale and reflects the narrator's own limits. But it also means that the concentration camp lacks any context. Wiesel argues strenuously that the world of Auschwitz is outside of time and place. But as some of the other books in our Guide demonstrate, the concentration camps were very much products of human facilitation, from the villagers to the politicians, from the guards to the factory supervisors and all the willing enactors of Nazi regulation. These are missing from *Night*. That is not to say that Wiesel is at fault for not including them, but rather that any reading of Holocaust literature needs to assure a broader, more varied context. However much the universe of the concentration camp was a world apart, it was part of a larger world. Many people who later claimed complete ignorance knew at least something about what was happening in these places. Certainly, it was widely known that no one emerged alive from the camps.

Wiesel's *Night* was not the first book to come out of the Holocaust, but it was the first to arrive with the imprimatur of the French literary establishment. The preface by François Mauriac, academician and literary arbiter, put Wiesel's book squarely into the literary mainstream and presented the book as a saga of death and resurrection, domesticating the experiences described (and the culpability of the bystanders, who, in the early 1960s, were still in the prime of life) into a Christological martyrology.

Wiesel has gone on to become the archetypal survivor. He admonishes presidents (Reagan, about the visit to Bitburg) and acts as a moral authority on issues of nuclear disarmament and torture. At the outset, there were many survivors, and many of them wrote accounts of their experiences and went on to live their lives in different registers. Wiesel alone has attained an international authority based on his victimhood and survival. Through his writing and his persona, Wiesel has rendered the Jewish victim accessible to a Christian audience. He is the archetypal translator figure, a sort of John the Baptist to the Holocaust. (ND)

[1959]

Hana Volavková, ed. *Children's Drawings and Poems, Terezín, 1942–1944*.
Epilogue by Jiří Weil. translated from the Czech by Jeanne Němcová.
Prague: Státní židovské muzeum. Republished as *I Never Saw Another*

Butterfly: Children's Drawings and Poems from Terezín Concentration Camp, 1942–1944 (New York: Schocken, 1978).

This is the iconic anthology of and on the Holocaust. The Holocaust rendered adults childlike and endowed children with visionary powers. If this was the universal rule, how much more so in the small garrison town of Terezín, where in the words of Jiří Weil, "everything . . . was false, invented; everyone of its inhabitants was condemned in advance to die." Here, as part of a comprehensive curriculum, children were taught to draw, sketch, and paint from a very young age—first animals and everyday objects, and eventually landscapes; and in the children's homes, poetry contests and recitation evenings of children's poems were held. Here boys and girls went their separate but equal ways: girls depicting nature, both real and remembered; boys more tied to industrial reality, such as steamboats, warships, battles, and action adventure. But when properly preserved and assembled, these seemingly most ephemeral, marginal, and minimal units of memory reveal the most truthful and compelling response of the victims.

Except in one respect. Although Terezín was a city of Jews—Jews from Bohemia and Moravia, then from far and wide, on their way to Auschwitz—this anthology of children's art and poetry is completely deracinated. The notes may tell us that Eva Meitner's "most interesting" art work was a pastel of a Passover seder, but she is represented instead by a pencil drawing of a "Man with a Long Beard," who might just as well be a likeness of Moses. And the pastel on semi-glossy paper of a "Candlestick" by Irena Karpeles looks suspiciously like a Hanukkah menorah, with all nine candles brightly lit. For all that this anthology is annotated, arranged, and reproduced with meticulous care, it betrays the telltale signs of Communist rule.

Yet there is no better proof that children are antitotalitarian. Children want above all to let their imagination roam free, beyond the ghetto walls, even while they like to draw and versify life exactly as they see it: the black potatoes, filthy floors, "the sound of shouting, cries, / And oh, so many flies." When they dream of being free ("Maybe more of us, / A thousand strong, / Will reach this goal / Before too long."), the dream begins in the first person singular:

> I'd like to go away alone
> Where there are other, nicer people,
> Somewhere into the far unknown,
> There, where no one kills another.

This anthology is no less a tribute to their dedicated teachers, who encouraged the children to draw what they saw and to write what they dreamed—a remarkable group of painters and pedagogues, who could do nothing to protect either their young charges or themselves from death. (DGR)

André Schwarz-Bart. *The Last of the Just*. Translated from the French by
    Stephen Becker. New York: Atheneum, 1960. First published as *Le dernier
    des Justes*, 1959.

A wall at Yad Vashem intersperses several words from the kaddish with the names of Nazi extermination and concentration camps. The words are taken from the very end of André Schwarz-Bart's *The Last of the Just*, a novel published in 1959 by a young, unknown, but soon to be famous author. The book caused a furor and was awarded the 1959 Prix Goncourt, one of the most important literary prizes in France.

Schwarz-Bart was a French Jew born of Polish Jewish parents. His parents and siblings were deported before him, not being of French birth. The teenage boy joined the resistance, was arrested, escaped, rejoined, and survived the war. He drifted from job to job, largely educating himself, and finally used his veteran's benefits to go to college.

Schwarz-Bart structures his novel around the trope of the thirty-six (*lamed vav* in Hebrew) righteous men in each generation who exist in humble anonymity. These men, unknown except in moments of extreme crisis, are guarantors of at least the minimal level of righteousness sufficient to keep the Almighty from losing hope in humanity.

Schwarz-Bart builds a thousand years of family history that account for the life of a Lamed-vovnik born in successive generations of the Levy family, starting from the destruction of the Jews of York in the twelfth century and ending with the death of Ernie Levy at Auschwitz in 1943. The Levy family thus stands for the history of the Jewish people in Europe, each chapter outlining the persecution that befalls the community in which the Levys live and die.

The Last of the Just was greeted with acclaim as a marvelous interpretation of the sweep of Jewish history; it was also reviled as a Christological martyrology that turned Jews into Christ-like figures, thereby effacing the very history that the book purported to restore. Despite moments of melodrama, the book remains credible because it refuses to let anyone off the hook—the Jews of the Hebraic persuasion who want to show that they are good Frenchmen; the Frenchwoman who tolerates an Israelite (as Jews were known in the best French secular tradition) in her bed but cannot accept the fact that she has been screwing a Jew; even Ernie himself for his attempt to transform himself into anything (Frenchman, dog, madman) other than the Jew he is.

In 1959, the Eichmann trial had yet to occur. Jean-Paul Sartre ruled the intellectual world of Paris. The French Communist party had refused to acknowledge Stalin's atrocities. Ninety percent of the French identified themselves as having resisted the Nazis. General Charles de Gaulle had recreated the pride of French nationalism by insisting against all evidence that France had been liberated by the French Résistance. The French lexicon of the war surrounded the political prisoners—many of Jewish origin—who had been deported. No one was willing to describe the capture and deportation of Jews, men, women, children, the elderly, the sick, the dying. Frenchness trumped everything.

Against this background, *The Last of the Just* had the impact of a grenade, shattering the surface to insist on the deep cultural roots of European anti-semitism, articulated and promoted by centuries of Christian theology. Jew-ishness was steeped in Western culture, and in effacing it, Christian culture had suffered a loss of monstrous proportions. In the loss of Ernie Levy in his convoy of frightened children, in fact, Western civilization had lost its own claim to rehabilitation. The attack on the culture of the West would be refined and rearticulated by the generations of 1968 and beyond, but Schwarz-Bart, as a hugely popular novelist, was there first. (ND)

[1960]

Vasily Grossman. *Life and Fate: A Novel.* Translated from the Russian with an introduction by Robert Chandler. New York: Harper and Row, 1985. First published as *Zhizn' i sud'ba: roman.*

Every copy but one, miraculously rescued, of *Life and Fate* was confiscated by the Soviet secret police. The author was told that it would not be published for another two hundred years, and he himself was driven to an early grave. What made the novel so scandalous in the eyes of the state was not its depiction of the Holocaust—although Grossman violated the rule against "dividing the victims." From beginning to end—with its multiple settings and symmetrical plot, and the tragic fate of its huge cast of characters—the novel drew an absolute equivalency between Soviet and Nazi totalitarianism, between the Gulag and the German concentration and death camps, between Hitler and Stalin.

Holding its many voices together is the epic narrator, who sometimes speaks with prophetic cadence, as when he reveals the double enslavement of Soviet POWs in a German concentration camp: "And in this silence of the dumb and these speeches of the blind, in this medley of people bound together by the same grief, terror and hope, in this hatred and lack of understanding between men who spoke the same tongue, you could see much of the tragedy of the twentieth century." How is it, he asks, that during the campaigns to liquidate the kulaks, the great purges of 1937, and, finally, the extermination of the Ukrainian and Belorussian Jews, the surrounding populations became obedient witnesses to the slaughter? It is because they were ensnared in the net of baseless hatred and revulsion that had been prepared for them in advance. Yet let there be no mistake. Those who allowed themselves to be ruled by fate, those who succumbed to state-sponsored evil—from Eichmann, who master-minded the annihilation, to Sturmbannführer Kaltluft and Private Roze, who carried it out—all are guilty: "Yes, there are men in this terrible world who are guilty." *Life and Fate*—presciently written before Eichmann was captured and put on trial—is the great rebuttal of the banality of evil.

The novel is the outstanding example of reading the Holocaust through a national lens. Grossman, who was the most widely read Soviet war corre-spondent and who immortalized the battle of Stalingrad, also produced the first journalistic account of Treblinka and became the coauthor of the Soviet Black Book. In the novel, the fate of a mother and son is emblematic of that of Soviet Jewry as a whole. Victor Shtrum's mother is murdered in the Ber-dichev ghetto, while he, the decorated Soviet physicist, is made to feel the stigma of his national identity. But it is Shtrum's act of self-betrayal that marks his undoing, as is the case with many other characters—male and female, old and young—who must bear the guilt of denunciation, indifference, and self-interest. *Life and Fate* called its readers to spontaneous acts of national self-cleansing. In Grossman's view, the future of the past rested on a moral vision of life that preceded and transcended historical fate. (DGR)

Anna Langfus. *The Whole Land Brimstone*. Translated from the French by
    Peter Wiles. New York: Pantheon, 1962. First published as *Le Sel et le Soufre*.

The narrator of Anna Langfus's novel is a young middle-class woman, married very young and still not grown up. Even as the family is moved into the ghetto and then finds its way to Warsaw and the ghetto there, she continues to behave like a spoiled teenager. The situation worsens. The family is split up, with the narrator, her husband, and her mother escaping to the non-Jewish section of Warsaw while her father remains behind.

The early scenes of the novel convey the way in which the bizarre becomes normal (to go to a party where you will drink champagne, you have to jump over a corpse). The Jews hidden on the Aryan side are at the mercy of their hosts, who exploit them for money, sex, or emotional support. Eventually the family is split again: the husband and his parents are hidden on the Aryan side; the protagonist's mother goes back to the ghetto to be with her husband; and the narrator is left to fend for herself.

This is yet another bildungsroman, a story of maturation, yet the narrator seems to be more a passive watcher than a full participant in her own destiny. Left by her husband's family to find her own shelter, she puts herself at the mercy of a man with whom she has had tea several times. He turns out to be an important figure in the Polish resistance. Later, she and her husband are in the forest, dying of cold and hunger. A German officer, who had been demoted for his lack of antisemitic zeal, finds them, takes them in, and—giving them a strong cover story—has them protected within his army unit. Later in the book, Maria, as she is now called, is arrested as a Russian spy—her German protector having hidden a copy of the map to Nazi minefields in their rooms. Jailed as a Pole and then condemned to death, her life continues in the same suspension as before, except punctuated at first by torture (the torturer making sure to disinfect her wounds each day) and later by prison labor and starvation.

While in prison, she communicates with her husband through the intermediary of a hunchback who has the cell between them. When her husband is shot, the hunchback tries to ease the blow by creating imaginary messages to her from her husband. That mode of existence—where all action and reaction is mediated through individuals, walls, brutality, bitter hunger, or freezing cold—is a constant throughout the novel.

At the end of the book, Maria returns to her childhood home only to have the door shut in her face. She finds herself in the cellar of the house, draped over her nanny's traveling trunk, as if ready for a journey whose next stage is always beginning and whose end will never come. (ND)

Provisional Memory, 1960–85

[1961]

Piotr Rawicz. *Blood from the Sky*. Introduction by Lawrence Langer.
Translated from the French by Peter Wiles. 1st paperback ed. New
Haven: Yale University Press, 2003. First published as *Le Sang du Ciel*.
First English edition 1964.

Imagine a novel that crosses James Joyce with Dostoevsky, add a large dose of André Breton, and then situate that novel in the early 1940s in an unspecified part of Eastern Europe—and *Blood from the Sky* might well be the result.

Although Rawicz survived three years in Auschwitz, imprisoned as a Ukrainian, not a Jew, his novel doesn't describe the concentration camp directly. Instead, the novel creates a hallucinatory universe, in which the narrative voice is consistently decentered; the text is a collection of dubious recollections; and a protagonist, Count Boris, may or may not also be one of the shabby survivors in Paris. The first-person voice is thoroughly unreliable, the victims themselves despicable and grotesque. There are moments of slapstick savagery (LL, the president of the ghetto council, is forced to dress as a clown and dance for the

Nazis' amusement) and a persistent recalcitrance in the face of conventional morality (the janitor in the ghetto hospital steals his father's cyanide so that the old man will not be able to cheat the Nazis of his death; the great Talmud scholar has a fine collection of pornographic postcards).

Out of the vertigo of the reading experience, one grasps at voices that recall or prefigure other writers. There is Tadeusz Borowski's sardonic self-hatred, Curzio Malaparte's aestheticized atrocity, Patrick Modiano's chameleon narrator, Michel Tournier's self-enclosed mythologies: the pastiche of the book leaves the reader struggling for context but also aware that this struggle to grasp, to understand, is at the very heart of Rawicz's vision of the Holocaust. None of it makes sense. The victims are not hallowed martyrs. They are human and flawed and have no recourse. Boris and Naomi are endlessly in transit, fleeing ahead of themselves and the fate that awaits them. So, too, are the various narrative voices in constant flight, even from their own narrative.

In Rawicz's hands, the surrealist rejection of the real becomes the most realistic of literary schools for its ability to make sense of the events of the ghettos and the camps, the life of a fugitive, the casual cruelty of the Germans and Poles and Ukrainians, the breakdown in social mores, the absurdity, the hideousness, and the ongoing devaluation of human culture. Ultimately, these all find their expression in the narrator's refusal at one point to speak and talking irrepressibly at other points. Both are telling options. The fact that the narrator survives the war is just as arbitrary as the narrative itself. (ND)

[1962]

Giorgio Bassani. *The Garden of the Finzi Continis*. Translated from the Italian by Isabel Quigly. New York: Atheneum, 1965. First published as *Il Giardino dei Finzi Contini*. Movie version directed by Vittorio de Sica (Italy, 1970).

Framed by a first-person narrative set in 1957, Bassani's novel describes the effect of ever-tightening racial legislation on two Jewish families from Ferrara, the narrator's own, a middle-class professional family, and the aristocratic Finzi Continis, owners of a former D'Este palace at the heart of Ferrara, behind whose high walls they lead a mysterious and quite self-contained existence.

Only the racial laws break the barriers of class, allowing the young narrator to be invited into this family circle. There is a beautiful daughter, with whom, inevitably, he falls in (unrequited) love; an indolent son; the son's friend, a Communist engineer from the north of Italy; family retainers; and the father, mother, and grandmother.

Without the impending doom of the family's deportation, about which we are informed at the outset, the book would be a gentle, faded reproduction of many a coming-of-age story: a charming, affectionate portrait of a time and place that has long since ceased to exist, recalling the dreaminess of the young protagonist in Proust's *Un Amour de Swann*, whose imagination builds up a rich imaginary connection with glittering individuals whose true nature can only disappoint.

But that historical doom is ever present. The book's prologue takes us from some ancient Etruscan tombs to the living tomb of the Finzi Contini estate and then, as the antisemitic racial laws hit home, into the aching expectation of deportation and death—a death without dignity, burial, or tombstones.

The Finzi Continis are representatives of high Italian culture and the expectations of the Risorgimento and its aftermath. There is no ghetto in Ferrara. The Jewish community is extremely assimilated. Many (including the narrator's father) are early members of the Fascist Party.

In Bassani's book, the characters are pale, white-haired, lacking in vitality —they are already well on the path to death. Indeed, Alberto Finzi Contini, the son and heir, dies shortly before the deportation, not from fascist or Nazi actions but from lung cancer. The narrator's father, in the last embrace that closes the prewar section of the story, has aged fifteen years in the few months since his expulsion from the Fascist Party. Even the garden becomes a doubly lost paradise, as the narrator is expelled from it when Micol does not return his affection, and then as the garden is ransacked, its exquisite arboretum chopped down for firewood. The deaths of the Finzi Continis and the neglected tomb mark the final failure of the Italian Jewish cultural experiment. Only the narrator's recollection remains to mark the existence of a cultural compromise that Fascist racial laws and Nazi murder effaced. (ND)

Jakov Lind. *Soul of Wood*. Translated from the German by Ralph Manheim. New York: Grove, 1964. First published as *Ein Seele aus Holz*.

Soul of Wood is a collection of seven short stories, the longest of which is the title story. Some cultures turn wood into totem poles, centers of ritual, sources of spiritual power and cultural authority. In other cultures, to call someone *a shtik holts* is an expression of contempt: to be so bereft of intelligence, responsiveness, and wit that one is nothing more than a block of wood.

In Jakov Lind's story, parody and farce mingle in a world literally reduced to nothing. Expecting to be deported, the Jewish parents of a severely handicapped boy—who is completely paralyzed, cannot speak, and cannot respond except by blinking—pay an elderly working-class man named Wohlbrecht to hide the boy and take care of him. Diligent according to his lights, the caregiver carries the boy on his back up a mountain path to hide him in a hikers' cabin that will be vacant during the winter. Wohlbrecht ends up as an orderly in a psychiatric institution, where patients are euthanized. As the war draws to a close, it becomes clear that a single Jew, even a completely paralyzed Jew, has enormous value. No matter how many Jews one has killed, one saved Jew may well serve as a free pass for the implementers of the Final Solution. Wohlbrecht locates his soul in his own wooden leg. His co-conspirators rip off his wooden leg and shoot him, leaving the leg to stand sentry, while they make off with the trussed-up Jew, who meanwhile has been magnificently reconstituted and lives like a centaur among the deer.

In "The Judgment," two men—a father and a son, the latter convicted of murdering twelve women—are locked together in a cell. The government's justice will be imposed in two hours, the murderer sentenced to be hanged. But the murderer plans to murder his last victim, his father, from whom he has requested a final visit. The father, meanwhile, plans to strangle his own son, because the son belongs to him and not to the government. The old man's grip is stronger; the young man never gets his final victim.

In "The Window," Lind presents a dystopia governed by a Faustus who wears red striped pajamas over his suit and presents himself as redeemer to his anarchist followers. The symbolism is inverted, laughable, and parodic, yet haunting.

Lind's universe is allegorical in the sense that objects stand for elements of the human soul or . . . they don't, being simply solid objects endowed by the reader with a misleading depth that is the narrator's final joke on the reader. The discomfort induced by this serious farce is intentional, and parody at least avoids hypocrisy. That, in the post-Holocaust world, may be achievement enough. (ND)

[1963]

Yehuda Amichai. *Not of This Time, Not of This Place*. Abridged translation
   from the Hebrew by Shlomo Katz. New York: Harper and Row, 1968.
   First published as *Lo me'akhshav, velo mikan*.

The Hebrew poet Yehuda Amichai was the voice of modern Israel. His themes were war, peace, love, and the precariousness of life. But Amichai, born Ludwig Pfeuffer in Würzburg, was raised in a German-speaking home steeped in Jewish tradition. He fled Germany with his parents at the age of twelve and did not return to the city of his birth for nearly a quarter-century. The return of the banished son to the fictional town of Weinburg is the subject of this important and innovative novel.

West Germany in the early 1960s was both the easiest and most problematic of all European landscapes to which to return. Can one trust the people over thirty not to have blood on their hands? And why return at all? To settle old scores? To demand restitution? To commune with the dead? To start over and forget the past? Amichai's pilgrim is himself split, literally, in two. One half, named Joel, a successful archeologist estranged from his wife, Ruth, remains behind in Jerusalem to pursue a new love, while the other half, Joel's double, leaves for Weinburg to avenge the death of his first love, also named Ruth. From then on, Joel and his double are torn between two cities, two loves, two saintly figures from the past, two tattoos designed to cover the scars of war, and two identities. The secular, cosmopolitan identity of an adult Israeli squares off against the sacred, communal identity of a German Jewish child.

Joel's revenge fantasy quickly founders on the shoals of postwar fakery. Weinburg, rebuilt from the ruins, is an ersatz Teutonic city, with no vestige of its Jewish landmarks, while the Jews who have taken up residence there make up an ersatz dying community. Besides, Joel's real struggle is with himself, obsessed as he still is with Ruth's bicycle accident in the snow during the festival of Hanukkah, when she lost her leg. There is no way to reinhabit an amputated childhood.

Nor can there be time travel for a German Jew without reliving, at least vicariously, *Kristallnacht*. In Joel's religious imagination, the burning of the Weinburg synagogue on *Kristallnacht* is another *hurban*, a destruction of the Jerusalem Temple. In Joel's moral odyssey, taking responsibility for Ruth's accident means tracking her fate all the way to the crematorium.

Joel, the German Jewish man-child, is engaged in an act of *teshuvah*—penitent return or spiritual cleansing—as numerous allusions to the Neilah, or closing prayer on Yom Kippur, make clear. To remember is to forget. To return is to long for closure.

When his romantic fling comes to an end, however, his Jerusalem double embarks on an act of ascent. Joel joins an academic convoy to Jordanian-occupied Mount Scopus. There are still many ruins to sort through in a divided city, in our time, and in our place. (DGR)

Hannah Arendt. *Eichmann in Jerusalem: A Report on the Banality of Evil.* New York: Viking. 1963.

The phrase "the banality of evil" has entered the language as shorthand for the diminished standing of mass murderers and torturers once stripped of their political power. Saddam Hussein, Radovan Karadžić, the murderers of Rwanda—all seem negligible as individuals. The elderly concentration camp guards who are brought to justice even today, old men in their late eighties, are absurdly ordinary, limited, even dull. We want our killers to be endowed with the flamboyance of Mephistopheles and the insouciance of Don Giovanni, who shouts his defiance even as the shades pull him down into hell. Otherwise the trial and the punishment leave one with a sense of anticlimax. The crimes are disproportionate to the individual who has committed them. Yet when

Hannah Arendt first published *Eichmann in Jerusalem*, initially as a series of essays in the *New Yorker* and shortly thereafter as a book, a wave of outrage swept through both the Jewish and also the literary and cultural world. In this respect, at least, *Eichmann in Jerusalem* is an important book in the history of Holocaust literature.

Primo Levi has written of the relentless depersonalization of the camps and, in the case of Dr. Pannwitz, the chemist who administers his chemistry exam, the absolute severing of human and moral connections between people. The basic question that remains for today's reader is how to measure guilt and dole out accountability in the context of a bureaucracy of murder. How responsible is the upper-middle-level bureaucrat? Where does moral responsibility fall? Does a figure like Adolf Eichmann, without whose careful command of rolling stock and community lists the concentration camps might have stood empty, deserve a minute parsing of his level of responsibility?

In attempting to answer these questions, and with an exaggerated insistence of evenhandedness that was responsible, more than anything else, for the rage unleashed by the book, Arendt tried to reset the stage. And a stage, she insisted, it was. She accused Ben-Gurion of conducting a show trial (an especially inflammatory charge since, at that time, the Stalinist show trials of the 1930s and late 1940s were within popular memory). Her distaste for Gideon Hausner, the chief prosecutor, is unconcealed.

Arendt excoriated Jewish officials for trying to shield their communities from the truth about their ultimate fate, thereby becoming an integral element in the mechanisms of annihilation. She criticized the prosecutor for turning Eichmann into a mastermind of destruction, which she believed from the evidence to be an overstatement. (Eichmann, in her view, was a cog—an important one, but certainly not a planner in the destruction of the Jews.) She deplored what she viewed as the misappropriation of the Eichmann trial for use as a restatement of the millennia-long persecution of the Jews. She viewed Israel's claim to prosecute Eichmann as a wasted opportunity. The new state ought to have declined the claim to prosecution in favor of an international tribunal. Instead, by claiming Eichmann as the perpetrator of a specifically Jewish tragedy, the Jews had lost some kind of moral superiority. She pointed to the fact that defense witnesses could not be called to give testimony because, since they were all wanted war criminals in their own right, they would have been subject to immediate arrest. These were positions that were unpopular at the time and to this reader appear now as insensitive at best, and downright inflammatory at worst.

Rereading Arendt's book some fifty years after its publication, one is struck by how pedestrian much of it is and how some of its contentions seem just plain wrong, others obvious, and still others confirmed by subsequent catastrophes.

The Eichmann trial was a true landmark for many different reasons. It took place at a time when, for virtually the first time, Israel's Holocaust survivors were invited to recount their tragedies for the public. It brought a certain period of Holocaust memory to a close, on the one hand, and opened up an area of discourse, on the other. Important trials frequently offer signals that are read very differently in retrospect than they were at the time. They are set pieces from which cultural attitudes, shifts, and obscurantism frequently emerge. The Dred Scott trial, the Sacco and Vanzetti trial, and the Dreyfus trial are examples: they set public discourse on a particular path. What emerges from Arendt's reading of the Eichmann trial, despite a certain bombast, is how critical the act of recounting the past becomes to the construction of a public memory endorsed and expounded by the trial itself. (ND)

Ladislav Fuks. *Mr. Theodore Mundstock*. Translated from the Czech by
Iris Urwin. New York: Orion, 1968. Originally published as *Pan Theodor
Mundstock*.

An elderly man rushes home to check his mailbox but is so agitated that his shadow, Mon, beats him to it. He is waiting for a summons from the authorities that is sure to come: Will he be sent to Terezín (still in his native land) or all the way to Łódź? Because this story takes place in Prague, the reader is not surprised to learn that Mr. Theodore Mundstock has committed no crime, but—unlike *The Trial*, where Kafka went to great lengths to erase all ethnic markers and even had Josef K. end up in church—here the innocent man is identifiably Jewish. For one thing, he has a yellow star sewn to the front of his coat, which is even more conspicuous when he walks around town clutching a bag to his breast. For another, he is punctilious about observing the Jewish holidays and attends the synagogue with regularity. Prague is also a place where miracles can happen, especially to Jews, ever since Rabbi Judah Loew fashioned a golem back in the sixteenth century. So readers are more likely to suspend their disbelief when Mr. Mundstock discovers that he too may be endowed with the power to foresee—and forestall—the future. If a man's shadow can act independently of its master, then a thirty-year employee with the firm of Lowy and Rezmovitch, String and Rope, can be the new messiah.

This time, it is not a summons for deportation but rather an invitation to visit his old friends, the Sterns, who are in desperate need of solace. Through them—the grandmother who speaks in biblical cadences, the husband and wife who are at odds with one another, their jilted daughter and precocious son—Mr. Mundstock discovers his new calling. With consummate skill, Fuks creates a mock messiah who is both silly and sublime. Mundstock begins to believe in his own white lies (performing as a fortune teller whose cards are stacked in everyone's favor) and in the curative power of time, even as everyone he has ever courted or communed with is deported or commits suicide. Becoming proactive, Mr. Mundstock adopts a fantastic regimen of simulated tortures, from carrying a heavy valise, living on stale bread, and sleeping on a plank, to being beaten, gassed, and burned to death. Thinking he is prepared for all eventualities, he strides joyfully to the deportation point when the summons finally comes. What he did not plan for are the vagaries of chance. Killed by accident, he is mourned by his shadow and his chief disciple, the Stern boy.

Fuks, a non-Jew whose identification with the plight of the Jews began when he was still in high school, wrote this tribute to their memory. He reanimated the streets of Prague with Jews: a caring, law-abiding, God-serving, naïve, and impractical people whose choices in life were reduced one by one to none. (DGR)

Rolf Hochhuth. *The Deputy*. Preface by Albert Schweitzer. Translated from the German by Richard Winston and Clara Winston. 1st paperback ed. New York: Grove, 1964. First published as *Der Stellvertreter: Ein christliches Trauerspiel*. Movie version, *Amen*, directed by Costa-Gavras (Germany, Romania, France, 2002).

Every now and then a play is produced that sparks keen interest and controversy about the Holocaust. This happened in 1943, with Ben Hecht's protest pageant *We Will Never Die!*; in 1955, with the stage adaptation of *The Diary of Anne Frank*; in 1992, with Joshua Sobol's *Geto* (1992); and, most spectacularly, in 1963 with *The Deputy*. Hochhuth's play was banned in Rome, picketed in New York, and interrupted in Basle. There were riots when the play hit Paris. As late as 1988, during a state visit by Pope John Paul II, protesters disrupted a performance in Vienna (Whitfield 2010). In these plays, the Holocaust evil was either offstage or on. Hochhuth alone placed Eichmann and Dr. Mengele center stage, and in Act 5 brought all his main characters together in Auschwitz, complete with sound effects. Challenging Celan's "Todesfuge," the playwright refused to translate the gassing of Jews into metaphors, for "metaphors still screen the infernal cynicism of what really took place." Appearing for the first time on the same stage were the officers and foot soldiers of the Final Solution alongside the giants of German industry, cardinals, abbots, and Pope Pius XII.

The protestors and picketers were, of course, Roman Catholics, most scandalized by a play billed (in German) as "A Christian Tragedy." *The Deputy* is a modern morality play in which the world is split into cynics and saints. The saints are those prepared to die *in imitatio Dei* by performing the ultimate Christian act of vicarious sacrifice—or those, like the ss officer Kurt Gerstein,

who risk all by operating in disguise. Father Maximilian Kolbe, who was martyred at Auschwitz and to whom the play is dedicated, is represented on stage
by the young Father Riccardo Fontana S.J., the playwright's mouthpiece. Riccardo affixes a yellow star to his cassock and (implausibly) joins a transport of
Jews to Auschwitz in order to minister to the Christian converts. "A poor priest
. . . if need be," he explains his desperate plan, "can also represent the Pope—
there / Where the Pope ought to be standing today." In Auschwitz, Riccardo
comes face to face with the Doctor, the purest embodiment of "infernal cynicism." "I cremate life," the Doctor boasts, "I create life— / and always I create
suffering." Riccardo replies with equal conviction, "Since / the devil exists,
God also exists."

Hochhuth opened his Christian tragedy with an epigraph from Albert
Camus, the French existentialist, whom he credited as the first to blame Pope
Pius XII for his unaccountable silence. The crime of complicity and bad faith,
he learned from Camus, transcended differences of ethnicity, religion, class,
or gender. From the Holy See to the front office at Auschwitz, the evil of the
Holocaust defiled the entire world. (DGR)

Jorge Semprún. *The Long Voyage.* Translated from the French by Richard
    Seaver. New York: Grove, 1964. First published as *Le grand voyage,* 1963.

Eastern European Jewish survivors' accounts of the Holocaust fall into certain
distinct chapters: the move to the ghetto, the roundup, the arrival at the camp,
at the camp, Liberation, and after. The chapters change for the Jews of Western Europe, where the ghetto experience doesn't occur before deportation.
For political prisoners, the narrative begins with a sequence of resistance, betrayal, and capture before it merges with the rest of the account—at the camp,
Liberation, and after. But Jorge Semprún's two novels about his experiences
in the concentration camps are different. Both are heavily autobiographical
novels that explode the periodicity of survivor narrative.

The Long Voyage was Semprún's first novel, and a tour de force. It won both
the Prix Formentor and the Prix littéraire de la Résistance. The book takes
the classical Western motif of the journey and turns it into an unendingly
recursive moment. There is nothing to find; there is no end; the journey is
an experience of loss refracted through further disillusionment, losses, and
ungovernable memories. The journey is from life to death (the camp, since
it is an account of the excruciating multiday train ride from France to Buchenwald) and back to life because the protagonist, in recounting this journey,
keeps articulating the experience through thoughts, memories, and experiences that are at one and the same time real and imagined, successive in time,
and completely out of sequence.

As might be expected from a writer who was a strongly ideological Communist for much of his life, the book also explores how solidarity develops between two men manacled together in a cattle car that holds more than a hundred people. He and another Frenchman, whose name we never learn, share the journey, exchange thoughts, ideas, memories, and aspirations—and also a couple of plums that "le type de Saumur" has thought to bring with him. The narrator's companion dies as the train finally arrives at the camp.

Semprún's book insists that linearity cannot apply to the experience of the concentration camps, not only because the experiences themselves are so confusing and so outside accepted norms, but also because past atrocity does not remain in the past. It becomes a constant companion in shaping present experience. In this respect, departure and liberation are on the same plane, like some odd manifestation of string theory, folded in on themselves once, and again, and yet again, and the narrator has no choice but to continue using the tools of language, which are essentially linear in construction, to describe the involutions of time and memory.

For the narrator of *The Long Voyage*, the end of the book is both the entry into the camp and also the final loss of innocence. He now has as concrete experiences in his imagination what might formerly have been classified as unimaginable. All contained in memory, refracted, distorted, rearranged, and reassembled, but always in transit toward an arrival that is not a beginning but an infinitely repeated and tragic ending. (ND)

[1965]

Hanoch Bartov. *The Brigade*. Translated from the Hebrew by David S. Segal. New York: Holt, Rinehart and Winston, 1968. First published as *Pits'ei bagrut*.

A seventeen-year-old fakes his age in order to join the army. At nineteen, he has served two years; is half-man, half-boy; worries about the girl back home who hasn't been writing to him; doesn't fit in with his platoon mates; worries about sex and taking his GED; and feels guilty because his family wants him to come home now that the war is won. This is a coming-of-age story, one of thousands generated by every war, and the book's title reflects that focus: in Hebrew, it is a play on words that translates as "acne" but literally means "the wounds of maturity." In this instance, the decisive turns toward adulthood are taken by a young man in the Jewish Brigade, formed by the British from Jewish volunteers in Mandatory Palestine. The year is 1945. The brigade is moving into occupied territory. The soldiers are about to encounter the Germans and Austrians, the peoples who—actively or passively—enabled the annihilation of the Jews of Europe.

Hovering over the protagonist's adolescent angst are the larger questions that agitate the whole brigade: how to deal with the enemy as individual people, how to exorcise their hatred for the Nazis, their desire to be active participants in the war against the enemies of the Jewish people, and their need to avenge their families and the communities from which they came. The soldiers also have to come to terms with the survivors, their brethren, the ones they joined up to save. Initially the kids in the brigade are so eager to encounter survivors that they hitch rides on military transport to get to the closest DP camps. The survivors treat these Zionist boys with messianic fervor. But to the soldiers the survivors in the flesh are so broken, so strange looking, so disturbing that the solders find themselves disgusted and then shamed by that repulsion.

At the other end of the spectrum from the refugees are the local people, who believe, with some satisfaction, that the Jews as both individuals and a people have been wiped out. The young men of the brigade want to force an acknowledgement from these people that they exist, as both Jews and soldiers. But how can they break through the apparently impenetrable barrier of ignorance, prejudice, and hostility? Even acts of violence are insufficient. At one point, the protagonist intervenes and stops some of his platoon mates from raping German women. The rape is supposed to be an assertion of agency by the Jewish soldiers, but to the protagonist, it is morally intolerable. His act of principle only serves to alienate him further from his fellow soldiers.

Bartov's book captures with economy and a lack of sentimentality the otherness of the encounter between the Jews of Palestine and the survivors. What makes the book so powerful is his insistence on situating the Zionist Jews, the New Jews, between the persecutors and the victims, literally in the no man's land of the army camp, where the conventional pieties of pity on the one hand and desire for vengeance on the other seem unable to gain any traction on reality. (ND)

Charlotte Delbo. *Auschwitz and After*. Introduction by Lawrence L. Langer. Translated from the French by Rosette C. Lamont. New Haven: Yale University Press, 1995. First published as *Auschwitz et après*. First English edition of *None of Us Will Return* translated by John Githens, 1968.

Charlotte Delbo, a member of the French resistance, was captured by the Gestapo in 1942 and sent to Auschwitz in 1943. Altogether she spent twenty-seven months in Auschwitz and other concentration camps. She was liberated and taken to Sweden, from which she returned to France.

Auschwitz and After is a trilogy of three works, the first two written in 1946 and 1947, and the last toward the end of her life; *None of Us Will Return* is the first work. The form of the books moves from prose-poetry toward prose as the content shifts from an attempt to communicate the immediacy of her wartime experience toward a more reflective, discursive engagement with her past. All three of the books grapple with the need to find ways of getting outsiders, those who were not there, to understand the enormity of the experience. In ways that are reminiscent of Jean Améry and Levi, Delbo tries to make space within ordinary words for the extremity of the experience in Auschwitz. No one who has read her description of thirst, hunger, or cold can ever again use those words in the same way in the ordinary world.

Delbo's work also insists on the immediacy and continuation of the memory of atrocity into Liberation and beyond. In her pages, she and her fellow survivors are pale simulacra of free people. Their true selves are those past selves annealed by the concentration camp experience. This is the essence of the second volume, *Useless Knowledge*. There are critically important things to be learned from the survivors, but they do not have any use or value in a postwar world because there isn't a context in which they apply. Similarly, blood relationships implode. The women who survive together are true relatives, their time in the camp coming to supersede blood ties with those who were not there.

Less sustaining is the role of human culture. Like Primo Levi in the "Canto of Ulysses" section of *Survival in Auschwitz*, Delbo describes a performance of Molière's *Le Misanthrope* painstakingly reconstructed from memory as a moment of cultural and personal retrieval. Yet these moments are tenuous in the extreme. A festive Christmas meal is brought to a shattering end when Delbo and the reader realize that a teddy bear could have been retrieved by the prisoners only if it was brought into the camp by a Jewish child sent to the gas chamber.

Delbo's work is unsparing and hauntingly sad. The formal experiments— poems, fragments, narrations in the first and third persons, short stories—and the recursion—the narrator's going back over certain key events, trying to present them from a different angle—are part of her insistence that however impossible to share, the experience of Auschwitz, broken down into constituent fragments, can and must be communicated, that memory, even flawed memory, can and must be passed on. (ND)

Henryk Grynberg. *The Jewish War*. In *The Jewish War and The Victory*. With an author's note. Afterword by Richard Lourie. Translated from the Polish by Celina Wieniewska and Richard Lourie. Evanston, IL: Northwestern University Press, 2001. First published as *Żydowska wojna*. Inspiration for the documentary *Miejsce urodzenia* (Place of birth), directed by Paweł Łoziński (Poland, 1992).

For *The Jewish War*, his first full-length prose work, Henryk Grynberg was awarded the Tadeusz Borowski Prize for Young Writers. As a Polish novelist, he stood on the shoulders of giants, heir to the naturalist school of Holocaust writing established by Borowski and Nałkowska, with its minimalism, matter-of-fact style, gaps, and silences. As a Polish Jew, he stood on the shoulders of his Old World grandparents, his courageous parents, and a stepfather hardened by history, to all of whom he dedicated his work. In *The Jewish War* and its 1969 sequel, *The Victory*, Grynberg adopted the perspective of a child, one who did not look back and who learned the art of survival by rote and mimicry. Father taught him to trust no one and to always carry money. Hanka taught him to knock forcefully, not like a Jew. Mother taught him to walk upright and always look people straight in the eye. The Jewish war could be won only by those who successfully un-Jewed themselves.

This was a novel of the great outdoors. "For we were country folk," they assured themselves, "and we knew that, no matter what, one does not perish so quickly in the country as in a town." Always on the run, they had dozens of places to hide. "Men alone," the narrator learned, "they held out in the forest longer than anyone else." Yet by the time the family was liberated by the Red Army there were few survivors. The baby brother, given over to peasants, had perished. One set of grandparents had gone willingly to the trains. The forester made his living hunting Jews. And as for the peasants among whom they found shelter, the word "forest" was always associated with loot, stolen lumber, and hidden Jews: "In the forest people and animals look and act alike." When, despite his manifold survival skills, Father too fell prey to a Polish peasant somewhere in the forest, the mother and son sought refuge in cosmopolitan Warsaw, where the narrator learned to recite his Hail Marys and his mother dyed her hair red. They went on to the tiny and utterly impoverished village of Kończany, where neither of their hosts had a cottage or land of his own. The Germans burned it down before beating a hasty retreat.

The dark irony and narrator's deadpan style are informed by a different perspective from that of the child. It is the perspective of an adult who has learned to suspect people who "studied philosophy" and therefore could justify flushing Jews out of hiding as a way of shortening the pain of living. Even though Jewish life was cheap and, as a rule, the forest folk behaved like animals, some thought it a sin not to help. That is how two Jews out of countless others managed to "win" the war—simply by surviving it.

The Holocaust as recounted by a child is a twice-told tale, a kind of postmemory that becomes allowable in the chronology of Holocaust narrative, now that the basic story has been told. It is usually told in two voices: the naïve or no-nonsense voice of the child subtly informed by the consciousness of the adult. Because adults are children when it comes to "knowing" the Holocaust, the child can speak for all victims trapped in the hunt for Jews. There are still masterpieces of this genre yet to come. (DGR)

Jerzy Kosinski. *The Painted Bird*. Boston: Houghton Mifflin, 1965.

The Painted Bird is a novel whose protagonist, a small Jewish child, is left adrift, fleeing from village to forest, from one abuser to another, in an attempt to survive the war. The novel is written in the register of a grotesque Breughel woodcut. There are no grays here. The lines are harsh and undifferentiated, the paper deeply scarred by the embedding of the wood into the paper fiber. Here is casual violence, constant brutality, sexual exploitation, bestiality, and superstition that one associates with the Middle Ages.

Until the very end of the book, when the boy is liberated by the Red Army and taken into the care of two Russian soldiers, there are no normal relationships. Death, rape, torture, and violation are as casual and everyday as drawing water from a well or walking in the woods. The perpetrators, who attack the child as a gypsy, are ignorant peasants whose religion is a strange mixture of superstition, folklore, and aggression. In a world devoid of kindness, it is no surprise that the child turns into a mute, unable to speak or respond, a figure of suffering and surprisingly agile escape.

In a sense, the child has learned the lessons of his environment all too thoroughly. For him, casual massacre is a daily spectacle, the ordinariness of which is reinforced by postwar life in an orphanage until, at the end of the book, he is reunited with his parents and a younger adopted brother. The only way the child, now a young boy of eleven, can relate to anyone is through violence—at one point he breaks his brother's arm—about which his parents say nothing at all. They send him to live in the mountains with a ski instructor, where he recovers his health and also his desire and ability to speak.

When it was first published, the book was greeted as a masterpiece by reviewers, including Elie Wiesel. But although the gratuitous violence continues to shock and the sexual depravity repel, the book has not withstood the test of time. Read at a distance, it seems exploitative and overly simplistic. Later revelations also worked to undermine Kosinski's credibility as a survivor and the value of a book that had been read as at least semi-autobiographical. Instead, it turned out that Kosinski himself was able to hide with his parents during the war. He also claimed to have written the book in English. Later evidence revealed that he had written the novel in Polish and never acknowledged his translators. Although true to his particular vision of human nature, *The Painted Bird* was not drawn from lived memory as he insisted (even in the preface to the 1976 edition, in which he shifted the blame from himself to his critics).

The Painted Bird is an example of a Holocaust novel that was prominent at a particular period (one thinks, also, of the novels of Ka-Tzetnik, similar in their almost pornographic submersion in sexual violence). The books shocked readers, their graphic detail suggesting an immediacy that is no longer apparent. Koskinki's is a "then" book, a product of that late 1960s convulsion that forced the discourse of the Holocaust and Holocaust literature to the surface. (ND)

[1966]

Jean Améry. *At the Mind's Limits: Contemplations by a Survivor on Auschwitz and Its Realities.* With a preface to the 1966 and 1977 editions by the author. Foreword by Alexander Stille. Afterword by Sydney Rosenfeld. Translated from the German by Sidney Rosenfeld and Stella P. Rosenfeld. Bloomington: Indiana University Press, 1980. First published as *Jehnseits von Schuld und Suhne.*

Jean Améry was born Hans Mayer, an Austrian Jew from a family so assimilated that he was sent to Catholic schools. Mayer rearranged the letters of his German name to produce Améry. It is a fitting representation of the fragmentation and reassembly that he underwent as a young Austrian, identified as Jew, denationalized, and deported to Auschwitz as a Belgian resistant and Jew.

Améry's pitiless lucidity is an attack on the pieties that have come to underlie Holocaust survivor identity. There is no triumphalist narrative here because the Nazi destruction of the self destroys even the means of self-reconstitution. In five essays, Amery explores various aspects of identity: the value of the intellect, the individual reduced to a body, home and homelessness, passion and anger, and, finally, the nature of being a Jew, the condition that makes him a victim of the kind of knowledge that the Holocaust will force on him. The original German title (Beyond guilt and expiation) suggests the intellectual drive behind Améry's project. Both these responses operate within a moral framework with implications for the broader society. For Améry, the isolation of a mind and body that have seen their own division and collapse can never be breached. What holds the fragments together is an unyielding anger that turns into smoldering resentment as the immediate fires of rage are banked.

Like Levi, Améry sees that the intellectual impulse, the wish to understand and master the world through the exercise of reason, is worthless after the concentration camps. Worse, the intellect weakens the individual and makes him more vulnerable, for not only is he reduced to nothing, he sees and recognizes—and can never forget—himself in this abject state. A man stripped of nationality, home, and language recovers a sense of at-homeness in the world only as an experience of loss, even if, as Améry did, he is later able to recover citizenship in his country of origin.

Améry found both the German economic miracle and postwar pieties intolerable. The Cold War turned recent enemies into fast friends. Ideology offered no support—the new Left, with its fiercely anti-Zionist position, seemed to be repeating the antisemitism of just twenty years earlier, and the anti-intellectual violence of the 1968 student uprisings seemed to be leading straight toward anarchy.

In this context, Améry's writings on surviving Auschwitz show enormous courage. Even though he wrote movingly of the fragility and insubstantiality of the mind faced with atrocity, he was still engaged as a public intellectual, still wrote, argued, and insisted on the value of language as a means of forcing the self to engage with atrocity. (ND)

A. Anatoli [Anatolii Kuznetsov]. *Babi Yar: A Document in the Form of a Novel.* New, complete, uncensored version translated from the Russian by David Floyd. New York: Farrar, Straus and Giroux, 1970. First published as *Babii Yar: roman-dokument.* First English translation from the Russian by Jacob Guralsky, 1967.

Babi Yar is a palimpsest. It begins after the war with local children scavenging among the bones of the dead for remainders of melted gold. Absent any memorial or landmark to the 33,774 Jews whom the Germans massacred there during two days in September 1941, the young narrator backtracks to when it all began, to the Soviet retreat and the beginning of the German occupation, and then farther back to the great famine, Stalin's prelude to the Holocaust. *Babi Yar,* then, is a coming-of-age story, skillfully juxtaposed with family history, interviews, and contemporary documents. It presents a landscape of multiple atrocities and state-sponsored crimes, one laid across another.

Typographically, too, the "new, complete, uncensored version" is a palimpsest. What passed the Soviet censor when *Babi Yar* was published, first in a widely read journal called *Youth* and then, to great acclaim, in book form a year later, is printed in regular typeface. What the censor excised appears in boldface. What Kuznetsov added after defecting to the West appears in square brackets: metamemory layered on scandalous memory layered on state-authorized memory. Thus, expunged from the harrowing eyewitness account of Dina Pronicheva, one of a handful of survivors who escaped from the killing field, are most references to Ukrainian complicity and all references to sexual violence. This is immediately followed by "A Chapter of Reminiscences," almost entirely in boldface, which recounts how the narrator's father, a loyal Communist, unmasked acts of cannibalism during the great famine, and how Stalin's reign of terror affected the home and school life of an eight-year-old. The child experiences the burning of his favorite books as the second most awful happening after the cannibalism. At this point the adult narrator interrupts to ask "what people knew about what was going on in those days," and he concludes that everyone knew the truth about Stalinism but would later protest their ignorance. Loyal Communists denied their complicity exactly as loyal Nazis would.

Babi Yar honors the ancillary victims alongside the main victims of Hitler's war against the Jews. Defying Socialist realism, it dwells on Stalin's war against his own people. In keeping with a magazine dedicated to Soviet youth, it is narrated by a sensitive young man of conscience. Defying the ideals of pioneering youth, the young man remains deeply attached to his anti-Soviet, pious grandparents. Such screaming contradictions could not be reconciled while the Soviet Union continued to exist. (DGR)

Isaac Bashevis Singer. *Enemies: A Love Story*. Translated from the Yiddish by Aliza Shevrin and Elizabeth Shub. New York: Farrar, Straus and Giroux, 1972. Movie version directed by Paul Mazursky (United States, 1989). Originally published as *Sonim: di geshikhte fun a libe*.

All of Isaac Bashevis Singer's characters are haunted by the past, especially those who survived Hitler's Europe and Stalin's camps. In 1957, he concentrated them on the Upper West Side of Manhattan in *Shadows on the Hudson* (1998), a sprawling novel of ideas that he did not consider appropriate for translation. (It appeared posthumously, in 1998.) *Enemies: A Love Story* was also unusual for its time because, as Singer explained in the preface to the English translation, he was not a survivor himself; instead of adhering to the facts, he implied, he would follow his usual novelistic practice. True to form, *Enemies* was the story of a social misfit, a man simultaneously involved with three women. As much as the characters were traumatized by their historical experience, the preface went on to explain, they were also victims of their own nature. Herman Broder, in other words, was a species of the ugly survivor.

Singer's complicated plot enabled him to provide the American reader with a panorama of responses to historical catastrophe. The year is 1946, and the place is Coney Island, long past its prime. In the place where America once came to find welcome release from daily drudgery, Herman Broder has created an ersatz Jewish home with his Polish Christian wife, Jadwiga, who rescued him from death. She represents a future that is too good to be true. Living in a derelict house in the Bronx are the mercurial Masha, a burning cigarette in her mouth at all times, and her saintly mother, Shifra Puah, always dressed in black. Mother and daughter represent the demonic present. Then one day Herman discovers that his first wife, Tamara, presumably killed by the Nazis, has risen from the dead and has found her way to the Lower East Side, where the smells and rhythms are the same as they were in prewar Poland. Tamara preserves the memory of their two murdered children; the not-so-severed past. Cameo appearances by Masha's husband, Leon Tortschiner, who recalls the Holocaust as a wholly negative experience, and by the Yiddish comic, Yasha Kotik, who defied death through his laughter, round out the portrait gallery of Polish Jewish refugees.

It is Masha, in the end, who claims Herman for herself—his Angel of Death, his demon wife. As in the medieval tale of a man who married a demoness, their offspring cannot inhabit the world of the living, leaving Jadwiga and Tamara to raise the only offspring, a girl, also named Masha. America is Coney Island writ large, a place where everything is fake, none more so than Herman the ghost writer, who works for a fake rabbi peddling ideas he doesn't believe in. Most real are the demons that pursue the survivors day and night, without regard for calendars, and their antitheses, those few saintly individuals who remain loyal to the past.

Enemies can profitably be read as the fourth volume in Singer's Holocaust Library, beginning in 1950 with *The Family Moskat*, which ends with German bombs falling on Warsaw, and continuing with *Shadows on the Hudson* in 1957 and *The Slave* in 1960, a tale of catastrophe and captivity set in the seventeenth century, inserted as a prequel. (DGR)

Jean-François Steiner. *Treblinka: The Revolt of an Extermination Camp*. Preface by Simone de Beauvoir. Translated from the French by Helen Weaver. New York: Simon and Schuster, 1967. First published as *Treblinka: la révolte d'un camp d'extermination*, 1966.

Perhaps the most offensive of Hannah Arendt's comments about the death of European Jewry was the assertion that they had gone like sheep to the slaughter. The figure of the Jew as fighter was more palatable to postwar Jewish and Zionist culture. Thus in Israel, it was the few fighters of the Warsaw ghetto with whom the memorial culture connected. The millions of anonymous dead, the industrial dead—whose output was mounds of gold fillings, warehouses of hair, and mind-numbing piles of clothes—were much more problematic.

Steiner's book is an attempt to correct that view, to create an understanding of the process by which the Technicians, his term for the Nazis, dehumanized the Jews. Hope, that most corrosive of emotions, was kept alive both by the Nazis and the individual tenacity of the victims in sufficient quantities to postpone any realization by the victims of their ultimate, ineluctable fate. As for that fate, Steiner works up a heroic portrayal of the revolt at Treblinka, one of the few instances of an insurrection from within a concentration camp, the other being the uprising of the Sonderkommando at Auschwitz-Birkenau.

In pursuit of a documentary "feel," Steiner uses the techniques of the New Journalism: dramatizing reportage, manufacturing dialogue, adapting the techniques of fiction to shape character. At the time of its publication, some of those interviewed for the book strongly objected to the way that Steiner had portrayed them and criticized the fictionalizing techniques as unfaithful to the documentary evidence.

Read from a distance of fifty years, Steiner's book is something of a pot-boiler. Despite his best intentions, in valorizing the rebels, he reinforces the stereotype of the Jews as passive victims, since only very few had the ability and strength even to consider resistance. It is from among the privileged Jews in the concentration camps—the Kapos, the Hofjuden—that the notion of rebellion arises. (Virtually every survivor account establishes that the Kapos were reviled for their inhumanity and brutality. Many were murdered after the war by survivors who were settling past scores.)

What makes Steiner's book important is its place in the postwar French discourse surrounding the Jews and the war. In this respect it serves as a book-end to *The Last of the Just*, the furious controversy surrounding both books embedding the content into popular consciousness. From a distance of fifty years, when people complain of a sense of "Holocaust exhaustion," *Treblinka* is a salutary reminder of how much it took to force the Jewish experience of the Second World War into French cultural discourse. Steiner's book may seem dated now, but the impassioned and sometimes virulent responses that it produced set the terms for much of the writing to come. (ND)

[1967]

Romain Gary. *The Dance of Genghis Cohn*. Translated from the French by
    Romain Gary with the assistance of Camilla Sykes. New York: World,
    1968. First published as *La danse de Genghis Cohn*, 1967.

Hans Helmut Schatz, previously a Nazi storm trooper, and now police chief of a small town called Licht, is inhabited by a dybbuk, the spirit of one of his victims, named Genghis Cohn. Dybbuks, as we know from Yiddish literature, and particularly from S. Ansky's 1914 play, *Between Two Worlds, or The Dybbuk*, are dislocated spirits of the dead who take over the bodies of their hosts. In Gary's hands, the dybbuk becomes the source of a monstrous and monstrously funny comedy in which slapstick, savage parody, and mordant irony bite through the pieties of Holocaust remembrance to force the reader into an engagement with mass murder stripped of the comforts of cliché.

Genghis, formerly Moishe, is an old-time Yiddish comedian, the product, as he points out on the first page of the book, of the Yiddish burlesque theater. The former ss man, now a police chief, is dealing with a spate of murders. Genghis Cohn is free with advice and conversation, and in responding to this unseen interlocutor, Schatzie (meaning sweetie, Genghis's nickname for him) seems more and more unhinged to his subordinates.

What is a comedy of atrocity? Can those words even coexist? Gary's novel adopts what one might term "the insanity defense"; that is, in a world where the realities exceed the parameters of normality, only insanity—and its literary form, surrealist parody—has the capacity to engage effectively with the past.

It is intensely discomforting for the reader to find him- or herself laughing out loud ("Gott in Himmler," Schatz says) at the situations that Genghis provokes. Gary's book is neither trivial nor inappropriate, and mass executions are not typically the stuff of comedy.

The act of parody insists on bringing back the reader to the particularity of that moment, of a Jewish comedian mooning the ss man who is about to shoot him, for example. It also explodes the postwar German attempt to cover up the Second World War in a frenzied drive toward affluence. The late 1960s, when Gary's book was published, was also in Germany the period of the Baader-Meinhoff gang and of the rebellion of the postwar generation against the amnesia that their parents had insisted on as the foundation of the new German reality. And France had just survived the great shock of the 1968 student uprisings when the pieties of the fathers (in which every Frenchman, seemingly, was a resistance fighter, and the Vichy state had ostensibly come into being without any assistance from the French themselves) were shattered.

Gary himself was a creator of multiple identities. He was a Polish Jew who wrote as a Frenchman, and he won the Prix Goncourt, France's premier literary prize, twice, using two different names—the second revealed only in a posthumous publication. For Gary, Jewishness is a form of burlesque identity. It infuses, defuses, confuses, and refuses. It insists on a perspective that unsettles, and in so doing makes it impossible for the reader to settle for received wisdoms. (ND)

Anthony Hecht. *The Hard Hours: Poems.* New York: Atheneum, 1967.

Born of German Jewish parents who had already immigrated to the United States, the American poet Anthony Hecht returned to his European roots while serving with the 97th infantry division. On April 23, 1945, he helped liberate Flossenbürg concentration camp. Then began the hardest hours, of confronting and readmitting the full meaning of the annihilation; hours which grew to be decades before he was able to bear witness. This Pulitzer Prize–winning book established Hecht as a major poetic voice.

The book's title derives from the poem "More light! More light!"—a quotation of Goethe's putative last words, and a deathbed legacy that captured the essence of his enlightened faith. For Hecht, the reach of the Holocaust is transhistorical, not political. Casting his net back to the sixteenth century, Hecht opens with the dying words of another crusader for truth, executed for heresy in the Tower of London. Another execution, of a Christian Pole by a "German Lüger," closes the historical arc. Before being shot, the Pole is forced to bury two Jews alive. This execution and sadistic shuffling of victims and perpetrators take place in a "German wood" adjacent to Goethe's Weimar, the unnamed wood of Buchenwald, which admits "No light, no light in the blue Polish eye."

No prayers or incense rose up in those hours
Which grew to be years, and every day came mute
Ghosts from the ovens, sifting through crisp air,
And settled upon his eyes in a black soot.

Not only does the victim's corpse miraculously resist decomposition in this, the poem's final stanza, but the black soot from the crematoria continues to sift through the crisp air long after the ovens stopped being stoked with Jewish bodies.

The Holocaust, then, is the ultimate challenge to any faith in enlightenment—perhaps, even, the culminating act of the Enlightenment in the heart of Christian Europe. Just as Hecht's vision is panhistorical, embracing many centuries, so his formal virtuosity embraces many genres. "More light! More light!" is written in ballad form, to mimic and parody the German master himself, while "Rites and Ceremonies," the central chapter on the theme of the Holocaust, is overtly liturgical, mixing Jewish and Christian symbolism and language. After twenty years of silence, the witness is now ready to confess and profess before "Father, adonoi, author of all things."

"The contemplation of horror is not edifying," he states in classical register, "Neither does it strengthen the soul," whether you are just a curious bystander during the dark Middle Ages or a sensitive and sorrowful French poet. Casting his net forward, Hecht locates the matrix of memory, mystery, and awe in "The Room," the inner sanctum, containing roomfuls of hair, shoes, and valises.

From Weimar to Buchenwald, from the room of horrors to the children's room, from formal to light verse—the dark hours embrace them all in their deathly embrace. (DGR)

Yoram Kaniuk. *Adam Resurrected*. Translated from the Hebrew by Seymour
Simckes. New York: Atheneum, 1971. First published as *Adam ben kelev*.
Movie version directed by Paul Schrader (Israel, Germany, and the United
States, 2008).

Twenty-five years after the end of the Second World War, one of the most lav-
ishly endowed and comfortable, if eccentric, mental hospitals in Israel houses
a group of elderly inmates, all but two of whom have blue numbers tattooed
on their arms. They are survivors. In a country that is home to the largest
number of Holocaust survivors, many suffering from war-related illnesses,
nightmares, and ongoing trauma, these inmates are the worst stricken. They
cannot function in the outside world. The asylum, their home and prison,
turns into the mise-en-scène for their lives, replaying dramas of the past,
which the characters process or do not process through their own distorted
personae. None more so than the dramaturge in chief, Adam Stein, once a
world-famous clown and the owner of a circus for whose loss he was reim-
bursed half a million US dollars, a colossal fortune in Berlin right after the war.

In an exchange of roles reminiscent of *The Dance of Genghis Cohn*, Adam
Stein, who has been forced to play the human-as-dog to Commandant Klein's
killer dog, Rex, (hence the Hebrew title, Adam, son of dog), also becomes
Klein's master and keeper after the war. He is an inspired mountebank whose
brilliance and effortless creativity literally captivates everyone around him,
from his fellow inmates to his nurse, Jenny; the psychiatrist; the chef; and
everyone else he meets, including a boy who behaves like a dog and a landlady
who is his mistress (both before and after he tries to strangle her).

By the book's end, Adam Stein has led his fellow inmates on a march into
the desert to seek divine revelation; he has domesticated the dog-child into a
human boy; and he has dismissed his various alter egos. And he has become
sane: diminished, ordinary, satisfied, and completely devoid of distinction.

Stein's is a world of amorality resting on the atrocities of his past, a past
that in the present offers him the excuse to avoid being a mensch. He has
the choice between sanity and madness. He chooses madness for as long as
it suits him, adopting it as a disguise that renders him powerful. Drawn increasingly into Adam Stein's alternative worlds, the reader cannot help but
be disappointed by the supposedly happy ending. At the same time, the "insanity gambit" that is Adam's claim to grandeur is deeply suspect. After all,
Stein the circus master is the same man who turns every place into a stage
and every aspect of human intercourse into a theatrical script that he himself
controls, dispensing moments of sanity only at those extreme points when his
performance becomes untenable. In this framework, the Holocaust survivor

as madman is a pointed morality symbol. Kaniuk's Stein prefigures the mountebank of Binjamin Wilkomirski's *Fragments*, who—taking the gambit into real life—turned himself into a prize-winning and entirely false survivor. (ND)

Patrick Modiano. *La Place de l'Etoile*. Paris: Gallimard, 1968. Never translated.

La Place de l'Etoile is a Paris landmark like Piccadilly Circus in London or Times Square in New York. A joke that made the rounds during the Occupation has a Gestapo officer approaching a Parisian. "Pardon me, sir," the officer asks. "Where can I find La Place de l'Etoile?" The man silently taps his chest, where Jews are required to affix the yellow star.

The joke encapsulates Modiano's undertaking. *La Place de l'Etoile* is his first novel and the first of a trilogy of novels that take the Nazi Occupation as their theme and starting point. *La Place de l'Etoile* both articulates and prefigures many of the themes that will come to dominate the ethos of 1968, characterized by student and union upheavals across Europe, antiwar protests in the United States, and the temporary flowering of the countercultural movement.

In Europe, the events of 1968 represented the revolt of the postwar generation against the crimes of their parents and the repression of any genuine political and moral discussion about the Second World War. This is a seminal period in the postwar culture wars. The year saw the emergence of the New Left, the efflorescence of what would turn into deconstruction in the realm of literary theory, and also the rise of the *nouveaux philosophes* like Bernard-Henri Lévy, who would challenge the hegemony of the Left in French politics.

Into this combustible atmosphere, *La Place de l'Etoile* detonates like a depth charge under the political posturing and animosity surrounding issues of collaboration, Frenchness, and, inevitably, antisemitism. (It is worth noting that before the political awakening of the Beurs—French citizens of Arab descent—it was Jews who occupied the position of official Other.)

Modiano adopts all the antisemitic language and stereotypes long embedded in French culture and brought to their peak during the years of Vichy. (Perhaps not surprisingly, English-language publishers have steered away from this work. It is the only volume of his Occupation trilogy to remain untranslated.) He creates a phantasmagoric figure, Raphael Schlemielovitch, who inhabits, subverts, and seduces every aspect of the true France and the true French. Like Woody Allen's Zelig, Schlemielovitch associates with the great figures of French politics and culture, sometimes extravagantly philosemitic, at other times, antisemitic to an extreme degree.

The protagonist is a white slaver, miscegenist, thief, fraud, cheat, usurer, and murderer—all roles that fulfill the expectations and, indeed, the needs of those prototypical antisemites, Abetz, the head of the ss in Paris; Drieu La

Rochelle; Robert Brasillach; and Bardamu. The novel moves back in time to the Dreyfus trial and forward to the existence of the State of Israel.

Modiano creates a vertiginous experience of language as itself collaborator, copyist, fraud, inventor, and exorcist. The high culture of France becomes a comic pawn in the hands of a villain so extreme in his villainy that the reader is shocked, discomforted, and also seduced. It's hard not to laugh, and harder not to find one's laughter distasteful. This is taking the creation of the false self to such an extreme that no identity retains particular value.

It's worth thinking about *La Place de l'Etoile* in relation to Irène Némirovsky's *Suite Française*. The latter, writing in the midst of the developing catastrophe, creates a sense of a France that continues in its round of petty grievances, betrayals, and practices as it has for centuries. For Modiano, a generation later, reverence is immediately subverted by pastiche. Not even the impulse to political engagement can avoid immediate translation into self-parody.

For the reader of *La Place de l'Etoile*, if there is a point of stability at all, it is the time frame of the German occupation and the cultural location of French high culture. From there, the novel works its way both backward and forward into the very warp and weft of Frenchness. Identity based on such uncertain ground obviously cannot be orchestrated into anything other than parody because there is not even a provisionally stable point of beginning. All that is left is a series of unwindings, bizarre and pointless excursions, hallucinatory fantasies of murder and betrayal, and the act of parody itself, constantly pointing to its own instabilities. (ND)

[1969]

Jurek Becker. *Jacob the Liar*. Translated by Leila Vennewitz. New York: Plume, 1997. First English edition translated from the German by Melvin Kornfeld, 1975. Second revised edition translated from the German by Leila Vennewitz, 1990. First published as *Jakob der Lügner*. Movie version of original screenplay directed by Frank Beyer (East Germany, 1974); remade and directed by Peter Kassovitz (United States, 1999).

Much of the literature that emerged from the Holocaust is focused on communicating some essential truth, trying to get to the root of an experience that defies all the norms of received culture and morality. Jurek Becker's *Jacob the Liar* takes this impetus a step further by using untruth as a key element in the day-to-day existence of people in a small ghetto in the weeks before its final liquidation. Levi's initial descent into the world of Auschwitz is contained in the phrase *"Hier ist kein warum"* ("There is no why here"). Becker's ghetto is instead a world whose motto should be "There is no hope here." Indeed, hope is like Iago, both close friend and treacherous betrayer.

Jacob Heym overhears a snippet of news at the Gestapo headquarters indicating that the Russian front has advanced to a mere 250 kilometers from the ghetto. From this snippet he creates a world of fable in which, as narrator, he spins tales in order to keep the ghetto inhabitants hopeful and positive. Of course, his motives are more complicated. Jacob reaps celebrity (although it soon becomes an oppressive burden). He becomes an important person in the community. He sees himself as a savior of sorts: because his stories give people hope, the number of suicides drops sharply.

Are they better off for the illusion? That question leads to another equally profound question: what is the value of prophetic knowledge in a condition of imminent catastrophe?

Mischa, a ghetto inhabitant with whom Jacob works in the ghetto factory, is the first recipient of Jacob's news. He promises to keep Jacob's secret, only to spill it out as a form of self-validation in meeting with the Frankfurters, the parents of his girlfriend (later his fiancée). The ghetto lives on gossip and is starved for news. Inevitably, word spreads, and Jacob's fictitious radio provokes widespread debate. Is he being irresponsible, since radios are forbidden by the Nazis and the discovery of his will bring savage reprisals down on the whole ghetto? Or is he refusing to submit to irrational regulation, knowing that even complete obedience will not propitiate the murderers? As it happens, Frankfurter actually owns a radio. On hearing the rumors based on Jacob's fabrications, he goes down to the cellar and methodically destroys the radio so that any blame will not fall on him. The ghetto's appetite for hope feeds on itself, and Jacob is under constant pressure to share news from the radio. The lies—ludicrous as they are, because Jacob's powers of invention are severely tested in the absence of new information—have value, at least in maintaining the illusion that information is available and hope still exists.

Hope is a fairy tale, the tale that Jacob spins for the orphan girl, Lina, whom he looks after. When Jacob, finally unable to sustain the deception, confesses his inventions to Kowalski, his close friend and enemy, an avowed skeptic, the latter hangs himself. The removal of illusion is too much to bear.

The book is told in the first person by a narrator who assures us of his credentials. He was there. He heard certain things. What he hasn't seen himself, he has on good authority. He seeks verification of the reputed suicide of the eminent Jewish physician who is taken out of the ghetto to treat the local Gestapo chief for heart disease by consulting the doctor's Gestapo guard. At the end, he offers the reader the possibility of further hope: two alternate endings to the novel. Jacob Heym dies in both versions: in the first, as a hero (shot before the Russians liberate the ghetto); in the second, deported with the rest of the ghetto to certain death. The choice is the reader's.

The Nazis refined choiceless choice as a form of psychological torture.

Victims were made to choose between two intolerable options, one of which might offer temporary survival. Becker catches the reader in a similar bind. We want to choose the hopeful ending because it is the temptation of hope that we, like the ghetto inhabitants, cannot refuse. But the real ending is there, forcing us to confront our own desire for illusion over fact. (ND)

Saul Bellow. *Mr. Sammler's Planet*. New York: Viking, 1970.

Mr. Sammler is a half-blind visionary in a dystopian world. Brought up as the sheltered child of a classic Central European bourgeois family, he spends many years in London with his wife and daughter, becoming an acquaintance of H. G. Wells, then at the height of his fame, and supporting himself as a respected journalist for the Polish press. From this high point, Sammler's life unravels. Caught by the outbreak of war in Poland, he and his wife are machine-gunned by the Nazis. Sammler escapes the mass grave, taking shelter in a tomb from which he emerges blind in one eye (a blow from a rifle butt), his humanist ideals shattered by the experience of the war. In fact, he embodies the proverb "in the land of the blind, the one-eyed man is king."

Now, in the 1960s, Sammler lives in New York City, a city in decline, characterized by irrationality and crime, supported by Elya Gruner, a well-to-do distant relative who found and brought Sammler and his daughter, Shula, to America after the war. Elya is dying. He and his children each want something different from Sammler before Elya dies—hidden money, absolution, an acknowledgement of value—none of which Sammler feels qualified to give, nor does he wish to do so. Meanwhile, Shula, eccentric, irrational, and childlike, steals the only existing manuscript of a study by an Indian scientist, Govinda Lal, about how human beings might exist on the moon. Shula is convinced that her father is writing a great work about H. G. Wells and requires the manuscript for his study. The theft brings Sammler and Lal together for a long conversation about the value of existence, a conversation that one might well believe articulates the author's own views.

Sammler is a reluctant prophet, honest enough to understand that his random survival should not and does not bestow any privileged knowledge on him. But to his relatives he is, despite himself, a moral arbiter, whose approval they seek while at the same time resenting the detachment that allows him to judge them.

Such detachment is costly. Sammler understands that he was overtaken by history, but at the same time, he views his prewar self dispassionately as self-centered and cold. In this context the demands of the outside world, including the requirement that he connect with people despite their foibles and weaknesses, turn Sammler from a bleak prophetic figure into a human being with his own weaknesses, desires, griefs, and impulses of generosity.

Bellow's is an apocalyptic vision of decadence and decline. New York City in the heat of the summer is a city full of garbage, violence, self-indulgence, and irrationality propelled by a postwar generation that, long shielded from true disaster, chooses to flirt with it in the present.

Almost twenty-five years after the end of the Second World War, Sammler is the Holocaust survivor writ large, a figure whom society needs to see as privy to a hidden, almost sacerdotal, knowledge about individuals, human nature, and life itself. But Bellow also understands how the morally superior survivor figure is merely the repository for needs and responsibilities that ordinary people living in ordinary times ought properly to take on themselves. As is often the case with his work, Bellow is ahead of the cultural curve, delineating the creation of the survivor as moral arbiter that will only become more marked with the passing of the survivor generations. (ND)

[1970]

Dan Pagis. *Metamorphosis*. Selections in *Points of Departure*. Introduction by
 Robert Alter. Translated from the Hebrew by Stephen Mitchell. Bilingual
 ed. Philadelphia: Jewish Publication Society of America, 1981. First
 published as *Gilgul*.

In 1970 the classical scholar and Israeli poet Dan Pagis broke his silence about the Second World War. Like his compatriot Aharon Appelfeld, who turned to writing fantastical tales about a Jew-centered world without Jews, and like his fellow poet Yehuda Amichai, who split his identity in two, Pagis took the memory work of the Holocaust onto a new plane. Eight poems that appeared in *Gilgul* were Pagis's first attempt to revisit the subject of the Holocaust. They depend on the reader's knowledge of what smoke, smokestacks, boots, yellow stars, bills sewn into the soles of shoes, sealed railway cars, roll call, and reparations signify in the context of twentieth-century Europe. Just as the Romanian-born Pagis had mastered biblical, medieval, and modern Hebrew from scratch, so his reader is expected to parse sentences, dissociate words from their colloquial context, and keep one ear open to classical echoes.

Seven short poems in *Gilgul* (six of which appear in *Points of Departure*) follow a loose narrative line. They begin with the complacency of the victims-to-be who do not realize that they are living on the brink of catastrophe ("Europe, Late"), move on to the catastrophe itself and its witnesses, and end with a debate on reparations (Yacobi 2005, 223). "Footprints," the longest poem and the first written, is pseudo-autobiographical. It takes the survivor ("It's true,

I was a mistake, I was forgotten, / in the sealed car, my body tied up / in the sack of life") on a parallel journey through the clouds and smoke above and the cattle cars below until the memory cloud descends over his ancestral home, "this ball of the earth, / scarred, covered with footprints."

Among the various devices that Pagis uses to scramble the universe and displace space into time is the Jewish art of countercommentary. As memory is fraught and fractured in these remarkably condensed and layered poems, so too are the sacred texts. "Draft of a Reparations Agreement" presents a fantastic proposal to reverse the movement of time and history so that the victims will still be living before the annihilation. But when the exasperated speaker of the poem promises the dead that "Nothing is too late," that their bones "will be covered with skin and sinews," he arrives at no more than a ferocious parody of Ezekiel's vision of the dry bones. So too the survivor's tortured voyage in "Footprints," accompanied by the exalted words of the liturgical poet Yannai in praise of God's dominion over the heavenly spheres—including the night, including the smoke. And the body left behind in the sealed railway car "tied up / in the sack of life" is of course the same "sack of life" that appears in the fervent *yizkor* (memorial) prayer. The memory traces of the Holocaust take up all of sacerdotal space even while all of time is recalibrated according to the years of the Holocaust. (DGR)

Michel Tournier. *The Ogre*. Translated from the French by Barbara Bray. New York: Doubleday, 1972. First published as *Le Roi des Aulnes*. Movie version *Der Unhold* (The ogre), directed by Volker Schlöndorff (Germany, 1996).

Abel Tiffauges, the ogre of Michel Tournier's novel, is a reclusive garage mechanic who is accused of raping a girl. The declaration of war in 1939 saves him from what appears to be certain conviction. He joins the French army, is taken prisoner by the Germans in 1940, and is transported to the East as a POW and forced laborer. As the novel progresses, he becomes a trusted ally of the Nazis, works for Himmler's chief forester, and eventually becomes a driver, factotum, and recruiter at a Nazi *napola* (Hitlerjugend training facility). A few days before the Russians reach Kaltenborn Castle, Tiffauges comes across a Jewish child survivor of the concentration camps and, carrying the child on his shoulder while escaping from the Russians, drowns in the marshes of East Prussia.

This bald summary of the book's plot bears almost no relation to its preoccupations, and herein lies the novel's power. In order to understand the novel, the reader has to enter into Tiffauges's obscure but internally coherent universe of symbolism writ large on human history and destiny.

Tiffauges knows with absolute conviction that he is the sole scribe of a world structured around inversion. Defeat is victory. Excrement is the script of destiny. Apotheosis is drowning.

The moral uncertainties of the book—Is Tiffauges a pedophile or a man locked into his child self, a hateful collaborator or woeful innocent?—are matched by the unsettlingly long account of the Second World War itself. This is a book about the war that doesn't have any battles and barely any refugees, and that is filled rather with exaltation than terror. Yet, caught in Tiffauges's universe, the reader somehow understands something truly profound about the Nazi universe: that their ideology was based on a deep inversion of social values, where death is valued over life and metaphor (the Jews as vermin) becomes real (exterminate them).

Tournier's account of the war undermines any triumphalist recovery. Tiffauges drowns in the marshes near Kaltenborn. The ogre who has seen his destiny as the gentle porter of destiny is overwhelmed by the feather-light weight of the starving Jewish child. Will he become yet another of the bodies lying intact in the acidic waters of the marshes, only to be revealed by some accident of time and exposure to the incredulous eyes of people hundreds of years hence?

Tournier's is one of several books discussed here that was awarded the Prix Goncourt, France's highest literary award. They are all fine novels, but what they have in common is an attempt to find a symbolic structure to contain the moral uncertainties and discomfortures of the French experience in the Second World War. The ogre is a nightmare figure made real. We sympathize with him on some level, revile him on others. But we cannot walk away from him, because Tournier's sense of the universe enters into our own world of personal myth. It insists that we keep trying to find a means of understanding the series of actions that add up to atrocity; that we struggle to identify the multiple individual concessions that add up eventually to genocide. (ND)

[1971]

Bogdan Wojdowski. *Bread for the Departed*. Foreword by Henryk Grynberg.
  Translated from the Polish by Madeline C. Levine. Evanston, IL:
  Northwestern University Press, 1997. First published as *Chleb rzucony
  umarłym*, 1971.

Bogdan Wojdowski placed maximal demands on himself as a writer because in a very real sense he was the last Jew who would bear witness. As a child survivor of the Warsaw ghetto, the last who could still remember the sights and especially the sounds of the largest city of Jews in Europe; and as one of the few Jews who was not forcibly expelled from Poland in 1968, in a state-sponsored campaign against the "Zionist" Fifth Column, he was among the last who could remind his fellow Poles of the civilization that had been destroyed before their very eyes. Thousands of homes throughout Poland still had indentations in their doorposts for a scroll of parchment called a mezuzah. In *Bread for the Departed*, these mezuzahs are the talismans that failed.

Within the confines of one courtyard in the Small Ghetto of Warsaw the young protagonist, David Fremde (the surname means stranger or foreigner), comes of age. "You could discern people's disdain for the authorities or their fear and docility," he notes, "by the way they wore their armbands." "It turned out," he says at the end, summarizing two and a half years of slow dying, "that bravery is the same as the desire for life." Yet no two deaths are alike. Overwhelmed with grief at the death of his daughter, the janitor hacks to pieces one of the last horses still left in the ghetto—and its carcass is devoured by the people in the yard. On that day also died the horse's owner, Mordechai the coachman, for when the police vans invaded Krochmalna Street in that "famous July of nineteen hundred forty-two," he put himself first in line to go to Umschlagplatz.

Bread for the Departed represents the Holocaust as a two-stage progression from concentration to annihilation. So when the great deportation begins, the street gangs of which David was a part march to their death in a boisterous procession. Rojzele and Haskiel Ajzen get all dressed up for the journey. The debauched Count Grandi joins the Jewish police and aids in the roundup, but when ordered to execute his father, he refuses and is shot. The most resilient are the rats, "because no one has yet proclaimed *Rattenrein*." Amid the orchestration of voices, we also hear Sturmbannführer Hölfe deliver a victory speech on the joys of a *Judenrein* world. Perhaps it was hearing the same rhetoric in 1968 that impelled the grownup "David" to restore all the lost voices in this polyphonic novel.

Bread for the Departed is a patriarchal narrative. With no gods for David to worship, he is left to reassemble the pieces of a shattered covenant—from Genesis to Job and Jonah—and to observe for the last time in the ghetto the full cycle of Jewish festivals, from Purim to the Feast of Tabernacles. As a child turned breadwinner in the grotesque, rat-infested reality of the ghetto, and with his father's disappearance during the great deportation, David inherits his grandfather's prophetic mantle. Patriarchy is both a blessing and a curse. (DGR)

[1972]

Danilo Kiš. *Hourglass*. Translated from the Serbo-Croatian by Ralph Manheim. Evanston, IL: Northwestern University Press, 1997. First published as *Peščanik*.

After extensive interrogation and cross-examination, a retired railway official named Eduard Sam, but identified only as E.S., is about to be sentenced and punished for the capital crime of being born a Jew. The absurdity and hilarity of his crime become apparent to the reader, who is privy in exhaustive detail and in a virtuoso display of narrative styles to his every deed and misdeed over the course of a lifetime. Descriptive "Travel Scenes" alternate with idiosyncratic "Notes of a Madman"; dry and accurate notes from his "Criminal Investigation" with evidence elicited against him from "A Witness Interrogated." E.S. is the same unstable father who has appeared and disappeared throughout Kiš's Family Cycle, of which *Hourglass* is the third and last installment; here alone he is presented in a near-infinity of interior time, relived on the night before his deportation to Auschwitz. If this sounds vaguely familiar, it is because this novel by the Serbo-Croatian Danilo Kiš hearkens back to Borges's 1943 "An Everyday Miracle" and can be read as a tribute to its author, Kiš's favorite (Stavans 2001, 75–82). As in Borges's story, in Kiš's novel a tangential, off-center participant in the large events of history wrestles with those events as they are filtered through a single consciousness. The faceless interrogators are as implacable and imperious as the Nazis of Borges's imagination. But E.S., unlike Jaromír Hladík, is no playwright. The most he can manage is an unsent letter to his sister, Olga, complaining bitterly about his niece and nephew. He does keep a diary, however, much like Gogol's *Diary of a Madman*—so in a way, Kiš returns Borges to the scene of the crime: to the Slavic outback, home of the hapless, petty, and grotesquely funny little man.

Hourglass can also be read as the author's loving portrait of his Jewish father, also named Eduard and also a retired railway official. But E.S. the madman actively discourages such a reading. Only philistines read "for cheap adventure stories." The "new reader" will agree that "so-called plot is not the soul and essence of a literary work" and will appreciate that the protagonist's "war with the world is in reality a war with death, whose approach he senses"—and a war with words, as well. Averting a comical near-death experience, when beams and tiles would have crashed down on his head (like the ice pick that less accidentally was thrust through the skull of another Jew, named Lev Trotsky, just a year earlier), E.S. sees things both inside and out. Given a choice between these two faces of reality, he greatly prefers to lose himself in dreams and drunkenness. In his rescue fantasy, he roams the map, from Switzerland to the Gulf of Kotor, from the burning bush to (his favorite image of) Noah's ark. For the hourglass is merely "an empty space, negative, hence an illusion," in which the only positive "is the two profiles turned toward each other, face to face as in a mirror." E.S. is never more lucid than when he is mad. (This most famous of psychological optical illusions, known as Rubin's Vase, is reproduced in the novel.)

Hourglass ends with Eduard's last, unsent letter, a cantankerous, spectacularly ordinary and apparently authentic missive. It is a fitting conclusion to a darkly comic novel that celebrates "the egoism of life." Reunited therein are the few people and the bits of love that made up his life, a distillation of grit at the bottom of the hourglass that stubbornly resists the outrage of death.

With Rawicz, Modiani, and Wojdowski, Kiš marks the experimental, postmodern turn in Holocaust fiction. Still addressed to a communal audience and thoroughly situated within a national landscape, these writers adopt a wildly eclectic and cosmopolitan style. (DGR)

[1975]

Aharon Appelfeld. *Badenheim 1939*. Translated from the Hebrew by Dalya
  Bilu. Boston: Godine, 1980. First published as *Badenheim 'ir nofesh*, 1979.

The height of the prewar Central European summer experience was the holiday trip to one of the great spa resorts of the region. For those of modest means, there were boarding houses. For the affluent, there were lavish hotels. A stroll around Carlsbad, called Karlovy Vary in Czech, still hints at its splendid past. Here, business and marriage alliances were secured, social networks expanded (within the limits of the acceptable), and the pursuit of the secular god of health was undertaken through daily modest bathing, huge breakfasts, brisk massages, enormous lunches, afternoon naps, and unending dinners.

The English title of the book, *Badenheim 1939*, situates the novel in history. But even without that indicator, the book captures the overripeness of a spa community preparing for high season. Then, as the book proceeds, the Department of Sanitation begins asking questions and making lists, while the spa's inhabitants revel in the beauty and amplitude of the town. Each of them plays their expected role—Pappenheim the impresario, the lazy musicians, the pastry chef, the head waiter. Each of them stands for a type: the traveling salesman, the tortured artist, the playboy, the withdrawn academic. The sick are there, too. All of them feel an almost mystical pull back to Eastern Europe, even if they have lived in Austria for generations. They become Jews because the Department of Sanitation requires it. As death approaches for everyone in Badenheim, only one holidaymaker—Trude, the pharmacist's wife—becomes more peaceful, for her constant fear of dying is about to be confirmed.

Like D. M. Thomas's alpine hotel guests, Badenheim's Jews do not and cannot know the end that awaits them. They are all drifting toward imminent disaster. In Appelfeld's hands, the balance between allegory and reality is minutely calibrated. One can smell the richness of the strawberry tarts and the heady ripeness of the roses. One appreciates these as metaphors for a community in full flower, and for the richness and fullness of individual experience in the instant before collective disaster.

There are harbingers—the hotel owner introduces a beautiful breed of fish into his fish tank. For a day or two the new and old fish coexist. Then the blue fish kill all the green fish. But the humans do not draw any conclusions. Even as conditions worsen, the spa's inhabitants are still trying to convince themselves that what is coming will be an improvement over what they are currently experiencing. If the train cars are filthy, then the distance to be covered must be short. In Warsaw, the level of discourse will be higher because the academics there will have connections to the great universities of Berlin or Vienna. There will be cigarettes, chocolate, toy trains. The Polish audience will be more musical, more discerning, than Austrian audiences.

Certainly, there are points of contention. Peter, the pastry chef, blames all the troubles on the impresario, a Jew from the East (that is, not a proper bourgeois). But the rest embrace the move East. They view the Department of Sanitation's sweep as a new beginning. This is the pathos of the book, especially read against the historical background that every reader brings to it. Are the characters truly ignorant, or are they entering willfully into a state of suspended disbelief? Is foreknowledge better than blindness? The same end awaits the anxious and the phlegmatic, the intuitive and the impassive. (ND)

Imre Kertész. *Fatelessness*. Translated from the Hungarian by Tim Wilkinson. New York: Vintage International, 2004. First published as *Sorstalanság*. First English translation from the Hungarian by Christopher C. Wilson and Katharina M. Wilson, 1992. Movie version, for which Kertész wrote the screenplay, directed by Lajos Koltai (Hungary, 2005).

Imre Kertész received the 2002 Nobel Prize for Literature "for writing that upholds the fragile experience of the individual against the barbaric arbitrariness of history." Yet for the reader of *Fatelessness*, his first book, what dominates is not the individual as actor but rather the strangely detached and personless voice of the narrator. Any writing about historical disaster—except for a diary (and sometimes even then)—is caught up in what we know to be the ending: the writer lives or dies, the town is destroyed, the books are burned, there is no one left and no place to which to return. Our knowledge of the end inevitably shapes our reading.

Kertész postpones this inevitability by creating a narrative strategy that engages only with what is known moment by moment. Each datum of information or experience is assessed in a curiously detached fashion, so that the logic of the concentration camp slowly emerges from successive pages in all its sadistic and hallucinatory reality.

This is hardly the technique of Levi, who sets out the categories of experience that make up the social laboratory; neither is it the empathetic technique of Delbo, who explores the individual at an almost cellular level. Here the key is the neuron, the way that each firing of a nerve transmits information about work, hunger, or pain. Everything arises at the same level of excitation, even good fortune. People give the narrator food: he eats it. They take away his contacts and his additional food: he accepts the deprivation as a given.

Throughout, Kertész articulates the depletion of human agency experienced by concentration camp prisoners. When the narrator returns to Budapest, one of his interlocutors is angered by the way that the boy, still only sixteen years old, responds to questions about his ill treatment. "Naturally," the boy says. "Naturally." To the questioner, there was never anything natural about Auschwitz. To the survivor, the deprivation and abnegation of experience was only natural. What follows, followed. How could it not?

Yes, the boy survives, but we have no sense of what he survives as, what kind of person he can be in the aftermath of such fateful fatelessness. To know, in Kertész's world, does not bring power, nor does it automatically bring the possibility of action. It simply marks the coming and going of a time made endless and endlessly painful by its passing. This is a true condition of death in life, like Coleridge's Ancient Mariner as most memorably referenced in Levi's *The Drowned and the Saved*. (ND)

Primo Levi. *The Periodic Table*. Translated from the Italian by Raymond Rosenthal. New York: Schocken, 1984. First published as *Il sistema periodico*.

The Periodic Table is built around an extended metaphor, the idea that the fragments of a life can cohere into the building blocks of existence because each of them is irreducible, a basic element. Taken together, they may constitute the narrative of a life. In Levi's case, the metaphor is even more powerful because the stories that make up *The Periodic Table* circle around but only briefly touch on the concentration camp experience that is at the heart of his own life story.

The book consists of twenty-one stories. The first, "Argon," is a witty and affectionate introduction to the Levi family. It sets up expectations: despite the odd, allusive title, this is to be an autobiography, starting, as is conventional, with the author's family background. But those expectations are quickly undone.

The Periodic Table indeed challenges the reader's expectations about what properly constitutes a work of Holocaust literature. What should he or she make of bagatelles like "Mercury," a fantasy, written in the third person? Or "Lead," another imaginative exercise that takes off from traditional quest narratives? Why are these stories significant enough to be collected together with "Gold," the story that introduces Sandro, Levi's school friend, rock-climbing mentor, and brave partisan?

The wartime experience resurfaces in "Vanadium," the story most clearly rooted in Levi's concentration camp experience. It concerns an unconsummated postwar meeting between Levi and a German chemist who worked in the same laboratory where Levi, a concentration camp prisoner, worked during the last year of the war. The encounter had begun with an exchange of professional correspondence about a defective varnish. A spelling error leads Levi to ask if the chemist is the same individual he recalls from Auschwitz Monowitz. The correspondence continues until Müller writes to set up a meeting in Italy, but he dies a few days before the two men are due to meet. We are left wondering whether Müller died of natural causes, suicide, or even murder.

The Periodic Table draws its narrative energy from the tension between continuity and discontinuity. The reader—and sometimes the writer—reaches for an overarching narrative of existence, something that will mend the fundamental disjunction of a life marked by the concentration camp experience. But the continuity is itself a fiction, just as the periodic table as a chemical taxonomy of existence can never be complete. At any point, a scientific breakthrough might reveal a new element, one whose existence has been unknown to science, and whose surfacing forces a reconsideration of the various internal connections that the previous versions of the periodic table have established. Similarly, for the concentration camp survivor, fragments of the past, resurfacing, can divide previously constructed narratives back into their constituent parts.

At the end, the reader has to ask about the value of continuity and, indeed, of autobiography as a form. Is autobiography the mode in which a fragmented existence can be narrated, or is the creation of continuity itself the greatest and most seductive fiction of all? (ND)

[1979]

Leslie Epstein. *King of the Jews*. New York: Coward, McCann and Geoghehan, 1979.

Chaim Rumkowski made himself the king of the Łódź ghetto, printed money with his likeness on it, gave up countless Jews to the Nazis, and rode to Auschwitz in a private rail car. Adam Czerniakow, the head of the Warsaw Ghetto Jewish Council, committed suicide rather than preside over the destruction of his community. Between these two extremes lay an infinite range of human behavior in which people tried to save themselves, their families, and sometimes their communities. Of course, the situation was rigged. Everyone was going to die. That was the Nazi plan. Yet the gradualist strategy was enough to foster hope, that most treacherous of emotions, for with hope came a devil's brew of compromises, choices, and moral destruction. This is the terrain that Epstein chooses for his novel.

It is fair to say that the great novel on the subject of the Judenrat and collaboration has yet to be written. Epstein's attempt is written in the register of burlesque, an approach used by other writers in this Guide (Romain Gary, Patrick Modiano). In Epstein's hands, however, the central character, I. C. Trumpelman, becomes a paper cutout, mountebank, con man, self-proclaimed healer, fabulist, and egomaniac. Surrounding him are a set of equally two-dimensional figures: the scheming and ambitious members of the Jewish Council; the Stalinist resistance; the Volksdeutch who is a "friend" to Trumpelman; the former kept woman, now queen of the ghetto; the orphans whom Trumpelman protects in his magical safe haven, known as the Summer Palace (after the tsars' retreat).

Trumpelman is a quasimagical figure. He heals, survives, betrays, creates myths of his own origins, and turns himself into the parody of an absolute monarch. His people, seeking hope wherever they can find it, bow before him and his white stallion. So absorbed is he in his role as absolute monarch that he engineers the defeat of both the revolutionary underground fighters and his opponents on the Jewish Council—ignoring the fact that the common enemy is the Germans. In the end, of course, as we have come to expect, the ghetto is liquidated, but a question remains as to whether Trumpelman miraculously survives.

Epstein's novel tackles with limited success the enormous difficulties of engaging with the facts of communal survival and betrayal. Although burlesque is certainly a traditional tool of the powerless, in this instance, it is an insufficient vehicle to delineate and understand the choices made by the Judenrat. What this novel lacks is something about the complexities of hope and its constant disappointment. The novel misses an important opportunity to address the choices made by people who cannot know that choice is the one action that is denied them. (ND)

Philip Roth. *The Ghost Writer*. New York: Farrar, Straus and Giroux, 1979.

Beginning with *Portnoy's Complaint* and *Goodbye, Columbus*, and moving through the Zuckerman series and novels like *Operation Shylock*, Philip Roth has spent his career as a mordant chronicler of the American Jewish sensibility. In *The Ghost Writer*, Roth introduces his alter ego, Nathan Zuckerman, an aspiring writer whose first published short story has garnered an invitation from the reclusive and much admired writer, E. I. Lonoff.

In the book's first paragraph, the narrator describes himself as a bildungs-roman hero in the making, self-conscious enough about his process of grow-ing into selfhood to understand that everything—all thoughts, encounters, hesitations, and betrayals—will be grist to the bildungsroman mill. Nathan hopes that Lonoff will offer him some important and secret knowledge about writing that will be the making of him as a writer. But he finds that Lonoff is a self-enclosed, uncommunicative man, as bewildered by his own gift as by his inability to experience true human connection.

Also staying at the Lonoff house is a young woman, Lonoff's mistress and one of his former students. In Nathan's imagination, she becomes Anne Frank, not the sweet young girl of popular imagination, but a strong, vibrant, and even vengeful figure. This Anne Frank adopts a new identity to escape her diarist self. Not having revealed herself as a survivor, she is now a victim of the very myth that has made her an iconic figure. For Nathan, "Anne" is the ultimate trophy bride, the innocent, virginal face of the Holocaust victim. In winning her affections, Nathan will be forever inoculated against accusations of betrayal—of family (a sore point, since his recently published story draws attention to his grandfather's stint in jail), his origins (the Jewish kid from Newark who thinks he can be a writer in the modernist mode), and the Jew-ish people (themselves forever above satire because of the tragedy that has befallen their brethren in Europe).

This early work in the Roth canon identifies with the unsettling precision what will characterize the rest of his work: the heart of postwar American Jewish anxiety. The United States sent large numbers of troops to fight in Eu-rope, but for the most part, American Jews were fortunate enough to have been shielded from the depredations and depravities of the Nazi regime. With that survival comes a certain uncertainty—a lack of self-confidence, for lack of a better word.

This is the source of Roth's characterization of Judge Leopold Wapter, a distant family connection of Nathan's who is an important person (a judge, no less). When Nathan wants to publish a short story that may bring some tempo-rary embarrassment to the family, Judge Wapter puts together a questionnaire that turns Nathan's fictional impulse into an act of communal betrayal, whose cost is nothing less than the moral—and, indeed, physical—survival of the Jewish people. For the reader, the excess is both comical and discomforting.

Just as Nathan Zuckerman advances his fantasy bride, Anne Frank, as his shield, protector, and justification, so American Jews find themselves locked into an identity based on survival of a catastrophe that, for the most part, they experienced only at second hand, a disaster that is still, and perhaps always will be, at the center of American Jewish identity. (ND)

William Styron. *Sophie's Choice*. New York: Random House, 1979. Movie
version directed by Alan Jay Pakula (United States, 1982).

Set in 1947, *Sophie's Choice* is narrated by Stingo, a twenty-two-year-old Southerner who has moved to New York City and embarked on the life of a novelist.
It is a traditional coming-of-age story that also describes the relationship between Stingo's two friends, Sophie Zawitowski, a Polish Catholic, and Nathan
Landau, a Brooklyn Jew. Sophie has recently arrived in the United States from
a Swedish DP camp. She bears a tattoo on her arm, indicating that she survived
Auschwitz. Nathan—her lover, savior, and tormentor—is brilliant, charming,
and generous as well as brutal, sadistic, and consumed with jealousy.

The novel recounts Stingo's infatuation with both characters. Polish survivor and Brooklyn Jew are equally foreign to him. Nathan, it turns out, is a
fabulist, having created a megalomaniac image of himself as a research chemist perennially on the brink of a major medical discovery. But he is a drug
addict, and his mental illness is intensified by amphetamines and cocaine into
a suicidal brew.

Sophie, too, is a fabulist. She has created a series of fantasies about her
life and family, each of which Styron gradually peels back to reveal the bitter
truths around her proto-Nazi and viciously antisemitic father and husband,
her moral cowardice, and the devastating facts underlying her survival. Ultimately Sophie's choice concerns not only the "choiceless choice" inflicted
on her by the Nazi doctor, who forced her to decide which of her children to
send to the gas chamber, but the other choices that she made and continues to
make in her life, including whether to live or to die.

Styron's book was very well received (it won the 1980 National Book Award
for Fiction) but also created a backlash. In a discourse shaped by claims of
unspeakability, the mere fact that Styron, a non-Jew, had written a novel about
the Holocaust with a non-Jewish survivor as its heroine was taken by some to
indicate a lack of respect for the specifically Jewish nature of the catastrophe.
Political correctness was moving toward an assertion that the Holocaust was
off-limits to those who had not experienced it directly or through religious
affiliation. Yet Styron was making no claims or appropriations. He and this
novel's protagonists, each in his or her own way, were clearly outsiders.

In this respect, *Sophie's Choice* continues to be a lightning rod for the iden-
tity politics of victimhood. As Styron's novel demonstrates, the sacralizing of
Holocaust memory should not stand in the way of the literary imagination.
No one owns the literary rights to history. (ND)

D. M. Thomas. *The White Hotel*. New York: Viking, 1981.

Is there a way to think about the experience of twentieth-century Europe without the decisive rupture of the Holocaust? D. M. Thomas's novel uses the formal tools of psychoanalysis (the case study, the psychoanalytic session, the notion of transference) to create a world in which the tools exist to understand atrocity before, during, and after its occurrence. The novel is a complex inter-weaving of narrative voices. Long before we meet the protagonist Lisa Erd-man (or Anna G., in Freud's casebook) in person, we encounter her through her imagination, which is vivid, pornographic, and infused with catastrophic experiences recounted in a disturbingly dream-like register in which death, sex, and the aesthetic are melded together.

The classic psychoanalytic encounter may begin its narrative at any point in a patient's life because the unconscious does not operate within linear time. *The White Hotel* eschews a direct chronological account of events in favor of a set of layered narratives that make sense only in retrospect. Even the later por-tions of the novel, where the protagonist comments on Freud's case study, are compromised by self-censorship, partial truths, and oblique references. For the reader, the dates and locations situate the fantasies of the patient in a context that can function only proleptically. The fantasies foreshadow future events. As a result, one reads about the fires, the destruction, the railways, even the hotel itself as both metaphors and facts of what will happen during the Ho-locaust. The protagonist, too, believes that her premonitions will be true, and Freud comes to agree with her.

As the book moves into a traditional third-person narrative for the case study, some of the reader's questions are answered. Lisa Erdman becomes less of an abstraction ("the patient") and more of a person. Yet her premonitions, combined with what the reader knows about the Holocaust, create a tension based on convergences between imagination and history. All events conspire to ensure that Lisa will die in the great killing grounds of Babi Yar. After the killing, the pickers and gleaners are sent in to harvest anything of value from the bodies. Here one expects the book to end.

But it doesn't. The corpses have an afterlife in this novel, and not just in the case of the single woman who escapes from the mass grave to be a witness to this history (the testimony of Dina Pronicheva from Kuznetsov's *Babi Yar*, discussed above). A further ending, cast in a mythic mode, brings us full circle, back to the psychoanalytic material that begins the book. In this last chapter, the narration gently and tenderly resolves the protagonist's conflicts and fears. As time slows in the grip of psychoanalysis, myth settles flashback and fore-shadowing within a bearable present. (ND)

Cynthia Ozick. *The Shawl*. New York: Vintage, 1983.

When is the Holocaust over? Was it when the Allied troops liberated the camps? When the surviving remnant was brought up to normal weight and took up the routines of daily life? Is there a time frame for decent closure? Ten years? Twenty? Fifty?

In the first of the two short stories that make up *The Shawl*, Rosa, a teenager, and her niece, Stella, are in a concentration camp. Rosa has a baby, Magda, whom she tries to keep alive by hiding her under a shawl. But Stella takes the shawl to cover herself. The infant child wanders out of the barracks, and an ss man throws her onto the electrified fence. The second story, "Rosa," takes us to the United States. Now middle-aged, Stella lives in Queens and supports her aunt, who has moved to Florida after an episode in which she smashed up her own store in New York City.

Rosa runs against the type that is already well established at this point in the literature. She refuses to concede anything to anyone, including herself. On the one hand, the war is never over. On the other, she claims the right to construct a present that addresses her own needs rather than adapting to the realities around her. An invitation to a date with Persky, a persistent and flirtatious retiree, causes her to reaffirm the immediacy of the past: she won't go out with him because of what happened to her during the Holocaust. She also insists that her infant daughter, murdered in the camp, actually survived and is now a professor of Greek at Columbia University.

Ozick refuses the platitudes that by the early 1980s are already coalescing around the survivor figure. Rosa is no moral visionary, no exemplar, no incarnation of the triumph of the self over adversity. Instead, she is held together by an implacable anger, no matter how uncomfortable or even arid this makes her own life and those of others around her. She avoids human contact, living in a dirty rooming house. Her life is sordid and distasteful. The only transforming element in her life is the shawl—the shawl that protected her baby, whose theft was the trigger for her daughter's death and the marker of her niece's betrayal. By the time Stella sends it to Rosa, it has faded to blankness, a palimpsest of grief and loss.

Ozick's writing is perhaps strongest when informed by indignation. Rosa's intransigence forces one to draw uncomfortable conclusions about one's own need for a set of comfortable metaphorical and social conventions with which to circumscribe the literature of atrocity. The survivor, writ large, is one such convention. But Rosa is no such character, and in her obduracy is a life force at once admirable and unnerving. (ND)

Ida Fink. *A Scrap of Time and Other Stories*. Translated from the Polish by
Madeline Levine and Francine Prose. New York: Pantheon, 1987. First
published as *Skrawek czasu*.

Ida Fink was born in Poland in 1921 and survived the war in the ghetto and
in hiding. The twenty-two stories that make up this collection are like photographs taken with a microscope. They magnify aspects of the narrator's
wartime experience until they fill a whole frame, drawing the reader's attention to tiny details that come to contain within themselves a universe of loss
and grief.

Fink's is an unsparing voice. The title story, "A Scrap of Time," addresses
the language of destruction: what does an "Action" mean? (*Aktion* was the
Nazi term for roundup and massacre). There is a world of experience in that
first *Aktion*. There is the birth of a native caution that leads the narrator to hide
from the roundup. There is the psychology behind Cousin David's insistence
on joining the group. He is, the narrator says, from the race of "impatient
ones," a figure whom we will recognize from Lustig's Tausig—those who
need to be part of the group and therefore eschew escape in favor of death.
And then, in the bitterest fragment of all, Cousin David embraces a tree at his
death, driven to hold a living thing in the moment of dying.

In Fink's hands, compassion cuts like acid on the skin. The story "Jean
Christophe" is about a group of ghetto workers, one of whom is reading Romain Rolland's great *roman-fleuve* about a genius who takes refuge in Switzerland from his life in Germany. The overseer assures the girl that she will
have time to finish the book—time, that is, before her inevitable death as a
prisoner. In "The Shelter," a Jewish couple is sheltered in a one-room hut by
an older Polish couple in exchange for a promise that after the war, the Jews
will give them enough money to build a proper house. Visiting them for the
first time after the war, the couple finds that the Poles have built themselves a
nice house, and in an act of generosity, they have made provision for "their"
Jews, a nicely furnished bunker in which they will be able to pass their future
imprisonment in greater comfort.

The act of recounting is sharp as cut crystal. There is no sentimentality
in the account of the survivor describing the footsteps in the snow, the only
remains of a group of children hidden in the Judenrat building. Words, fragile
and insufficient as they may be, are the scraps of time that the memory retains.

Fink's stories together assemble an account of the war and postwar survival
that is acutely painful in its lack of self-indulgence. There are no heroes. There
are no victors. There is just time, grasped in fragments that, like the footsteps
in the snow, have long since melted. (ND)

Authorized Memory: 1985–Present

[1985]

Claude Lanzmann. *Shoah: An Oral History of the Holocaust; The Complete Text of the Film.* Preface by Simone de Beauvoir. New York: Pantheon, 1985.

Shoah is the complete text of the nine-and-a-half-hour documentary that took Lanzmann eleven years to create. In this respect it is unique in this Guide. A number of books here, as we have seen, were later made into films, such as *The Garden of the Finzi Continis, Sophie's Choice, Enemies: A Love Story, Fatelessness,* and *Adam Resurrected.* In contrast, this is a film rendered into written words. Much has been written about Lanzmann's film, perhaps the greatest documentary ever created. Yet the text of the film is no mere transcript. It is, on its own terms, a tragic masterpiece. Indeed, if the film had never existed, this book would still stand as one of the great works of Holocaust literature. In it, Lanzmann creates a complex counterpoint of fact, self-incrimination, self-exculpation, loss, unbearable memory recovered, willed ignorance, and unyielding bigotry. He shows the intimate details of destruction, from the bureaucratic memos that established the necessary machinery of destruction to the words of the few survivors—Simon Srebnik, Rudolf Vrba, Abraham Bomba, Filip Muller, Jan Karski, Antek Zuckerman, and others. And there is the work of Raul Hilberg, not himself a survivor, but the author of the keystone work that first outlined, in precise details drawn from the Nazi archives, what went into the destruction of the Jews.

The film moves through multiple languages, and Lanzmann as the interviewer sometimes works through translators. Nonetheless, ever alert to narrative interference, he is quick to insist on returning to the words spoken by his interviewees. Whatever the language, the subject resists and the questioner is insistent, refusing evasions. It is the small and intimate details that survive emotion. And it is those details that are needed to create the armature for both viewers' experience and survivors' memory.

In their own words, even as they try to excuse themselves, the perpetrators lay bare what one can only call wickedness, a depth of inhumanity that makes real the evil at the heart of the Nazi system. Here is the answer to Arendt's assertion of the banality of evil. What she terms banality is, in Lanzmann's absolute insistence on specificity, the bureaucracy of death. It is the cumulative detail, not the emotion, that overwhelms the viewer's defenses. Here are no heaps of bodies, piles of human hair, lampshades made of human skin. Rather, here are the plans of Treblinka, the technical details of killing ten thousand Jews in three hours, the lies needed to keep the machinery of death moving smoothly. Equally telling and unbearable are Lanzmann's interviews with

Franz Suchomel, a functionary at Treblinka; and Abraham Bomba, a Jewish survivor and a barber who cut women's hair on the way to the gas chamber, because the details—the fact that women lost control of their bowels while waiting for death at Treblinka, but men didn't; Bomba's cutting the hair of his loved ones—allow no escape. Here is no flight into the generic or symbolic. Without exception, the perpetrators and bystanders claim not to remember the details, while the survivors have forgotten nothing. "If you could lick my heart," Zuckerman tells Lanzmann, "it would poison you."

Even as the survivors talk about the disbelief with which they faced their own experience—Muller, for example, tells of his work in the Sonderkommando, clearing out the gas chambers and burning the dead in crematoria— they remember everything and in great detail, and the narrator is there to prompt them. The work of memory rests not only on what is said, but on how it is said, its precise words. The pace of the conversation emerges from the text without any of the normal screenplay edits or stage directions.

This book is one of the greatest masterpieces of postwar Holocaust literature for two reasons. First, it insists on the past as past—it includes no recreations of place, only the maps of the time and the pacing out of spaces in their contemporary shapes: here where these trees are, this was where the gas chambers were. And second, it reminds us how truly miraculous is the ability of memory to recover even tragic time. (ND)

[1986]

David Grossman. *See Under: Love*. Translated from the Hebrew by Betsy Rosenberg. New York: Washington Square, 1989. First published as *'Ayyen 'erekh: 'ahava,'* 1986.

The impetus to write *See Under: Love*, David Grossman told an American interviewer, was to redeem the "needless, brutal death" of the Polish Jewish fiction writer Bruno Schulz (D. Grossman 2010). To that end, Grossman created a believable fantasy about a man who joins a shoal of salmon while he searches underwater for Schulz's lost masterpiece, which in turn, inspired other rescue fantasies that comprise this spectacularly innovative four-part novel. *See Under: Love* marked the breakthrough of Hebrew fiction into magic realism, the marriage of magic realism with the hallowed subject of the Holocaust, and the coming of age of the second generation (*dor sheni lasho'ah*). Thanks to Grossman, the second generation signified the experience of growing up in Israel, in the shadow of the Shoah, which transfused the fear and collective neurosis into one's system (Milner 2003).

For the Israeli reader, however, it was the first, entirely realistic section of the novel that conveyed the existential burden of the Shoah, and the character of nine-year-old Shlomo (Momik) Neuman (the "new man") whom the reader anxiously followed into adulthood. In the "Momik" section, since republished as a separate book, Grossman created a symbolic space that was local, not foreign: the cellar of Momik's apartment building in a new immigrant quarter of Jerusalem. Here Momik staged his feverish imaginings and deepest fears, uniquely his own, learned not in school or a youth movement but within a home obsessed with banishing the Nazi beast, once master "Over There."

As an improved version of Sholem Aleichem's devil-may-care orphan, Motl the cantor's son, Momik begins to teach himself the rudiments of the language of Over There. Grossman then casts his net backward in time to resuscitate the pastiche of nineteenth-century literary Hebrew and the ironic register of Jewspeak through Momik's grandfather, Anshel Wasserman—a broken, babbling survivor who turns out to be none other than Scheherazade, the legendary author of action adventure stories about the Children of the Heart, so popular in their day that even the commandant at Auschwitz remembers them fondly. Writing fantasy, for children of all ages, becomes the ultimate death-defying activity.

In 1986, two young authors, David Grossman and Art Spiegelman, both practiced in fantastical genres and writing from the perspective of only children of survivors, turned the Holocaust into the crucible of their usable pasts. (DGR)

Art Spiegelman. *Maus: A Survivor's Tale. I: My Father Bleeds History*. New York: Pantheon, 1986.

Maus is a graphic novel that operates on three different levels. The first is a father's account of what happened to him and his family in Poland from 1935 to his arrival in Auschwitz. The second describes the son's difficult relationship with his father, his mother's death by suicide, and the impact of the parents' experience on their son, the book's author. The third is the father's postwar existence, how he justifies his way of life, explains his own actions to himself, and complains about his difficult relationship with his second wife, Mala, who knew both of the son's parents in Poland.

All of this would be somewhat conventional except for the medium—the comic strip, an unusual choice, rendered even more striking by a critical artistic choice. In this book, Jews are drawn as mice, Poles as pigs, and Germans as cats, each in a coherent and self-contained reality. On the one hand, the animal figures defamiliarize the characters, creating a disconcerting alternate universe through which to engage with a set of circumstances wholly beyond lived norms. On the other, *Maus* is startlingly hyperreal, taking Nazi metaphors at face value. If Jews are vermin, then they have to be trapped, caught, and killed.

Spiegelman's book brings the question of medium to the forefront. What is an appropriate form for engaging with atrocity? Spiegelman's family history recalls the political graphic novel, a form that was particularly popular during the 1920s and 1930s, and cross-fertilizes it with the tradition of American comic books. At the height of the American comic book, artists like Frans Masereel and Lyndon Ward, for example, were engaged in creating graphic novels using woodcuts (a favorite medium of German expressionism) to create extended politically engaged narratives. Just as the family story of survival and its aftermath links the European past with the American present, so, too, the choice of medium connects the act of American comic-book storytelling to genres and forms of storytelling that are embedded in the European political tradition. Alternatively, Spiegelman's hybrid will be a harbinger of further experimentation and engender its own tradition. (ND)

Andrzej Szczypiorski. *The Beautiful Mrs. Seidenman*. Translated from the Polish by Klara Glowczewska. New York: Vintage International, 1989. First published as *Początek*.

An adolescent male, his hormones raging, is fatally attracted to an older woman. More than age and gender divide them. He stands on one side of the abyss called the Holocaust, and she stands on the other. Artificial though this bed's-eye view of the Holocaust may be, it has proved to be indispensable for fiction and film. In the French film by Louis Malle, the young man goes by the name of *Lacombe, Lucien* (1974), in America he is played by a young Southerner named Stingo (Styron 1979), and in Germany he first appears as fifteen-year-old Michael Berg (Schlink 1997). Pawel Kryński, their Polish counterpart, is about to turn nineteen in 1943, and this work is very much a coming-of-age story; the original title (*Początek*) means "the beginning." First love is last love when the object of desire is the beautiful Mrs. Seidenman.

This plot always serves an ecumenical purpose: to cast the moral net as wide as possible. As much as the war divided people by race, nationality, political allegiance, and sexual orientation, the alchemy of love and desire makes all things seem possible. Pawel is only one of many characters in this novel—noble and venal; old and young; intellectuals and salt of the earth; Christian, Jewish, and German—who take sides over whether Irma Seidenman will live or die. "All Jews are prewar," says the railwayman, yet he will put his life on the line to try and save her. Bronek Blutman lives by the credo "I can betray everyone, because I was betrayed myself," yet when it comes to betraying Mrs. Seidenman to the Gestapo, he will be forced to admit defeat. And even though her eventual rescue is the result of the "fears and efforts of many people," she will ultimately be robbed of something more than her life. As the novel mixes prewar, wartime, and postwar perspectives, the Polish Communist regime that will expel the last 60,000 Jews from Poland in 1968 stands accused of robbing Irma of "her right to be herself, the right to self-determination." Szczypiorski has cast his net very wide indeed. The moral upheavals wrought by the war continue after the war, as one totalitarian regime is replaced by another.

Because Irma survives, thanks in some measure to Pawel, and because his love is revealed thirty years later to be nothing more than an adolescent crush, Pawel's real coming of age is not about her. Rather, it is about Henryk Fichtelbaum, his one true friend, the Jewish classmate who, after a delicious initiation into sex at the deft hands of a kindly whore, decides to return to the ghetto to die among his own people. Their final farewell signals for Pawel the loss of hope in a future built together by Christians and Jews. So what starts out as a flimsy plot device ends up delivering love, sex, and heroism where one least expects to find them. As this Holocaust love story is left open-ended, so too is Poland's love-hate relationship with the Jews. (DGR)

[1988]

Jarosław Marek Rymkiewicz. *The Final Station: Umschlagplatz.* Translated from the Polish by Nina Taylor. New York: Farrar, Straus and Giroux, 1994. First published as *Umschlagplatz.*

Rymkiewicz is the latest in a series of poets who turned to prose in order to do the memory work that the Holocaust required. Like Sutzkever and Amichai before him, he mixed and matched—in this case, combining journalism and personal confession, biography and fiction, the dead and the living. As someone "limited to a spiritual rather than a practical experience of Polish-Jewish life," the neoclassical poet and scholar of Polish literature could write neither straight testimony nor straight fiction. So he combined the two for his existential remapping of the severed past.

The main fictional device, which adds a Yiddish inflection to the dialogue and much comic relief, is the character of Icyk Mandelbaum, an obvious stand-in for the Polish Yiddish and American author Isaac Bashevis Singer, and a not-so-obvious Jewish double for the author himself. Halfway through this documentary novel, Rymkiewicz invites Mandelbaum on an imaginary return trip to Poland, where the Nobel Prize–winning author visits his old haunts and makes out with his old flames. Both the narrator and his double find Jewish women irresistible. Both use sexual flirtation to escape their personal grief over the overwhelming absence of Polish Jewry. "O God," the narrator breaks with his usual banter to exclaim, "let me just once in my life travel by train to Świder amid the pandemonium and uproar issuing from Sheol, from history's abyss. But this clearly exceeds Thy scope, so I withdraw my request."

A second patron saint is Czesław Miłosz, whose poem "A Poor Christian Looks at the Ghetto," written in 1943, was the direct inspiration for Rymkiewicz's memory project. Like Miłosz, the narrator witnessed the tragic fate of the Jews, and, like his fellow poet, it is only as a Christian that he can address the problem, "out of a sense of shared suffering." This sets the moral bar very high, and non-Christian readers may find it hard to comprehend or credit the narrator's final gesture of trying to change places with the Jewish boy with his arms raised in surrender, in the iconic photograph of the liquidation of the Warsaw ghetto.

What further drives the book's moral passion, however, is something that Miłosz did not witness. Rymkiewicz was "there in October 1968, as the last Polish Jews stood on the platforms at Gdańsk Station waiting for the trains to Vienna." This book, then, must serve as their final requiem.

Fiction and theology are the armature for the book's stated purpose: the meticulous reconstruction of the complex of buildings in the very heart of Warsaw (likened to an Umschlagplatz in Central Park) where the ghetto Jews were rounded up for the Treblinka death camp. Here every reader has much to gain from following the often frustrating efforts of a nonspecialist as he pores over all available testimony. Rymkiewicz sees wartime diaries and the earliest historical monographs as the bedrock of Holocaust memory and casts a skeptical eye on later acts of retrieval. Where precise detail is at stake, he prefers the Marek Edelman testimony from 1950 to the Marek Edelman testimony from 1988. Above all, what he cannot abide is the use of documentation—who did what to whom, and when—to escape from assuming moral responsibility in the present, and the easy evasions of later generations through theory and abstraction. To remember and to mourn, it is vital to confront the past in all its messy, concrete particularity. (DGR)

János Nyiri. *Battlefields and Playgrounds*. Translated from the Hungarian by
    William Brandon and the author. Waltham, MA: Brandeis University Press,
    1989. First published as *Madarorzság*.

Watch Joszka Sondor live his life, from the age of six to the age of twelve and a half. He's a tough little tyke, throws a mean punch, always faces up to bullies, and never finds a rule he shouldn't break. For a child from a peasant family, struggling through urban poverty with his mother and brother, life means mastering soccer well enough eventually to play for Ferencvaros, the champion (and fascist) team, dodging school where possible, tormenting his *heder* teacher, scheming to scare off his mother's non-Jewish lover, holding his deadbeat father accountable for ditching the family—and asking impossible questions of almost everyone. In the story of the prince and the pauper, for example, why is it so much harder for the prince to be poor than it is for the pauper to be rich? Joszka's family is poor, and it's hard enough for them. Life also means fighting the antisemites, trawling for food and clothes and shoes, figuring out how to establish himself as a goy where necessary, coping with starvation, determining where the Russian front actually is, and always refusing to concede anything to adult authority.

For Joszka, every question is immediate: How best can he face down a fascist functionary? Should he take money from his father, and if so, should he give it all to his mother, or can he buy himself a soccer ball and give her the rest? Every question entails the decoding of the multiple ways in which adults lie and observing with a pitiless eye the encroachment and final arrival of the Germans in Budapest.

Joszka takes things as they come. People behave well or they behave badly. Sometimes they do both. The storekeepers gouge the poorest customers. Rich people always have it better—there's no way that he, Joszka, would qualify for Wallenberg papers (allowing Jews to emigrate to Sweden, and avoid the prospect of transportation to concentration camp and almost certain death). Those are reserved for the children of the very rich, like Arnold Kohn. Sometimes people do amazingly good things, like Ferenc Jager, a Hungarian noncommissioned officer, who provides Joszka's mother with authentic Christian papers that belong to his own family, and the Lutheran couple who take in people without papers (Jews), without asking questions, placing them in accommodations where they can continue their lives under cover. Sometimes even fascists behave with compassion. Most times, though, they don't.

The child's skepticism is wonderful, funny, engaging, and also devastating—sometimes even to himself. At one point, his mother, desperate to stop her bright, cocky son from taking on a fight that will endanger them all, takes him to see Aunty Sarolta, the doctor. She introduces the boy to a Warsaw ghetto survivor. The small, emaciated, gray figure speaks in a colorless voice, translated without affect by Aunty Sarolta. As transcribed in the novel, the account reads like a summary of the literature of the ghetto—the concentration, deportation, the ss, the Jewish Community's engagement. "Don't trust the Jewish community," says the survivor. "Don't even trust God too much."

The child responds to the trust placed in him by the doctor and the Pole and realizes the deep truth of what has been revealed to him. In some sense, it doesn't surprise him because he has never trusted adults and has long since had his doubts about God.

Together, Joszka and his brother, David, make up a survival game, called "the Lying Game," in which they build a deep cover story to answer any questions that might be asked by anyone. Ultimately, in Nyiri's book, solidarity occurs between children, even if they punch each other, throw stones at each other, and insult each other. Adults cannot be trusted, and the Almighty deserves only the deepest skepticism. In this sense, lessons learned on the playground prepare the child to survive and help his family survive the worst of the German invasion. But, as survivors, they return to nothing. They are the only Jews left in the village. The two boys spend their days shoveling out the manure left behind by the occupying Germans. (ND)

Abraham Sutzkever. *Di nevue fun shvartsaplen: dertseylungen* (Prophecy of the inner eye: stories). Introduction by Ruth Wisse. Jerusalem: Magnes, 1989. Thirteen of the thirty-two stories are translated in *A. Sutzkever: Selected Poetry and Prose*, introduction by Benjamin Harshav, translated by Barbara and Benjamin Harshav (Berkeley: University of California Press, 1991), 373–422.

The fantastic, as famously defined by Tzvetan Todorov, creates a hole in the fabric of reality; it must be neither "poetic" nor "allegorical" (Todorov 1975, 32). Abraham Sutzkever arrived at the writing of poetic fantastical stories in the 1970s, after a twenty-year-long battle that he waged against the enemy called time. He began in the mid-1950s with *Green Aquarium* (1982), a cycle of fifteen prose poems in which, through cyclical and simultaneous time frames, with syncopated sentences and highly figurative language, he set forth the terms of engagement: the finality of death, the disappearance of the dead versus the life-giving potential of art. The poems followed a loose chronology from the first *Aktionen* in the Vilna ghetto to the Liberation (Sutzkever 1982). In the 1975 "Messiah's Diary," as the title suggests, Sutzkever turned to mythopoetic narratives, where the plots of fairytales like Beauty and the Beast and Little Red Riding Hood were thrown into the crucible of Holocaust time: before, during, and after the slaughter. Finally, in *Dortn vu es nekhtikn di shtern* (Where the stars spend the night; 1979b) and this work, Sutzkever pulled out all the stops. These were stories set in present-day Tel Aviv, but they were autobiography experienced as bizarre, paradoxical, and portentous struggles between the living and the dead.

In "Faithful Needles," the yearning of one of three sisters for their lost father is so powerful that it can bring him back to life just long enough for one last reunion, accompanied by a cup of tea. In "Lupus," narrated with macabre humor, the seller of cyanide during the slaughter emerges from the mirror. When death was so much more valuable than life, as he says when justifying his illicit trade, the best way to compete was by turning oneself into a wolf. In "Glikele," a love story, the object of desire is not attainable, either in the hallucinatory present or the luminous past. In "The Black Angel with a Pin in His Hand," the bohemian poet Moyshe-Itske does not succeed in defying death, but neither does he succumb. In "The Gunpowder Brigade," the narrator and Dr. Horacy Dik, in straw hat and pince-nez, are forced to transport unexploded bombs as punishment for starting the Second World War. Dik, a descendant of the first professional Yiddish storyteller, is director of the lunatic asylum, who narrates his story of survival. Only by accepting the madman on his own terms, he instructs the narrator, can one escape his knives.

The survivor lives in transcendent communion with the dead. Each of the dead has some divine lunacy to impart, like "The Beggar with the Blue Eyeglasses," who proclaims that Cosmic Man must change so that death will not find him. Each must seek an heir on this side of life if the White-Headed Worm of mutability is ever to be vanquished. For the only way to engage the angel of destruction in combat is through the power of the poetic word and the fantastical tale. (DGR)

[1990]

Salomon Isacovici and Juan Manuel Rodríguez. *Man of Ashes*. Translated from the Spanish by Dick Gerdes, Lincoln: University of Nebraska Press, 1999. First published as *A7393: Hombre de cenizas*.

Salomon Isacovici was born in Sighet, Hungary, a part of the world that belonged at different times to Romania and Hungary and then was occupied by Germany and liberated by Russians. Sighet is also Elie Wiesel's hometown, by now a mythic place that has come to symbolize Eastern European Jewish existence before the Holocaust. Young Isacovici's Sighet is a vibrant, down-to-earth agricultural community. He comes from a large family. He goes to *heder*. His mother takes food to the poor Jews in the area. He plays pranks. And then, in the caesura that is both historical fact and also literary trope in the literature of the Holocaust, war is declared. The border is closed. Life becomes a great deal harder. But the Nazis have not yet invaded, and as bad as the Romanians are, they are not yet conducting routine massacres.

Isacovici's strength lies in his ability to articulate the stages of social ostracism that affected the Jews of Sighet, from the onset of a certain indifference through willed ignorance to murderous destruction. Then come the deportation and the arrival at Auschwitz, the final glimpses of mother and sister, and the dreadful physical realities: the smell of burned flesh, the greasy soot that covers the palm of his hand and through which he sees the lines of his hand in a dreadful parody of the fortuneteller's craft.

Most Holocaust memoirs end with the Liberation. Survival is a natural endpoint. For Isacovici, postwar existence occupies half the book. He is fortunate in finding three of his brothers and therefore being able to reconstitute at least some family connection. But, unlike that of Odysseus, his homecoming is a bitter one. The Romanian who is living in his house threatens him, and he runs away, his dream of return forsaken. He leaves Sighet to try his luck elsewhere, becomes a *makher* (a mover and shaker) in the DP camp and an active Zionist. Ultimately he decides not to emigrate to Palestine, feeling that he has been through enough wars. And then he meets the woman who becomes his wife, makes his way to Ecuador, and builds a life for himself there.

If this were the full account, one would read the book as something of a curiosity. Jews migrated all over the world. This one established himself on a hacienda in Quito, felt deep compassion for the maltreated Indian *campesinos*, and pulled himself up by his bootstraps to become a well-respected businessman. There are family photographs and reproductions of identity documents in Isacovici's name, but also photographs of corpses in the liberated Auschwitz that clearly have a different source. His memoir is not so different from hundreds of other accounts that have survived.

But then there was the threat of litigation over the English-language translation that was averted by crediting Isacovici with a coauthor, Juan Manuel Rodríguez. Isacovici claimed that he had asked Rodríguez, a Roman Catholic priest and friend, for assistance in smoothing out the prose, since Spanish was not Isacovici's first language. But Rodríguez claimed instead that the book was his. Isacovici had recounted his story and shown Rodríguez various documents over the course of several months. Rodríguez claimed that he had written what he called "the novel," infusing it with his own philosophy and view of the world. So successful had he been, Rodríguez insisted, that he claimed the narrative as his own.

Whose book is it? Whose narrative? Whose memoir? Is this a memoir or a work of Holocaust fiction? Given this nonliterary frame, where should the book be situated within our temporary canon of Holocaust writing? Very few writers truly write alone. They are influenced by the people around them. Their views of the world and of their own past are undoubtedly shaped by their personal contexts, but they share their drafts with trusted readers, often incorporating editorial comments and suggestions along the way.

Isacovici never presented the book as anything other than his own life story. There are other cases of extensive editing in the literary existence of important works of Holocaust literature (most prominently, Elie Wiesel's *Night*). But even significant editorial interventions do not constitute ownership of the narrative. In this context, Rodríguez's claims seem dubious at best.

The struggle in this case between subject and editor over the rights to the narrative shows how unstable the line between memoir and fiction can become. Other books in our list—Wilkomirski's, for example—raise similar issues. They are important for this very reason. The struggle for ownership is not over Holocaust memory as such, but rather over the moral honors that go with narrating that experience. That struggle becomes more acute as the survivor generation dies and the work of Holocaust memory becomes ever more deeply indebted to fictional impulses. (ND)

[1991]

Louis Begley. *Wartime Lies*. New York: Knopf, 1991.

Our study of Holocaust literature begins with direct, first-person testimony, written at the very time of catastrophe, perhaps in the ghetto or on the run, or extracted from a burial place meant to keep memory for those to come. At the other end of the literary and chronological spectrum comes this novel, written long after the war has ended. It is somewhat autobiographical. The reader has to accept both the author's veracity and the autobiographical underpinning of the fiction. It is an intelligent, understated, and compelling story of a small boy, his aunt, and their struggle to survive in Poland under the Nazis. The canvas is modest here, at least in part because the protagonists live such limited lives—in hiding, with restricted mobility and endless secrets, and, as the title indicates, a depth of lying that comes to reshape the boy's identity permanently. As the narrator acknowledges, theirs is a privileged existence compared to that faced by other Jews during the war. It is part of the novel's power that the reader is not able to dismiss this story as just one more with a happy ending. Every survival story comes with its own costs. Begley's book keeps an accurate accounting that is unsentimental and undramatic, yet compelling.

One of the reasons for its success is the series of frames that, like the lies of the title, shape the protagonists' cover stories and the novel as a whole. The outermost is the narrator as a "sad-eyed" adult, a grown-up who has survived but with significant damage. The second is the overarching frame of the Western classical tradition. Virgil and Dante are the reader's companions throughout the book, even as the family history reveals the superficiality of the classical ideals that those works present.

The protagonists survive because they look relatively Aryan and can blend into the host culture, have valuables to trade, and, perhaps most important, have few illusions about people in general. In order to live, they assume mask after mask, layering them one on top of the other. Like the lead soldiers that the little boy melts down and reconstitutes as different soldiers in different armies, he, guided by his formidable aunt, takes on different names and identities. His name changes, along with his usable past and his self. In their place he acquires a secular *gymnasium* and a Catholic education. He gets to know about cows and pigs. He learns to take off the split second he perceives a threat, to shuck off his previous self and adopt a new one.

This frame is disconcerting. Aunt and nephew live their lives as good Polish Roman Catholics while observing the smoke rising from the ghetto and hearing the Nazi bombardments as if in the distance. Toward the end of the book, hiding with other Poles from the retreating Germans, who are even more vicious in defeat than in victory, the boy's aunt leads the women in a prayer to the Virgin Mary.

Even Liberation is not the end of the disguise, for the boy and his aunt are in Kielce, site of virulent postwar pogroms. We know that the disguise is eventually removed because otherwise the book couldn't be written. But we never learn how and where and when. Those questions are left hanging at the end, an ending that is, by its very nature, provisional. (ND)

Arnold Zable. *Jewels and Ashes*. San Diego: Harcourt Brace, 1994.

By the end of the twentieth century, the Second World War had been over for more than fifty years. Many wars had intervened, with new genocides in Biafra, Rwanda, Bosnia, and elsewhere. Empires other than the Third Reich had fallen while prosecuting foreign wars (the French, the British, the Soviet). The world was full of survivors—the *desesparecidos*, the migrants living in intolerable conditions at the edges of the second great industrial revolution, the San people confined to ever smaller areas of desert southern Africa. Hundreds of languages had died out because their community of speakers no longer existed. For the survivors of the Holocaust and their children, there remains but one war and the facts of their own survival. The "then" literature of the Holocaust, written as the events themselves were occurring, has become the province of scholars, able—with access to former Soviet archives—to continue the work of recovery. But the attempt to recover the prelapsarian prewar period remains a preoccupation for the children and grandchildren of survivors who want to place the oblique statements, half-told reminiscences, fragments, and behavioral patterns that are their inheritance into a larger perspective. Arnold Zable's book was written in the late 1980s, when the generation of those who survived the war as adults was, though frail, still alert and active.

The central figure in Zable's family account is his grandfather, Bishke Zabludowski, the news crier of Białystok, famous for decades as the man who sold papers in the central square under the town clock, the man who knew the news before everyone else did. He was a character, as Dickens might have said. Meier Zabludowski, Arnold's father, leaves Poland in the 1930s, joining his wife, who has acquired a visa to go to her sister in Melbourne, Australia. They are the fortunate ones. What they pass on to their son is the emptiness of survival, of deaths expected or confirmed in passing, of farewells that never took place, of life after effacement. Zable's father has no time for introspection, he tells us repeatedly. "One foot after the other," he says. But by the end of the book, we realize that for Meier Zabludowski, the past hovers like the shadow of his father and mother at the foot of his bed every single morning. He is the archivist of lost fragments, holding onto every scrap of paper that relates to his life before the war. He marks each important entry in red ballpoint pen, underlining and commenting like a scholar of secular documents that, by force of absence and allusion, have acquired the power of the sacred.

Zable undertakes a journey that is both recovery and restitution. He visits the last fragments of the Jewish community in various parts of Poland. He meets the unofficial historian of Jewish Białystok, Simon Datner, with his pre-war maps and directories of a missing community. As the book progresses, Zable reconstructs the family existence, what he calls the "fragile romance of the shtetl." The narrator knows that his version of the shtetl is a fantasy. Meeting the last few remaining Jews in Warsaw and Białystok, leading marginal existences in the present, only reinforces the illusion.

Zable's recovery of Białystok as it survives in the memories of a handful of elderly survivors coincides in his narrative with his father's acceptance of the pastness of the past. Only words survive, his father tells him, words that are both the jewels and the ashes of the book's title. Holocaust literature as a category undertakes to reverse the centrifugal impact of death and dispersal by bringing back to a lost center the fragments spun off into fractured families and dispersed geography. (ND)

[**1992**]

W. G. Sebald. *The Emigrants.* Translated from the German by Michael Hulse. New York: New Directions, 1996. First published as *Die Ausgewanderten.*

For writers, enormity is both a problem and an opportunity. Over and over, writers, students, and teachers struggle with what is appropriate, consonant, and possible in relation to events like genocide that challenge traditional moral, historical, and artistic tools. As living memory approached the long tail of its existence—that is, with the decline and death of the generations of survivors—these questions become more acute and more the focus of the writer's undertaking.

Indirection as a means of addressing the Holocaust is an approach used by other writers—Aharon Appelfeld comes to mind. In Sebald's hands, indirection is structured not only around the four stories that make up *The Emigrants,* but also around the introduction of what, in other contexts, might be considered material of directly evidentiary nature: photographs of people and places, diary pages, and objects. The structuring irony, of course, is that the introduction of the photographs—apparent proofs of the verifiable—serves, because of the ambiguity surrounding them and their inclusion in a work of fiction, to destabilize any direct historical connection. These images could be, but are not necessarily, factual. Yet they bring a certain heft to the narratives in which they are contained. They support and validate the pervasive sense of time lost, lives created in disjunction with themselves, moral ambiguity and compromise, and a profound melancholy that goes far beyond the more histrionic exhibitions of loss that might characterize other kinds of Holocaust narratives.

The chapters of *The Emigrants* take four individuals as their central focus: Dr. Henry Selwyn, Paul Bereyter, Ambros Adelwarth, and Max Ferber. The narrator functions as historian and interlocutor for each of them. In Selwyn's case, the narrator is a lodger; in Bereyter's, a former student; in Adelwarth's, a young relative; and in Ferber's, something between a student and someone for whom Ferber is a mentor. Each chapter is a story of reconstruction. Sometimes it is the subject of the chapter who is revealed as putting pieces of himself back into some kind of order (for example, Bereyter, the teacher); in others, as in the family narrative constructed around the major-domo Ambros Adelwarth, it is the narrator who performs the reconstruction. In all four stories, rebuilding a narrative from past fragments is profoundly unsatisfactory, yet it is the best that can be accomplished because there are so many missing pieces that will never be found, that can never be accounted for.

The title itself calls the reader to order. These are not refugees, nor are they émigrés, with all the overtones of intellectual exile and class advantage. There is nothing romantic about the condition of emigration. It is a term of location. These are those who have left. It is not a coincidence that they are also all that is left of what happened "back there."

In the book's last story, the decline of a great industrial city and the minute details of a childhood remembered *in minimus* as defense against murder, seen all too clearly by its victim, come together in the charcoal fragments that remain from Max's drawings that come into being through a series of erasures. A small pile of dust is all that is left, too, of the mother who wrote an account of her childhood, of Ambros Adelwarth who committed himself to a serial destruction of his memory through electroshock therapy, and of Selwyn and Bereyter, as well. For Sebald, all life ends in a form of murder-suicide. There is nothing to recover. What remains is reconstruction—flawed, fictionalized, but compelling. (ND)

[1994]

Sarah Kofman. *Rue Ordener, Rue Labat.* Translated from the French by Ann Smock. Lincoln: University of Nebraska Press, 1996.

Two streets, only two metro stations apart but two different worlds. Sarah Kofman's brief and lapidary recollection of her wartime childhood and its aftermath takes the reader between the two poles of her childhood in a wrenching but unsentimental account. Many works about the Holocaust are fragmentary, whether collections of short stories (Borowski's *This Way for the Gas, Ladies and Gentlemen*), episodic (Semprún's *Quelle beau dimanche*), or scraps of text cobbled together (Charlotte Delbo's *Aucun de nous de reviendra*, part of her *Auschwitz and After*). All seek a form with which to pull together the disjointed remnants of trauma and external displacement. In Kofman's case, the fragmentation emerges oddly enough from a duplication: two mothers, one her birth mother, the other the French gentile woman who takes in mother and daughter, appropriating the daughter's affections while saving both their lives.

Kofman's father, whose arrest begins her story and ends the Rue Ordener experience, remains in the book through his fountain pen, the object by which she remembers him and which she herself uses until it gives out. Her siblings are dispersed and in hiding, leaving Kofman's mother and the small girl together. Her mother tries repeatedly to hide her, but she refuses to be separated from her mother. On the brief occasions when she is sent away, she refuses to eat nonkosher food, putting herself at great risk of exposure. Eventually, her mother takes the child to an acquaintance who risks her own life to hide them both. But altruism is a treacherous value, as Kofman's book demonstrates. She is seduced by the woman who wishes to displace her birth mother. Her birth mother is in an invidious position, dependent on her host for survival and therefore unable to challenge her for alienating her daughter's affections. The child is irretrievably marked by her divided loyalties, internally fragmented, and forced into the position of betrayer and collaborator in her mother's displacement by the family's savior.

The larger canvas of family and community destruction is writ small in this book. Homes are stripped, people are taken away, fear and desolation dominate existence. In the child's world, hunger and feeding are reflections of her family affiliations. When she begins to eat and enjoy the nonkosher and thoroughly *treyf* delicacies prepared by her adoptive mother, she is implicitly taking into herself everything that her mother and father rejected. The relationship between the birth mother and daughter becomes irretrievably embittered.

Many accounts of survival end with the end of the war itself. In this case, the family war continues well past the Liberation. There is an ugly court case in which, as the child wishes, the state awards custody of her to the interloper. But her mother literally hires some muscle to wrench the child back.

The child reconstitutes herself, reappropriates her religious Jewish persona, is a gifted student—and, as the reader knows, becomes a famous academic, a philosopher and student of Freudianism.

Sarah Kofman committed suicide in 1994 at the age of sixty. This book is one of the last pieces she wrote. Just as the text itself almost dares the reader to impose a Freudian framework on the bare account, the end of the life described in part in this volume begs the question about the reconstituted self. For Kofman, in any case, childhood remains unresolved. Guilt, shame, fear, humiliation, and loss are the war's only legacy. (ND)

[1995]

Bernhard Schlink. *The Reader*. Translated from the German by Carol Brown Janeway. New York: Pantheon, 1997. Movie version directed by Stephen Daldry (United States, 2008). First published as *Die Vorleser*.

By the turn of the millennium, the seminal works of Holocaust literature in the West—by Tadeusz Borowski, Primo Levi, and Elie Wiesel—were at least a generation in the past. The topic of Holocaust literature had finally become domesticated. Oprah Winfrey selected Elie Wiesel's *Night* as one of her book-of-the-month choices. Berhard Schlink's novel, *The Reader*, was also selected for this honor (which guarantees a mass audience), as well as other, more literary, awards. Made into a movie starring Kate Winslet and Ralph Fiennes, it won Kate Winslet the Oscar for Best Actress in 2008.

The book is divided into three sections: a boy's first love affair with an older woman, his growing disillusion, and her disappearance before that disillusion is complete; the same boy's time in law school, when he attends the trial of several female ss guards accused of wartime atrocities, of whom his former lover is one, in the course of which he realizes that the woman is illiterate and would rather be condemned for war crimes than diminish her guilt by revealing her secret; and the last section, in which the protagonist reconnects with the woman by sending her books that he has read on tape. The woman commits suicide the night before her release from prison.

The book has been widely viewed as a sensitive rendering of a generational dilemma—how the postwar German generation can come to terms with the crimes of the Nazi generation—and also as a careful exploration of the moral dilemmas facing both the boy (Should he reveal his lover's illiteracy? Did he betray her trust as a boy?) and the woman, who in prison, learns how to read and write and engage her past.

But despite the writer's insistence that he is not blurring the categories of victim and victimizer, that blurring is essentially the outcome of the book. The woman, the ss guard, is victimized by her fellow defendants, who heap all the blame on her. She takes young Jewish girls to read to her in her room in the camp, giving them food and warmth and sparing them a little from the inevitable outcome. Is this a form of compassion or of exploitation? And then there is the protagonist, so earnestly concerned with his own moral choices and betrayals.

By the end of the novel, Hanna the prison guard is a figure of pity and of a certain moral standing: she has overcome her illiteracy, she has studied books about the Nazi period, she has served as a moral arbiter within the prison. She leaves a small amount of money to be given to the remaining plaintiff in her case.

The novel has brought the reader to this point, but it is a distasteful moral position. One does not wish to forgive the cruelties, even as the persecutor is humanized. The boy, grown into a man, reads his former lover "into" the great literature of the West, almost in the way that a spy is "read into" the details of a secret case. But what does that knowledge bring? And to whom?

It is perhaps a sign of the ineluctable movement of the Holocaust into the historical past that Schlink's book can be viewed in a redemptive light. After all, whether Hanna could read or not, she did her duty when the doors were locked and the women burned to death. No text, whether the *Odyssey* read on tape or books about the Holocaust read by Hanna in prison, can change that historical fact or exculpate the human beings responsible for enacting mass murder. (ND)

Binjamin Wilkomirski [Bruno Dössekker]. *Fragments: Memories of a Wartime Childhood*. Translated from the German by Carol Brown Janeway. New York: Schocken, 1996. First published as *Bruchstücke*.

The facts underlying *Fragments* are by now well known. The book and the experiences it describes are untrue. Why, then, include Wilkomirski's book in this Guide? Surely there are other, authentic works that deserve the reader's attention. This is an important question. Wilkomirski's fraud is far from the first literary hoax to embarrass reviewers and critics and take advantage of the credulity of the reading public. Why should this one matter? Why not just move the book from the column of memoir over to the category of fiction (like many another supposed memoir)? If the book is as good as the reviewers insisted, then shouldn't it be just as valuable as a work of fiction? Just asking the question provides the answer. "No," one feels. "That shouldn't be a permeable boundary." It is precisely this reflex and the reasons for it that make *Fragments* an important element in the history of Holocaust literature's reception.

Fragments marks a particular period in Holocaust remembrance. The book was first published exactly fifty years after the end of the Second World War. It represents a kind of completion of the survivor narrative trajectory. By 1995, the life span of most Holocaust survivors was reaching its endpoint. Only those who survived the war as children—younger and younger children as time progressed—could be looked to as the real-life authenticators of this great personal and historical trauma. But what were the limits of memory? How much does a very young child remember? What kind of authorizing figures would the remaining survivors constitute? *Fragments* was one kind of answer, even though there were questions about its veracity even before publication—inconsistencies that in retrospect are conclusive. Yet the book was published and had a great public success precisely because it filled a particular kind of need.

This was the generational transition. Wilkomirski's broken, confused, and heart-rending account suggested the consequences of Holocaust experience in the formation of memory that did not yet have consolidated language with which to articulate and experience itself.

Further, the narrative contains a set of tropes, what might be described as the formalized notation of authentic, first-person Holocaust narration: the ghastly experiences in the camps; the hardships of postwar existence; survivor guilt; the inability to establish true human connection; the audience's unwillingness to listen to so terrible a story; the permanently fragmented self; the act of writing as a form of self-reconstitution; trauma so deep and permanent that the past could never be mastered. These are all important and recognizable elements of verifiable and fundamental works of Holocaust literature. One reason, then, for the initially overwhelmingly positive reception of Wilkomirski's book is that it fulfilled the existing expectations for a work of Holocaust autobiography. The conditions for its acceptance had already been set by fifty years of post-Holocaust writing.

Does *Fragments* undermine the genre of Holocaust memoir? Not in and of itself. Levi, whose literary and moral authority grows as the years pass, wrote movingly of his friend and comrade Alberto, lost in the death march. A survivor who claimed to know Alberto and insisted that he had survived soaked Alberto's family for money. They paid, in the hopes that the fiction was true.

Such is the case for the readers whose trust was abused by Wilkomirski. The need for authentic voices is so great that literary fraud becomes possible and profitable. In the contract between autobiographer and reader, if the writer betrays his or her side of the contract, it is up to the reader to fight back—by challenging his or her own expectations and needs, as well as the texts themselves. (ND)

Theo Richmond. *Konin: A Quest*. New York: Pantheon, 1995.

At the other end of the spectrum from the documents written during the Holocaust are works of recovery, restoration, and reintegration—topographies that are spatial, generational, and affiliational. Topography is a mathematical field whose insights explain the ability to fold ever more complex notions of dimensionality within space and time. Similarly, Theo Richmond, Daniel Mendelsohn, Arnold Zable and others write in order to return to lost space and find within it both lost time and lost communities.

Konin is a country town in Poland, at one time prosperous because of a broad river that made it a transportation and trade hub. At the town's height in the late nineteenth century, almost half of its population was Jewish. The depredations of the First World War and then the Great Depression, matched by the centrifugal pull of alternate ideologies (socialism, communism, Zionism) and economics (emigration) eroded the community. Like so many Polish Jewish towns, Konin was barely surviving when the fascist and antisemitic onslaught hit home.

Richmond's book begins with the Konin *yizkor* book, the official memory book compiled by the remaining Jewish Koniners, those who had emigrated before the Second World War and those few who managed to survive the Shoah. The *yizkor* books were meant to capture something concrete and lasting about the life of the Jews of their towns, but they turn out to have a very short life in social memory. They may outlive the survivors as documents, but the lived substance captured in two dimensions does not survive as text connected with direct human experience more than half a generation beyond that survival.

Like Arnold Zable with his map of Białystok, Richmond goes from continent to continent, listening to old voices, marking the known parameters of a lost Jewish existence. His project is a personal memory quest; in effect, he is seeking to create a set of marginalia and footnotes to expand and supplement the official memory of a community. In this sense it differs from both Zable's and Mendelsohn's undertakings. Richmond's is a book profoundly embedded in the notion of Jewish community; its interrelationships; and its religious, social, economic, and ideological bases.

One of the Konin survivors, an architect, does not speak his memories, but rather creates detailed and intricate architectural drawings of his house, his childhood secret space, and the paths between the synagogue and the study house. His memory takes his own childhood spaces and builds them into the sacred communal spaces described in the memory book. He restores space to the time that Richmond is recovering, just as Richmond's questions about that time cause the architect to revisit and recreate past spaces.

Piecing the fragments together—connecting a name with a street that had a view over the river, a distant relative, or a child's prank—the survivor him- or herself is at least making a gesture at restoring the whole community, trying to demonstrate that in this place and time, the parts must stand for the whole, the folded maps and torn fragments of paper and almost overwritten voices of the past restore space and thus recover time.

One of the survivors tells Richmond that he is "twenty-five years too late." Richmond responds with the image of a ragged old siddur (prayer book). The book as object is still valuable, even if the text is torn and incomplete. So, too, is Richmond's family story. There might be large gaps, but there is enough to embed that one extended family into the lost Konin Jewish community. Like the fragments of Jewish text entombed in a *genizah* (a repository for fragments of writing that may not be destroyed because they may contain God's name), these memories are interred in a stratum of experience that will be available only as fragments and byproducts, never the thing in itself—not the family, the community, or the past. (ND)

[1999]

Michał Głowiński. *The Black Seasons*. Foreword by Jan T. Gross. Translated from the Polish with preface and notes by Marci Shore. Evanston, IL: Northwesern University Press, 2005. First published as *Czarne sezony*.

Michał Głowiński is one of the most eminent literary scholars of Poland. He waited fifty years to tell this story and, for that matter, to reveal his identity as a Jew. *The Black Seasons* is the great summation of Holocaust literature, in which the child survivor recapitulates the many "seasons of death" both during and after the war, and his adult counterpart tests his memory against that of many others, including Paul Celan, whose "Todesfuge" inspired the title: "black milk of daybreak we drink you at night." Like Celan, Głowiński presents fragmented memories and experiences, giving images, colors, sounds, and snatches of conversation without trying to achieve coherence. At the great remove of half a century, the only reliable sources of memory are radical metonymies, each of which cries out to be interpreted.

"Even the cruelest episodes of the Bible bear no comparison to the stories comprising the Holocaust," writes Głowiński in the spirit of Primo Levi. In one chapter, the nine-year-old boy is playing chess with death, in the person of a *szmalcownik* (a professional blackmailer) "with a roguishly trimmed moustache." As contrived as this may sound, it was a time "when the most extraordinarily diabolical things could happen." How can one distinguish between the "season of great dying," when close to 300,000 Jews were dragged off to Umschlagplatz, the child and his parents among them, and "The Black Hour" of this chess game, played in an attic on the Aryan side? In either time frame, the child's survival depended on the vagaries of chance. Whether on the road to Umschlagplatz or during "A Quarter Hour Passed in a Pastry Shop," the child has the status of an object at best, a monster at worst.

Głowiński's carefully crafted twenty tales are more than a seasonal guide. Through fragments, stops and starts, and relived traumas and terrors, the adult-as-child pieces together a vivid and precise guide to the Jew-Zone as he knew it, with its colors, sounds (he devotes a whole chapter to the phenomenology of knocking), and mental landscape. It is a landscape not devoid of humor (the flamboyant figure of Długi and his ugly, domineering, and heroic lover, Natka) or of Christian charity ("the wonderful Irena Senderowa, the guardian angel of those in hiding"). Those divinely bestowed with "good looks," like Aunt Maria, can travel freely on the Aryan side, while Krystał, with "a Jewish eye," is better able to assess "bad looks"—that is, those people who are not worth the risk of being smuggled out of the ghetto. More than a dozen years after the war, when his family moves from Pruszków to Warsaw, his mother categorically refuses to agree to a new apartment built on the ghetto ruins. It is impossible, she claims, to live a calm life in a cemetery, even one without any graves. The Jew-Zone remains a perilous terrain, even after it ceases to exist. But one man, emerging from underground after fifty years, set out to excavate the ruins of memory. (DGR)

[**2000**]

Michael Chabon. *The Amazing Adventures of Kavalier & Clay: A Novel.*
New York: Random House, 2000.

The Amazing Adventures of Kavalier & Clay, published to great acclaim in 2000 and awarded the Pulitzer Prize for fiction, is a huge, ambitious novel, informed both by the ample spirit of the great nineteenth-century novelists—Hugo, Balzac, Dickens—and the edgy, wisecracking American and American Jewish writers of the mid-twentieth century. Part borscht-belt humor, part vaudeville; infused by the movies and, of course, the spirit of the comic book, it is that rare compendium: a graphic novel written in words.

Joseph Kavalier and Sam Clay are cousins. The former a refugee from Prague, the latter a quintessential Brooklyn boy, they pool their talents to create a new superhero, the Escapist, who is able to accomplish everything that Joseph would like to do in order to save his family—defeat Hitler, punish the antisemites, kill the spies, make his fortune, and justify his survival.

This is a retelling of the refugee story from week to week in the pages of the comic book, and from chapter to chapter within the novel as a whole. Each week needs terrible dangers so that the hero and his friends can overcome them. Being a refugee is a condition of life that repeats itself at every level of the novel. It is the recursive experience of the twentieth century, invoking profound sadness, a sense of vertigo, and the constant sense of foreboding that is justified by later events.

Just as Kavalier changes the shape of the comic's panels, stretching and compressing them in pursuit of narration that is suitable to their own materials, so Chabon uses an intricate set of frames within frames to put the reader in different relationships to the characters and the plot. At some points, Chabon draws on the conventions of academic prose (footnotes, references to books that don't exist). At others, he invokes a narrator who knows everything about the characters, how they will feel at the end of their lives, and how their work will be perceived and valued. But most powerful of all is prolepsis, the narrative tool that foreshadows what we know is to come, that the family in Prague will be turned into ashes, just as the golem delivered finally to a house on Long Island has long since disintegrated into flakes of soil that bear with them the smell of the Moldava River.

For all its broad humor, memorable characters, great one-liners, and absolute fealty to the lost world of midcentury comic books, this is ultimately a tragedy built around the escapes that couldn't or didn't take place.

It is interesting to compare Chabon's novel to Art Spiegelman's *Maus*. In Spiegelman's account, the weight of language and prolepsis gives his metaphor its validity. In Chabon's book, the dizzying multiplicity of metaphors, languages, characters, emotions, canvasses, and creations serves to render the metaphor of the Escapist as light as air. The Escapist, then, is *luftmentsh*, floating on a column of ash above the fictive creations of the imagination. (ND)

Amir Gutfreund. *Our Holocaust*. Translated from the Hebrew by Jessica Cohen. New Milford, CT: Toby, 2006. First published as *Shoah shelanu*.

This is the quintessential Israeli novel on the Holocaust. Hilarious, irreverent, and secular, it situates "our" Shoah within the warp and woof of everyday life. Yet because it is so deeply embedded within the collective psyche, the real story must be deciphered before it can be owned by the next generation. Like David Grossman before him, Gutfreund skips a generation and lavishes a great deal of attention on the lovable, avuncular Grandpa Yosef, himself a spinoff of Tevye the Dairyman, along with a bevy of other adopted uncles, aunts, and grandparents. In the course of *Our Holocaust*, the children of Katzenelson Street age from not old enough to old enough, which, in a sense, is also the story of modern-day Israel.

In the national psyche as well as among the children, the Holocaust started out as action adventure: "Above us the Carmel mountains towered, and behind them the woods of Minsk. We were partisans and we were American-Indians and we were ghetto-fighters, day in and day out." Playing Buchenwald meant going without food or drink. Puberty fed the passion for pornography, so Levertov, after much prodding, finally revealed to them the "Doll's" atrocities in Treblinka. From firsthand experience the children knew that some survivors were stark raving mad, like Crazy Hirsch, who went around screaming,

"Only saints were gassed?" Once they got older, Attorney Perl tried to explain that you didn't need a Holocaust for there to be bad Jews. His *idée fixe* was keeping all the war criminals alive so as to squeeze the last bit of testimony out of them. Grandpa Yosef, in contrast, didn't need much prodding to launch into his incredible journey from ghetto to death camp, partly in the company of a high-ranking ss officer nicknamed Ahasuerus. Later there came the realization that everyone in the neighborhood had a story to tell, but could they, even in the aggregate, explain the Big Bang: in the beginning was the Shoah?

Quickening the pace of discovery was the illness and death of the informants. As the old-timers died out, so too would their rivalry over who had suffered more. Just when their stories were more or less wrapped up, moreover, a good German appeared on the scene, with a harrowing story of his own to tell. Seen from a grown-up perspective, the Holocaust was knowable, accountable, and communicable.

Katzenelson Street, Israel, stands at the farthest possible remove from the street on Long Island where Daniel Mendelsohn grew up. Our Guide ends with Mendelsohn's personal odyssey into the darkest family secrets; a search for origins that leads via Belechow in present-day Ukraine all the way back to Scripture. As the memory of the Holocaust is serious, reverential, and familial for one, it is grotesquely funny, mundane, and communal for the other. Thanks to autobiographical works of great literary merit, these two paths of Holocaust memory have been mapped to perfection. (DGR)

[**2001**]

Jan T. Gross. *Neighbors: The Destruction of the Jewish Community in Jedwabne, Poland*. Princeton: Princeton University Press, 2001. Preceding documentary version, *Sasiedzi* (Neighbors), directed by Agnieszka Arnold (Poland, 2001).

As the Second World War and the Holocaust recede into the historical past, two divergent trends reveal themselves. On the one hand, there is an increased emphasis on memorialization—the atrocity is far enough in the past to be safely revisited in the sanitized forms of public memory. On the other, there is an attempt to hold onto the past by parsing smaller and narrower areas, from the wide-angle perspective of synoptic history and the collective accounts of the *yizkor* books to the extremely specific—Lanzmann's *Shoah*, in this as in so many other ways, is a precursor. Cases in point are Zable's fragments of prewar Białystok, Mendelsohn's family of six lost, and Jan Gross's *Neighbors*. Gross painstakingly studies the destruction of the Jewish population of one small Polish town, half of whose prewar population of 3,000 were Jews. By the end of the war, there are only twelve Jewish survivors, seven of whom were saved by one family.

The numbers of mass destruction are numbing—one and a half million children dead; six million Jews murdered; twenty million Russian civilians and soldiers killed. In comparison, the numbers in Gross's village are infinitesimal. Yet his account is more shocking than the images to which we are now inured—the mounds of cadavers; pyramids of shoes; heaps of clothes, luggage, and books. In Gross's account, each person is a name, reinforced by the black and white photographs at the end of the book. And the names are assigned not just to the victims—as in, say, Daniel Mendelsohn's study of his own family—but also to the perpetrators. Furthermore, the perpetrators have a postwar existence. Some are brought to trial and complain about the unfairness of the accusations. Others are not, and they and their descendants live on in Jedwabne. This last is the most disturbing part of the book. For Gross is asking us to try to imagine a world in which intimate strangers deal out death, and then return to live in the area after the war as if their actions never happened. Toward the end of the book, Gross remarks that in any Polish village, everyone, even today's children, know where the Jews are buried. Yet the general view today is that Poles were as much victims as Jews, that the Polish killers were limited to the riffraff, and that the Germans conducted the killing. Two memorials exist in the village, each misleading for different reasons. One incorrectly blames the Nazis for the murder of Jedwabne's Jews. The other commemorates victims of the Soviet NKVD. None holds the perpetrators accountable, and therefore none truly memorializes the lost community.

We are barely ten years beyond the orgy of hatred in the Balkans that led to similar massacres by people of their own neighbors. Gross shows us that there are no answers to the question of what motivates racial hatred. It is a disease borne of the constituent elements of ethnic identity, nurtured by greed, and brought to fruition by the lifting of moral restraints. At several points in Gross's narrative, village worthies are asked to intervene. None is willing to do so. Such is the irony that some of Jedwabne's Jews survive the Polish pogrom by taking refuge in the German police station. Hatred is immune to amnesia, even if collective memory tries to occlude the past.

In the context of Holocaust literature, Gross's work is important because it shows the intersection between individual, collective, and archival accounting. *Neighbors* tells the story of the events and their aftermath. It is a simple account that is anything but simple in its outcome and implications. It suggests that what has been buried are not only the corpses of the victims but also the documentation of their murder. And then it takes the final step and shows how contemporary narratives reject the historical document as well as the living and transmitted memory of communities that enacted hatred on their neighbors. (ND)

[2006]

Daniel Adam Mendelsohn. *The Lost: A Search for Six of Six Million.*
    Photographs by Matt Mendelsohn. New York: HarperCollins, 2006.

Sixty-five years after the end of the Second World War, witnesses in the first degree—survivors, perpetrators, bystanders, and all the categories in between—have only the most tenuous grasp on life. The search of their descendants for the facts related to the past can emerge only from an act of imagination. The armature of detail is too fragile for anything else. For Mendelsohn, the search for the truth about his Great Uncle Shmiel, his wife, and their daughters has to be excavated, almost literally, since he seeks and ultimately finds an underground space in which his relatives were hidden before they were betrayed.

As with so many of the books in this Guide, autobiography and bildungsroman coexist here. The author's grandfather tells him family stories that the child accepts but that in retrospect don't quite make sense. The author, now an adult, begins with some photographs, a few truncated stories from his grandfather, and scattered details from various relatives that are confusing in their internal contradictions. In what is a familiar trope in such accounts from the third generation, he comes almost too late. There are questions that were never asked, inconsistencies that could have been explained, facts that should have been revealed. The narrator speculates about relationships, about when particular individuals died, and by whose hand. In the process, he reconstructs a different understanding of his own family and how and why its dynamics operate in the way that they do. So the historian's work is also a personal quest, a story about rebuilding his relationship with his brother, reconnecting with branches of the family in Israel and beyond. Beyond that intimate framework, between six and six million, there is an enormous gap. Here, the writer affiliates himself not with communities but with culture, broadly described. Proust provides the epigraph, Homer and Virgil the connection to a richly imagined foundational past, and the Hebrew Bible the connection to the ancestral past and through that, indirect ties with the Jewish tradition that underlay the destroyed towns and villages of Jewish Eastern Europe. The book is a plethora of structuring possibilities, their very multiplicity suggesting the difficulty of connecting to the Holocaust past when two and a half generations have passed. To the classicist, a century is an insignificant length of time. But to the grandson and second cousin, it is too long. It moves family history beyond the scope of transmission.

What, then, of community? Arnold Zable's Białystok and Theo Richmond's

Konin are both vibrant and engaging centers of human endeavor. Those authors cannot engage with their own family members without the community, and indeed their work of recuperation uses the individual to get to that larger religious cultural and social whole. But for Mendelsohn, that notion of community no longer exists, and he knows it: that is why the book's subtitle is "a search for six of six million." The limits are a given.

Mendelsohn has a refined intellect and is a gifted and self-aware writer. But what makes the book so poignant is his understanding that the work of recovery with the survivor as interlocutor can go no further. (ND)

Acknowledgments

It is now my privilege and pleasure to thank those who have accompanied this book through its eight-year birthing process.

In 2004 I was commissioned by Laurie E. Fialkoff to write a thousand-word book review for *Studies in Contemporary Jewry* that—with the blessing of the volume editor, my friend and colleague, Eli Lederhendler—grew into the longest review essay in that journal's history. "What Is Holocaust Literature?" appeared in 2005, 21:157–212. The idea of expanding that review essay into a short history of Holocaust literature came from Sylvia Fuks Fried, the executive director of the Tauber Institute at Brandeis University. Sylvia has supported this project from its inception, as have her able assistants, Talia Graff and Golan Moskowitz. Phyllis D. Deutsch, editor in chief of the University Press of New England, encouraged me to unpack a cramped "communal" narrative into something more portable. Of the incomparable copy editor, Jeanne Ferris, I can only say that all writers should be so lucky.

Before the contract was signed and sealed, however, I picked up the phone to Naomi Diamant. A former student and colleague, Naomi was the only person I trusted to do all three of the following things: cover French, Italian, and American Holocaust literature; think British; and speak the truth. The idea of compiling a guide to the first hundred books was born out of our collaboration, turning a monologue into a storytelling round. The dialogue between DGR and ND in that guide is but the formal aspect of our lunches at Saigon Grill and the Do-Jo Café in Greenwich Village, where a comment from Naomi would challenge and change the direction of whatever chapter we were going over.

Other voices that echo through these pages come from the members of the Jack and Anita Hess Faculty Seminar on Literature and the Holocaust, held in January 2007 at the US Holocaust Memorial Museum. A more ideal learning environment can hardly be imagined. Sitting in the seminar room were twenty-one handpicked professionals from across the United States and Canada, and directing the seminar with me was Professor Sara R. Horowitz of York University. Her critical approaches to gender, the second generation, and the ethics of reading inform parts of this book, as do the comments and questions of other participants, notably Professors Eric Rose and Brad Prager. But that was not all. A guest participant in the seminar was Professor Monika Adamczyk-Garbowska of Marie Curie University in Lublin, who has done so much to bring Polish Holocaust writing to the attention of American readers, and she in turn brought the writer and survivor Henryk Grynberg before the group. Monika and I stayed on in Washington, I to serve as the J. B. and Maurice C. Shapiro Senior Scholar-in-Residence at the museum. This enabled us to continue conversations about Polish-Jewish relations in life and literature that had begun two decades before and were to continue—in New York, Lublin, Tel Aviv, and cyberspace. The first fruit of my tenure at the museum is this book. The other has still to be harvested.

Another set of conversations were ongoing in my second home, Jerusalem: in-depth discussions about the literature and history of the Holocaust with Havi Ben-Sasson Dreyfus, Amos Goldberg, Alan Rosen, and Shira Wolosky. Alan's support has been especially important. Tel Aviv was my third home, thanks to the hospitality and unflagging energy of Hana Wirth-Nesher.

In cyberspace—the new symposium—the following people have selflessly responded to queries large and small: Mark Baker, Bryan Cheyette, Henryk Grynberg, Jack Kugelmass, Alina Molisak, Jeffrey Shandler, Maxim Shrayer, Ilán Stavans, Miriam Udel, and Annette Wieviorka. My students Ofer Dynes and Saul Zaritt were always ready and able to search and find.

The word "colleague" hardly describes the role that five people have played in the shaping of this book. Precision, love of language, and the refusal to suffer nonsense are the triple attributes of Hillel Schwartz, who critiqued and line edited the entire manuscript as only he can. Samuel Kassow, Avrom Novershtern, and my sister Ruth Wisse set the gold standard by their very presence, as did Alan Mintz, my next-door neighbor at the Jewish Theological Seminary, through his writing, teaching, and discreet prodding, over many years.

I owe a special debt of thanks to my soul mate, Shana. The first thirty years of our life together has been bracketed by big books on the theme of Jewish catastrophe. May the next thirty be bracketed by something else.

This book was made possible in part by funds granted to the author through the J. B. and Maurice C. Shapiro Senior Scholar-in-Residence Fellowship at the Center for Advanced Holocaust Studies, US Holocaust Memorial Museum. The statements made and views expressed, however, are solely the responsibility of the author.

DAVID G. ROSKIES
New York City
February 1, 2012

Works Cited

Adamczyk-Garbowska, Monika. 1999. "The Return of the Troublesome Bird: Jerzy Kosinski and Polish-Jewish Relations." Polin 12:284–94.

———. 2009. "'Smutno mi Boże . . .' Pożegnania z Polskš w literaturze jidysz." In Honor—Bóg—Ojczyzna, edited by Monika Rudace-Grodzka and Dorota Krawczyńska, 205–11. Warsaw: Fundacja Odnawiania Znaczeę/Dom Spotkaę z Historiš.

——— and Henryk Duda. 2003. "Terminy 'Holocaust,' 'Zagłada' i 'Szoa' oraz ich konotacje leksykalno-kulturowe w polszczyznie potocznej i dyskursie aukowym." In Żydzi i judaizm we współczesnych badaniach polskich, edited by Krzysztof Pilarczyk, 3:237–53. Kraków: PAU/PSTŻ.

Adelson, Alan, and Robert Lapides, eds. 1989. Lodz Ghetto: Inside a Community under Siege. New York: Viking.

Adler, Stanisław. 1982. In the Warsaw Ghetto 1949–1943: An Account of a Witness. Translated by Sara Chmielewska Philip. Jerusalem: Yad Vashem.

Agnon, S. Y. 1971. "The Lady and the Peddler." Translated by Robert Alter. In Modern Hebrew Literature, edited by Robert Alter, 201–12. New York: Behrman House.

———. 1973. 'Ir umlo'ah. Jerusalem: Schocken.

———. 1989. "The Sign." Translated by Arthur Green. In The Literature of Destruction: Jewish Responses to Catastrophe, edited by David G. Roskies, 585–604. Philadelphia: Jewish Publication Society of America.

Alter, Robert. 1981. Introduction to Dan Pagis, Points of Departure, translated by Stephen Mitchell, xi–xv. Philadelphia: Jewish Publication Society of America.

Alterman, Natan. 1954. "Yom hazikaron vehamordim." Davar, April 30, 4.

———. 1961. "Klaster-hapanim." In Natan Alterman, Hatur hashvi'i, 2:522–26. Tel Aviv: Hakibbutz Hameuchad, 1975.

Améry, Jean. 1980. At the Mind's Limits: Contemplations by a Survivor on Auschwitz and Its Realities. Preface to the 1966 and 1977 editions by the author. Foreword by Alexander Stille. Afterword by Sydney Rosenfeld. Translated by Sidney Rosenfeld and Stella P. Rosenfeld. Bloomington: Indiana University Press.

———. 1999. On Suicide: A Discourse on Voluntary Death. Translated by John D. Barlow. Bloomington: Indiana University Press.

Amichai, Yehuda. 1968. Not of This Time, Not of This Place. Translated by Shlomo Katz. New York: Harper and Row.

Anatoli, A. [Anatolii Kuznetsov]. 1970. Babi Yar: A Document in the Form of a Novel. New, complete, uncensored version. Translated by David Floyd. New York: Farrar, Straus and Giroux.

Antelme, Robert. 1992. The Human Race. Homage to Robert Antelme by Edgar Morin. Translated by Jeffrey Haight and Annie Mahler. Marlboro, VT: Marlboro.

Appelfeld, Aharon. 1980. Badenheim 1939. Translated by Dalya Bilu. Boston: Godine.

———. 1983. Introduction to Leyb Rochman, *The Pit and the Trap: A Chronicle of Survival*, 7–9, translated by Moshe Kohn and Sheila Friedling. New York: Holocaust Library.

———. 1994. "Conversation with Philip Roth." In Aharon Appelfeld, *Beyond Despair: Three Lectures and a Conversation with Philip Roth*, translated by Jeffrey M. Green, 57–80. New York: Fromm International.

———. 1999. "Bertha." Translated by Tirza Zandbank. In *When Night Fell: An Anthology of Holocaust Short Stories*, edited by Linda Schermer Raphael and Marc Lee Raphael, 18–28. New Brunswick, NJ: Rutgers University Press.

Appenszlak, Jakub, ed. 1945. *Z otchłani: Poezja ghetto i podziemia w Polsce*. 2nd ed. New York: Association of Friends of "Our Tribune."

Arendt, Hannah. 1963. *Eichmann in Jerusalem: A Report on the Banality of Evil*. New York: Viking.

———. 2007. "We Refugees." In Hannah Arendt, *The Jewish Writings*, edited by Jerome Kohn and Ron H. Feldman, 264–74. New York: Schocken.

Auerbach, Rachel. 1954. *Behutsot Varsha: 1939–1943*. Tel Aviv: Am Oved.

———. 1989. "Yizkor, 1943." Translated by Leonard Wolf. In *The Literature of Destruction: Jewish Responses to Catastrophe*, edited by David G. Roskies, 459–64. Philadelphia: Jewish Publication Society of America.

Baker, Zachary M., editorial advisor. 1990. *Jewish Displaced Persons Periodicals from the Collections of the YIVO Institute*. Microform. Bethesda, MD: University Publications of America.

Barrett, William. 1952. "To Save Their Own." Review of *The Skin*, by Curzio Malaparte. *New York Times*, September 21.

Bartov, Hanoch. 1968. *The Brigade*. Translated by David S. Segal. New York: Holt, Rinehart and Winston.

Bartov, Omer. 1997. "Kitsch and Sadism in Ka-Tzetnik's Other Planet: Israeli Youth Imagining the Holocaust." *Jewish Social Studies* 3:42–76.

Bassani, Giorgio. 1965. *The Garden of the Finzi Continis*. Translated by Isabel Quigly. New York: Atheneum.

Bauer, Yehuda. 1970. *Flight and Rescue: Brichah*. New York: Random House.

Baumel, Judith Tydor. 2005. *The "Bergson Boys" and the Origins of Contemporary Zionist Militancy*. Foreword by Moshe Arens. Translated by Dena Ordan. Syracuse, NY: Syracuse University Press.

Baumel-Schwartz, Judith Tydor. 2010. *Perfect Heroes: The World War II Parachutists and the Making of Israeli Collective Memory*. Madison: University of Wisconsin Press.

Becker, Jurek. 1997. *Jacob the Liar*. Translated by Leila Vennewitz. New York: Plume.

Beevor, Antony, and Luba Vinogradova, eds. 2005. *A Writer at War: Vasily Grossman with the Red Army*. New York: Pantheon.

Begley, Louis. 1991. *Wartime Lies*. New York: Knopf.

Belis, Shloyme. 1964. *Portretn un problemen*. Warsaw: Yidish bukh.

Bell, Lenore. 1996. *LC Holocaust Headings Survey: Analysis of Results*. Washington: Library of Congress, June 12.

Bellow, Saul. 1970. *Mr. Sammler's Planet*. New York: Viking.

Berakhot. The Babylonian Talmud. 1989. 61b. Translated by Maurice Simon. In *The

Literature of Destruction: Jewish Responses to Catastrophe, edited by David G. Roskies, 48. Philadelphia: Jewish Publication Society of America.

Berenbaum, Michael. 2009. "When the Last Survivor Is Gone." *Forward*, April 24.

Berg, Mary. 1945. *Warsaw Ghetto: A Diary*. Edited by S. L. Shneiderman. Translated by Norbert Gutterman. New York: L. B. Fischer.

Bern, Alan. 2004. *Who Is Weiskopf? Joshua Sobol's "Ghetto" on East & West German Stages*. Bloomington: Robert A. and Sandra S. Borns Jewish Studies Program, Indiana University.

Bettelheim, Bruno. 1960. "Individual and Mass Behavior in Extreme Situations." In Bruno Bettelheim, *The Informed Heart: Autonomy in a Mass Age*, 48–83. Glencoe, IL: Free Press.

Bialik, Hayyim Nahman. 1989. "In the City of Slaughter." Translated by A. M. Klein. In *The Literature of Destruction: Jewish Responses to Catastrophe*, edited by David G. Roskies, 160–68. Philadelphia: Jewish Publication Society of America.

Biermann, Wolf. 1999. "Epilogue: A Bridge between Władysław Szpilman and Wilm Hosenfeld." In Władysław Szpilman, *The Pianist: The Extraordinary Story of One Man's Survival in Warsaw, 1939–45*, translated by Anthea Bell, 209–22. New York: Picador.

Blumental, Nachman. 1981. *Verter un vertlekh fun der khurbn-tkufe*. Tel Aviv: Y. L. Perets.

Boder, David P. 1948. *I Did Not Interview the Dead*. Urbana: University of Illinois Press.

Borges, Jorge Luis. 1964. "Kafka and His Precursors." In Jorge Luis Borges, *Other Inquisitions, 1937–1952*, introduction by James E. Irby, translated by Ruth L. C. Simms, 106–8. Austin: University of Texas Press.

———. 1998. "The Secret Miracle." Translated by Andrew Hurley. In Jorge Luis Borges, *Collected Fictions*, 157–62. New York: Viking.

Borowski, Tadeusz. 1976. *This Way for the Gas, Ladies and Gentlemen*. Introduction by Jan Kott. Translated by Barbara Vedder. Harmondsworth, England: Penguin.

———. 2000. "Preface." In Janusz Nel Siedlecki, Krystyn Olszewski, and Tadeusz Borowski, *We Were in Auschwitz*, 3–4. [Edited by Tadeusz Borowski.] Translated by Alicia Nitecki. New York: Welcome Rain.

———. 2005. "Rozmowy: Dla towarzyszy Jerzego Andrzejewskiego i Wiktora Woroszylskiego." In Tadeusz Borowski, *Krytyka*, edited by Tadeusz Drewnowski, 246–65. Kraków, Wydawnictwo Literackie.

Borwicz, Michał M, ed. 1947. *"Pieśę ujdzie cało . . ."* Warsaw: Centralna Żydowska Komisja Historyczna.

———. 1954–55. *Arishe papirn*. 3 vols. Buenos Aires: Tsentral-farband fun poylishe yidn in Argentine.

———. 1955. "Der apokrif u.n. 'Yosl Rakover redt tsu got.'" *Almanakh* (Paris): 193–203.

———. 1973. *Écrits des condamnés à mort sous l'occupation nazie, 1939–1945*. Preface by René Cassin. 2nd ed. Paris: Gallimard.

Bower, Kathrin M. 2003. "Nelly Sachs." In *Holocaust Literature: An Encyclopedia of Writers and Their Work*, edited by S. Lillian Kremer 2:1067–74. New York: Routledge.

Celan, Paul. 2001. *Selected Poems and Prose of Paul Celan*. Translated by John Felstiner. New York: W. W. Norton.

———. 2002. *Poems of Paul Celan*. Translated by Michael Hamburger. Rev. and expanded ed. New York: Persea.

Chabon, Michael. 2000. *The Amazing Adventures of Kavalier & Clay: A Novel*. New York: Random House.

Cheyette, Bryan. 2007. "Appropriating Primo Levi." In *The Cambridge Companion to Primo Levi*, edited by Robert S. C. Gordon, 67–85. Cambridge: Cambridge University Press.

Cohen, Boaz. 2003. "Holocaust Heroics: Ghetto Fighters and Partisans in Israeli Society and Historiography." *Journal of Political and Military Sociology* 31:197–213.

———. 2010. "Representing the Experience of Children in the Holocaust Children's Survivor Testimonies Published in *Fun Letsten Hurbn*, Munich 1946–49." In *"We Are Here": New Approaches to Displaced Persons in Postwar Germany*, edited by Avinoam J. Patt and Michael Berkowitz, 74–97. Detroit: Wayne State University Press.

Cohen, Nathan. 1994. "Diaries of the Sonderkommando." In *Anatomy of the Auschwitz Death Camp*, edited by Yisrael Gutman and Michael Berenbaum, 522–34. Bloomington: Indiana University Press.

Consonni, Manuela. 2010. *Rezistentsa o shoah: zikaron hagreush vehahashmada be'Italia 1945-1985*. Edited by Ilana Shamir. Jerusalem: Magnes.

Davidson Draenger, Gusta. 1976. "From Justina's Diary: Resistance in Cracow." Translated by Ted Hudes and Mark Nowogrodzki. In *A Holocaust Reader*, edited by Lucy S. Dawidowicz, 340–47. New York: Behrman House.

———. 1996. *Justyna's Narrative*. Edited with an introduction by Eli Pfefferkorn and David H. Hirsch. Translated by Roslyn Hirsch and David H. Hirsch. Amherst: University of Massachusetts Press.

Davison, Neil R. 2004. "André Schwarz-Bart." In *Holocaust Novelists*, edited by Efraim Sicher, 297–303. Detroit: Gale.

Dawidowicz, Lucy S. 1975. *The War against the Jews, 1933–1945*. New York: Holt, Rinehart and Winston.

———, ed. 1976. *A Holocaust Reader*. New York: Behrman House.

Delbo, Charlotte. 1995. *Auschwitz and After*. Introduction by Lawrence L. Langer. Translated by Rosette C. Lamont. New Haven: Yale University Press.

Der Nister. 2011. *Regrowth: Seven Tales of Jewish Life before, during, and after Nazi Occupation*. Translated with an afterword by Erik Butler. Evanston, IL: Northwestern University Press.

Des Pres, Terrence. 1976. *The Survivor: An Anatomy of Life in the Death Camps*. New York: Oxford University Press.

Dobroszycki, Lucjan, ed. 1984. *The Chronicle of the Łódź Ghetto 1941–1944*. Translated by Richard Lourie, Joachim Neugroschel, et al. New Haven: Yale University Press.

Draenger, Shimshon. 2006. *Hechalutz Halochem: bit'on hano'ar hayehudi haḥalutsi bemaḥteret Krakov, ogust-oktober 1943*. Edited by Michal Uffenheimer and Tsvi Oren. Translated by Tsvi Arad. 2nd rev. ed. Tel Aviv: Beit Loḥamei Hageta'ot.

Drewnowski, Tadeusz, ed. 2007. *Postal Indiscretions: The Correspondence of Tadeusz Borowski*. Translated by Alicia Nitecki. Evanston, IL: Northwestern University Press.

Ehrenburg, Ilya. 2007. "Babi Yar." In *An Anthology of Jewish-Russian Literature: Two Centuries of Dual Identity in Prose and Poetry*, edited by Maxim D. Shrayer, 1:530–31. Armonk, NY: M. E. Sharpe.

———— and Vasily Grossman, eds. 2002. *The Complete Black Book of Russian Jewry*. Translated and edited by David Patterson. New Brunswick, NJ: Transaction.

Eliav, Mordecai, ed. 1965. *Ani ma'amin: Eiduyot 'al ḥayeihem umotam shel anshei emunah biymei hasho'ah*. Jerusalem: Mosad Harav Kook.

Engel, David. 1999. "'Will They Dare?': Perceptions of Threat in Diaries from the Warsaw Ghetto." In *Holocaust Chronicles: Individualizing the Holocaust through Diaries and Other Contemporaneous Personal Accounts*, introduction by Ruth R. Wisse and edited by Robert Moses Shapiro, 71–82. Hoboken, NJ: Ktav.

Engelking, Barbara. 2009. "Culture and Entertainment." In *The Warsaw Ghetto: A Guide to the Vanished City*, edited by Barbara Engelking and Jacek Leociak, translated by Emma Harris, 530–640. New Haven: Yale University Press.

———— and Jacek Leociak, eds. 2009. *The Warsaw Ghetto: A Guide to the Vanished City*. Translated by Emma Harris. New Haven: Yale University Press.

Epstein, Helen. 1979. *Children of the Holocaust: Conversations with Sons and Daughters of Survivors*. New York: Putnam.

Epstein, Leslie. 1979. *King of the Jews*. New York: Coward, McCann and Geoghegan.

Ezrahi, Sidra DeKoven. 1980. *By Words Alone: The Holocaust in Literature*. Foreword by Alfred Kazin. Chicago: University of Chicago Press.

————. 1994. "Conversations in the Cemetery: Dan Pagis and the Prosaics of Memory." In *Holocaust Remembrance: The Shapes of Memory*, edited by Geoffrey H. Hartman, 121–33. Oxford: Blackwell.

————. 2003. "Representing Auschwitz." In *The Holocaust: Theoretical Writings*, edited by Neil Levi and Michael Rothberg, 318–22. New Brunswick, NJ: Rutgers University Press.

Feffer, Itzik. 1964. "Ikh bin a yid!" In *A shpigl oyf a shteyn: antologye poezye un proze fun tsvelf farshnitene yidishe shraybers in Ratn-farband*, edited by Khone Shmeruk, 694–97. Tel Aviv: Di goldene keyt and Y. L. Perets.

Feldman, Jackie. 2001. "In the Footsteps of the Israeli Holocaust Survivor: Israeli Youth Pilgrimages to Poland, Shoah Memory and National Identity." In *Building History: The Shoah in Art, Memory, and Myth*, edited by P. Daly, K. Filser, C. Goldschlager, and N. Kramer, 4:36–63. New York: Peter Lang.

Fink, Ida. 1987. *A Scrap of Time and Other Stories*. Translated by Madeline Levine and Francine Prose. New York: Pantheon.

Flanzbaum, Hilene A. 2003. "Gerald Green." In *Holocaust Literature: An Encyclopedia of Writers and their Work*, edited by S. Lillian Kremer, 1:468–70. New York: Routledge.

Feldstein, Zemach. 1997. "'Tsum moment': Dr. Tsemakh Feldtshyens editoryaln in vilner geto 1942–1943." Edited by David G. Roskies. *YIVO-bleter*, n.s., 3:114–205.

Felstiner, John. 1995. *Paul Celan: Poet, Survivor, Jew*. New Haven: Yale University Press.

Fenster, Hersh, ed. 1951. *Undzere farpaynikte kinstler*. Foreword by Marc Chagall. Paris: H. Fenster.

Feuchtwanger, Lion. 1944. "The Working Problems of the Writer in Exile." In *Writers' Congress: The Proceedings of the Conference Held in October 1943 under the Sponsorship of the Hollywood Writers' Mobilization and the University of California*, 345–49. Berkeley: University of California Press.

Fink, Ida. 1987. *A Scrap of Time and Other Stories*. Translated by Madeline Levine and Francine Prose. New York: Pantheon.

Flam, Gila. 1992. *Singing for Survival: Songs of the Lodz Ghetto, 1940–45*. Urbana: University of Illinois Press.

Flinker, Moshe. 1965. *Young Moshe's Diary: The Spiritual Torment of a Jewish Boy in Nazi Europe*. Introductions by Shaul Esh and Geoffrey Wigoder. Jerusalem: Yad Vashem.

Fogelman, Eva, and Bella Savran. 1979. "Therapeutic Groups for Children of Holocaust Survivors." *International Journal of Group Psychotherapy* 29, no. 2: 211–35.

Frank, Anne. 1952. *The Diary of a Young Girl*. Introduction by Eleanor Roosevelt. Translated by B. M. Mooyaart-Doubleday. Garden City, NY: Doubleday.

———. 1995. *The Diary of a Young Girl*. Definitive ed. Edited by Otto H. Frank and Mirjam Pressler. Translated by Susan Massotty. New York: Doubleday.

Franklin, Ruth. 2011. *A Thousand Darknesses: Lies and Truth in Holocaust Fiction*. Oxford: Oxford University Press.

Friedlander, Albert H., ed. 1968. *Out of the Whirlwind: A Reader of Holocaust Literature*. New York: Union of American Hebrew Congregations.

Friedlander, Saul. 1992. "Afterword: The *Shoah* between Memory and History." In *Breaking Crystal: Writing and Memory after Auschwitz*, edited by Efraim Sicher, 345–57. Urbana: University of Illinois Press.

Fuks, Ladislav. 1968. *Mr. Theodore Mundstock*. Translated by Iris Urwin. New York: Orion.

Garbarini, Alexandra. 2006. *Numbered Days: Diaries and the Holocaust*. New Haven: Yale University Press.

Garrard, John Gordon, and Carol Garrard. 1996. *The Bones of Berdichev: The Life and Fate of Vasily Grossman*. New York: Free Press.

Gary, Romain. 1968. *The Dance of Genghis Cohn*. Translated by Romain Gary with the assistance of Camilla Sykes. New York: World.

Gebirtig, Mordecai. 1989. "Fire!" Translated by David G. Roskies. In *The Literature of Destruction: Jewish Responses to Catastrophe*, edited by David G. Roskies, 371–73. Philadelphia: Jewish Publication Society of America.

Gillon, Adam. 1965. "'Here Too as in Jerusalem': Selected Poems of the Ghetto." *Polish Review* 10, no. 3: 22–45.

Gilman, Sander L. 1986. *Jewish Self-Hatred: Anti-Semitism and the Hidden Language of the Jews*. Baltimore: Johns Hopkins University Press.

Girs, Anatol. 2000. "Note from the Publisher." In Janusz Nel Sieldecki, Krystyn Olszewski, and Tadeusz Borowski, *We Were in Auschwitz*, 1–2. Edited by Tadeusz Borowski. Translated by Alicia Nitecki. New York: Welcome Rain.

Glatstein, Jacob. 1943. *Gedenklider*. New York: Yidisher kemfer.

———. 1946. *Shtralndike yidn*. New York: Matones.

———. 1987a. "Good Night, World." Translated by Richard Fein. In *Selected Poems of Yankev Glatshteyn*, edited by Richard J. Fein, 101–3. Philadelphia: Jewish Publication Society of America.

———. 1987b. *Selected Poems of Yankev Glatshteyn*. Translated and edited, with an introduction, by Richard J. Fein. Philadelphia: Jewish Publication Society of America.

———. 1987c. "I Have Never Been Here Before." Translated by Richard Fein. In *Selected Poems of Yankev Glatshteyn*, edited by Richard J. Fein, 111–13. Philadelphia: Jewish Publication Society of America.

————. 1993. *I Keep Recalling: The Holocaust Poems of Jacob Glatstein*. Introduction by Emanuel S. Goldsmith. Translated by Barnett Zumoff. Hoboken, NJ: Ktav.

————. 2006. *Emil and Karl*. Translated with a foreword and afterword by Jeffrey Shandler. New Milford, CT: Roaring Brook.

————. 2010. *The Glatstein Chronicles*. Edited by Ruth R. Wisse. Translated by Norbert Guterman and Meier Deschell. New Haven: Yale University Press.

Głowiński, Michał. 2005. *The Black Seasons*. Foreword by Jan T. Gross. Translated with preface and notes by Marci Shore. Evanston, IL: Northwestern University Press.

Gold, Nili Sharf. 2008. *Yehuda Amichai: The Making of Israel's National Poet*. Waltham, MA: Brandeis University Press.

Goldberg, Amos. 2005. "If This Is a Man: The Image of Man in Autobiographical and Historical Writing during and after the Holocaust." *Yad Vashem Studies* 33:381–429.

————. 2009. "The Victim's Voice and Melodramatic Aesthetics in History." *History and Theory* 48:219–36.

Goldberg, Leah. 1996. "Lady of the Castle." Translated by T. Carmi. In *Israeli Holocaust Drama*, edited by Michael Taub, 21–78. Syracuse, NY: Syracuse University Press.

Goldin, Leyb. 1989. "Chronicle of a Single Day." Translated by Elinor Robinson. In *The Literature of Destruction: Jewish Responses to Catastrophe*, edited by David G. Roskies, 424–34. Philadelphia: Jewish Publication Society of America.

Goldstein, Judith. 2003. "Anne Frank: The Redemptive Myth." *Partisan Review*, January 1. Accessed January 17, 2012; http://www.bu.edu/partisanreview/archive/2003/1/index.html.

Gorny, Yosef. 2012. *The Jewish Press and the Holocaust, 1939–1945: Palestine, Britain, the United States, and the Soviet Union*. Translated by Naftali Greenwood. Cambridge: Cambridge University Press.

Gordon, Robert S. C. 1999. "Primo Levi's *If This Is a Man* and Responses to the *Lager* in Italy 1945–47." *Judaism* 48, no. 1: 49–57.

Gouri, Haim. 2004. *Facing the Glass Booth: The Jerusalem Trial of Adolf Eichmann*. Foreword by Alan Mintz. Translated by Michael Swirsky. Detroit: Wayne State University Press.

Grade, Chaim. 1999. "My Quarrel with Hersh Rasseyner." Translated by Milton Himmelfarb. In *When Night Fell: An Anthology of Holocaust Short Stories*, edited by Linda Schermer Raphael and Marc Lee Raphael, 161–84. New Brunswick, NJ: Rutgers University Press.

Gradowski, Zalmen. 1977. "Fartseykhenungen." In *Megeles Oysvits*, edited by Ber Mark, 288–346. Tel-Aviv: Yisroel-bukh.

————. 1985. "Writings." In *The Scrolls of Auschwitz*, edited by Ber Mark, 173–205. Translated by Sharon Neemani. Adapted from the original Yiddish text. Tel Aviv: Am Oved.

————. 1989. "The Czech Transport: A Chronicle of the Auschwitz *Sonderkommando*." Translated by Robert Wolf. In *The Literature of Destruction: Jewish Responses to Catastrophe*, edited by David G. Roskies, 548–64. Philadelphia: Jewish Publication Society of America.

Green, Gerald. 1969. *The Artists of Terezin*. New York: Hawthorn.

Greenberg, Uri Zvi. 1951. *Reḥovot hanahar: sefer ha'iliyot vehakoaḥ*. Jerusalem: Schocken.

————. 1989. "To God in Europe." Translated by Robert Friend. In *The Literature of*

Destruction: Jewish Responses to Catastrophe, edited by David G. Roskies, 571–77. Philadelphia: Jewish Publication Society of America.

Greenstein, Edward L. 2008. "The Book of Lamentations: Response to Destruction or Ritual of Rebuilding?" In *Religious Responses to Political Crisis*, edited by Henning Graf Reventlow and Yair Hoffman, 52–71. New York: T. and T. Clark.

Gris, Noah, ed. 1947. *Kinder-martirologye: zamlung fun dokumentn*. Buenos Aires: Tsentral-farband fun poylishe yidn in Argentine.

Gross, Jan T. 2001. *Neighbors: The Destruction of the Jewish Community in Jedwabne, Poland*. Princeton: Princeton University Press.

Grossman, David. 1989. *See Under: Love*. Translated by Betsy Rosenberg. New York: Washington Square.

———. 2010. "The Art of Fiction." Interviewed by Jonathan Shainin. *Paris Review*, Fall. Accessed January 17, 2012; http://www.theparisreview.org/interviews/5794/the-art-of-fiction-no-194-david-grossman.

Grossman, Mendel. 1972. *With a Camera in the Ghetto*. Edited by Zvi Szner and Alexander Sened. Translated by Mendel Kohansky. Israel: Ghetto Fighters' House.

Grossman, Vasily. 1985. *Life and Fate: A Novel*. Translated with an introduction by Robert Chandler. New York: Harper and Row.

———. 2002a. "The Murder of the Jews of Berdichev." In *The Complete Black Book of Russian Jewry*, edited by Ilya Ehrenburg and Vasily Grossman, 12–20. Translated and edited by David Patterson. New Brunswick, NJ: Transaction.

———. 2002b. "The Hell of Treblinka." In *The Complete Black Book of Russian Jewry*, edited by Ilya Ehrenburg and Vasily Grossman, 462–83. Translated and edited by David Patterson. New Brunswick, NJ: Transaction.

Grynberg, Henryk. 2001. *The Jewish War and the Victory*. With an author's note. Afterword by Richard Lourie. Translated by Celina Wieniewska and Richard Lourie. Evanston, IL: Northwestern University Press.

———. 2002. *Drohobycz, Drohobycz and Other Stories: True Tales from the Holocaust and Life After*. Edited by Theodosia Robertson. Translated by Alicia Nitecki. New York: Penguin.

———. 2004. *The Holocaust as a Literary Experience*. Washington: US Holocaust Memorial Museum.

Gutfreund, Amir. 2006. *Our Holocaust*. Translated by Jessica Cohen. New Milford, CT: Toby.

Habas, Bracha, ed. 1943. *Mikhtavim min hageta'ot*. Tel Aviv: Am Oved.

Halbwachs, Maurice. 1992. *On Collective Memory*. Edited, translated, and with an introduction by Lewis A. Coser. Chicago: University of Chicago Press.

Harshav, Benjamin. 2002. "Introduction: Herman Kruk's Holocaust Writings." In Herman Kruk, *The Last Days of the Jerusalem of Lithuania: Chronicles from the Vilna Ghetto and the Camps, 1939–1944*, edited by Benjamin Harshav and translated by Barbara Harshav, xxi–lii. New Haven: Yale University Press.

———. 2004. *Marc Chagall and His Times: A Documentary Narrative*. Stanford: Stanford University Press.

——— and Barbara Harshav, eds. 1986. *American Yiddish Poetry: A Bilingual Anthology*. Berkeley: University of California Press.

Hecht, Anthony. 1967. *The Hard Hours: Poems*. New York: Atheneum.

Hecht, Ben. 1943. "We Will Never Die: A Memorial Dedicated to the 2,000,000 Jewish Dead of Europe." *Liberal Judaism*, June, 39–63.

Herman, Ora. 2004. "Shidurim miplaneta aḥeret: mishpat Eichmann, hamimshal, ukhlei hatikshoret ha'elektronit." MA thesis, Hebrew University.

Hersey, John. 1950. *The Wall*. New York: Knopf.

Hever, Hanan. 1999. *Sifrut shenikhtevet mikan: kitsur hasifrut hayisre'elit*. Tel Aviv: Yediot Aharonot.

Hillesum, Etty. 1983. *An Interrupted Life: The Diaries of Etty Hillesum, 1941–1943*. Introduction by J. G. Gaarlandt. Translated by Arno Pomerans. New York: Pantheon.

———. 1986. *Letters from Westerbork*. Introduction and notes by Jan G. Gaarlandt. Translated by Arnold J. Pomerans. New York: Pantheon.

Hilsenrath, Edgar. 1966. *Night: A Novel*. Translated by Michael Roloff. Garden City, NY: Doubleday.

Hoberman, J. 1991. *Bridge of Light: Yiddish Film between Two Worlds*. New York: Museum of Modern Art.

Hochhuth, Rolf. 1964. *The Deputy*. Preface by Albert Schweitzer. Translated by Richard Winston and Clara Winston. New York: Grove.

Hofstadter, Dan. 2005. "Afterword." In Curzio Malaparte, *Kaputt*, translated by Cesare Foligno, 431–37. New York: New York Review of Books.

Horowitz, Sara R. 1994. "Voices from the Killing Ground." In *Holocaust Remembrance: The Shapes of Memory*, edited by Geoffrey H. Hartman, 42–58. Oxford: Blackwell.

———. 1997. "But Is It Good for the Jews? Spielberg's Schindler and the Aesthetics of Atrocity." In *Spielberg's Holocaust: Critical Perspectives on Schindler's List*, edited by Yosefa Loshitzky, 119–39. Bloomington: Indiana University Press.

Huberband, Shimon. 1969. *Kiddush hashem: ketavim miyemei hasho'ah*. Edited by. Nachman Blumental. Tel Aviv: Zakhor.

———. 1987. *Kiddush Hashem: Jewish Religious and Cultural Life in Poland during the Holocaust*. Edited by Jeffrey S. Gurock and Robert Hirt. Translated by David E. Fishman. Hoboken, NJ: Ktav.

Isacovici, Salomon, and Juan Manuel Rodríguez. 1999. *Man of Ashes*. Translated by Dick Gerdes. Lincoln: University of Nebraska Press.

Jockusch, Laura. 2010. "A Folk Monument to Our Destruction and Heroism: Jewish Historical Commissions in the Displaced Persons Camps of Germany, Austria and Italy." In *"We Are Here": New Approaches to Displaced Persons in Postwar Germany*, edited by Avinoam J. Patt and Michael Berkowitz, 31–73. Detroit: Wayne State University Press.

Kaczerginski, Shmerke. 1948. *Lider fun di getos un lagern*. Edited by H. Leivick. New York: CYCO.

Kalmanovitsh, Zelig. 1989. "Three Sermons." Translated by Shlomo Noble. In *The Literature of Destruction: Jewish Responses to Catastrophe*, edited by David G. Roskies, 509–13. Philadelphia: Jewish Publication Society of America.

Kaniuk, Yoram. 1971. *Adam Resurrected*. Translated by Seymour Simckes. New York: Atheneum.

Kantor, Alfred. 1971. *The Book of Alfred Kantor: Terezin-Auschwitz-Schwarzheide, December 1941–May 1945*. Preface by John Wykert. New York: McGraw-Hill.

Kaplan, Chaim A. 1973. *Scroll of Agony: The Warsaw Diary of Chaim A. Kaplan*. Edited and translated by Abraham I. Katsh. 2nd rev. ed. New York: Colliers.

Kassow, Samuel D. 1999. "Vilna and Warsaw, Two Ghetto Diaries: Herman Kruk and Emanuel Ringelblum." In *Holocaust Chronicles: Individualizing the Holocaust through Diaries and Other Contemporaneous Personal Accounts*, introduction by Ruth R. Wisse and edited by Robert Moses Shapiro, 171–215. Hoboken, NJ: Ktav.

———. 2007. *Who Will Write Our History? Emanuel Ringelblum, the Warsaw Ghetto, and the Oyneg Shabes Archive*. Bloomington: Indiana University Press.

Katz, Steven T., ed. 2007. *Wrestling with God: Jewish Theological Responses during and after the Holocaust*. Shlomo Biderman and Gershon Greenberg, associate editors. Oxford: Oxford University Press.

Katzenelson, Yitzhak. 1958. "Letter to Berl Katznelson and Yitzhak Tabenkin." In *Extermination and Resistance: Historical Records and Source Material*, edited by Zvi Szner, and translated by I. M. Lask, 27. Israel: Ghetto Fighters' House.

———. 1964. *Vittel Diary [22.5.43–16.9.43]*. Translated by Myer Cohen. Israel: Ghetto Fighters' House.

———. 1980. *The Song of the Murdered Jewish People*. Translated by Noah H. Rosenbloom. Bilingual edition. Israel: Ghetto Fighters' House.

———. 1984. *Yidishe geto-ksovim Varshe 1940–1943*. Edited by Yechiel Szeintuch. Tel Aviv: Beit Lohamei Hageta'ot and Hakibbutz Hameuchad.

———. 1988. *Ktavim aharonim: begeto Varsha uvemahane Vitel*. Vol. 5, *Ktavim*. Edited by Menahem Dorman. Tel Aviv: Beit Lohamei Hageta'ot and Hakibbutz Hameuchad.

Ka-Tzetnik 135633. 1955. *House of Dolls*. Translated by Moshe Kohn. New York: Simon and Schuster.

Kazdan, Chaim S., ed. 1954. *Lerer-yizker-bukh: di umgekumene lerer fun Tsisho shuln in Poyln*. New York: Komitet tsu fareybikn dem ondenk fun di umgekumene lerer fun di Tsisho shuln in Poyln.

Kdoyshim: lider fun farpaynikte. 1947. Melodies by Henech Kon and paintings by Isaac Lichtensten. New York: Machmadim Art Editions.

Keilson, Hans. 2010. *Comedy in a Minor Key*. Translated by Damion Searls. New York: Farrar, Straus and Giroux.

Kermish, Joseph, ed. 1986. *To Live with Honor and Die with Honor: Selected Documents from the Warsaw Ghetto Underground Archives "O.S." (Oneg Shabbath)*. Jerusalem: Yad Vashem.

——— and Yisrael Bialostocki, eds. 1979. *'Itonut-hamahteret hayehudit beVarsha*. Vols. 1–2. Jerusalem: Yad Vashem.

Kertész, Imre. 2004. *Fatelessness*. Translated by Tim Wilkinson. New York: Vintage International.

Kiš, Danilo. 1997. *Hourglass*. Translated by Ralph Manheim. Evanston, IL: Northwestern University Press.

Kligsberg, Moshe. 1974. "Di yidishe yugnt-bavegung in Poyln tsvishn beyde velt-milkhomes (a sotsyologishe shtudye)." In *Studies on Polish Jewry 1919–1939*, edited by Joshua A. Fishman, 137–228. New York: YIVO.

Klingenstein, Susanne. 2004. "Edgar Hilsenrath." In *Holocaust Novelists*, edited by Efraim Sicher, 138–44. Detroit: Gale.

Koestler, Arthur. 1945. "On Disbelieving Atrocities." In Arthur Koestler, *The Yogi and the Commissar and Other Essays*, 88–92. New York: Macmillan.

———. 1969. *Arrival and Departure*. London: Penguin.

Kofman, Sarah. 1996. *Rue Ordener, Rue Labat*. Translated by Ann Smock. Lincoln: University of Nebraska Press.

Kolitz, Zvi. 1947. *Tiger beneath the Skin: Stories and Parables of the Years of Death*. Translated by Shmuel Katz. New York: Creative Age.

———. 1994. "Yossel Rakover's Appeal to God." Newly translated with an afterword by Jeffrey V. Mallow and Frans Jozef van Beeck. *Cross Currents*, Fall, 362–73.

———. 1999. *Yosl Rakover Talks to God*. Afterwords by Emmanuel Lévinas and Leon Wieseltier. Edited by Paul Badde. Translated by Carol Brown Janeway. New York: Pantheon.

Kosinski, Jerzy. 1965. *The Painted Bird*. Boston: Houghton Mifflin.

Kott, Jan. 1976. Introduction to Tadeusz Borowski, *This Way for the Gas, Ladies and Gentlemen*. Introduction translated by Michael Kandel, 11–26. Harmondsworth, England: Penguin.

Kovner, Abba. 1986. *My Little Sister and Selected Poems, 1965–1985*. Selected and translated by Shirley Kaufman. Oberlin, OH: Oberlin College.

Krawczyęska, Dorota, and Grzegorz Wołowiec. 2000. "Fazy i sposoby pisania o Zagładzie w literaturze polskiej." In *Literatura polska wobec zagłady: praca zbiorowa*, edited by Alina Brodzkiej-Wald, Dorota Krawczyęskiej, and Jacek Leociak, 11–28. Warsaw: Żydowski Instytut Historyczny.

Kremer, S. Lillian, ed. 2003. *Holocaust Literature: An Encyclopedia of Writers and their Work*. 2 vols. New York: Routledge.

Kruk, Herman. 2002. *The Last Days of the Jerusalem of Lithuania: Chronicles from the Vilna Ghetto and the Camps, 1939–1944*. Edited by Benjamin Harshav. Translated by Barbara Harshav. New Haven: Yale University Press.

Kugelmass, Jack, and Jonathan Boyarin, eds. 1998. *From a Ruined Garden: The Memorial Books of Polish Jewry*, Bibliography and geographical index by Zachary M. Baker. 2nd ed. Bloomington: Indiana University Press.

Kuprel, Diana. 2000. Introduction to Zofia Nałkowska, *Medallions*, xi–xxi. Translated by Diana Kuprel. Evanston, IL: Northwestern University Press.

Kushner, Tony. 2006. "Holocaust Testimony, Ethics, and the Problem of Representation." In "The Humanities of Testimony," edited by Geoffrey Hartman. Special issue, *Poetics Today* 27, no. 2: 275–95.

Lamdan, Isaac. 1989. "Masada." Translated by Leon I. Yudkin. In *The Literature of Destruction: Jewish Responses to Catastrophe*, edited by David G. Roskies, 367–70. Philadelphia: Jewish Publication Society of America.

Langer, Lawrence L. 1982. *Versions of Survival: The Holocaust and the Human Spirit*. Albany: State University of New York Press.

———. 1995. *Admitting the Holocaust: Collected Essays*. New York: Oxford University Press.

Langfus, Anna. 1962. *The Whole Land Brimstone*. Translated by Peter Wiles. New York: Pantheon.

Lanzmann, Claude. 1985. *Shoah: An Oral History of the Holocaust; The Complete Text of the Film*. Preface by Simone de Beauvoir. New York: Pantheon.

Laor, Dan. 2007. "How Are We Expected to Remember the Holocaust? Szenesz versus Kasztner." In *On Memory: An Interdisciplinary Approach*, edited by Doron Mendels, 195–213. Oxford: Peter Lang.

Leivick, H. 1940. *Lider un poemes*. Vol. 1, *Ale verk fun H. Leyvik*. New York: H. Leyvik yubiley-komitet.

———. 1947. *Mit der sheyris hapleyte*. Toronto: H. Leyvik yubiley-fond.

———. 1949. *Di khasene in Fernvald*. New York: CYCO.

Levi, Neil, and Michael Rothberg. 2003a. "General Introduction: Theory and the Holocaust." In *The Holocaust: Theoretical Readings*, edited by Neil Levi and Michael Rothberg, 1–22. New Brunswick, NJ: Rutgers University Press.

———, eds. 2003b. *The Holocaust: Theoretical Readings*. New Brunswick, NJ: Rutgers University Press.

Levi, Primo. 1947. *Se questo è un uomo*. Turin: De Silva.

———. 1984. *The Periodic Table*. Translated by Raymond Rosenthal. New York: Schocken.

———. 1985. *Survival in Auschwitz and The Reawakening: Two Memoirs*. Translated by Stuart Woolf. New York: Summit.

———. 1988. *The Collected Poems of Primo Levi*. Translated by Ruth Feldman and Brian Swann. Boston: Faber and Faber.

———. 1996. *Survival in Auschwitz: The Nazi Assault on Humanity*. Including "A Conversation with Primo Levi," by Philip Roth. Translated by Stuart Woolf. New York: Touchstone.

Levin, Meyer. 1950. *In Search: An Autobiography*. New York: Horizon.

Lewin, Abraham. 1988. *A Cup of Tears: A Diary of the Warsaw Ghetto*. Edited with an introduction by Antony Polonsky. Translated by Christopher Hutton. Oxford, UK: Basil Blackwell in association with the Institute for Polish-Jewish Studies.

Lewinsky, Tamar. 2010. "Dangling Roots? Yiddish Language and Culture in the German Diaspora." In *"We Are Here": New Approaches to Displaced Persons in Postwar Germany*, edited by Avinoam J. Patt and Michael Berkowitz, 308–34. Detroit: Wayne State University Press.

Lilly, Paul R., Jr. 2004. "Jerzy Kosinski." In *Holocaust Novelists*, edited by Efraim Sicher, 181–94. Detroit: Gale.

Lind, Jakov. 1964. *Soul of Wood*. Translated by Ralph Manheim. New York: Grove.

Lipstadt, Deborah E. 2011. *The Eichmann Trial*. New York: Schocken.

Lisek, Joanna. 2005. *Jung Wilne: żydowska grupa artystyczna*. Wrocław, Poland: Wydawnictwo Uniwersytetu Wrocławskiego.

Livneh, Anat. 2010. "'The Cry of the Desperate and the Fortitude of the Remaining Will Suffice': Commemorative Literature, Documentation and the Study of the Holocaust." *Dapim* 24:177–222.

Lukert, Steven. 2002. *The Art and Politics of Arthur Szyk*. Washington: US Holocaust Memorial Museum.

Lustig, Arnošt. 1962. *Night and Hope*. Translated by George Theiner. New York: Dutton.

Malamud, Bernard. 1997. "The Jewbird." In Bernard Malamud, *The Complete Stories*, 322–30. New York: Farrar, Straus and Giroux.

Malaparte, Curzio. 1946. *Kaputt*. Translated by Cesare Foligno. New York: Dutton.

———. 2005. *Kaputt.* Afterword by Dan Hofstadter. Translated by Cesare Foligno. 3rd ed. New York: New York Review of Books.

Mallow, Jeffrey V., and Frans Jozef van Beeck. 1994. Afterword to Zvi Kolitz, "Yossel Rakover's Appeal to God," newly translated by Jeffrey V. Mallow and Frans Jozef van Beeck. *Cross Currents*, Fall, 373–77.

Mandela, Nelson. 2009. "Nelson Mandela about Anne Frank." Accessed April 1, 2012; http://www.youtube.com/watch?v=PHd2Y98pvbc.

Mark, Ber. 1950. *Di yidishe tragedye in der poylisher literatur.* Warsaw: Yidish bukh.

———. 1952. "Yudenratishe 'ahves-yisroel' (an entfer afn bilbl fun H. Leyvik)." *Bleter far geshikhte* 5, no. 3: 63–115.

———, ed 1977. *Megiles Oyshvits.* Tel Aviv: Yisroel-bukh.

———, ed. 1985. *The Scrolls of Auschwitz.* Translated by Sharon Neemani. Adapted from the original Yiddish text. Tel Aviv: Am Oved.

Markish, Peretz. 1964a. "Dem yidishn shlakhtman." In *A shpigl oyf a shteyn: antologye poezye un proze fun tsvelf farshnitene yidishe shraybers in Ratn-farband,* edited by Khone Shmeruk, 490–92. Tel Aviv: Di goldene keyt and Y. L. Perets.

———. 1964b. "Ho lakhmo." In *A shpigl oyf a shteyn: antologye poezye un proze fun tsvelf farshnitene yidishe shraybers in Ratn-farband,* edited by Khone Shmeruk, 487–88. Tel Aviv: Di goldene keyt and Y. L. Perets.

Marrus, Michael Robert. 2001. "Killing Time: Jewish Perceptions during the Holocaust." In *Hasho'ah: historyah vezikaron: kovets ma'amarim shai leYisrael Gutman,* edited by Shemuel Almog, Daniel Blatman, David Bankier, and Dalia Ofer, 10–38. Jerusalem: Yad Vashem and the Institute for Contemporary Jewry.

Megged, Aharon. 1950. "The Name." Translated by Minna Givton. In *Facing the Holocaust: Selected Israeli Fiction,* edited by Gila Ramras-Rauch and Joseph Michman-Melkman, 21–36. Philadelphia: Jewish Publication Society of America.

———. 1996. "Hanna Senesh." Translated by Michael Taub. In *Israeli Holocaust Drama,* edited by Michael Taub, 79–126. Syracuse, NY: Syracuse University Press.

Mendelsohn, Daniel Adam. 2006. *The Lost: A Search for Six of Six Million.* Photographs by Matt Mendelsohn. New York: HarperCollins.

Michlic-Coren, Joanna. 2000. "Polish Jews during and after the Kielce Pogrom: Reports from the Communist Archives." *Polin* 13:253–67.

Michman, Dan. 2011. *The Emergence of Jewish Ghettos during the Holocaust.* Translated by Lenn J. Schramm. New York: Cambridge University Press and Yad Vashem.

Mikhoels, Solomon, and Itzik Feffer. 1943. "Di ershte redes fun di yidishe sovetishe shlukhim." *Yidishe kultur,* June–July, 63–65.

Mikics, David. 2003. "Underground Comics and Survival Tales: *Maus* in Context." In *Considering Maus: Approaches to Art Spiegelman's "Survivor's Tale" of the Holocaust,* edited by Deborah R. Geis, 15–25. Tuscaloosa: University of Alabama Press.

Milch, Baruch. 2003. *Can Heaven Be Void?* Edited with a foreword by Shosh Milch-Avigal. Translated by Helen Kaye. Jerusalem: Yad Vashem.

Millu, Liana. 1991. *Smoke over Birkenau.* Translated by Lynne Sharon Schwartz. Philadelphia: Jewish Publication Society of America.

Milner, Iris. 2003. "Writing and the Holocaust: Problematics of Representation in Second-Generation Literature in Israel." *Journal of Israeli History* 22:91–108.

Miłosz, Czesław. 1981. *The Captive Mind.* Translated with a foreword by Jane Zielonko. New York: Octagon.

———. 1988. *The Collected Poems 1931–87.* New York: HarperCollins.

Mintz, Alan L. 1984. *Hurban: Responses to Catastrophe in Hebrew Literature.* New York: Columbia University Press.

———, ed. 1997. *The Boom in Contemporary Israeli Fiction.* Waltham, MA: Brandeis University Press.

Miron, Dan. 2000. *The Image of the Shtetl and Other Studies of Modern Jewish Literary Imagination.* Syracuse, NY: Syracuse University Press.

———. 2005. "Bein sefer le'efer." In Dan Miron, *Hasifriya ha'iveret: proza me'urevet 1980–2005,* 147–83. Tel Aviv: Yediot Aharonot.

———. 2010. *The Prophetic Mode in Modern Hebrew Poetry.* Milford, CT: Toby.

Mlotek, Eleanor, and Malke Gottlieb, comps. 1983. *Mir zaynen do: lider fun di getos un lagern; We Are Here: Songs of the Holocaust.* Foreword by Elie Wiesel. Singable translations by Roslyn Bresnick-Perry. Illustrated by Tsirl Waletzky. New York: Educational Department of the Workmen's Circle and Hippocrene Books.

Modiano, Patrick. 1968. *La Place de l'Etoile.* Paris: Gallimard.

Molodowski, Kadia. 1988. "God of Mercy." Translated by Irving Howe. In *The Penguin Book of Modern Yiddish Verse,* edited by Irving Howe, Ruth R. Wisse, and Khone Shmeruk, 330–33. New York: Penguin.

Moyn, Samuel. 2005. *A Holocaust Controversy: The Treblinka Affair in Postwar France.* Waltham, MA: Brandeis University Press.

Murav, Harriet. 2011. *Music from a Speeding Train: Jewish Literature in Post-Revolution Russia.* Stanford: Stanford University Press.

Nałkowska, Zofia. 2000. *Medallions.* Translated with an introduction by Diana Kuprel. Evanston, IL: Northwestern University Press.

Natter, Wolfgang G. 1999. *Literature at War, 1914–1940: Representing the "Time of Greatness" in Germany.* New Haven: Yale University Press.

Némirovsky, Irène. 2006. *Suite Française.* Translated by Sandra Smith, with appendices and preface to the French edition. New York: Alfred A. Knopf.

Niger, Shmuel. 1948. *Kidesh hashem: a zamlung geklibene, oft gekirtste barikhtn, briv, khronikes, tsavoes, oyfshriftn, legendes, lider, dertseylungen, dramatishe stsenes, eseyen, vos moln oys mesires-nefesh in undzere un oykh in frierdike tsaytn.* New York: CYCO.

Nitecki, Alicia. 2007. "Translator's Preface." In Tadeusz Drewnowski, ed., *Postal Indiscretions: The Correspondence of Tadeusz Borowski,* translated by Alicia Nitecki, ix–xi. Evanston, IL: Northwestern University Press.

Norich, Anita. 2007. *Discovering Exile: Yiddish and Jewish American Culture during the Holocaust.* Stanford: Stanford University Press.

Novershtern, Abraham, ed. 1983. *Avraham Sutskever bimelot lo shiv'im: ta'arukha* and *Avrom Sutskever tsum vern a ben-shivim: oysshtelung.* 2 vols. in 1. Jerusalem: National and University Library.

Novick, Peter. 1999. *The Holocaust in American Life.* Boston: Houghton Mifflin.

Nyiri, János. 1989. *Battlefields and Playgrounds.* Translated by William Brandon and the author. Waltham, MA: Brandeis University Press.

Ofer, Dalia. 2000. "The Strength of Remembrance: Commemorating the Holocaust during the First Decade of Israel." *Jewish Social Studies* 6:24–55.

Ohad, Meir, ed. 1977. *Yizkor leyaldei Teheran shenaflu bema'arakhot Yisrael veshehalkhu le'olamam.* Israel: Hava'adah hatsiburit lehantsaḥat "Yaldei Teheran."

Opoczynski, Peretz. 1951. *Gezamlte shriftn.* Biography by Rina Oper-Opochinsky. Edited by Shiye Tenenboym. New York: Rina Oper-Opochinsky.

———. 1969. "The Letter Carrier." Translated by E. Chase. In *Anthology of Holocaust Literature,* edited by Jacob Glatstein, Israel Knox, and Samuel Margoshes, 57–70. Philadelphia: Jewish Publication Society of America.

———. 1970. *Reshimot.* Edited by Zvi Szner. Translated by Avraham Yeivin. Tel Aviv: Hakibbutz Hameuchad.

———. 1976. "Smuggling in the Warsaw Ghetto." Translated by Adah B. Fogel. In *A Holocaust Reader,* edited by Lucy S. Dawidowicz, 197–207. New York: Behrman House.

———. 1989. "House No. 21." Translated by Robert Wolf. In *The Literature of Destruction: Jewish Responses to Catastrophe,* edited by David G. Roskies, 408–24. Philadelphia: Jewish Publication Society of America.

Orlev, Uri. 1980. *The Lead Soldiers.* Translated by Hillel Halkin. New York: Taplinger.

Ozerov, Lev. 2007. "Babi Yar." In *An Anthology of Jewish-Russian Literature: Two Centuries of Dual Identity in Prose and Poetry,* edited by Maxim D. Shrayer, 1:575–79. Armonk, NY: M. E. Sharpe.

Ozick, Cynthia. 1983. *The Shawl.* New York: Vintage.

Pagis, Dan. 1981. *Points of Departure.* Introduction by Robert Alter. Translated by Stephen Mitchell. Bilingual ed. Philadelphia: Jewish Publication Society of America.

Papiernik, Charles. 2004. *Unbroken: From Auschwitz to Buenos Aires.* Introduction by Ilán Stavans. Translated by Stephen A. Sadow. Albuquerque: University of New Mexico Press.

Perechodnik, Calel. 1993. *Czy ja jestem mordercą?* Edited by Paweł Szapiro. Warsaw: KARTA.

———. 1996. *Am I a Murderer? Testament of a Jewish Ghetto Policeman.* Edited and translated from the censored Polish edition of 1993 by Frank Fox. Boulder, CO: Westview.

———. 2004. *Spowiedź: dzieje rodziny żydowskiej podczas okupacji hitlerowskiej w Polsce.* Revised and edited by David Engel. Warsaw: Ośrodek Karta.

Peretz, I. L. 2002. "Three Gifts." In *The I. L. Peretz Reader,* edited with an introduction by Ruth R. Wisse, 222–30. 2nd rev. ed. New Haven: Yale University Press.

Perle, Yehoshue. 1955. "Khurbn Varshe." In *Tsvishn lebn un toyt,* edited by Leyb Olicki, 100–41. Warsaw: Yidish bukh.

———. 1989. "4580." Translated by Elinor Robinson. In *The Literature of Destruction: Jewish Responses to Catastrophe,* edited by David G. Roskies, 450–54. Philadelphia: Jewish Publication Society of America.

Polonsky, Antony. 1988. Introduction to Abraham Lewin, *A Cup of Tears: A Diary of the Warsaw Ghetto,* edited with an introduction by Antony Polonsky and translated by Christopher Hutton, 1–54. Oxford, UK: Basil Blackwell in association with the Institute for Polish-Jewish Studies.

——— and Monika Adamczyk-Garbowska. 2001. Introduction to *Contemporary Jewish Writing in Poland: An Anthology,* edited by Antony Polonsky and Monika Adamczyk-Garbowska, ix–l. Lincoln: University of Nebraska Press.

Porat, Dina. 1983. "'Al-Domi'—anshe-ruaḥ be'erets-yisrael nokhaḥ hashoah, 1943–1945." In *Hatsiyonut* 8:245–75.

Prager, Brad. 2005. "The Good German as Narrator: On W. G. Sebald and the Risks of Holocaust Writing." *New German Critique* 96:75–102.

Prager, Moshe. 1954. *Antologye fun religyeze lider un dertseylungen: shafungen fun shrayber, umgekumene in di yorn fun yidish khurbn in Eyrope*. New York: Research Institute of Religious Jewry.

President's Commission on the Holocaust. 1979. *The Report of the President's Commission on the Holocaust*. Washington: Government Printing Office.

Pressler, Mirjam. 1995. "Foreword." In Anne Frank, *The Diary of a Young Girl*, edited by Otto H. Frank and Mirjam Pressler, translated by Susan Massotty, v–viii. Definitive ed. New York: Doubleday.

Rawicz, Piotr. 2003. *Blood from the Sky*. Introduction by Lawrence Langer. Translated by Peter Wiles. 1st paperback ed. New Haven: Yale University Press.

Reagan, Ronald. 1986. "Remarks of President Ronald Reagan to Regional Editors, White House, April 18, 1985." In *Bitburg in Moral and Political Perspective*, edited by Geoffrey H. Hartman, 239–40. Bloomington: Indiana University Press.

Redlich, Shimon. 1995. *War, Holocaust, and Stalinism: A Documented Study of the Jewish Anti-Fascist Committee in the USSR*. Luxembourg: Harwood Academic.

Reznikoff, Charles. 1945. "Kaddish." In *Jewish Frontier Anthology, 1934–1944*, 438–39. New York: Jewish Frontier Association.

Richmond, Theo. 1995. *Konin: A Quest*. New York: Pantheon.

Ringelblum, Emanuel. 1958. *Notes from the Warsaw Ghetto: The Journal of Emmanuel Ringelblum*. Edited and translated by Jacob Sloan. New York: McGraw-Hill.

———. 1985. *Ksovim fun geto*. Edited by Yosef Kermish. Photo-offset edition of 1962 Warsaw edition, edited by Artur Eisenbach. 2 vols. Tel Aviv: Y. L. Perets.

———. 1989. "Oyneg Shabbes." Translated by Elinor Robinson. In *The Literature of Destruction: Jewish Responses to Catastrophe*, edited by David G. Roskies, 386–98. Philadelphia: Jewish Publication Society of America.

———. 1992. *Polish-Jewish Relations during the Second World War*. Foreword by Yehuda Bauer. Edited by Joseph Kermish and Shmuel Krakowski. Translated by Dafna Allon, Danuta Dabrowska, and Dana Keren. Evanston, IL: Northwestern University Press.

Rivkin, Isaac, ed. 1959. *Yidishe gelt in lebnsshteyger kultur-geshikhte un folklor*. New York: American Academy for Jewish Research.

Rochman, Leyb. 1949. *Un in dayn blut zolstu lebn: togbukh 1943–1944*. Paris: Farlag-komisye bay der gezelshaft "Fraynt fun Minsk-Mazovyetsk" in Pariz.

———. 1961. *Bedamayikh ḥayyi*. Translated by Hanoch Kela'i. Jerusalem: Yesodot.

———. 1983. *The Pit and the Trap: A Chronicle of Survival*. Introduction by Aharon Appelfeld. Edited by Sheila Friedling. Translated by Moshe Kohn and Sheila Friedling. New York: Holocaust Library.

Rosen, Alan. 2005. *Sounds of Defiance: The Holocaust, Multilingualism, and the Problem of English*. Lincoln: University of Nebraska Press.

———. 2010. *The Wonder of Their Voices: The 1946 Holocaust Interviews of David Boder*. Oxford: Oxford University Press.

Rosenfarb, Chava. 1973. "A vide fun a mekhaber." *Di goldene keyt* 81:127–41.

————. 1985. *The Tree of Life: A Novel about Life in the Lodz Ghetto*. Translated by the author in collaboration with Goldie Morgentaler. Melbourne, Australia: Scribe.

Rosenfeld, Alvin H. 2005. *Anne Frank and the Future of Holocaust Memory*. Washington: Center for Advanced Holocaust Studies, US Holocaust Memorial Museum. Accessed January 15, 2012; http://www.ushmm.org/research/center/publications/occasional/2005-04-01/paper.pdf.

Rosenfeld, Oskar. 2002. *In the Beginning Was the Ghetto*. Edited with an introduction by Hanno Loewy. Translated by Brigitte M. Goldstein. Evanston, IL: Northwestern University Press.

Rosental, Leyb. 1989. "Yisrolik." Translated by Hillel Schwartz and David G. Roskies. In *The Literature of Destruction: Jewish Responses to Catastrophe*, edited by David G. Roskies, 476–78. Philadelphia: Jewish Publication Society of America.

Roskies, David G. 1984. *Against the Apocalypse: Responses to Catastrophe in Modern Jewish Culture*. Cambridge: Harvard University Press.

————, ed. 1989. *The Literature of Destruction: Jewish Responses to Catastrophe*. Philadelphia: Jewish Publication Society of America.

————. 1995. *A Bridge of Longing: The Lost Art of Yiddish Storytelling*. Cambridge: Harvard University Press.

————. 1999. *The Jewish Search for a Usable Past*. Bloomington: Indiana University Press.

————. 2004. "Jewish Cultural Life in the Vilna Ghetto." In Michael MacQueen, Jürgen Matthäus, and David G. Roskies, *Lithuania and the Jews, the Holocaust Chapter: Symposium Presentations*, 33–44. Washington: US Holocaust Memorial Museum.

Roth, Philip. 1979. *The Ghost Writer*. New York: Farrar, Straus and Giroux.

Rothberg, Michael. 2000. *Traumatic Realism: The Demands of Holocaust Representation*. Minneapolis: University of Minnesota Press.

————. 2009. *Multidirectional Memory: Remembering the Holocaust in the Age of Decolonization*. Stanford: Stanford University Press.

Rousset, David. 1982. *The Other Kingdom*. Translated with an introduction by Ramon Guthrie. New York: Fertig.

Rudashevski, Isaac. 1973. *Diary of the Vilna Ghetto June 1941–April 1943*. Translated and edited by Percy Matenko. Tel Aviv: Ghetto Fighters' House and Hakibbutz Hameuchad.

Rudnicki, Adolf. 1957. *The Dead and Living Sea and Other Stories*. Translated by Jadwiga Zwolska. Warsaw: Polonia.

————. 2001. "The Ascension." Translated by H. C. Stevens and revised by Monika Adamczyk-Garbowska. In *Contemporary Jewish Writing in Poland: An Anthology*, edited by Antony Polonsky and Monika Adamczyk-Garbowska, 87–131. Lincoln: University of Nebraska Press.

Rudolf, Anthony. 2004. "Piotr Rawicz." In *Holocaust Novelists*, edited by Efraim Sicher, 277–80. Detroit: Gale.

Rymkiewicz, Jarosław Marek. 1994. *The Final Station: Umschlagplatz*. Translated by Nina Taylor. New York: Farrar, Straus and Giroux.

Sachs, Nelly. 1967. *O the Chimneys: Selected Poems, Including the Verse Play, Eli*. Translated by Michael Hamburger. New York: Farrar, Straus and Giroux.

Sadow, Stephen A. 2004. Translator's preface to Charles Papiernik, *Unbroken: From Auschwitz to Buenos Aires*, ix–x. Albuquerque: University of New Mexico Press.

Schaumann, Caroline. 2004. "Jurek Becker." In *Holocaust Novelists*, edited by Efraim Sicher, 36–43. Detroit: Gale.

Schaver, Emma. 1954. "Songs of the Ghetto." In *From the Heart of a People*. Mercury Record MG 20052.

Schein, Ada. 2009. "'Everyone Can Hold a Pen': The Documentation Project in the DP Camps in Germany." In *Holocaust Historiography in Context: Emergence, Challenges, Polemics and Achievements*, edited by David Bankier and Dan Michman, 103–34. New York: Berghahn.

Schlink, Bernhard. 1997. *The Reader*. Translated by Carol Brown Janeway. New York: Pantheon.

Scholem, Gershom. 1971. *The Messianic Idea in Judaism and Other Essays on Jewish Spirituality*. New York: Schocken.

Schwarz, Jan. 2007a. "A Library of Hope and Destruction: The Yiddish Book Series *Dos poylishe yidntum* (Polish Jewry), 1946–1966." *Polin* 20:173–96.

———. 2007b. "The Original Yiddish Text and the Context of *Night*." In *Approaches to Teaching Wiesel's "Night,"* edited by Alan Rosen, 52–58. New York: Modern Language Society of America.

———. 2011. "Blood Ties: Leib Rochman's War Diary." In *Memorial Books of Eastern European Jewry: Essays on the History and Meanings of Yizker Volumes*, edited by Rosemary Horowitz, 163–79. Jefferson, NC: McFarland.

Schwarz, Leo W., ed. 1949. *The Root and the Bough: The Epic of an Enduring People*. New York: Rinehart.

Schwarz-Bart, André. 1960. *The Last of the Just*. Translated by Stephen Becker. New York: Atheneum.

Sebald, W. G. 1996. *The Emigrants*. Translated by Michael Hulse. New York: New Directions.

Segev, Tom. 2000. *The Seventh Million: The Israelis and the Holocaust*. Translated by Haim Watzman. New York: Henry Holt.

Semprún, Jorge. 1964. *The Long Voyage*. Translated by Richard Seaver. New York: Grove.

Shalev, Ziva. 1992. *Tosyah: Tosyah Altman, mehahanhaga harashit shel hashomer hatsa'ir lemifkedet ha'irgun hayehudi halohem*. Edited by Levi Dror. Tel Aviv: Moreshet and Tel Aviv University, Department of Jewish History.

Shamir-de-Leeuw, Elsje. 2004. "Harry Mulisch." In *Holocaust Novelists*, edited by Efraim Sicher, 245–52. Detroit: Gale.

Shandler, Jeffrey, ed. 2002. *Awakening Lives: Autobiographies of Jewish Youth in Poland before the Holocaust*. Introduction by Barbara Kirshenblatt-Gimblett, Marcus Moseley, and Michael Stanislawski. New Haven: Yale University Press.

Shapira, Anita. 2005. "The Eichman Trial: Changing Perspectives." In *After Eichmann: Collective Memory and the Holocaust since 1961*, edited by David Cesarani, 18–39. London: Routledge.

Shayevitsh, Simkhe Bunem. 1946. . . . *Lekh-lekho*. . . . Edited by Nachman Blumental. Łódź, Poland: Tsentrale yidishe historishe komisye baym tsentral-komitet fun poylishe yidn.

———. 1989. "Lekh-lekho." Translated by Leah Robinson. In *The Literature of*

Destruction: Jewish Responses to Catastrophe, edited by David G. Roskies, 520–30. Philadelphia: Jewish Publication Society of America.

Shedletzky, Ephraim, ed. 1977. *Seyfer minsk-mazovyetsk.* Jerusalem: Minsk Mazowiecki Societies in Israel and Abroad.

Sheinson, Yosef D. 2000. *Passover Service.* In *A Survivor's Haggadah.* With woodcuts by Miklos Adler. Edited with an introduction by Saul Touster. Translated by Yaron Peleg, Robert Szulkin, and Marc Samuels. Philadelphia: Jewish Publication Society of America.

Shenfeld, Ruth. 1991. *Adolf Rudnitski: sofer ben shnei 'olamot.* Jerusalem: Magnes.

Sherman, Joseph. 2003. *The Jewish Pope: Myth, Diaspora and Yiddish Literature.* Oxford: European Humanities Research Centre.

Shmeruk, Khone. 1964. Notes to *A shpigl oyf a shteyn: antologye poezye un proze fun tsvelf farshnitene yidishe shraybers in Ratn-farband*, edited by Khone Shmeruk, 773–804. Tel Aviv: Di goldene keyt and Y. L. Perets.

———. 1995. "A briv in redaktsye." *Di goldene keyt* 140: 214–16.

Shore, Marci. 2005. "Translator's Preface." In Michał Głowiński, *The Black Seasons*, foreword by Jan T. Gross, translated by Marci Shore, xi–xiv. Evanston, IL: Northwestern University Press.

Shrayer, Maxim D. 2012. "Jewish-Russian Poets Bearing Witness to the Shoah, 1941–1946: Textual Evidence and Preliminary Conclusions." In *Studies in Slavic Languages and Literatures (ICCEES Congress Stockholm Papers and Contributions)*, edited by Stefano Garzonio, 59–119. Faenza, Italy: Portal on Central Eastern and Balkan Europe.

———. 2013. *I Saw It: Ilya Selvinsky and the Legacy of Bearing Witness to the Shoah.* Boston: Academic Studies Press, forthcoming.

Siedlecki, Janusz Nel, Krystyn Olszewski, and Tadeusz Borowski. 2000. *We Were in Auschwitz.* [Edited by Tadeusz Borowski.] Translated by Alicia Nitecki. New York: Welcome Rain.

Sierakowiak, Dawid. 1996. *The Diary of Dawid Sierakowiak: Five Notebooks from the Łódź ghetto.* Foreword by Lawrence L. Langer. Edited by Alan Adelson. Translated by Kamil Turowski. New York: Oxford University Press.

Singer, Isaac Bashevis. 1972. *Enemies: A Love Story.* Translated by Aliza Shevrin and Elizabeth Shub. New York: Farrar, Straus and Giroux.

———. 1983a. "The Cafeteria." Translated by the author and Dorothea Straus. In *The Collected Stories of Isaac Bashevis Singer*, 287–300. New York: Farrar, Straus and Giroux.

———. 1983b. "The Last Demon." Translated by Martha Glicklich and Cecil Hemley. In *The Collected Stories of Isaac Bashevis Singer*, 179–87. New York: Farrar, Straus and Giroux.

———. 1995. "Concerning Yiddish Literature in Poland." Translated by Robert Wolf. *Prooftexts* 13, no. 2: 113–27.

———. 1998. *Shadows on the Hudson.* Translated by Joseph Sherman. New York: Farrar, Straus and Giroux.

———. 2004. "Zeidlus the Pope." Translated by Joel Blocker and Elizabeth Pollet. In Isaac Bashevis Singer, *Collected Stories: Gimpel the Fool to The Letter Writer*, edited by Ilan Stavans, 477–87. New York: Library of America.

Sobol, Joshua. 1992. *Geto.* 2nd ed. Tel Aviv: Or-Am.

———. 1995. "Ghetto." In *Art from the Ashes: A Holocaust Anthology,* edited by Lawrence L. Langer, 480–551. New York: Oxford University Press.

Sokoloff, Naomi B. 1988. "Reinventing Bruno Schulz: *The Messiah of Stockholm* and David Grossman's *See Under: Love.*" *AJS Review* 13, nos. 1–2: 171–99.

———. 2004. "Aharon Appelfeld." In *Holocaust Novelists,* edited by Efraim Sicher, 17–30. Detroit: Gale.

Spero, I., G. Kenig, M. Shulshteyn, and B. Shlevin, eds. 1946. *Yizker-bukh tsum ondenk fun 14 umgekumene parizer yidishe shrayber.* Paris: Oyfsnay.

Spiegel, Isaiah. 1947. *Malkhes geto: noveln.* Łódź: Dos naye lebn.

———. 1998. *Ghetto Kingdom: Tales of the Łódź Ghetto.* Translated by David H. Hirsch and Roslyn Hirsch. Evanston, IL: Northwestern University Press.

Spiegelman, Art. 1986. *Maus: A Survivor's Tale. I: My Father Bleeds History.* New York: Pantheon.

———. 1991. *Maus II: A Survivor's Tale: And Here My Troubles Began.* New York: Pantheon.

Spivak, Elye. 1946. *Di shprakh in di teg fun der foterlendisher milkhome (etyudn).* Kiev: Farlag fun der visnshaft-akademye fun USSR.

Stanislawski, Michael. 2004. *Autobiographical Jews: Essays in Jewish Self-Fashioning.* Seattle: University of Washington Press.

Stauber, Roni. 2009. "Philip Friedman and the Beginning of Holocaust Studies." In *Holocaust Historiography in Context: Emergence, Challenges, Polemics and Achievements,* edited by David Bankier and Dan Michman, 83–102. New York: Berghahn.

Stavans, Ilán. 2001. *The Inveterate Dreamer: Essays and Conversations on Jewish Culture.* Lincoln: University of Nebraska Press.

———. 2003. "A Comment on Borges's Response to Hitler." *Modern Judaism* 23, no. 1: 1–11.

———. 2004. Introduction to Charles Papiernik, *Unbroken: From Auschwitz to Buenos Aires,* xi–xiii. Translated by Stephen A. Sadow. Albuquerque: University of New Mexico Press.

Steiner, Jean-François. 1967. *Treblinka: The Revolt of an Extermination Camp.* Preface by Simone de Beauvoir. Translated by Helen Weaver. New York: Simon and Schuster.

Steinitz, Lucy Y., and David M. Szonyi, eds. 1976. *Living after the Holocaust: Reflections by the Post-War Generation in America.* New York: Bloch.

Steinlauf, Michael C. 1997. *Bondage to the Dead: Poland and the Memory of the Holocaust.* Syracuse, NY: Syracuse University Press.

Stern, David. 2004. *The Jewish Anthological Imagination.* New York: Oxford University Press.

Strigler, Mordecai. 1947. *Maydanek.* Preface by H. Leivick. Buenos Aires: Tsentral-farband fun poylishe yidn in Argentine.

———. 1948. *In di fabrikn fun toyt.* Buenos Aires: Tsentral-farband fun poylishe yidn in Argentine.

———. 1950. *Werk C.* 2 vols. Buenos Aires: Tsentral-farband fun poylishe yidn in Argentine.

———. 1952. *Goyroles.* 2 vols. Buenos Aires: Tsentral-farband fun poylishe yidn in Argentine.

Styron, William. 1979. *Sophie's Choice*. New York: Random House.

Sutzkever, Abraham. 1945a. *Di festung: lider un poemes geshribn in vilner geto un in vald 1941–1944*. Edited with a foreword by Nachman Mayzel. New York: YKUF.

———. 1945b. *Fun vilner geto*. Moscow: Der emes.

———. 1968a. *Lider fun yam hamoves: fun vilner geto, vald, un vander*. Tel Aviv: Remembrance Award Library.

———. 1968b. "Tsu Poyln." In Abraham Sutzkever, *Lider fun yam hamoves: fun vilner geto, vald, un vander*, 297–307. Tel Aviv: Remembrance Award Library.

———. 1979a. *Di ershte nakht in geto: lider, lidvariantn, fragmentn, geshribn in di khurbn-yorn 1941–1944*. Illustrated by Samuel Bak. Tel Aviv: Di goldene keyt.

———. 1979b. *Dortn vu es nekhtikn di shtern*. Illustrated by Yonia Fein. Tel Aviv: Yisroel-bukh.

———. 1981. "Mother." In *Burnt Pearls: Ghetto Poems of Abraham Sutzkever*, introduction by Ruth R. Wisse and translated by Seymour Mayne, 27–31. Oakville, ON: Mosaic.

———. 1982. "Green Aquarium." Translated by Ruth Wisse. *Prooftexts* 2, no. 1: 98–121.

———. 1988a. "1981: A letter arrived from the town of my birth." Translated by Cynthia Ozick. In *The Penguin Book of Modern Yiddish Verse*, edited by Irving Howe, Ruth R. Wisse, and Khone Shmeruk, 702. New York: Penguin.

———. 1988b. "Epitaphs." Translated by Neal Kozodoy. In *The Penguin Book of Modern Yiddish Verse*, edited by Irving Howe, Ruth R. Wisse, and Khone Shmeruk, 682–88. New York: Penguin.

———. 1988c. "Lead Plates at the Rom Press." Translated by Neal Kozodoy. In *The Penguin Book of Modern Yiddish Verse*, edited by Irving Howe, Ruth R. Wisse, and Khone Shmeruk, 678. New York: Penguin.

———. 1989a. *Di nevue fun shvartsaplen: dertseylungen*. Introduction by Ruth Wisse. Jerusalem: Magnes.

———. 1989b. "No Sad Songs Please." Translated by C. K. Williams. In *The Literature of Destruction: Jewish Responses to Catastrophe*, edited by David G. Roskies, 500–501. Philadelphia: Jewish Publication Society of America.

———. 1989c. "Song for the Last." Translated by C. K. Williams. In *The Literature of Destruction: Jewish Responses to Catastrophe*, edited by David G. Roskies, 497–99. Philadelphia: Jewish Publication Society of America.

———. 1989d. "To My Child." Translated by C. K. Williams. In *The Literature of Destruction: Jewish Responses to Catastrophe*, edited by David G. Roskies, 494–95. Philadelphia: Jewish Publication Society of America.

———. 1991a. "Frozen Jews." Translated by Barbara and Benjamin Harshav. In *A. Sutzkever: Selected Poetry and Prose*, introduction by Benjamin Harshav and translated by Barbara and Benjamin Harshav, 181–82. Berkeley: University of California Press.

———. 1991b. "Teacher Mira." In *A. Sutzkever: Selected Poetry and Prose*, introduction by Benjamin Harshav and translated by Barbara and Benjamin Harshav, 160–62. Berkeley: University of California Press.

———. 1991c. "Three Roses." In *A. Sutzkever: Selected Poetry and Prose*, introduction by Benjamin Harshav and translated by Barbara and Benjamin Harshav, 139–49. Berkeley: University of California Press.

———. 1991d. *A. Sutzkever: Selected Poetry and Prose*. Introduction by Benjamin Harshav. Translated by Barbara and Benjamin Harshav. Berkeley: University of California Press.

Syrkin, Marie. 1945. "The Flag on the Ghetto Wall." In *Jewish Frontier Anthology, 1934–1944*, 381–88. New York: Jewish Frontier Association.

Szczypiorski, Andrzej. 1989. *The Beautiful Mrs. Seidenman*. Translated by Klara Glowczewska. New York: Vintage International.

Szeintuch, Yechiel. 2006. "Al 'Tkhiyes-hameysim'—ha'iton harishon shel she'erit hapletah ve'orkho." *Khulyot* 10:191–218.

———. 2009. *Salamandra: mitos vehistoria bekitvei Ka. Tzetnik*. Edited by Carrie Friedman-Cohen. Jerusalem: Karmel.

Szlengel, Władysław. 1943. "What I Read to the Dead." Translated by Andrew Kobos. Accessed January 15, 2012; http://zchor.org/szlengel/prose.htm.

———. 2006. "Things." Translated by John R. Carpenter. *Chicago Review* 52, nos. 2–4: 283–86.

Szpilman, Władysław. 1999. *The Pianist: The Extraordinary Story of One Man's Survival in Warsaw, 1939–45*. With extracts from the diary of Wilm Hosenfeld, foreword by Andrzej Szpilman, and epilogue by Wolf Biermann. Translated by Anthea Bell. New York: Picador.

Tenebaum-Tamaroff, Mordecai. 1987. *Dapim min hadelekah pirkei yoman, mikhtavim ureshimot*. Edited by Bronka Klibanski and Zvi Szner. 2nd rev. ed. Jerusalem: Yad Vashem.

Tenenbaum, Binyamin, ed. 1948. *Eḥad me'ir ushnayim mimishpaḥa*. Tel-Aviv: Sifriat Po'alim.

Thomas, D. M. 1981. *The White Hotel*. New York: Viking.

Todorov, Tzvetan. 1975. *The Fantastic: A Structural Approach to a Literary Genre*. New foreword by Robert Scholes. Translated by Richard Howard. Ithaca: Cornell University Press.

Tory, Avraham. 1990. *Surviving the Holocaust: The Kovno Ghetto Diary*. Edited by Martin Gilbert and Dina Porat. Translated by Jerzy Michalowicz. Cambridge: Harvard University Press.

Tournier, Michel. 1972. *The Ogre*. Translated by Barbara Bray. New York: Doubleday.

Touster, Saul. 2000. Introduction to Y. D. Sheinson, *A Survivor's Haggadah*, edited with an introduction by Saul Touster, translated by Yaron Peleg, Robert Szulkin and Marc Samuels, xi–xxxii. Philadelphia: Jewish Publication Society of America.

Tych, Feliks. 2009. "The Emergence of Holocaust Research in Poland: The Jewish Historical Commission and the Jewish Historical Institute (ZIH), 1944–1989." In *Holocaust Historiography in Context: Emergence, Challenges, Polemics and Achievements*, edited by David Bankier and Dan Michman, 227–44. New York: Berghahn.

United Emergency Relief Committee for the City of Lodz. 1943. *Lodzer Yiskor Book*. New York: United Emergency Relief Committee for the City of Lodz.

Varga, Péter, and Thomas Nolden. 2008. "Writing along Borders: Contemporary Jewish Writing in Hungary." In *Contemporary Jewish Writing in Europe: A Guide*, edited by Vivian Liska and Thomas Nolden, 160–75. Bloomington: Indiana University Press.

Volavková, Hana, ed. 1959. *Children's Drawings and Poems, Terezín, 1942–1944.* Epilogue by Jiří Weil. Translated by Jeanne Němcová. Prague: Státní židovské muzeum.

Wallant, Edward Lewis. 1961. *The Pawnbroker.* New York: Harcourt, Brace and World.

Web, Marek. 1988. *The Documents of the Łódź Ghetto: An Inventory of the Nachman Zonabend Collection.* New York: YIVO.

Weil, Jiří. 1989. *Life with a Star.* Preface by Philip Roth. Translated by Rita Klímová with Roslyn Schloss. New York: Farrar, Straus and Giroux.

Weissberg, Liliane. 1997. "The Tale of a Good German: Reflections on the German Reception of *Schindler's List.*" In *Spielberg's Holocaust: Critical Perspectives on Schindler's List,* edited by Yosefa Loshitzky, 171–92. Bloomington: Indiana University Press.

Whitfield, Stephen J. 1996. "The Politics of Pageantry, 1936–1946." *American Jewish History* 84: 221–51.

———. 2010. "*The Deputy*: History, Morality, Art." *Modern Judaism* 30, no. 2: 153–71.

Wiesel, Elie. 1960. *Night.* Foreword by François Mauriac. Translated by Stella Rodway. New York: Hill and Wang.

———. 1972. "One Generation After." In Elie Wiesel, *One Generation After,* 8–17. New York: Avon.

———. 1986. "Remarks of Elie Wiesel at Ceremony for Jewish Heritage Week and Presentation of Congressional Gold Medal, White House, April 19, 1985." In *Bitburg in Moral and Political Perspective,* edited by Geoffrey H. Hartman, 241–44. Bloomington: Indiana University Press.

———. 2000. *Night.* New preface by the author. Translated by Marion Wiesel. New York: Hill and Wang.

Wiesel, Eliezer. 1956. *. . . un di velt hot geshvign.* Buenos Aires: Tsentral-farband fun poylishe yidn in Argentine.

Wieviorka, Annette. 1994. "Jewish Identity in the First Accounts by Extermination Camp Survivors from France." In "Discourses of Jewish Identity in Twentieth-Century France," edited by Alan Astro. Special issue, *Yale French Studies* 85:135–51.

———. 2006. *The Era of the Witness.* Translated by Jared Stark. Ithaca: Cornell University Press.

Wilkomirski, Benjamin [Bruno Dössekker]. 1996. *Fragments: Memories of a Wartime Childhood.* Translated by Carol Brown Janeway. New York: Schocken.

Wisse, Ruth R. 1971. *The Schlemiel as Modern Hero.* Chicago: University of Chicago Press.

———. 1975. "The Prose of Abraham Sutzkever." Introduction to Abraham Sutzkever, *Griner akvarium: dertseylungen,* v–xxxiii. Jerusalem: Tcherikover.

———. 1982. "Green Aquarium." *Prooftexts* 2, no. 1: 95–97.

———. 1996. "Language as Fate: Reflections on Jewish Literature in America." In *Literary Strategies: Jewish Texts and Contents,* edited by Ezra Mendelsohn, 129–47. Vol. 12, *Studies in Contemporary Jewry.* New York: Oxford University Press.

———. 2000. *The Modern Jewish Canon: A Journey through Language and Culture.* New York: Free Press.

———. 2003. "Abraham Sutzkever." In *Holocaust Literature: An Encyclopedia of Writers and their Work,* edited by S. Lillian Kremer, 2:1234–40. New York: Routledge.

Wojdowski, Bogdan. 1997. *Bread for the Departed.* Foreword by Henryk Grynberg. Translated by Madeline C. Levine. Evanston, IL: Northwestern University Press.

Woolf, Judith. 2007. "From *If This Is a Man* to *The Drowned and the Saved.*" In *The Cambridge Companion to Primo Levi*, edited by Robert S. C. Gordon, 33–49. Cambridge: Cambridge University Press.

Wróbel, Józef. 1998. "Jewish Martyrdom in the Works of Adolf Rudnicki." *Polin* 11: 247–62.

Wygodski, Yehoshua [Stanysław]. 1977. "A vort fun a gevezenem osir in Oyshvits." In *In harts fun genem: a dokument fun oyshvitser zonder-komando, 1944*, by Zalmen Gradowski, preface by David Sfard and edited by Chaim Wolnerman, 9–15. Jerusalem: Chaim Wolnerman.

Wyman, David S., ed. 1996. *The World Reacts to the Holocaust.* Baltimore: Johns Hopkins University Press.

Yablonka, Hannah. 2004. *The State of Israel vs. Adolf Eichmann.* Translated by Ora Cummings and David Herman. New York: Schocken.

Yacobi, Tamar. 2005. "Fiction and Silence as Testimony: The Rhetoric of Holocaust in Dan Pagis." *Poetics Today* 26, no. 2: 209–55.

Yehoshua, A. B. 1980. "On Hebrew Literature." *Jerusalem Quarterly* 16:97.

Young, James E. 1988. "Holocaust Documentary Fiction: The Novelist as Eyewitness." In *Writing and the Holocaust*, edited by Berel Lang, 200–15. New York: Holmes and Meier.

———. 1993. *The Texture of Memory: Holocaust Memorials and Meaning.* New Haven: Yale University Press.

Zable, Arnold. 1994. *Jewels and Ashes.* San Diego: Harcourt Brace.

Zelkowicz, Josef. 1989a. "Twenty-Five Live Chickens and One Dead Document." Translated by Joachim Neogroschel. In *Lodz Ghetto: Inside a Community under Siege*, edited by Alan Adelson and Robert Lapides, 62–67. New York: Viking.

———. 1989b. "The Truth of His Fantasies." Translated by Joachim Neogroschel. In *Lodz Ghetto: Inside a Community under Siege*, edited by Alan Adelson and Robert Lapides, 342–46. New York: Viking.

———. 2002. *In Those Terrible Days: Writings from the Lodz Ghetto.* Edited by Michal Unger. Translated by Naftali Greenwood. Jerusalem: Yad Vashem.

Zlotnik, Dov, ed. and trans. 1989. "Mourning" (*Semahot*), chap. 8. In *The Literature of Destruction: Jewish Responses to Catastrophe*, edited by David G. Roskies, 46–47. Philadelphia: Jewish Publication Society of America.

Zuckerman, Yitzhak, and Moshe Basok, eds. 1954. *Sefer milḥamot hageta'ot: ben haḥomot, bamaḥanot baye'arot.* Tel Aviv: Hakibbutz Hameuchad and Beit hageta'ot 'al shem Yitshak Katsenelson.

Credits

Index

Note: Page numbers in *italics* refer to the illustrations. Wherever possible, names of persons are followed by their birth and death dates in parentheses.

pogroms, 32, 92, 199

Poland, 8–10; Communist Party and government, 89–90, 183; expulsion of Jews, 92, 275, 292–93; Jewish life and, 33, 47, 84–93, 195; as literary center, 26. *See also* Białystok, Poland; *The Black Seasons*; Buczacz, Poland; Jedwabne, Poland; Konin, Poland; Warsaw and Warsaw ghetto

police, Jewish, 99, 204

Poliker, Yehudah (b. 1950), 171

Polish language/literature, 84–85, 87, 89, 91. *See also* artists and writers; Holocaust literature; memorial literature; women in the Holocaust

Ponar (killing field), 150–51

Dos poylishe yidntum (library), 61, 107, 121

Prager, Moshe (1909–1984), 101

"In Praise of the Natural Response," 65

prolepsis, 309

Pronicheva, Dina, 262, 285

prose poems, 145–48. *See also* Sutzkever, Abraham

protest pageants and rallies, 9, 30–31, 34–35

Rabbi Binyamin. *See* Redler-Feldman, Yehoshua

racism, 169. *See also* antisemitism

rallies. *See* protest pageants and rallies

Rapoport, Nathan [publisher], 96

Rapoport, Nathan [sculptor] (1901–1987), 92–93, 96

Ratzkin, Lawrence, 185

Rawicz, Piotr (1919–1982), 138, 155, 247–48

The Reader, 303–4

readers and readership, 16–19, 54–55, 104, 181–84

Reagan, Ronald (1911–2004), 158

Rebbe of Radzyn [Shmuel Shloyme Leiner] (1909–1942), 59

Red army. *See* Soviet army

Redler-Feldman, Yehoshua (1880–1957), 37

refugees, 32–34, 308–9; in the ghettos,

46–47, 210, 214; in Israel, 96; in Paris, 94. *See also* survivors

Regrowth, 219–20

Reḥovot hanahar, 118, 183

reparations, 9

reportage, 53–54, 98–99, 199–200. *See also* Goldin, Leyb; Gradowski, Zalmen; Malaparte, Curzio [Kurt Erich Suckert]; New Journalism; Opoczynski, Peretz; Perle, Yehoshue; Rosenfeld, Oskar; Zelkowicz, Josef

The Report of the President's Commission on the Holocaust, 152–53

resistance, 43–44, 60–64, 96–97, 134, 264–65. *See also* heroism; women in the Holocaust

Reznikoff, Charles (1894–1976), 31

Richmond, Theo, 161–63, 305–7

Ringelblum, Emanuel (1900–1944), 46–47, 53, 61–62, 195, 208–9. *See also* Oyneg Shabes (archive)

Rochman, Leyb (1918–1978), 94–96, 108, 183, 233–34

Rodríguez, Juan Manuel (b. 1945), 166, 296–97

Roosevelt, Eleanor (1884–1962), 18

The Root and the Bough: The Epic of an Enduring People, 83

Rosen, Alan, 172

Rosenfarb, Chava (1923–2011), 136, 138

Rosenfeld, Oskar (1884–1944), 24–25, 55, 58, 214–15

Rosental, Leyb (1916–1945), 48–49

Roth, Philip (b. 1933), 18, 155–56, 282–83

roundups and massacres. See *Aktionen*; atrocities

Rousset, David (1912–1997), 114

Rubenstein, Richard L. (b. 1924), 152

Rudashevski, Isaac (1927–1943), 59, 103

Rudnicki, Adolf [Aron Hirschhorn] (1909–1990), 84, 86–90, 155

Rue Ordener, Rue Labat, 177, 301–3

Rumkowski, Mordecai Chaim (1877–1944), 46, 135, 200, 205, 281–82

Russian Jews. *See* Soviet Jews

The Wall, 235–36

Wallant, Edward Lewis (1926–1962), 169

Warsaw and Warsaw ghetto, 196–97,
235–36; burning of, 85; cultural, political, and religious life, 44–48, 58–59
(see also youth movements); as literary
center, 50, 90–91, 208–9; uprising, 22,
90, 97, 220 (see also Warsaw Ghetto
Memorial). See also Głowiński,
Michal; Great Deportation; Miłosz,
Czesław; Nałkowska, Zofia; Oyneg
Shabes (archive); reportage; Rudnicki,
Adolf

Warsaw Ghetto Memorial, 92–93, 96, 158

Wartime Lies, 298–99

wartime literature, 190–217. See also diaries and diarists; Holocaust literature;
letters (genre); memorial literature

Wasserman, Anshel (fictional), 173–74, 290

We Are Here: Songs of the Holocaust, 231–32

Weil, Jiří (1900–1959), 156, 234–35, 243

Wellers, George (1905–1991), 127

We Were in Auschwitz, 79, 82, 181–82, 187,
222–23

We Will Never Die, 30–31, 254

"What I Read to the Dead," 66

The White Hotel, 285

White Paper (British), 80–81

The Whole Land Brimstone, 246–47

Wiesel, Elie (b. 1928), 107–8, 126–27, 158;
Night, 121–22, 167, 170, 241–42; response
to the Holocaust, 151–54; un di velt hot
geshvign, 121, 184

Wieviorka, Annette (b. 1948), 113, 164

Wilkomirski, Binjamin. See Dössekker,
Bruno

Wisse, Ruth (b. 1936), 7, 44

witnessing (moral), 85–89. See also
survivors

Wojdowski, Bogdan (1930–1994), 8,
136–38, 275–76

women in the Holocaust: as chroniclers
or diarists (see Auerbach, Rachel;
Draenger, Gusta Davidson; Frank,
Anne; Holländer, Grete; Nałkowska,

Zofia); portrayal in fiction, 26, 140–42,
246–47, 284–86, 291–92, 303–4; as
resistance fighters, 63–64, 127 (see
also Altman, Tosia; Draenger, Gusta
Davidson); as survivors, 86, 228, 262
(see also portrayal in fiction; Sarah
Kofman); as victims, 59, 213–14, 217,
262, 285; as writers, 108, 113–14, 136,
138, 197–98, 229–30, 270, 287 (see also
Delbo, Charlotte; Hillesum, Etty)

writers. See artists and writers

Writers' Congress, 32

"Written in Pencil in the Sealed Railway
Car," 143–44

Würzburg, Germany, 130

Yad Vashem, 93

"Yad Vashem," 110

year 4 of the war. See 1943 (year)

Yehoshua, A. B. (b. 1936), 126

Yiddish language, 9, 71, 92, 96, 106–7, 119,
121–22

Yiddish literature. See Holocaust
literature

Yiddish press, 94–97, 104–5

Di yidishe tragedye in der poylisher literatur,
91

the Yishuv, 36–37. See also Israel

yizkor books, 100–103, 130, 160

"Yosl Rakover's Appeal to God," 97, 101,
110, 121

Yosl Rakover Talks to God, 220–21

youth movements, 61–62, 103. See also
Zionism and Zionists

Zable, Arnold (b. 1947), 160–61, 163,
299–300, 306

zagłada (destruction) and Zagłada (Holocaust, Jewish), 84–85

"Zeidlus the Pope," 39–40

Zeitlin, Aaron (1899–1974), 9

Zelkowicz, Josef (1897–1944), 25; In Those
Terrible Days, 199–200; "Twenty-Five
Live Chickens and One Dead Docu-
ment," 56–57